Cambodia
Handbook

John Colet, Joshua Eliot
and Jane Bickersteth

Footprint Handbooks

Out of the East there shone a sun
As the blood rose on the day
And it shone on the work of the warrior wind
And it shone on the heart
And it shone on the soul
And they call the sun Dismay, my friend,
They called the sun – Dismay

Out of the East, James Fenton

Footprint Handbooks

6 Riverside Court, Lower Bristol Road
Bath BA2 3DZ England
T 01225 469141 F 01225 469461
E mail handbooks@footprint.cix.co.uk
www.footprint-handbooks.co.uk

ISBN 0 900751 89 4 ISSN 1363-7452
CIP DATA: A catalogue record for this book is
available from the British Library

In North America, published by

PASSPORT BOOKS
a division of NTC *Publishing Group*

4255 West Touhy Avenue, Lincolnwood
(Chicago), Illinois 60646-1975, USA
T 847 679 5500 F 847 679 24941
E mail NTCPUB2@AOL.COM

ISBN 0-8442-4921-1
Library of Congress Catalog Card
Number: 96-72528
Passport Books and colophon are registered
trademarks of NTC Publishing group

First published in 1992 as part of *Thailand,
Indochina & Burma Handbook* by Trade &
Travel Publications Ltd

Every effort has been made to ensure that
the facts in this Handbook are accurate.
However travellers should still obtain
advice from consulates, airlines etc about
current travel and visa requirements and
conditions before travelling. The authors
and publishers cannot accept responsibility
for any loss, injury or inconvenience,
however caused.

The maps are not intended to have any
political significance.

Cover design by Newell and Sorrell; cover
photography by Life File/Richard Powers

Production: Design by Mytton Williams;
Typesetting by Jo Morgan, Ann Griffiths and
Melanie Mason-Fayon; Maps by Sebastian
Ballard, Alasdair Dawson and Kevin Feeney;
Charts by Ann Griffiths; Original line drawings
by Andrew Newton; Proofread by Rod Gray
and David Cotterell.

Printed and bound in Great Britain by
Clays Ltd., Bungay, Suffolk

959.6.
3

Contents

The Editors

Joshua Eliot

Joshua has a long-standing interest in Asia. He was born in India, brought up in Hong Kong and has spent the last two decades studying and working in the countries of Southeast Asian. He has undertaken research in Thailand, Laos and Sumatra (Indonesia) and as well as editing Footprint Handbooks' guides to Southeast Asia, has also written and edited six other books on the region. He speaks Thai, and some Lao and Indonesian.

Jane Bickersteth

Jane has worked on the guidebooks since the first edition in 1992. She has been visiting the region for over 10 years, spending a year there whilst she researched the first edition. Jane is an artist by training and is particularly inspired by the Khmer ruins of Thailand and the candis of Java and Bali.

John Colet

John Colet was Head of Geography at Eton College and St Paul's Girls' School, London. He has been living and working in Vietnam since 1995 from where he makes frequent visits to Cambodia. Besides editing the Cambodia and Vietnam Handbooks for Footprint his chief occupation is running an educational charity. He has contributed to and edited earlier editions of this Handbook.

Acknowledgements

Much help has been received from friends, colleagues, researchers and fellow travellers during the preparation of this edition. All contributions have been tremendously helpful and are acknowledged on page 219. However we would particularly like to acknowledge the help of Duncan Shearer in Phnom Penh who provided a 'resident's view' of the country and a great deal of invaluable comment and information.

Introduction and hints

CAMBODIA'S recent history has been one of appalling calamity and sadness. Before the Khmers Rouges took power in 1975 it was drawn into the conflict in Vietnam, a 'sideshow' where a greater geo-political end was pursued in the paddy fields of Cambodia. Pol Pot's Khmers Rouges then proceeded to tear the country and its people apart over a terrible 4 years. 'Year Zero' was built on the corpses of as many as 2 million of its inhabitants, many brutally murdered. With the Vietnamese invasion of Christmas Day 1975 the Khmers Rouges were ousted from Phnom Penh but not from large swathes of the countryside. One nightmare had ended, but another was set to begin. Cambodia descended into a vicious civil war as the Soviet Union, America and China, through their respective proxies, fought out the Cold War in a place that few people cared about. The Vietnamese-backed government in Cambodia was disowned and the country cut off from most international aid and support. A poor and wretched country was made more wretched still.

Only in 1989 did these successive nightmares begin to end. The Vietnamese withdrew in 1989 as the end of the Cold War made proxy wars obsolete. UN-sponsored elections were held in 1993. Since then, unsteadily, the country has begun to rebuild itself and the Cambodian people have started to experience something close to normal life for the first time in years. Tourists, too, have begun to arrive in numbers, most for just one reason: to see Angkor. The ruins of the great Khmer empire of Angkor are one of the world's greatest historical monuments and are, quite simply, stupendous. Other than Angkor much of the country still remains off limits and so Cambodia has become, in effect, a one destination country. Phnom Penh has its attractions; there are various memorials to the Khmer Rouge genocide which have a terrible macabre fascination; and the coastal resort of Sihanoukville is also a relaxing place to spend a few days. But it is hard to think that so many people – around a quarter of a million in 1995 – would visit Cambodia if it were not for Angkor.

Where to go

Most of Cambodia is off-limits to the tourist and there are really just three destinations worthy of mention: Phnom Penh (the capital), Siem Reap and the ruins of Angkor, and the coastal resort of Sihanoukville. Very few tourists venture further afield and many people in Phnom Penh would maintain that it is foolish to try.

TRANSPORT AND TRAVELLING

The main constraint to transport and travelling in Cambodia is one of **safety**. Road and rail travel outside the capital is simply not safe. The Khmers Rouges and troops belonging to the Royal Cambodian Army are trigger happy and seem to operate without any central control. Many residents in Phnom Penh will not even venture out into the city after around 2100. Hold-ups, armed robberies, muggings and the like are very common (see the section on Safety on page 211 at the end of the book). In addition to these risks, **mines** are also a hazard over large areas of the countryside (see page 211).

For the above reasons, long distance **bus travel** is not recommended. As the situation in Cambodia is in a state of flux it is best to check on road conditions on arrival. Many people do use Highway 1 linking Phnom Penh with Ho Chi Minh City (Saigon) in Vietnam, the cheapest way to travel between the two countries but there are risks associated even with taking this route.

The same advice applies to travelling by **train** in Cambodia. There are two lines, one running from Phnom Penh to Cambodia's second city of Battambang (and from there to the Thai border), and the second from Phnom Penh to Sihanoukville (Kompong Som) on the coast. However at the time of writing it was not possible for foreigners to purchase train tickets because of the risks involved in travelling by rail.

The Mekong provides a useful watery highway and some visitors opt to travel by **boat** to Siem Reap. Though there was an accident recently when a vessel overturned, boat travel is comparatively safe.

Given the dangers and limitations of overland transport in Cambodia, many people choose instead to travel by **air**. The national airline is Royal Air Cambodge which operates domestic services to Siem Reap (for Angkor), Battambang, Stung Treng, Rattanakiri, Koh Kong, Sihanoukville and Mondulkiri (see the route map and timetable on page 231). It also has a limited international network to regional centres.

TIMETABLING A VISIT

Most people fly into Cambodia via Phnom Penh's Pochentong Airport. However a significant number of budget travellers opt to take the bus from Ho Chi Minh City (Vietnam) to Phnom Penh, a considerably cheaper alternative. There are no other international border crossings currently open to foreigners.

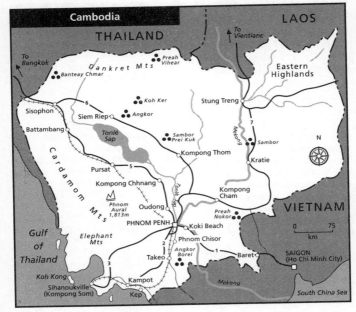

Visitors are still unable to travel freely in Cambodia and because there are just three principal destinations – Phnom Penh, Siem Reap/Angkor, and Sihanoukville – few people stay for more than a week to 10 days. They arrive and spend 2 days or so in Phnom Penh; fly to Siem Reap for 4-5 days; return to Phnom Penh; and then either leave the country or spend a few days on the coast at Sihanoukville.

HIGHLIGHTS

River trips
The boat trip from Phnom Penh to Siem Reap is enjoyable. It is also possible to take a day excursion to Mekong Island with its fishing villages and silk weavers.

Natural features
Siem Reap: the great lake or Tonlé Sap on which the economic vitality of the Angkor Empire was based.

Historical sites and ancient cities
Phnom Penh: the Royal Palace is open to the public. Wat Ounalom is Phnom Penh's most important monastery.

Phnom Penh environs: there are a number of lesser historical sites within a day's journey of the capital: Ta Phrom, Yeah Peau and Phnom Chisor.

Siem Reap and Angkor: the historical monuments of the Khmer Empire of Angkor are for most people the sole reason to come to Cambodia. Most see the temples in the vicinity of Siem Reap.

Vicinity of Angkor: There are many other sites within a day's journey of Siem Reap, but the outlying temples are not regarded as safe. Among the more notable are: the Roluos group, Phnom Krom, Banteay Samre, Banteay Srei, Phnom Kulen, Beng Mealea, Preah Vihear, and Banteay Chmar.

Coastal resorts

Sihanoukville or Kompong Som is Cambodia's only beach resort.

Shopping and handicrafts

Phnom Penh: handicrafts and antiques are best bought in Phnom Penh.

Cuisine and night life

Phnom Penh: the capital has a surprisingly good range of restaurants some serving fine food. There is also a lively nightlife and good bars.

Museums

Phnom Penh: The National Museum of Arts houses a notable collection of Khmer sculpture and other artefacts. It is worth visiting as the collection is complementary to the ruins of Angkor. The Tuol Sleng Museum is a memorial to the millions who died during the Khmers Rouges period. The museum, previously a school, was used by the Khmers Rouges as a torture and interrogation centre.

Phnom Penh environs: Choeung Ek was one of many Khmers Rouges execution grounds and has been preserved as a memorial to those who died (around 40,000 here alone).

NB The above is only a selection of places of interest and is not exhaustive. It is designed to assist in planning a trip to Cambodia. Any 'highlight' list is inevitably subjective.

How to go

BEST TIME TO VISIT

The best time to visit Cambodia is during the dry and comparatively cool months between Dec and Feb. After Feb, although it invariably remains dry, it becomes hot. The hottest time of year is just prior to the first rains, usually in Apr. The rainy season runs through until Nov, with the heaviest rain falling in the months of Sept and Oct. For more information on climate see the monthly climate graph for Phnom Penh on page 84 and the section on climate in the introduction on page 19.

HEALTH

Health care in Cambodia is poor and most foreign residents go to Thailand or Singapore for treatment beyond simple illnesses and injuries. For a roundup of health related issues, see page 225.

WHAT TO TAKE

Travellers usually tend to take too much, even to a place like Cambodia. In Phnom Penh it is possible to buy most toiletries and other personal items although they are imported and therefore pricier than elsewhere in the region.

Suitcases are not appropriate if you are intending to travel overland by bus. A backpack, or even better a travelpack (where the straps can be zipped out of sight), is recommended. Travelpacks have the advantage of being hybrid backpacks-suitcases; they can be carried on the back for easy porterage, but they can also be taken into hotels without the owner being labelled a 'hippy'.

In terms of clothing, dress in Cambodia is relatively casual – even at formal functions. Suits are not necessary. However, though formal attire may be the exception, dressing tidily is the norm. There is a tendency, rather than to take inappropriate articles of clothing, to take too many of the same article. Laundry services are cheap, and the turn-around rapid.

Checklist
Earplugs
First aid kit
Insect repellent and/or electric mosquito mats, coils
International driving licence
Passports (valid for at least 6 months)
Photocopies of essential documents
Short wave radio
Spare passport photographs
Sun protection
Sunglasses
Swiss Army knife
Torch
Umbrella
Wet wipes
Zip-lock bags

Those intending to stay in budget accommodation might also include:
Cotton sheet sleeping bag
Money belt
Padlock (for hotel room and pack)
Soap
Student card
Toilet paper
Towel
Travel wash

MONEY

Traveller's cheques are not easy to change in Cambodia, although banks in Phnom Penh will do so. US$ cash is most convenient. In Jan 1997, US$1 was worth 2,700 riel.

● ISIC

Anyone in full-time education is entitled to an International Student Identity Card (ISIC). These are issued by student travel offices and travel agencies across the world and offer special rates on all forms of transport and other concessions and services. The ISIC head office is: ISIC Association, Box 9048, 1000 Copenhagen, Denmark, T (45) 33 93 93 03.

GETTING THERE

AIR

Cambodia's only international airport is Phnom Penh's Pochentong Airport and most people arrive via Bangkok which has become a transport hub for the whole Indochina region. There are several flights a day between Bangkok and Phnom Penh. Many airlines offer nonstop or direct flights to Bangkok from Europe, North American and other cities within the Asian region. There are also direct air connections with Phnom Penh on *Royal Air Cambodge* from the following cities: Ho Chi Minh City/Saigon (Vietnam), Guangzhou (China), Hong Kong, Singapore, and Kuala Lumpur (Malaysia).

Discounts

It is possible to obtain significant discounts on flights to Bangkok, especially outside European holiday times, most notably in London. Shop around and book early. It is also possible to get discounts from Australasia, South Asia and Japan. Note that 'peak season' varies from airline to airline – many using 8-10 bands. This means one airline's high season may not be another's.

OVERLAND

Most international visitors arrive in Cambodia by air through Pochentong Airport in Phnom Penh. However, many budget travellers arrive by road from Vietnam, taking one of the buses that ply highway 1 between Ho Chi Minh City/Saigon and Phnom Penh.

BANGKOK (THAILAND) SECTION IN THIS GUIDE

Because so many people enter Cambodia via Bangkok, using Thailand as a way station to Cambodia, we have included a short section on Bangkok with basic general information on Thailand at the end of the book.

SAFETY

During recent months there has been a significant increase in the number of robberies and violent crimes in Phnom Penh. Many have been directed at Westerners and the *Phnom Penh Post* claimed that 70 foreigners had been robbed at gun-point in a 6-week period between Apr and May 1996. Many expatriate residents do not venture out on to the streets after 2100. Outside Phnom Penh, travelling by road or rail also has its risks and many areas of the country are effectively out of bounds. As safety in Cambodia is in a constant state of flux it is recommended that visitors check on security with their embassy/consulate in Phnom Penh before venturing anywhere other than Siem Reap.

WOMEN TRAVELLING ALONE

Women travelling alone face greater difficulties than men or couples although in Cambodia these problems are less pronounced than in many other countries. Women are nonetheless advised to dress modestly.

WHERE TO STAY

Though accommodation in Cambodia is limited, Phnom Penh and Siem Reap, the two principal destinations for foreign visitors, are relatively well provided for. Phnom Penh experienced something of a hotel building boom after the elections of 1993 and because the expected numbers of tourists have not materialized occupancy rates are low and room rates competitive. Siem Reap also has a reasonable selection of hotels and several more are under construction or in the pipeline. Outside these two places, accommodation is very limited.

FOOD AND DRINK

Food

Food in Cambodia is surprisingly good. One is tempted to think that this is a legacy of the French presence in the country. All towns of any size will have the requisite Chinese/Vietnamese restaurant as well as stalls selling simple single dish meals. In most towns it will also be possible to buy freshly baked baguettes and to order fresh and strong coffee. In Phnom Penh recreational eating is once more becoming an affordable pleasure and numerous restaurants are appearing to cater to local demand.

Water

Bottled water is easily obtainable in Cambodia – and cheap. It is not advisable to drink water straight from the tap. Soft drinks are also widely sold as well as locally brewed and imported beers.

GETTING AROUND

AIR

Royal Air Cambodge, the national airline, runs services to seven provincial destinations, with the capital Phnom Penh as the hub of this small network. They are: Siem Reap, Battambang, Koh Kong, Si-hanoukville, Stung Treng, Rattanakiri and Mondulkiri. See page 531 for a timetable and route map. *Royal Air Cambodge* flies new French-built ATR 72s.

ROAD

There are 2,000 km of highway in the country. Much of this is in a poor state of repair and there are also safety risks connected with travelling overland. As this book went to press many local residents would advise against using public transport to travel between provincial centres.

RAIL

Cambodia has a limited rail network consisting of two lines (Phnom Penh- Battambang, and Phnom Penh-Sihanoukville). The government prohibits foreigners from buying tickets because of the associated security risks of travelling by train.

CAR HIRE

Cars for self-drive hire are not available although it is sometimes possible to negotiate an informal arrangement. More common is to hire a driver as well as the car.

BOAT

The Mekong is an important artery of communication for both cargo and passengers. For overseas visitors the only route that is regularly used is between Phnom Penh and Siem Reap.

LANGUAGE

English is not widely spoken. There are rather more French speakers, but even they are small in number and will become relatively fewer as English catches on (which it looks like doing). Cambodian is hard to pick up.

Writing to the editor

Many people write to us - with corrections, new information, or simply comments. If you want to let us know something, we would be delighted to hear from you. Please give us as precise information as possible, quoting the edition and page number of the Handbook you are using and send as early in the year as you can. Your help will be greatly appreciated, especially by other travellers. In return we will send you details about our special guidebook offer.

For hotels and restaurants, please let us know:

- each establishment's name, address, phone and fax number
- number of rooms, whether a/c or air-cooled, attached (clean?) bathroom
- location - how far from the station or bus stand, or distance (walking time) from a prominent landmark
- if it's not already on one of our maps, can you place it?
- your comments - either good or bad - as to why it is distinctive
- tariff cards
- local transport used

For places of interest:

- location
- entry, camera charge
- access - by whatever means of transport is most approriate, eg time of main buses or trains to and from the site, journey time, fare
- facilities - nearby drinks stalls, restaurants, for the disabled
- any problems, eg steep climb, wildlife, unofficial guides
- opening hours
- site guides

Horizons

U NTIL the mid-19th century, the outside world knew almost nothing of the interior of Cambodia. From the 16th and 17th centuries, rumours began to surface in Europe – based on tales from Portuguese and French missionaries – about a magnificent city, hidden somewhere in the middle of the jungle. It is usually claimed that the ruins of Angkor were 'discovered' by the French naturalist and explorer Henri Mouhot in 1861. This is a travesty of history: Southeast Asians never forgot that Angkor existed. Truth, as they say, is determined by the powerful, and in this case the West determined that a westerner should 'discover' what was already known. In a sense, Angkor is a great weight on the collective shoulders of the Cambodian people. The usual refrain from visitors is: 'How could a people who created such magnificence have also nurtured Pol Pot and the Khmers Rouges?' A simple answer might be that only despotic rule could create anything on the scale of Angkor. The totalitarianism of the Khmers Rouges echoed that of the Khmer kings, but as the kings built, so the Khmers Rouges destroyed. Nonetheless, it is easy enough to see a stark disjuncture between the glory of Angkor and the horrors of recent history. As Elizabeth Becker wrote at the beginning of 1995: "Cambodia's recent history is one of breathtaking tragedy; by comparison its immediate future looks small and venal. Today Cambodia resembles many of the striving, corrupt, developing nations trying to make up for time lost behind the iron curtain. ... The nation that bore the horrors of the Khmers Rouges seemed ready for a kinder if not a more prosperous transformation."

In his book *Sideshow*, the British journalist William Shawcross says the diplomats, journalists and tourists who visited Cambodia in the 1950s and 1960s described it as "an idyllic, antique land unsullied by the brutalities of the modern world". Paddy farmers laboured in their ricefields, mystical ruins lay hidden in the jungle, the capital had the charm of a French provincial town and pagodas dotted the landscape. "Such was the illusion," writes Shawcross, of "bucolic plenty, Buddhist serenity, neutralist peace". This was an illusion because for centuries Cambodia had been in a state of continuous social and political upheaval. Since the demise of the Angkorian Empire in the 15th century, the country has been at the mercy of its much larger neighbours, Siam (Thailand) and Vietnam, and of various foreign powers – China, France, the US and the former Soviet Union. This history of foreign domination is starkly overshadowed by the so-called 'Pol Pot time'. Between 1975 and 1979, Cambodians suffered one of the worst human tragedies to afflict any country since WW2 – more than a million people died out of a total population of about 7 million. If the preceding period, during America's involvement in Indochina, is also taken into account, it is possible that up to a fifth of Cambodia's population was killed.

The relics and reminders of those days are now firmly on the tourist's sightseeing agenda. These include the chilling Tuol Sleng Genocide Museum, in the former high school where the Khmers Rouges tortured and killed at least 20,000 people and Choeung Ek, a series of mass graves, the 'Killing Fields', 15 km SW of Phnom Penh.

Cambodia: Provinces

The Land

GEOGRAPHY

Cambodia is all that remains of the once mighty Khmer Empire. Covering a land area of 181,035 sq km – about the size of England and Wales combined – the country is squeezed in between Thailand to the W, Vietnam to the E and Laos to the N. The **Mekong** is as central to life in Cambodia as the Nile is to life in Egypt. The river runs through Cambodia for about 500 km, bisecting the E lowlands, N to S. It is navigable by cargo ships from the delta in Vietnam, right up to Phnom Penh and beyond. Near the centre of the country is the **Tonlé Sap** – the 'Great Lake' – the largest freshwater lake in Southeast Asia. It is connected to the Mekong via the short channel-like Tonlé Sap River. When the Mekong floods between Jun and Oct – sometimes these floods can be devastating, as they were in 1991 – the Tonlé Sap River reverses its flow and the floodwaters fill the Great Lake, which doubles in size, covering the surrounding countryside (see page 135).

North of Phnom Penh, the Mekong is known as the Upper Mekong – or just the Mekong; downriver from the capital it divides into the Lower Mekong and the Bassac rivers. These two tributaries then swing to the SE across the fertile alluvial plain, towards the sprawling delta and the sea. The broad valley of the Mekong is a centuries-old trade route and its fertile central flood-plain is densely populated. The alluvial soils are irrigated but have an even greater potential for agricultural production than is

presently being realized. Throughout most of its course in Cambodia the river averages more than 1.6 km in width. There are viscous rapids at Kratie, NE of Phnom Penh, and a succession of dramatic waterfalls – Li Phi and Khong Phapheng Falls – on the border with Laos.

The **central lowlands** are surrounded by savanna; in S Cambodia these plains run all the way to the Vietnamese border. But to the N, E and W, Cambodia is enclosed by mountain chains: the Cardamom Mountains and Elephant Range to the W and SW, while the sandstone escarpment of the Dangrek Range forms a natural border with Thailand. The **Cardamom Mountains** (named after the spice) run in a gentle curve from just S of Battambang towards Phnom Penh. Phnom Aural, in the Cardamoms, is Cambodia's highest peak at 1,813m. The **Elephant Mountains** run along the S coastline. All these mountains are densely forested and sparsely inhabited, making them perfect operational bases for Cambodia's rebel guerrilla factions, who fought the Phnom Penh government throughout the 1980s. On the S coast around Kompong Som is a lowland area cut off from the rest of the country by mountains. Because the Mekong was a major thoroughfare, the **coastal region** never developed into a centre of trade until a road was built with American aid from Kompong Som to Phnom Penh in the 1960s.

CLIMATE

The monsoons determine rainfall and temperature patterns in Cambodia. The SW monsoon, from May to Oct, brings heavy rain throughout the country. This period accounts for between 75% and 80% of the total annual rainfall. The NW monsoon blows from Oct to Apr and ushers in the dry season. In the mountain areas the temperature is markedly cooler and the dry season only lasts 3 months.

Between the heat and rains there are transitional periods and the best time to visit the country is between Nov and Jan, before it gets too hot. Rainfall varies considerably from region to region. The Cardamom Mountains are the wettest. The mean temperature for Cambodia is 27.5°C. It is cooler – around 24°C – from Nov to Jan and hotter – around 32°C – between Feb and Apr. Humidity is generally high. (For a table of monthly temperature and rainfall in Phnom Penh, see page 84.)

FLORA AND FAUNA

The central plains are a predominantly agricultural area and are sparsely wooded but most of the rest of Cambodia

---

The Mekong: mother river of Southeast Asia

The Mekong River is one of the 12 great rivers of the world. It stretches 4,500 km from its source on the Tibet Plateau in China to its mouth (or mouths) in the Mekong Delta of Vietnam. (On 11 April 1995 a Franco-British expedition announced that they had discovered the source of the Mekong – 5,000m-high, at the head of the Rup-Sa Pass, and miles from anywhere.) Each year, the river empties 475 billion m^3 of water into the South China Sea. Along its course it flows through Burma, Laos, Thailand, Cambodia and Vietnam – all of the countries that constitute mainland Southeast Asia – as well as China. In both a symbolic and a physical sense then, it links the region. Bringing fertile silt to the land along its banks, but particularly to the Mekong Delta, the river contributes to Southeast Asia's agricultural wealth. In former times, a tributary of the Mekong which drains the Tonlé Sap (the Great Lake of Angkor and Cambodia), provided the rice surplus on which that fabulous empire was founded. The Tonlé Sap acts like a great regulator, storing water in time of flood and then releasing it when levels recede.

The first European to explore the Mekong River was the French naval officer Francis Garnier. His Mekong Expedition (1866-1868), followed the great river upstream from its delta in Cochin China. Of the 9,960 km that the expedition covered, 5,060 km were 'discovered' for the first time. The motivation for the trip was to find a southern route into the Heavenly Kingdom – China. But they failed. The river is navigable only as far as the Lao-Cambodian border where the Khone rapids make it impassable. Nonetheless, the report of the expedition is one of the finest of its genre.

Today the Mekong itself is perceived as a source of potential economic wealth – not just as a path to riches. The Mekong Secretariat was established in 1957 to harness the waters of the river for hydropower and irrigation. The Secretariat devised a grandiose plan incorporating a succession of seven huge dams which would store 142 billion m^3 of water, irrigate 4.3 million ha of riceland, and generate 24,200MW of power. But the Vietnam War intervened to disrupt construction. Only Laos' Nam Ngum Dam on a tributary of the Mekong was ever built – and even though this generates only 150MW of power, electricity exports to Thailand are one of Laos' largest export earners. Now that the countries of mainland Southeast Asia are on friendly terms once more, the Secretariat and its scheme have been given a new lease of life. But in the intervening years, fears about the environmental consequences of big dams have raised new questions. The Mekong Secretariat has moderated its plans and is now looking at less ambitious, and less contentious, ways to harness the Mekong River.

The tears of the Gods: rubies and sapphires

Major deposits of two of the world's most precious stones are found distributed right across mainland Southeast Asia: rubies and sapphires are mined in Thailand, Myanmar, Vietnam, Cambodia and Laos. During the civil war in Cambodia, thousands of Thais were mining gems in Khmers Rouges controlled territory (especially around Pailin) – with the protection of the vilified Khmers Rouges and the support of the Thai Army. Bangkok has become one of the centres of the world's gem business and Thailand is the largest exporter of cut stones.

Rubies and sapphires are different colours of corundum, the crystalline form of aluminium oxide. Small quantities of various trace elements give the gems their colour; in the case of rubies, chromium and for blue sapphires, titanium. Sapphires are also found in a spectrum of other colours including green and yellow. Rubies are among the rarest of gems, and command prices four times higher than equivalent diamonds.

The colour of sapphires can be changed through heat treatment (the most advanced form is called diffusion treatment) to 1,500-1,600°C (sapphires melt at 2,050°C). For example, relatively valueless colourless geuda sapphires from Sri Lanka, turn a brilliant blue or yellow after heating. The technique is an ancient one: Pliny the Elder described the heating of agate by Romans nearly 2,000 years ago, while the Arabs had developed heat treatment into almost a science by the 13th century. Today, almost all sapphires and rubies are heat treated. The most valued colour for sapphires is cornflower blue – dark, almost black, sapphires command a lower price. The value of a stone is based on the four 'C's: Colour, Clarity, Cut and Carat (1 carat = 200 mg). Note that almost all stones are heat treated to improve their colour.

– until recently – was still forested. In 1970, 73% of Cambodia's land area was thought to be forested; the figure in 1995 was less than 40%. In the SW, around the Cardamom and Elephant Mountains, there are still large tracts of primary forest where teak predominates. There are also tracts of virgin rainforest in the W and the NE. At higher elevations in these mountains there are areas of pine forest and in the N and E highlands, temperate forest.

Cambodia has a wide variety of fauna and, before war broke out in the 1970s, was on the international game-hunters' circuit; there were tigers (now an endangered species), buffalo, elephants, wild oxen, clouded leopards (also endangered) and bears including Malaysian sun bears. Even after all the fighting, game is still said to be abundant in forested areas, particularly in northeastern provinces of Mondulkiri and Rattanakiri. Smaller animals include monkeys, squirrels, tree rats and shrews, flying foxes and numerous species of reptile, including several varieties of poisonous snake, the most common being Russell's viper, the banded krait, cobra and king cobra. The kouprey (meaning 'jungle cow') is Cambodia's most famous animal and a symbol of the Worldwide Fund for Nature. A wild ox, it was first identified in 1939 but is now virtually extinct worldwide. In 1963, King Sihanouk declared the animal Cambodia's national animal. Small numbers are thought to inhabit the more remote areas of the country, although some experts fear that the last specimens were either killed by guerrillas for meat or are being fatally maimed after treading on anti-personnel mines laid by the Khmers Rouges. An effort to capture and breed the kouprey is underway in Vietnam.

Even around Phnom Penh one can see herons, cranes, grouse, pheasant, wild duck, pelicans, cormorants and egrets. The Tonlé Sap area is particularly rich in fish-eating waterfowl.

The Tonlé Sap is also rich in marine life, and supports possibly the largest inland fisheries industry in the world. The lower reaches of the Mekong, marking the border between Cambodia and Laos, is also the last place in Indochina where the rare Irrawaddy dolphin is to be found. Unfortunately, fishermen in the area have taken to fishing using dynamite and this threatens the survival of the mammal. Explosives are widely available, and evidently this method of fishing is quick and effective. It is also indiscriminate and wasteful, killing juvenile as well as mature fish, and animals like the dolphin which were hitherto left unharmed. The number of dolphins is put at between 100 and 200. It was also once found in Thailand's Chao Phraya River, but pollution put paid to that population years ago.

ILLEGAL LOGGING AND THE THAI CONNECTION

Ly Thuch, Under-Secretary for State for the Environment, told a meeting at the Foreign Correspondents Club in Phnom Penh that "the main destroyers of the environment are the Khmers Rouges and the rich and powerful". Thai logging companies, with the permission and connivance of the Khmers Rouges, have been logging large areas of valuable hardwood forest along Cambodia and Thailand's common border in the W – and generating revenue of US$10mn a month. Although the Thai government has consistently argued that Thai companies are not involved, and more to the point that the Thai army is not involved in this business, most independent commentators believe that the lucrative trade

has been based upon a triangular relationship including the Khmers Rouges, Thai businessmen, and the Thai army, the latter reputedly often paying for timber in arms and ammunition.

Nor is the Thai role in Cambodia restricted just to timber. When government forces captured the town of Pailin in the gem-rich W from the Khmers Rouges in 1994, they discovered six Thai companies working there in league with the rebels. The figure rose to 16 by the end of 1994. These reports flatly contradicted Thai government assurances that there were no Thai companies working in the area. The mining has devastated the area, with many of the rivers now filled with deep-red silt and poisoned with magnesium, potassium and iodine.

In 1995 the Cambodian government introduced a new Environment Law backed up by further laws such as the Environmental Impact Assessments Law. Experts stated that the Environment Law should be seen as a first step – and not, in itself, as a comprehensive solution to the problems of environmental degradation and exploitation. The lack of transparency in many of the regulations that exist, and the ease with which companies and individuals with political and economic power can circumvent those regulations, makes environmental protection weak. In Mar 1995, for example, the UK-based environmental NGO Global Witness released a report accusing the Khmers Rouges, Thai companies, and the Cambodian government, of profiting from the booming illegal timber trade which, they claim, continues apace despite Cambodia's logging ban. The then Prime Minister of Thailand, Chuan Leekpai, responded to the report saying, "If we knew logs were coming from the Khmers Rouges, we would not allow them in", to which Global Witness Investigator Patrick Alley replied, "If it is so easy for us to visit border areas and see hundreds of trucks loaded with logs coming in from Cambodia, how is it they [the Thais] can't?"

Despite the success of Global Witness in bringing the rape of Cambodia's forests to international attention in 1995, the following year saw little downturn in activity. New logging roads from Thailand into Cambodian territory were being cut, and old ones repaired. The government explained that all the timber being removed from Cambodia had already been cut, but few independent

The cycle of wet rice cultivation

There are an estimated 120,000 rice varieties. Rice seed – either selected from the previous harvest or, more commonly, purchased from a dealer or agricultural extension office – is soaked overnight before being sown into a carefully prepared nursery bed. Today farmers are likely to plant one of the Modern Varieties or MVs bred for their high yields.

The nursery bed into which the seeds are broadcast (scattered) is often a farmer's best land, with the most stable water supply. After a month the seedlings are up-rooted and taken out to the paddy fields. These will also have been ploughed, puddled and harrowed, turning the heavy clay soil into a saturated slime. Traditionally buffalo and cattle would have performed the task; today rotavators, and even tractors are becoming more common. The seedlings are transplanted into the mud in clumps. Before transplanting the tops of the seedlings are twisted off (this helps to increase yield) and then they are pushed in to the soil in neat rows. The work is back-breaking and it is not unusual to find labourers – both men and women – receiving a premium – either a bonus on top of the usual daily wage or a free meal at midday, to which marijuana is sometimes added to ease the pain.

After transplanting, it is essential that the water supply is carefully controlled. The key to high yields is a constant flow of water, regulated to take account of the growth of the rice plant. In 'rain-fed' systems where the farmer relies on rainfall to water the crop, he has to hope that it will be neither too much nor too little. Elaborate ceremonies are performed to appease the rice goddess and to ensure bountiful rainfall.

In areas where rice is grown in irrigated conditions, farmers need not concern themselves with the day-to-day pattern of rainfall, and in such areas 2 or even 3 crops can be grown each year. But such systems need to be carefully managed, and it is usual for one man to be in charge of irrigation. He decides when water should be released, organizes labour to repair dykes and dams and to clear channels, and decides which fields should receive the water first.

Traditionally, while waiting for the rice to mature, a farmer would do little except weed the crop from time to time. He and his family might move out of the village and live in a field hut to keep a close eye on the maturing rice. Today, farmers also apply chemical fertilisers and pesticides to protect the crop and ensure maximum yield. After 90–130 days, the crop should be ready for harvesting.

Harvesting also demands intensive labour. Traditionally, farmers in a village would secure their harvesters through systems of reciprocal labour exchange; now it is more likely for a harvester to be paid in cash. After harvesting, the rice is threshed, sometimes out in the field, and then brought back to the village to be stored in a rice barn or sold. It is only at the end of the harvest, with the rice safely stored in the barn, that the festivals begin.

The universal stimulant – the betel nut

Throughout the countryside in Southeast Asia, and in more remote towns, it is common to meet men and women whose teeth are stained black, and gums red, by continuous chewing of the 'betel nut'. This, though, is a misnomer. The betel 'nut' is not chewed at all: the three crucial ingredients that make up a betel 'wad' are the nut of the areca palm (*Areca catechu*), the leaf or catkin of the betel vine (*Piper betle*), and lime. When these three ingredients are combined with saliva they act as a mild stimulant. Other ingredients (people have their own recipes) are tobacco, gambier, various spices and the gum of *Acacia catechu*. The habit, though also common in South Asia and parts of China, seems to have evolved in Southeast Asia and it is mentioned in the very earliest chronicles. The lacquer betel boxes of Burma and Thailand, and the brass and silver ones of Indonesia, illustrate the importance of chewing betel in social intercourse. Galvao in his journal of 1544 noted: "They use it so continuously that they never take it from their mouths; therefore these people can be said to go around always ruminating". Among Westernized Southeast Asians the habit is frowned upon: the disfigurement and ageing that it causes, and the stained walls and floors that result from the constant spitting, are regarded as distasteful products of an earlier age. But beyond the élite it is still widely practised.

observers were convinced. International aid donors had become so worried about the failure of the Cambodian government to control logging that the IMF suspended a US$20 million budget-support payment in protest in mid-1996. The fact that Cambodia's two prime ministers have continued to sign logging contracts – without cabinet discussion and in contravention of their own environmental laws – illustrates the degree to which those in power ignore green concerns in the country. "The government's arguments just don't stand up on any count" argued Charmian Gooch of Global Witness in April 1996. "They are simply illegal deals signed in secret by the two Prime Ministers, carrying on what is becoming a Royal Government tradition, selling off Cambodia's forests at bargain basement prices, at the expense of the Cambodian people". A month later, Sam Rainsy, the President of the Khmer Nation Party, exposed the sham of government 'controls' on the cutting and export of timber to Thailand. Even as this book went to press, at the beginning of 1997, there were reports from people who had made the journey by boat from Phnom Penh to the Lao-Cambodian border that extensive logging was still underway, largely by the Cambodian military. In an interview published in Nov 1996, William Shawcross suggested that illegal logging is "perhaps the most serious crisis of corruption in the regime".

NATIONAL PARKS

Towards the end of 1993, King Sihanouk signed a decree setting in motion a process that should lead to the creation of 23 protected areas, covering 15% of Cambodia's land area. These will include seven national parks and 10 wildlife sanctuaries (see map). The country's first new national park in 25 years is to open in the timber rich province of Kompong Speu.

It may be rather ironic, but the dislocations caused by Cambodia's long-running civil war have probably helped to protect the environment, rather than destroy it. Although larger animals like the kouprey may have suffered from the profusion of land mines that dot the countryside, other animals havebenefited from the lack of development that has occurred. Unlike Thailand, and to a lesser degree Vietnam, forest has not been cleared for agriculture and many regions became 'no-go' areas to all except for the foolhardy and the well-armed. This created conditions in which wildlife could survive largely undisturbed by the forces of 'development'. Now wildlife experts and environmentalists are arguing that Cambodia has a unique asset that should be preserved at all costs – and not just because it might be the morally 'right' thing to do. In addition, the growth in eco-tourism world wide could create a considerable money-spinner for the country.

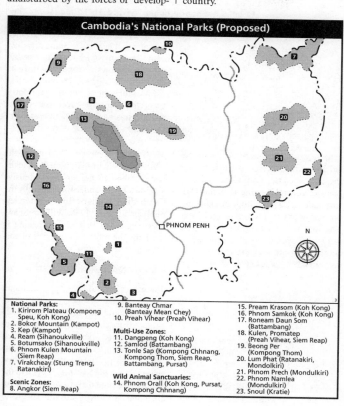

Cambodia's National Parks (Proposed)

National Parks:
1. Kirirom Plateau (Kompong Speu, Koh Kong)
2. Bokor Mountain (Kampot)
3. Kep (Kampot)
4. Ream (Sihanoukville)
5. Botumsako (Sihanoukville)
6. Phnom Kulen Mountain (Siem Reap)
7. Virakcheay (Stung Treng, Ratanakiri)

Scenic Zones:
8. Angkor (Siem Reap)

9. Banteay Chmar (Banteay Mean Chey)
10. Preah Vihear (Preah Vihear)

Multi-Use Zones:
11. Dangpeng (Koh Kong)
12. Samlod (Battambang)
13. Tonle Sap (Kompong Chhnang, Kompong Thom, Siem Reap, Battambang, Pursat)

Wild Animal Sanctuaries:
14. Phnom Orall (Koh Kong, Pursat, Kompong Chhnang)

15. Pream Krasom (Koh Kong)
16. Phnom Samkok (Koh Kong)
17. Roneam Daun Som (Battambang)
18. Kulen, Promatep (Preah Vihear, Siem Reap)
19. Beong Per (Kompong Thom)
20. Lum Phat (Ratanakiri, Mondolkiri)
21. Phnom Prech (Mondulkiri)
22. Phnom Namlea (Mondulkiri)
23. Snoul (Kratie)

History

PRE-HISTORY

Archaeological evidence suggests that the Mekong Delta and the lower reaches of the river – in modern-day Cambodia – have been inhabited since at least 4,000 BC. But the wet and humid climate has destroyed most of the physical remains of the early civilizations. Excavated remains of a settlement at Samrong Sen on the Tonlé Sap show that houses were built of bamboo and wood and raised on stilts – exactly as they are today. Where these people came from is uncertain. Anthropologists believe there were two waves of migration; one from the Malay peninsula/Indonesia and a second from Tibet/China.

RISE OF THE LUNAR AND SOLAR DYNASTIES

For thousands of years Indochina was isolated from the rest of the world and was virtually unaffected by the rise and fall of the early Chinese dynasties. India and China 'discovered' Southeast Asia early in the first millennium and trade networks were quickly established. The Indian influence was particularly strong in the Mekong basin area. The Khmers adopted and adapted Indian script as well as their ideas about astrology, religion (Buddhism and Hinduism) and royalty (the cult of the semidivine ruler). Today, several other aspects of Cambodian culture are recognizably Indian in origin – including classical literature and dance. Religious architecture also followed Indian models. These Indian cultural influences which took root in Indochina gave rise to a legend to which Cambodia traces its historical origins. An Indian Brahmin called Kaundinya, travelling in the Mekong Delta area, married Soma, daughter of the Naga (the serpent deity – see page 112), or Lord of the Soil. Their union, which founded the 'Lunar Dynasty' of Funan (a pre-Angkorian Kingdom), symbolized the fertility of the kingdom and occupies a central place in Khmer cosmology. The Naga, Soma's father, helpfully drank the floodwaters of the Mekong, enabling people to cultivate the land.

The kingdom of Funan – the forerunner of Kambuja – was established on the Mekong by tribal people from S China in the middle of the 3rd century AD and became the earliest Hindu state in Southeast Asia. Funan was known for its elaborate irrigation canals which controlled the Mekong floodwaters, irrigated the paddy fields and prevented the incursion of seawater. By the 5th century Funan had extended its influence over most of present day Cambodia, as well as Indochina and parts of the Malay Peninsula. Leadership was measured by success in battle and the ability to provide protection; in recognition of this fact, rulers from the Funan period onward incorporated the suffix – 'varman' (meaning protection) into their names. Records of a 3rd century Chinese embassy give an idea of what it was like: "There are walled villages, places and dwellings. The men ... go about naked and barefoot. ... Taxes are paid in gold, silver and perfume. There are books and libraries and they can use the alphabet." 20th century excavations suggest a seafaring people engaged in extensive trade with both India and China, and elsewhere.

The 'Solar Dynasty' of Chenla was a tributary kingdom of Funan, probably first based on the Mekong at the junction with the Mun tributary, but rapidly grew in power. It was the immediate predecessor of Kambuja and the great Khmer Empire. According to Khmer legend, the kingdom was the result of the marriage of Kambu, an ascetic, to a celestial nymph named Mera. The people of Chenla – the Kambuja, or the sons of Kambu – lent their name to the country. Chenla, was centred in the area of present day S Laos. In 540 AD a Funan prince married a Chenla princess, uniting the Solar and Lunar dynasties. But the prince sided with his wife, turning against his own people and Funan was swallowed by

Confusion in the name of the sons of Kambu

The word Cambodia derives from 'Kambuja' meaning 'the sons of Kambu' – the ascetic who, according to Khmer legend, married a celestial nymph and founded the kingdom of Chenla, the forerunner to the great Khmer Empire.

Khmers called the country Kambuja; the English, Cambodia; and the French, Cambodge. Kampuchea is the usual transliteration of Kambuja – although political inferences crept into the usage of the term when the Khmers Rouges insisted on calling the country Kampuchea. In the 4 decades since Cambodian independence in 1953, the name has changed several times.

On independence in 1953, it was called the kingdom of Cambodia. In 1970, the country was renamed the Khmer Republic following the overthrow of Prince Sihanouk. Then, in 1975 it was renamed Democratic Kampuchea following the Khmers Rouges take-over. 4 years later, in 1979, the Hanoi-backed regime renamed the country the People's Republic of Kampuchea. Finally, in 1989, it was renamed the State of Cambodia or *Roet Kampuchea*.

Chenla. The first capital of this fusion of Chenla and Funan was at Sambor. King Ishanavarman (616-635) established a new capital at Sambor Prei Kuk, 30 km from modern Kompong Thom, in the centre of the country (the monuments of which are some of the best preserved of this period). His successor, Jayavarman I, moved the capital to the region of Angkor Borei near Takeo.

Quarrels in the ruling family led to the break-up of the state in the 7th century: it was divided into 'Land Chenla', a farming culture located N of the Tonlé Sap (maybe centred around Champassak in Laos), and 'Water Chenla', a trading culture based along the Mekong. Towards the end of the 8th century Water Chenla became a vassal of Java's powerful Sailendra Dynasty and members of Chenla's ruling family were taken back to the Sailendra court. This period, from the fall of Funan until the 8th century, is known as the pre-Angkorian period – it is a hazy period of Cambodian history. The Khmers remained firmly under Javanese suzerainty until Jayavarman II (802-850), who was born in central Java, returned to the land of his ancestors around 800 AD to change the course of Cambodian history.

ANGKOR AND THE GOD-KINGS

Jayavarman II, the Khmer prince who had spent most of his life at the Sailendra court, claimed independence from Java and founded the Angkor Kingdom to the N of the Tonlé Sap in 802, at about the same time as Charlemagne became Holy Roman Emperor in Europe. They were men cast in the same mould, for both were empire builders. Jayavarman won immediate political popularity on his return and, to consolidate and legitimize his position, arranged his coronation by a Brahmin priest, declaring himself the first Khmer devaraja, or god-king. From then on, the reigning

Mekong exploration – slowly up the rapids

In 1866, 3 years after Cambodia became a French protectorate, the first Resident in Cambodia, Doudart de Lagrée and a 23-year-old naval lieutenant, Francis Garnier, set out on an expedition to explore the interior of Indochina by following the Mekong River. One of their first stops was to visit the ruins of Angkor which had been made famous by Henri Mouhot just 5 years earlier, after which they pushed N, consuming legendary quantities of alcohol in an effort to ease the discomforts of the terrain, climate, mosquitoes and disease. They made their way up past the Kratie rapids and Khong falls, finally reaching Vientiane (Laos) in Apr 1867. A fortnight later, they were in the old royal Lao capital of Luang Prabang. From there they pushed further N into China, where Lagrée collapsed and died. Garnier made it back to Saigon with the other survivors, via Shanghai. He had surveyed about 6,500 km of uncharted territory; his maps were published in his landmark atlas of Indochina – *Atlas d'Explorations en Indo-Chine* – in 1873, the year he was ambushed and killed by Chinese bandits just outside Hanoi.

monarch was identified with Siva, the king of the Hindu gods. In the centuries that followed, successive devaraja strove to outdo their predecessors by building bigger and finer temples to house the royal lingam (the symbol of Siva and the devaraja). The god-kings commanded the absolute allegiance of their subjects, allowing them control of a vast pool of labour which was used to build an advanced and prosperous agricultural civilization. For many years historians and archaeologists maintained that the key to this agricultural wealth lay in a sophisticated hydraulic – ie irrigated – system of agriculture (see page 122) which allowed the Khmers to produce up to three harvests a year. However, this view of Angkorian agriculture has come under increasing scrutiny in recent years and now there are many who believe that flood-retreat – rather than irrigated – agriculture was the key. Jayavarman II installed himself in successive capitals N of the Tonlé Sap, secure from attack by the Sailendras, and he ruled until 850. Indrapura was his first capital (to the E of Kompong Cham); later he moved his capital to Wat Phu (in S Laos) and the Roluos (Angkor).

Jayavarman III (850-877) continued his father's traditions and ruled for the

next 27 years. **Indravarman (877-889)**, his successor, was the first of the great temple-builders of Angkor. At the end of the 9th century **Yasovarman I (889-900)** moved the capital from Roluos and laid the foundations of Angkor itself. He called his new capital Yasodharapura and copied the water system his father had devised at Roluos on an even larger scale, using the waters of the Tonlé Sap. In 921, **Jayavarman IV** set up a rival capital about 65 km from Angkor at Koh Ker (see page 139) but 30 years later, **Rajendravarman** moved the court back to Angkor, where the Khmer kings remained. Rajendravarman (944-968) is believed to have been a tolerant king and allowed the establishment of several Mahayana Buddhist temples at Angkor.

The formidable warrior **King Suryavarman I (1002-1050)**, who may originally have come from the Malay peninsula, conquered the kingdom in the early 11th century and extended its influence as far as S Thailand and Laos. He continued the royal Hindu cult but also tolerated Mahayana Buddhism. Ta Keo (NW of Angkor Thom) and the Phimeanakas pyramid temples were Suryavarman's main contributions to Angkor's architectural heritage (see page 118). But on Suryavarman's death,

How to crown a god-king

The coronation ceremony of a Cambodian god-king, dating back to the kings of Angkor is steeped in historical ritual. On coronation day, the crown prince traditionally took possession of the city by circumambulating in imitation of a mythical king who inherited the world by encircling the outermost shore of the outermost ocean. On his circumambulation, the would-be king used four different types of transport and changed his headdress four times, each time assuming the traditional costume and mount of one of the kings of the four cardinal points. Water also played an important role, symbolizing allegiance and vassaldom. At the courts of Phnom Penh – as in Bangkok – holy water was gathered from the principal rivers in the scattered provinces of the kingdom. This water was used to annoint the new monarch during the coronation ceremony.

the Khmer Kingdom began to fragment due to internal revolt. His three successors had short, troubled reigns and the Chams (Champa was a rural kingdom based in present day Vietnam) captured, sacked and razed the capital.

In 1080 a new kingdom was founded by a northern provincial governor claiming aristocratic descent. He called himself **Jayavarman VI (1080-1107)**. He never settled at Angkor, living instead in the northern part of the kingdom. He left monuments at Wat Phou in southern Laos, and Preah Vihear (or Phra Viharn) and Phimai, both in Thailand. When Jayavarman VI died in 1107, the throne was protected by his brothers for his grand-nephew **Suryavarman II (1131-1150)**, who acceded to the throne 6 years later. He was the greatest of Angkor's god-kings, during whose reign the temple of Angkor Wat was built. It was an architectural masterpiece and represented the height of the Khmer's artistic genius (see page 125). Under him, the Khmer Kingdom encompassed a large part of Thailand, S Vietnam, Laos and part of the Malay peninsula. A network of roads was built to connect regional capitals, one of the most important being Phimai in NE Thailand.

Suryavarman II deposed the King of Champa in 1145 but the Chams regained their independence in 1149 and the following year, Suryavarman died after a disastrous attempt to conquer Annam (northern Vietnam). In 1177 the Chams seized their chance of revenge and sacked Angkor. But when the 50-year-old **Jayavarman VII** – a cousin of Suryavarman – attained power in 1181, he hit back, attacking the Chams and seizing their capital, Vijaya. He expanded the Khmer Kingdom further than ever before; its suzerainty stretched from the Malay peninsula in the S to the borders of Burma in the W and the Annamite chain to the NE.

Jayavarman's VII's first task was to plan a strong, spacious new capital – Angkor Thom; but while that work was being undertaken he set up a smaller, temporary seat of government where he and his court could live in the meantime – Preah Khan meaning 'Fortunate City of Victory' (see page 132). He also built 102 hospitals throughout his kingdom, as well as a network of roads, along which he constructed resthouses. But because they were built of wood, none of these secular structures survive; only the foundations of four larger ones have been unearthed at Angkor.

ANGKOR'S DECLINE

Jayavarman VII's principal architectural legacy was his capital, Angkor Thom (*Thom* literally translates as 'great'),

A Chinese Emissary's account of his stay at Angkor (1296-1297)

One of the most interesting documents of the great empire of Angkor is the Chinese emissary Chou Ta-kuan's short account of his stay there entitled *Notes on the customs of Cambodia*. The book was written in the late 13th or early 14th century, shortly after he had returned to China after a sojourn at Angkor between 1296 and 1297. His book describes the last days of the kingdom and his role was as male companion to the Chinese ambassador.

The book is divided into 40 short 'chapters' dealing with aspects of everyday and royal life ranging from childbirth, to justice, to clothing. The account also details aspects of the natural environment (fish and reptiles, birds), the economy of the empire (agriculture, trade, products), and technology (utensils, boats and oars). What makes the account so useful and unusual is that it describes not just the concerns and actions of great men and women, but of everyday life too. The extracts below are just a sample of the insights into everyday Cambodian life during the waning days of the Angkorian Empire. For those intending to visit the site of Angkor, the book is highly recommended reading. It brings to life the ruins of a city, helping the visitor to imagine a place – now so empty – full of people and life.

Cambodian dwellings Out of the [royal] palace rises a golden tower, to the top of which the ruler ascends nightly to sleep. It is common belief that in the tower dwells a genie, formed like a serpent with nine heads, which is Lord of the entire kingdom. Every night this genie appears in the shape of a woman, with whom the sovereign couples. Not even the wives of the King may enter here. At the second watch the King comes forth and is then free to sleep with his wives and his concubines. Should the genie fail to appear for a single night, it is a sign that the King's death is at hand.

Straw thatch covers the dwellings of the commoners, not one of whom would dare place the smallest bit of tile on his roof.

Clothing Every man or woman, from the sovereign down, knots the hair and leaves the shoulders bare. Round the waist they wear a small strip of cloth, over which a large piece is drawn when they leave their houses. Many rules, based on rank, govern the choice of materials. ... Only the ruler may wear fabrics woven in an all over pattern.

The natives Generally speaking, the women, like the men, wear only a strip of cloth, bound round the waist, showing bare breasts of milky whiteness. ... As for the concubines and palace girls, I have heard it said that there are from three to five thousand of these, separated into various categories. ... When a beautiful girl is born into a family, no time is lost in sending her to the palace.

Childbirth Once a Cambodian woman's child is born, she immediately makes a poultice of hot rice and salt and applies it to her private parts. This is taken off in 24 hrs, thus preventing any untoward after-effects and causing an astringency which seems to renew the young mother's virginity. When told of this for the first time, my credulity was sorely taxed. However, in the house where I lodged a girl gave birth to a child, and I was able to observe beyond peradventure that the next day she was up carrying the baby in her arms and going with him to bathe in the river. This seems truly amazing!

Everyone with whom I talked said that the Cambodian women are highly sexed. One or 2 days after giving birth they are ready for intercourse: if a husband is not responsive he will be discarded. When a man is called away on matters of business, they endure his absence for a while; but if he is gone as much as 10 days, the wife is apt to say, "I am no ghost; how can I be expected to sleep alone?"

Slaves Wild men from the hills can be bought to serve as slaves. Families of wealth may own more than 100; those of lesser means content themselves with 10 or 20; only the very poor have none. ... If a slave should run away and be captured, a blue mark would be tattooed on his face; moreover, an iron collar would be fitted to his neck, or shackles to his arms or legs.

Cambodian justice Points of dispute between citizens, however trifling, are taken to the ruler. ... In dealing with cases of great seriousness, recourse is not had to strangulation or beheading; outside the West Gate, however, a ditch is dug into which the criminal is placed, earth and stones are thrown back and heaped high, and all is over. ... Lesser crimes are dealt with by cutting off feet or hands, or by amputation of the nose.

When a thief is caught red-handed, he may be imprisoned and tortured. Recourse is also had to another curious procedure. If an object is missing, and accusation brought against someone who denies the charge, oil is brought to boil in a kettle and the suspected person forced to plunge his hand into it. If he is truly guilty, the hand is cooked to shreds; if not, skin and bones are unharmed. Such is the amazing way of these barbarians.

Products of Cambodia Many rare woods are to be found in the highlands. Unwooded regions are those where elephants and rhinoceros gather and breed. Exotic birds and strange animals abound. The most sought-after products are the feathers of the kingfisher, elephant tusks, rhinoceros horns, and beeswax.

Trade In Cambodia it is the women who take charge of trade. For this reason a Chinese arriving in the country, loses no time in getting himself a mate, for he will find her commercial instincts a great asset.

Utensils For sleeping only bamboo mats are used, laid on the wooden floors. Of late, certain families have adopted the use of low beds, which for the most part are made by the Chinese.

A prodigy Within the Walled City, near the East Gate, a Cambodian man committed fornication with his younger sister. Their skin and their flesh were fused beyond the power of separating them. After 3 days passed without food, both parties died. My compatriot Mr Hsieh, who spent 35 years in this country declares he has known this to happen twice. If such be the case, it shows how well the Cambodians are policed by the supernatural power of their holy Buddha.

● Notes on the customs of Cambodia was originally translated from the Chinese original into French by Paul Pelliot. J Gilman d'Arcy Paul translated the French version into English, and the Siam Society in Bangkok have republished this version with colour photographs and reproductions of Delaporte's fine lithographs of the monuments. *The customs of Cambodia*, Siam Society: Bangkok, 1993.

which was begun in 1200. The mysterious and visually powerful 12th century Bayon temple, was his most ambitious architectural feat. It is said that the Bayon was completed in 21 years and was the last of the fine monuments built at Angkor. Jayavarman took thousands of peasants from the rice fields to build it, which proved a fatal error, for rice yields decreased and the empire began its decline as resources were drained. Jayavarman VII adopted Mahayana Buddhism; Buddhist principles replaced the Hindu pantheon, and were invoked as the basis of royal authority. This spread of Buddhism is thought to have caused some of the earlier Hindu temples to be neglected, while others were converted to the new faith.

Jayavarman VII died in 1218 and the Kambujan Empire fell into progressive decline over the next 2 centuries. Territorially, it was eroded by the eastern migration of the Siamese. The Khmers were unable to prevent this gradual incursion but the diversion of labour to the military from temple building and rice farming helped seal the fate of Angkor. Another reason for the decline was the introduction of Theravada Buddhism in the 13th century, which undermined the prestige of the king and the priests. There is even a view that climatic change disrupted the agricultural system and led to Kambuja's demise. After Jayavarman VII, no king seems to have been able to unify the kingdom by force of arms or personality – internal dissent increased while the king's extravagance continued to place a crippling burden on state funds. With its temples decaying and its once-magnificent agricultural system in ruins, Angkor became virtually uninhabitable. In 1431 the royal capital was finally abandoned to the Siamese, who drove the Khmers out and made Cambodia a vassal of the Thai Sukhothai Kingdom.

EXPLAINING ANGKOR'S DECLINE

Why the Angkorian Empire should have declined has always fascinated scholars in the W – in the same way that the decline and fall of the Roman Empire has done. Numerous explanations have been offered, and still the debate remains unresolved. As Anthony Barnett argued in a paper in the *New Left Review* in 1990, perhaps the question should be "why did Angkor last so long? Inauspiciously sited, it was nonetheless a tropical imperium of 500 years' duration."

There are essentially five lines of argument in the 'Why did Angkor fall?' game. First, it has been argued that the building programmes became simply so arduous and demanding of ordinary people that they voted with their feet and moved out, depriving Angkor of the population necessary to support the great empire. Second, some scholars have presented an environmental argument: that the great irrigation works silted-up, undermining the agricultural wealth on which the empire was based. (This line of argument conflicts with recent work that maintains that Angkor's wealth was never based on hydraulic – or irrigated – agriculture.) Third, there are those who say that military defeat was the cause – although that begs the question of why they were defeated in the first place. Fourth, historians with a rather wider view, have offered the opinion that the centres of economic activity in Southeast Asia moved from land-based to sea-based foci, and that Angkor was poorly located to adapt to this shift in patterns of trade, wealth and, hence, power. Lastly, some scholars have argued that the religion on which kings demanded labour of their subjects became so corrupt as to corrode the empire from within.

AFTER ANGKOR – RUNNING SCARED

The next 500 years or so, until the arrival of the French in 1863, was an undistinguished period in Cambodian history. In 1434 the royal Khmer court under Ponheayat moved to Phnom Penh, where a replica of the cosmic Mt Meru was built. There was a short-lived period of revival in the mid-15th century until the Siamese invaded and sacked the capital again in 1473. One of the sons of the captured King Suryavarman drummed up enough Khmer support to oust the invaders and there were no subsequent invasions during the 16th century. The capital was established at Lovek (between Phnom Penh and Tonlé Sap) and then moved back to the ruins at Angkor. But a Siamese invasion in 1593 sent the royal court fleeing into Laos; finally, in 1603, the Thais released a captured prince to rule over their Cambodian vassal. There were at least 22 kings between 1603 and 1848.

Politically, the Cambodian court tried to steer a course between its powerful neighbours of Siam and Vietnam, seeking one's protection against the other. King Chey Chetta II (1618-1628), for example declared Cambodia's independence from Siam and in order to back up his actions he asked Vietnam for help. To cement the allegiance he was forced to marry a Vietnamese princess of the Nguyen Dynasty of Annam, and then obliged to pay tribute to Vietnam. His successors – hoping to rid themselves of Vietnamese domination – sought Siamese assistance and were then forced to pay for it by acknowledging Siam's suzerainty. Then in 1642, King Chan converted to Islam, and encouraged Malay and Javanese migrants to settle in Cambodia. Considering him guilty of apostasy, his cousins ousted him – with Vietnamese support. But 50 years later, the Cambodian Ang Eng was crowned in Bangkok. This see-saw pattern continued for years; only Siam's wars with Burma and Vietnam's internal disputes and long-running conflict with China prevented them from annexing the whole of Cambodia, although both took territorial advantage of the fragmented state.

By the early 1700s the kingdom was centred on Phnom Penh (there were periods when the king resided at Ondong). But when the Khmers lost their control over the Mekong Delta to the Vietnamese in the late 18th century, the capital's access to the sea was blocked. By 1750 the Khmer royal family had split into pro-Siamese and pro-Vietnamese factions. Between 1794-1811 and 1847-1863, Siamese influence was strongest; from 1835-1837 the Vietnamese dominated. In the 1840s, the Siamese and Vietnamese armies fought on Cambodian territory devastating the country. This provoked French intervention – and cost Cambodia its independence, even if it had been nominal for several centuries. On 17 April 1864 (the same day and month as the Khmers Rouges soldiers entered Phnom Penh) King Norodom agreed to French protection as he believed they would provide military assistance against the Siamese. The king was to be disappointed: France honoured Siam's claim to the western provinces of Battambang, Siem Reap and Sisophon, which Bangkok had captured in the late 1600s. (They were only returned to Cambodia in 1907.) And in 1884, King Norodom was persuaded by the French governor of the colony of Cochin China to sign another treaty that turned Cambodia into a French colony, along with Laos and Vietnam in the Union Indochinoise. The establishment of Cambodia as a French protectorate probably saved the country from being apportioned between Siam and Vietnam.

THE FRENCH COLONIAL PERIOD

The French did little to develop Cambodia, preferring instead for the territory to pay for itself. The French only invested income generated from tax revenue to build a communications network. In the 1920s French private-sector investors

King Norodom Sihanouk: latter day god-king

An uncomplimentary profile of Prince Norodom Sihanouk in The Economist *in 1990 said that over the preceding 20 years, he "twisted and turned, sulked, resigned many times, [was] humiliated and imprisoned. In one thing, however, he [was] consistent: his yearning to recover the face he lost in 1970, and return to Phnom Penh in triumph". The following year, on 14 Nov, Prince Sihanouk did exactly that, arriving in his former royal capital to a rapturous welcome, after 13 years of exile. In Nov 1991, as in 1953 when he returned from exile at Independence, he represented the one symbol Cambodia had of any semblance of national unity.*

Norodom Sihanouk was crowned King of Cambodia at the age of 18 in 1941. He owed his accession to the throne to a method of selection devised by the French colonial regime who hoped that the young, inexperienced Sihanouk would be a compliant puppet-king. But in the event he turned out to be something very different. Using his position to great advantage, he became a nationalist leader and crusaded for independence in 1953. But following independence, his royal title worked against him: the 1947 constitution restricted the role the monarch could play in politics. So, he abdicated in favour of his father, Norodom Suramarit, in 1955 and, as Prince Sihanouk, was free to enter politics. He immediately founded the *Sangkum Reastr Niyum* – the Popular Socialist Community (PSC). The same year, the PSC won every seat in the National Assembly – as it did in subsequent elections in 1958, 1962 and 1966.

The old king died in 1960, but Sihanouk side-stepped the problem of succession by declaring himself Head of State, without ascending to the throne. Michael Leifer, a British political scientist, writes: "As Head of State, Prince Sihanouk became literally the voice of Cambodia. He articulated its hopes and fears within the country and to the outside world... He appeared as a popular figure revered especially in the rural areas as the father figure of his country." He was a populist of the first order. Someth May, in his autobiography *Cambodian Witness*, describes Phnom Penh in the early 1960s:

"Sihanouk's portrait was everywhere around town: in uniform with a sword, in a suit, in monk's robes, dressed in white with a shaved head like an *achar*, on posters, on notebooks; framed in every classroom above the teacher's head; in the shops and offices. In the magazine that he edited himself we saw him helping

planted out rubber estates in Kompong Cham in E Cambodia. From a Cambodian perspective, the only benefit of colonial rule was that the French forestalled the total disintegration of the country, which would otherwise have been divided up between its warring neighbours. French cartographers also mapped Cambodia's borders for the first time and in so doing, the French forced the Thais to surrender the northwestern provinces of Battambang and Siem Reap.

For nearly a century the French alter-nately supported two branches of the royal family, the Norodoms and the Sisowaths, crowning the 18-year-old schoolboy **Prince Norodom Sihanouk** in 1941. The previous year, the Nazis had invaded and occupied France; French territories in Indochina were in turn occupied by the Japanese – although Cambodia was still formally governed and administered by the French. It was at this stage that a group of pro-independence Cambodians realized just how weak the French control of

a farmer dig an irrigation canal, reviewing the troops, shooting a film (for he was also a film-maker), addressing the National Assembly, giving presents to the monks, opening the annual regatta with his wife, Monique. On the radio we heard his speeches, and one year when he had a craze for singing you could hear his songs more than 10 times a day."

Sihanouk liked to run the show single-handedly and he is said to have treated his ministers like flunkies. In *Sideshow*, William Shawcross paints him as being vain – "a petulant showman who enjoyed boasting of his sexual successes. He would not tolerate criticism or dissent... At the same time he had enormous political skill, charm, tenacity and intelligence."

With an American-backed right-wing regime in power after the coup in 1970, the former king went into exile in China, where his supporters formed an alliance with his former enemies, the Khmers Rouges: the Royal Government of National Union of Cambodia – otherwise known as the Grunc. When the Khmers Rouges marched into Phnom Penh in 1975, they restored Prince Sihanouk as Head of State.

He resigned in Apr 1976 as he became increasingly marginalized, and the Grunc was dissolved. Sihanouk was kept under house-arrest until a few days before the Vietnamese army occupied Phnom Penh in Jan 1979, whereupon he fled to Beijing. There Sihanouk and his supporters once again joined forces with the Khmers Rouges in a tripartite coalition aimed at overthrowing the Hanoi-backed government.

The peace settlement which followed the eventual Vietnamese withdrawal in 1989 paved the way for Sihanouk's return from exile. His past association with the Khmers Rouges had tarnished the prince's image, but to many Cambodians, he represents one of their few hopes for a stable future. Following the elections of 1993, Sihanouk returned from Beijing to be crowned King on 24 Sep, thus reclaiming the throne he relinquished in 1955. Now an old man – he turned 74 in 1996, suffers from cancer of the prostate, and reportedly had a mild stroke in 1996 – many commentators wonder whether he will ever see his country truly at peace. Who his successor might be, and what his role might be, is far from clear. The next king will be nominated by the fractious Royal Council to the Throne. Currently three of Sihanouk's sons are all in the frame.

their country actually was. In 1942 two monks were arrested and accused of preaching anti-French sermons; within 2 days this sparked demonstrations by more than 1,000 monks in Phnom Penh. These demonstrations marked the beginning of Cambodian nationalism. In Mar 1945 Japanese forces ousted the colonial administration and persuaded King Norodom Sihanouk to proclaim independence. Following the Japanese surrender in Aug 1945, the French came back in force; Sihanouk tried to negoti-ate independence from France and they responded by abolishing the absolute monarchy in 1946 – although the king remained titular head of state. A new constitution was introduced allowing political activity and a National Assembly elected.

INDEPENDENCE AND NEUTRALITY

By the early 1950s the French army had suffered several defeats in the war in Indochina. Sihanouk dissolved the

National Assembly in mid-1952, which he was entitled to do under the constitution, and personally took charge of steering Cambodia towards independence from France. To publicize the cause, he travelled to Thailand, Japan and the United States, and said he would not return from self-imposed exile until his country was free. His audacity embarrassed the French into granting Cambodia independence on 9 November 1953 – and Sihanouk returned, triumphant.

The people of Cambodia did not want to return to absolute monarchy, and following his abdication in 1955, Sihanouk became a popular political leader. But political analysts believe that despite the apparent popularity of the former king's administration, different factions began to develop at this time, a process which was the root of the conflict in the years to come. During the 1960s, eg there was a growing rift between the Khmer majority and other ethnic groups, between the city dwellers and the farmers, as well as among the urban élites themselves. Even in the countryside, differences became marked between the rice-growing areas and the remoter mountain areas where people practised shifting cultivation supplementing their diet with lizards, snakes, roots and insects. As these problems intensified in the late 1960s and the economic situation deteriorated, the popular support base for the Khmers Rouges was put into place. With unchecked population growth, land ownership patterns became skewed, landlessness more widespread and food prices escalated. The Chinese community was increasingly resented as Chinese businessmen emerged as loan-sharks.

Sihanouk managed to keep Cambodia out of the war that enveloped Laos and Vietnam during the late 1950s and 1960s by following a neutral policy – which helped attract millions of dollars of economic aid to Cambodia from both the West and the Eastern Bloc. But when a full scale civil war broke out in S Vietnam in the early 1960s, Cambodia's survival – and Sihanouk's own survival – depended on its outcome. Sihanouk believed the rebels, the National Liberation Front (NLF) – allied to the Communist regime in Hanoi – would win; he openly courted and backed the NLF. It was an alliance which cost him dear. In 1965-66 the tide began to turn in S Vietnam, due to US military and economic intervention. This forced NLF troops to take refuge inside Cambodia (in 1966 half of Cambodia's rice supplies, normally sold abroad, were distributed to the NLF agents inside Cambodia). A peasant uprising in northwestern provinces in 1967 showed Sihanouk that he was sailing rather close to the wind; his forces brutally suppressed the rebellion by massacring as many as 10,000 peasants.

But slowly – and inevitably – he became the focus of resentment within Cambodia's political élite. He also incurred American wrath by allowing N Vietnamese forces to use Cambodian territory as an extension of the **Ho Chi Minh Trail**, ferrying arms and men into S Vietnam. This resulted in his former army Commander-in-Chief, **Marshal Lon Nol** masterminding his removal as Head of State while Sihanouk was in Moscow in 1970. Lon Nol abolished the monarchy and proclaimed a republic. One of the most auspicious creatures in Khmer mythology is the white crocodile. The crocodile is said to appear above the surface at important times. A white crocodile was sighted near Phnom Penh just before Lon Nol took over.

THE THIRD INDOCHINA WAR AND THE RISE OF THE KHMERS ROUGES

On 30 April 1970, following the overthrow of Prince Norodom Sihanouk, US President Richard Nixon officially announced **Washington's military intervention in Cambodia** – although in reality it had been going on for some time. The invasion aimed to deny the Vietnam-

The Ho Chi Minh Trail

ese Communists the use of Sihanoukville port through which 85% of their heavy arms were reaching S Vietnam. The US Air Force had been secretly bombing Cambodia using B-52s since Mar 1969. In 1973, facing defeat in Vietnam, the US Air Force B-52s began carpet bombing Communist-controlled areas to enable Lon Nol's inept regime to retain control of the besieged provincial cities. Historian David P Chandler writes:

"When the campaign was stopped by the US Congress at the end of the year, the B-52s had dropped over half a million tons of bombs on a country with which the United States was not at war – more than twice the tonnage dropped on Japan during WW2.

"The war in Cambodia was known as 'the sideshow' by journalists covering the war in Vietnam and by American policy-makers in London. Yet the intensity of US bombing in Cambodia was greater than it ever was in Vietnam; about 500,000 soldiers and civilians were killed over the 4-year period. It also caused about 2 million refugees to flee from the countryside to the capital."

By the end of the war, the country had become totally dependent on US aid and much of the population survived on American rice rations. Confidence in the Lon Nol government collapsed as taxes rose and even children were drafted into combat units. At the same time, the **Khmers Rouges** increased its military strength dramatically and began to make inroads into areas formerly controlled by government troops. Although officially the Khmers Rouges rebels represented the Beijing-based Royal Government of National Union of Cambodia (Grunc), which was headed by the exiled Prince Sihanouk. Grunc's *de facto* leaders were Pol Pot, Khieu Samphan (who today is the public face of the Khmers Rouges), Ieng Sary (later foreign minister) and Son Sen (Chief of General Staff) – all Khmers Rouges men. By the time the American bombing

stopped in 1973, the guerrillas dominated about 60% of Cambodian territory, while the government clung tenuously to towns and cities. Over the next 2 years the Khmers Rouges whittled away Phnom Penh's defence perimeter to the point that Lon Nol's government was sustained only by American airlifts into the capital.

Some commentators have suggested that the persistent heavy bombing of Cambodia, which forced the Communist guerrillas to live in terrible conditions – was in part, responsible for the notorious savagery of the Khmers Rouges in later years. Not only were they brutalized by the conflict itself, but they became resentful that the city-dwellers had no inkling of how unpleasant their experiences really were. This, writes US political scientist Wayne Bert, "created the perception among the Khmers Rouges that the bulk of the population did not take part in the revolution, was therefore not enthusiastic about it and could not be trusted to support it. The final step in this logic was to punish or eliminate all in these categories who showed either real or imagined tendencies toward disloyalty." And that, as anyone who has watched *The Killing Fields* will know, is what happened.

THE 'POL POT TIME': BUILDING YEAR ZERO

On 1 April 1975 President Lon Nol fled Cambodia to escape the rapidly advancing Khmers Rouges. Just over 2 weeks later, on 17 Apr, the victorious Khmers Rouges entered Phnom Penh. The capital's population had been swollen by refugees from 600,000 to over 2 million. The ragged conquering troops wearing Ho Chi Minh sandals made of used rubber tyres – which were *de rigueur* for guerrillas in Indochina – were welcomed as heroes. None in the crowds that lined the streets appreciated the horrors that the victory would also bring. Cambodia was renamed Democratic Kampuchea (DK) and Pol Pot set to work establishing a radical Maoist-style agrarian society. These ideas had been first sketched out by his longstanding colleague Khieu Samphan, whose 1959 doctoral thesis – at the Sorbonne University in Paris – analysed the effects of Cambodia's colonial and neo-colonial domination. In order to secure true economic and political independence he argued that it was necessary to isolate Cambodia completely and to go back to a self-sufficient agricultural economy.

It was Prince Norodom Sihanouk who had first coined the term 'Khmers Rouges' when he faced a peasant uprising in 1967; they called themselves *Angkar Loeu* – 'The Higher Organization'. Within days of the occupation, the rubber sandalled revolutionaries had forcibly evacuated many of the inhabitants of Phnom Penh to the countryside. A second major displacement was carried out at the end of the year, when hundreds of thousands of people from the area SE of Phnom Penh were forced to move to the NW. Prior to the Khmers Rouges coming to power, the Cambodian word for revolution had a conventional meaning: *bambahbambor* or 'uprising'. Under Pol Pot's regime, the word *pativattana* was used instead; it meant 'return to the past'. The Khmers Rouges did this by obliterating everything that did not subscribe to their vision of the past glories of ancient Khmer culture. Pol Pot wanted to return the country to **'Year Zero'** – he wanted to begin again. One of the many revolutionary slogans was "we will burn the old grass and new will grow"; money, modern technology, education and newspapers were outlawed. Khieu Samphan, who became the Khmers Rouges Head of State, following Prince Sihanouk's resignation in 1976, said at the time: "No, we have no machines. We do everything by mainly relying on the strength of our people. We work completely self-

sufficiently. This shows the overwhelming heroism of our people. This also shows the great force of our people. Though bare-handed, they can do everything".

Food was scarce under Pol Pot's inefficient system of collective farming and administration was based on fear, torture and summary execution. A veil of secrecy shrouded Cambodia and, until a few desperate refugees began to trickle over the border into Thailand, the outside world was largely ignorant of what was going on. The refugees' stories of atrocities were, at first, disbelieved. Jewish refugees who escaped from Nazi occupied Poland in the 1940s had encountered a similarly disbelieving reception simply because (like the Cambodians) what they had to say was, to most people, unbelievable. Jan Karski, a Pole, escaped from a concentration camp in 1942 and made his way to America. He described to a Supreme Court Judge the conditions he had experienced. The Judge replied "I do not believe you". Not unnaturally Karski protested. The Judge replied "I do not mean that you are lying, I simply said I cannot believe you." Some left wing academics initially viewed the revolution as an inspired and brave attempt to break the shackles of dependency and neo-colonial domination. Others, such as Noam Chomsky, dismissed the allegations as right wing press propoganda.

It was not until the Vietnamese 'liberation' of Phnom Penh in 1979 that the scale of the Khmers Rouges carnage emerged and the **atrocities** witnessed by the survivors became known. The stories turned the Khmers Rouges into international pariahs – but only until 1982 when, remarkably, their American and Chinese sympathisers secured them a voice at the United Nations. Wives has been encouraged to denounce their husbands; children their mothers. Anyone who had smoked an American cigarette was a CIA operative; anyone with a taste

Pol Pot – the idealistic psychopath

Prince Norodom Sihanouk once referred to Pol Pot as "a more fortunate Hitler". Unlike his erstwhile fascist counterpart, the man whose troops were responsible for the deaths of perhaps 2 million fellow Cambodians has managed to get away with it. Pol Pot's real name is Saloth Sar – he adopted his *nom de guerre* when he became Secretary-General of the Cambodian Communist Party in 1963. He was born in 1928 into a peasant family in Kompong Thom, central Cambodia, and is believed to have lived as a novice monk for 9 months when he was a child. His services to the Democrat Party won him a scholarship to study electronics in Paris. But he became a Communist in France in 1949 and spent more time at meetings of Marxist revolutionary societies than in classes. In his 1986 book *Sideshow*, William Shawcross notes that at that time the French Communist Party, which was known for its dogmatic adherence to orthodox Marxism, "taught hatred of the bourgeoisie and uncritical admiration of Stalinism, including the collectivization of agriculture". Pol Pot finally lost his scholarship in 1953.

Returning to newly independent Cambodia, Pol Pot started working as a school teacher in Phnom Penh and continued his revolutionary activities in the underground Cambodian Communist Party (which, remarkably kept its existence a secret until 1977). In 1963, he fled the capital for the countryside, fearing a crackdown of the left by Sihanouk. There he rose to become Secretary-General of the Central Committee of the Communist Party of Kampuchea. He was trained in guerrilla warfare and he became a leader of the Khmers Rouges forces, advocating armed resistance to Sihanouk and his 'feudal entourage'. In 1975 when the Khmers Rouges marched into Phnom Penh, Pol Pot was forced out of the shadows to take the role of leader, 'Brother Number One'. Although he took the title of Prime Minister, he ruled as a dictator and set about reshaping Cambodia with his mentor, Khieu Samphan, the Head of State. Yet during the years he was in power, hardly any Cambodians – save those in the top echelons of the Khmers Rouges – had even heard of him.

The Vietnam-backed Hun Sen government, which took over the country after the overthrow of the Khmers Rouges in Dec 1978, calculated that by demonizing Pol Pot as the mastermind of the genocide, it would avert the possibility of the Khmers Rouges ever making a comeback. The Hun Sen regime showed no interest in analysing the complex factors which combined to bring Pol Pot to power. Within Cambodia, he has been portrayed simply as a tyrannical bogey-man. During the 1980s, 20 May was declared National Hate Day, when everyone reaffirmed their hatred of Pol Pot.

Pol Pot and what Hun Sen dubbed 'his genocidal clique' of close associates are thought still to control the movement, which continues to hold some areas of rural Cambodia. (Ieng Sary, confirmed Pol Pot was still alive when he surrendered to the government in late 1996.) In a review of David Chandler's biography of Pol Pot (*Brother Number One: A Political Biography of Pol Pot*, Westview Press, 1992), Peter Carey – the co-director of the British-based Cambodia Trust – was struck by what he called "the sinister disjunction between the man's evident charisma ... and the monumental suffering wrought by his regime". Carey concludes: "one is left with the image of a man consumed by his own vision, a vision of empowerment and liberation that has little anchorage in Cambodian reality".

for café crème was a French collaborator. During the Khmers Rouge's 44-month reign of terror, it had hitherto been generally accepted that around a million people died. This is a horrendous figure when one considers that the population of the country in 1975 was around 7 million. What is truly shocking is that new work being undertaken by a team from Yale University indicates that this figure is far too low.

Although the Khmers Rouges era in Cambodia may have been a period of unprecedented economic, political and human turmoil, they still managed to keep meticulous records of what they were doing. In this regard the KR were rather like the Chinese during the Cultural Revolution, or the Nazis in Germany. Using Australian satellite data, the team were expecting to uncover around 200 mass graves; instead they think they have found several thousand. The Khmers Rouges themselves have claimed that around 20,000 people died because of their 'mistakes'. The Vietnamese have traditionally put the figure at 2-3 million, although their estimates have generally been rejected as too high and politically motivated (being a means to justify their invasion of the country in 1978/79 and subsequent occupation). But the Yale work seems to indicate that the Vietnamese figures may well be closer to the truth, and that 1 million deaths is a significant underestimate. (Academics are congenitally argumentative, but the worst – or best – seem to work on Cambodia for some reason. Steven Heder, Ben Kiernan, Craig Etcheson, Michael Vickery and others trade thinly veiled insults and engage in the art of the finely worded riposte. Much of the debate centres on their views of the various Cambodian factions and how blame should be apportioned. *The Phnom Penh Post* carries their numerous letters and articles.

How such a large slice of Cambodia's people died in so short a time (between 1975 and the end of 1978) staggers belief. Some were shot, strangled or suffocated; many more starved; while others died from disease – malaria was rife – and overwork. The Khmers Rouges transformed Cambodia into what the British journalist, William Shawcross, described as:

"a vast and sombre work camp where toil was unending, where respite and rewards were nonexistent, where families were abolished and where murder was used as a tool of social discipline... The manner of execution was often brutal. Babies were torn apart limb from limb, pregnant women were disemboweled. Men and women were buried up to their necks in sand and left to die slowly. A common form of execution was by axe handles to the back of the neck. That saved ammunition."

The Khmers Rouges revolution was primarily a class-based one, fed by years of growing resentment against the privileged élites. The revolution pitted the least-literate, poorest rural peasants against the educated, skilled and foreign-influenced urban population. Through a series of **terrible purges**, the members of the former governing and mercantile classes were liquidated or sent to work as forced labourers. But Peter Carey, Oxford historian and Chairman of the Cambodia Trust, argues that not all Pol Pot's victims were townspeople and merchants. "Under the terms of the 1948 Genocide Convention, the Khmers Rouges stands accused of genocide," he wrote in a letter to a British newspaper in 1990. "Of 64,000 Buddhist monks, 62,000 perished; of 250,000 Islamic Chams, 100,000; of 200,000 Vietnamese still left in 1975, 100,000; of 20,000 Thai, 12,000; of 1,800 Lao, 1,000. Of 2,000 Kola, not a trace remained." American political scientist Wayne Bert noted that: "The methods and behaviour compare to that of the Nazis and Stalinists, but in the percentage of the population killed by a revolutionary movement, the Khmers Rouges holds an unchallenged record."

It is still unclear the degree to which these 'genocidal' actions were controlled by those at the centre. Many of the killings took place at the discretion of local leaders, but there were some notably cruel leaders in the upper echelons of the Khmers Rouges and none can have been ignorant of what was going on. Ta Mok, who administered the region SW of Phnom Penh, oversaw many mass-executions for example. There is also evidence that the central government was directly involved in the running of the Tuol Sleng detention centre in which at least 20,000 people died. It has now been turned into the Cambodian version of Auschwitz, as a memorial to Pol Pot's holocaust (see page 91).

In addition to the legacy left by centres such as Tuol Sleng, there is the impact of the mass killings upon the Cambodian psyche. One of which is – to western eyes – the startling openness with which Khmer people will, if asked, matter-of-factly relate their family history in detail: this usually involves telling how the Khmers Rouges era meant they lost one or several members of their family. Whereas death is talked about in hushed terms in western society, Khmers have no such reservations, perhaps because it touched, and touches them all.

THE VIETNAMESE INVASION

The first border clashes over offshore islands between Khmers Rouges forces and the Vietnamese army were reported just a month after the Khmers Rouges came to power. These erupted into a minor war in Jan 1977 when the Phnom Penh government accused Vietnam of seeking to incorporate Kampuchea with an Indochinese federation. Hanoi's determination to oust Pol Pot only really became apparent however, on Christmas Day 1978 when 120,000 Vietnamese

troops invaded. By 7 Jan (the day of Phnom Penh's liberation) they had installed a puppet government which proclaimed the foundation of the People's Republic of Kampuchea (PRK); Heng Samrin, a former member of the Khmers Rouges, was appointed president. The Vietnamese compared their invasion to the liberation of Uganda from Idi Amin – but for the western world it was an unwelcome Christmas present. The new government was accorded scant recognition abroad, while the toppled government of Democratic Kampuchea retained the country's seat at the United Nations.

But the country's 'liberation' by Vietnam did not end the misery; in 1979 nearly half Cambodia's population was in transit, either searching for their former homes or fleeing across the Thai border into refugee camps. The country reverted to a state of outright war again, for the Vietnamese were not greatly loved in Cambodia – especially by the Khmers Rouges. American political scientist Wayne Bert writes: "The Vietnamese had long seen a special role for themselves in uniting and leading a greater Indochina Communist movement and the Cambodian Communists had seen with clarity that such a role for the Vietnamese could only be at the expense of their independence and prestige." Under the Lon Nol and Khmers Rouges regimes, Vietnamese living in Cambodia were expelled or exterminated. Resentment had built up over the years in Hanoi – exacerbated by the apparent ingratitude of the Khmers Rouges for Vietnamese assistance in fighting Lon Nol's US-supported Khmer Republic in the early 1970s. As relations between the Khmers Rouges and the Vietnamese deteriorated, the Communist superpowers, China and the Soviet Union, polarized too – the former siding with the Khmers Rouges and the latter with Hanoi. The Vietnamese invasion had the full backing of Moscow. While the Chinese and Americans

Cambodian refugees

The Paris Peace Accord charged the UN's Transitional Authority in Cambodia (UNTAC) with overseeing one of the biggest population shifts in modern history. By May 1993 it resettled more than 360,000 Cambodian refugees – about 5% of the Cambodian population – from six refugee camps in Thailand at a cost of more than US$800mn. The resettlement programme was hailed as one of the most successful aspects of the UN's mission in Cambodia. It was supervised by the UN High Commissioner for Refugees (UNHCR) which organized the resettlement of up to 10,000 people a week between Mar 1992 and Apr 1993. The refugees moved to UN-built reception centres before being dispatched to their resettlement sites. The Geneva-based organization decided to let the refugees choose their resettlement location; it also promised that each should be given a plot of land, materials to build a house, land to farm, tools, cooking utensils and food for 1 year – until the first rice crop was harvested. But the UN soon discovered that it could not stand by its word; such a large area of farmland had been mined that there simply was not enough safe land to go round. Many went instead for cash handouts of US$300 each.

Like the country's physical infrastructure which lies in ruins, Cambodia's social infrastructure has been virtually destroyed by the years of civil war. Families have been split up and family members are often unaware of whether their parents, children, brothers or sisters are alive or dead. Even if they are still alive, they could be just about anywhere – in Cambodia, Thailand or the United States. The 360,000 refugees who have returned face a lengthy and difficult period of adjustment after nearly 14 years in camps on the Thai border. Observers note that the conditions in some of the Thai camps were markedly better than those in Cambodia, where banditry is rife, and land mines are everywhere. Nearly half of the returnees are under the age of 15 – most grew up in the Thai camps and have no experience of life outside them; their understanding of the outside world is limited. In 1991 a British newspaper report quoted a UNHCR official as saying: "Many of the children don't know that rice grows in paddies. They think it comes off the back of a lorry every Tuesday."

began their support for the anti-Vietnamese rebels.

Following the Vietnamese invasion, three main anti-Hanoi factions were formed. In Jun 1982 they banded together in an unholy and unlikely alliance of convenience to fight the PRK and called themselves the Coalition Government of Democratic Kampuchea (CGDK), which was immediately recognized by the United Nations. The three factions of the CGDK were:

● The Communist **Khmers Rouges**, whose field forces had recovered to at least 18,000 by the late 1980s. Supplied with weapons by China, they were concentrated in the Cardamom Mountains in the SW and were also in control of some of the refugee camps along the Thai border.

● The National United Front for an Independent Neutral Peaceful and Cooperative Cambodia (Funcinpec) – known by most people as the **Armée Nationale Sihanoukiste** (ANS). It was headed by Prince Sihanouk – although he spent most of his time exiled in Beijing; the group had under 15,000 well-equipped troops – most of whom took orders from Khmers Rouges commanders.

● The anti-Communist **Khmer People's National Liberation Front**

Cambodia 1953-1993

1953	Cambodian independence from France.
1965	Prince Sihanouk's government cuts links with the United States following deployment of US troops in Vietnam.
1966	Right-wing beats Sihanouk in the election; Lon Nol elected Prime Minister.
1967	Lon Nol toppled following left-wing demonstrations.
1969	Lon Nol becomes Prime Minister again.
1970	Lon Nol topples Sihanouk in US-backed coup; US bombs Communist bases in Cambodia.
1972	Lon Nol becomes first President of the Khmer Republic.
1975	Lon Nol flees as Khmers Rouges seizes power; Sihanouk made Head of Government.
1976	Cambodia renamed Democratic Kampuchea; Sihanouk resigns and Khieu Samphan becomes Head of State, with Pol Pot as Prime Minister. Government moves people from towns to labour camps in the countryside.
1975	Lon Nol flees as Khmers Rouges government recognized by UN. Dec: Vietnam invades.
1981	Country renamed the People's Republic of Kampuchea (PRK).
1982	Coalition government-in-exile formed by anti-Hanoi resistance comprising Sihanoukists, Khmers Rouges and KPNLF. Sihanouk appointed President; Khieu Samphan, Vice-President and Son Sann, Prime Minister. Coalition backed by China and ASEAN.
1984	Vietnam gains rebel-held territory along Thai border; Vietnamese civilians settle in Kampuchea.
1989	Peoples Republic of Kampuchea renamed the State of Cambodia. Sep: last of the Vietnamese troops leave.
1991	International Conference on Cambodia leads to peace treaty and deployment of UN.
1993	In May elections were held under the auspices of the United Nations Transitional Authority in Cambodia. A coalition government was formed and Norodom Sihanouk was re-crowned King in Sep.

(KPNLF), headed by Son Sann, a former prime minister under Sihanouk. Its 5,000 troops were reportedly ill-disciplined in comparison with the Khmers Rouges and the ANS.

The three CGDK factions were ranged against the 70,000 troops loyal to the government of President Heng Samrin and Prime Minister Hun Sen (previously a Khmers Rouges cadre). They were backed by Vietnamese forces until Sep 1989. Within the forces of the Phnom Penh government there were reported to be problems of discipline and desertion. But the rebel guerrilla coalition was itself seriously weakened by rivalries and hatred between the different factions: in reality, the idea of a 'coalition' was fiction. Throughout most of the 1980s the war followed the progress of the seasons: during the dry season from Nov to Apr the PRK forces with their tanks and heavy arms took the offensive but during the wet season this heavy equipment was ineffective and the guerrilla resistance made advances.

THE ROAD TOWARDS PEACE

In the late 1980s the Association of Southeast Asian Nations (ASEAN) – for which the Cambodian conflict had almost become its *raison d'être* – began steps to bring the warring factions together over the negotiating table. ASEAN countries were united primarily in wanting the Vietnamese out of Cambodia. While publicly deploring the Khmers Rouges record, ASEAN tacitly supported the guerrillas. Thailand, an ASEAN member-state, which has had a centuries-long suspicion of the Vietnamese, cooperated closely with China to ensure that the Khmers Rouges guerrillas over the border were well-supplied with weapons.

After Mikhail Gorbachev had come to power in the Soviet Union, Moscow's support for the Vietnamese presence in Cambodia gradually evaporated. Gorbachev began leaning on Vietnam, as early as 1987, to withdraw its troops. Despite saying their presence in Cambodia was 'irreversible', Vietnam completed its withdrawal in Sep 1989, ending nearly 11 years of Hanoi's direct military involvement. The withdrawal led to an immediate upsurge in political and military activity, as forces of the exiled CGDK put increased pressure on the now weakened Phnom Penh regime to begin power-sharing negotiations (see page 65).

Art and architecture

The art of modern Cambodia is almost completely overshadowed by the greatness of its past. The influence of the Khmers at the height of the empire spread as far as the Malay peninsula in the S, to the Burmese border in the W and the Vietnamese frontier in the N and E. But ancient Khmer culture was itself inherited. Indian influence was particularly strong in the Mekong basin area and the Khmers accepted Indian ideas about astrology, religion and royalty – including the cult of the god-king (deva-raja). Other elements of Cambodian culture which are recognizably Indian in origin include classical literature and dance, as well as religious architecture. Hindu deities inspired the iconography in much of Cambodian (and Southeast Asian) art and Sanskrit gave the Khmers access to a whole new world of ideas, which were tailored and transformed to the Cambodian way of thinking. Cambodian influence is very strong in Thai culture as Siam's capture of a large part of the Khmer Empire in the 15th century resulted in many of Cambodia's best scholars, artists and craftsmen being transported to Siam (Thailand).

The richness of their culture remains a great source of pride for the Khmer people and in the past it has helped forge a sense of national identity. There has been an artistic revival since 1979 and the government has devoted resources to the restoration of monuments and

Mudras and the Buddha image

An artist producing an image of the Buddha does not try to create an original piece of art; he is trying to be faithful to a tradition which can be traced back over centuries. It is important to appreciate that the Buddha image is not merely a work of art but an object of, and for, worship. Sanskrit poetry even sets down the characteristics of the Buddha – albeit in rather unlikely terms: legs like a deer, arms like an elephant's trunk, a chin like a mango stone and hair like the stings of scorpions. The Pali texts of Theravada Buddhism add the 108 auspicious signs; long toes and fingers of equal length, body like a banyan tree and eyelashes like a cow's. The Buddha can be represented either sitting, lying (indicating *paranirvana*), or standing, and occasionally walking. He is often represented standing on an open lotus flower: the Buddha was born into an impure world, and likewise the lotus germinates in mud but rises above the filth to flower. Each image will be represented in a particular *mudra* or 'attitude', of which there are 40. The most common are:

Abhayamudra – dispelling fear or giving protection; right hand (sometimes both hands) raised, palm outwards, usually with the Buddha in a standing position.

Varamudra – giving blessing or charity; the right hand pointing downwards, the palm facing outwards, with the Buddha either seated or standing.

Vitarkamudra – preaching mudra; the ends of the thumb and index finger of the right hand touch to form a circle, symbolizing the Wheel of Law. The Buddha can either be seated or standing.

Dharmacakramudra – 'spinning the Wheel of Law'; a preaching mudra symbolizing the teaching of the first sermon. The hands are held in front of the chest, thumbs and index fingers of both joined, one facing inwards and one outwards.

Bhumisparcamudra – 'calling the earth goddess to witness' or 'touching the earth'; the right hand rests on the right knee with the tips of the fingers 'touching ground', thus calling the earth goddess Dharani/Thoranee to witness his enlightenment and victory over Mara, the king of demons. The Buddha is always seated.

Dhyanamudra – meditation; both hands resting open, palms upwards, in the lap, right over left.

Buddha calling for rain – a common image in Laos but very rare elsewhere; the Buddha is depicted standing, both arms held stiffly at the side of the body, fingers pointing downwards.

Other points of note:

Vajrasana – yogic posture of meditation; cross-legged, both soles of the feet visible.

Virasana – yogic posture of meditation; cross-legged, but with the right leg on top of the left, covering the left foot (also known as *paryankasana*).

Buddha under Naga – a common image in Khmer art; the Buddha is shown seated in an attitude of meditation with a cobra rearing up over his head. This refers to an episode in the Buddha's life when he was meditating; a rain storm broke and Nagaraja, the king of the nagas (snakes), curled up under the Buddha (seven coils) and then used his seven-headed hood to protect the Holy One from the falling rain.

ZTB 201

Bhumisparcamudra – calling
the earth goddess to witness.

Dhyanamudra – meditation.

Abhayamudra –
dispelling fear or giving
protection.

Vitarkamudra –
preaching, "spinning the
Wheel of Law" seated in
the "European" manner.

Abhayamudra –
dispelling fear or giving
protection; subduing
Mara position.

Stupa

after Stratton & Scott, 1981

1. Umbrella spire
2. Shaft
3. Harmika
4. Bell
5. Mouldings
6. Base or plinth

pagodas. (Many local wats have been repaired by local subscription; it is estimated that one fifth of rural disposable income is given to the upkeep of wats.) The resurgence of Buddhism has been paralleled in recent years by a revival of traditional Khmer culture, which was actively undermined during the Pol Pot years. Today Phnom Penh's two Fine Arts Schools are flourishing again; one teaches music and dance, the other specializes in architecture and archaeology. There is a surprisingly good collection of artefacts in the National Museum of Arts even though huge quantities of treasure and antiques have been stolen and much of the remainder destroyed by the Khmers Rouges.

The height of Khmer art and architecture dates from the Angkor period spanning the 8th to 13th centuries. All the surviving monuments are built of stone or brick, and all are religious buildings. The culture and art of the early kingdoms of **Funan** and **Chenla** were central to the evolution of Angkorian art and architecture. Art historian Philip Rawson writes that these two kingdoms were the foundation of Khmer art, "just as archaic Greek sculpture was the foundation of later classical Greek art". Funan's centre was to the SW of the Mekong Delta but extended into present day Cambodia. The only remains that definitely came from the early kingdom of Funan are limited to

four Sanskrit inscriptions and a few sculptures. The earliest surviving statues from Funan are at Angkor Borei and date from the 6th century; but by then Funan was a vassal of Chenla. The kingdom of Chenla – based at Sambor and later at Sambor Prei Kuk – expanded at the expense of Funan. It refined and developed Funan's earlier artistic styles.

Relics of the pre-Angkorian periods have been found all over S Cambodia and between the Mekong and the Tonlé Sap. The principal monuments are brick towers with square ground plans, false doors and mounting storeys of decreasing size. They were characterized by strong sculptural work, based on Indian ideas but carved in a unique style. Many of the statues from this era are in the National Museum of Arts at Phnom Penh (see page 90). Most of the art from the pre-Angkorian kingdoms is Hindu but it seems that Mahayana Buddhism was briefly introduced into the country as a number of images of Bodhisattvas have been found. In the late 8th century, the Chenla Kingdom collapsed and Jayavarman II, who had lived most of his life in the Sailendra court in Java, returned to declare himself devaraja in 802.

During the Angkor period, Javanese and neighbouring Champa architectural influences were incorporated into Khmer designs. The architecture and its decoration were governed by a series of mystical and religious beliefs. Temples were designed to represent the cosmic Mt Meru, surrounded by oceans. For a detailed account of the typical design features and evolution of Angkor temple architecture, as well as the development of Khmer sculpture, see page 107.

TEXTILES

Cambodia is not well known for the quality and range of its textiles, especially when compared with the industry in neighbouring Thailand and Laos. In Chou Ta-kuan's account of life at Angkor written in 1296-1297, he claimed that "Not only do the Khmer women lack skill with needle and thread for mending and sewing, they only know how to weave fabrics of cotton, not of silk". However by the time the French arrived in the second half of the 19th century, weaving in silk and cotton was well-established. The Cambodian royal court had a large retinue of weavers producing sumptuous, richly patterned and coloured silk cloth. Even as recently as the 1940s, weaving was still a craft practised in just about every village, and every woman worth her salt was expected to be able to weave. Then, in the 1950s, cheap imported silk and cotton cloth began to undermine the local product and people began to turn to other occupations. One elderly silk weaver, Liv Sa Em, explained in 1995, "you could earn more selling cakes in two days than you could earn weaving in five months". But it was the Khmers Rouges period which finally sealed the fate of Cambodia's textile industry. Apart from producing the familiar checked cloth used as a head scarf, or *kramar*, weaving virtually died out between 1975 and 1979. Many of the most skilled weavers, especially those associated with the Cambodian court, were either murdered or fled the country.

Now the government and many NGOs see a bright future for silk weaving and resources are being directed towards its revitalization. Many women find weaving attractive: it can be built around the demands of housework and childcare; it can be done at home; and it can provide an important supplementary source of income. However, because the domestic industry was so withered after years of neglect, NGOs are finding it necessary to bring in foreign weaving experts from Thailand, Laos, Vietnam and China to teach people anew how to raise silkworms and train women in more advanced weaving techniques.

The Cambodian national dress is the *samphot*, a long rectangle of cloth (about twice as long as a sarong length) which is wrapped around the body and then taken up between the legs to be tucked in at the waist. Traditionally women wore this with a simple breast cloth and men with a jacket. *Samphot* are woven in rich, warm colours. Sometimes the warp and weft are different colours giving the finished cloth a shimmering appearance. Weft ikat (see box) is used to produce the well-known *samphot hol* and it is thought that this process influenced Thai designs after Siam conquered Angkor in the mid-15th century taking many of the most skilled weavers back to the capital, Ayutthaya, as booty.

Ikat production

Ikat is a technique of patterning cloth characteristic of Southeast Asia and is produced from the hills of Burma to the islands of Eastern Indonesia. The word comes from the Malay word *mengikat* which means to bind or tie. Very simply, groups of warp or weft, and in one case both, are tied with material or fibre (or more often plastic string these days) so that they resist the action of the dye. Hence the technique's name – resist dyeing. By dyeing, retieing and dyeing again through a number of cycles it is possible to build up complex patterns. This initial pre-weaving process can take anything from 2-10 days, depending on the complexity of the design. Ikat is distinguishable by the bleeding of the dye which inevitably occurs no matter how carefully the threads are tied; this gives the finished cloth a blurred finish. The earliest ikats so far found date from the 14th-15th centuries.

To prepare the cloth for dyeing, the warp or weft is strung tight on a frame. Individual threads, or groups of threads are then tied together with fibre and leaves. In some areas wax is then smeared on top to help in the resist process. The main colour is usually dyed first, secondary colours later. With complex patterns (which are done from memory, plans are only required for new designs) and using natural dyes, it may take up to 6 months to produce a piece of cloth. Today, the pressures of the market place mean that it is more likely that cloth is produced using chemical dyes (which need only one short soaking, not multiple long ones – 6 hrs or so – as with some natural dyes), and design motifs have generally become larger and less complex. Traditionally, warp ikat used cotton (rarely silk) and weft ikat, silk. Silk in many areas has given way to cotton, and cotton sometimes to synthetic yarns.

Culture and life

PEOPLE

Before 1975, Cambodia had a population of about 7.2 million; within 4 years this had dropped to around 6 million (some were the victims of genocide, others became refugees). The population topped 10 million in 1995. The Khmers are the dominant group and there are significant Chinese and Vietnamese minorities as well as a small percentage of tribal groups – most of whom suffered badly during the Pol Pot years.

Khmers
The Khmers are believed to have lived in the region from about the 2nd century AD but there is some argument as to from where they migrated. They may constitute a fusion of Mongul and Melanesian elements. The Khmers now constitute 85% of the population. They have been mainly influenced over the centuries by the powerful Indian and Javanese kingdoms.

Khmer Loeu
The Khmer Loeu, or Upland Khmer (divided into the Saoch, Pear, Brao and Kui), are one of the main tribal groups and live in the forested mountain zones, mainly in the NE. The Saoch live in the Elephant Mountains to the SW; the Pear occupy the Cardamom Mountains to the W; while the Brao are settled along the Lao border to the NE. Traditionally the Khmer Loeu were semi-nomadic and practised slash and burn agriculture. Like many tribal groups in Southeast Asia they were also mainly animist. In recent years, however, increasing numbers have turned to settled agriculture and adopted many of the customs of the lowland Khmers.

Chinese
In the 18th and 19th centuries large numbers of ethnic Chinese migrated to Southeast Asia, where most became involved in commerce. The Chinese settled in the countryside as well as in cities and towns. Until the Khmers Rouges takeover in 1975, the Chinese played a central role in the economy, controlling trade, banking and transport. As in neighbouring Thailand, they assimilated to a greater degree than in other parts of Southeast Asia. In recent decades, most of Cambodia's urban and governing élite has had at least some Chinese blood – Lon Nol, for example had a Chinese grandparent. The Chinese started leaving the country when civil war broke out in 1970 – and many of those who did not get out before 1975 were killed during the Pol Pot years. The few who survived the Khmers Rouges were emigrated during the first months of the pro-Vietnam PRK rule. Officially, the Chinese population of Cambodia today (1995) is 50,000, although some unofficial sources put the number as high as 400,000.

Vietnamese
The southern part of Cambodia, particularly along the Mekong, has always had many inhabitants of Vietnamese descent as well as the area around Phnom Penh. The Vietnamese live very separate lives to the Cambodians due to centuries of mistrust and animosity between the two groups. They are known by the Khmers as 'youn', a derogatory term meaning 'people from the N'. The Cambodian Vietnamese can be distinguished from the Khmers by their typical two-piece pyjama suits of black cotton. Many of the Vietnamese population left following the takeover of the Khmers Rouges as they were a target of special persecution. A large percentage returned after

1979 with the Vietnamese military presence in the country. As in neighbouring Laos, the Hanoi government encouraged an active resettlement programme for Vietnamese in Cambodia. Most estimates currently put Cambodia's Vietnamese population at 6% of the total. Many Vietnamese have traditionally been businessmen and money changers; some work in skilled jobs and are tailors, mechanics and electricians but those living around the Tonlé Sap are mainly fishermen.

It is the Vietnamese in Cambodia who have suffered most in recent years, and who are most at risk. There are thought to be about 200-500,000 Vietnamese in the country, and some sources put the figure as high as 1 million. However officially the Vietnamese population is less than 100,000 (see table). Not only have they been specifically targeted by the Khmers Rouges, but it is hard to find a single Cambodian who has anything positive to say about Vietnamese settlers in the country. One human rights official was quoted as saying at the end of 1994 in the *Far Eastern Economic Review* that "Give a choice, a lot of people in this country would expel every single Vietnamese". This dislike of the Vietnamese stems partly from historical fears – Vietnam absorbed large areas of the former Cambodian Empire in the 18th and 19th centuries; partly from Vietnam's role in Cambodia between 1979 and 1989; and partly from the shear size of Vietnam – some 70 million inhabitants – when set against Cambodia's population of 9 million. As a result anti-Vietnamese sentiment is mainstream politics in the country. Inventing fanciful stories about Vietnamese commandos infiltrating the country, or Vietnamese control of the economy, is never likely to do harm to a budding populist politician.

The possibility that the Vietnamese, as an ethnic group, might simply be legislated into exile seemed to come closer to

Minority ethnic groups in Cambodia (1995)	
Cham	203,88
Vietnamese	95,597
Chinese	47,180
Lao	19,819
Tumpoun	15,861
Kui	14,186
Jarai	11,549
Kroeng	7,854
Phnong	5,323
Kavet	3,585
Steang	3,234
Prov	2,585
Thai	2,454
Kraol	1,962
Rabel	1,640
Por	1,440
Thmaun	453
Loemoun	280
Saoch	72
Kachok	6
Others	3,708
Total:	**370,463**

Source: Ministry of the Interior figures (Mar 1995) quoted in the *Phnom Penh Post* (4: 15, Jul/Aug 1995).

NB These are the official (Ministry of the Interior) population figures for ethnic minorities in Cambodia. Many unofficial sources put the numbers of Vietnamese and Chinese considerably higher.

reality when a controversial immigration law was passed by the National Assembly in Aug 1994. Some commentators saw the law as permitting the expulsion of ethnic Vietnamese residents.

Cham-Malays

There are about 200,000 Cham-Malays, descended from the Chams of the royal kingdom of Champa based in present day central Vietnam. They now constitute the single largest ethnic minority in the country. In the 15th century the Vietnamese moving S drove many of the

Chams living in the lower Mekong area into Cambodia. They now mainly live along the Mekong, N of Phnom Penh. The Chams were badly persecuted during the Pol Pot years and their population more than halved, from about 800,000 during the rule of King Norodom Sihanouk to 350,000 by the end of the Khmers Rouges period. They are Muslim people and their spiritual centre is Chur-Changvra near Phnom Penh. They adopted their faith and script from Malays who settled in Kampot and interior regions on the invitation of the Muslim Khmer King Chan in 1642, after he had converted to Islam. The Chams are traditionally cattle traders, silk weavers and butchers – Theravada Buddhism forbids the Khmer to slaughter animals. Their batik sarongs are very similar to those found in Malaysia.

Although the Cham are now free to pursue their faith largely free from persecution, they still suffer from the stigma of being viewed, by many Cambodians, as second class citizens. Strangely perhaps, there is a close affinity between Christians and Muslims in Cambodia – in the face of an overwhelmingly dominant Buddhist faith.

Other groups

There are also a small number of Shans, Thai and Lao, most who live near Battambang, the descendants of miners and jewellers who came to work the ruby mines of Pailin during the French colonial era (see table).

PROSTITUTION AND AIDS IN CAMBODIA

A survey undertaken in mid-1994 found there to be 418 brothels in Phnom Penh with 1,444 prostitutes. This is, in all likelihood, a gross under-estimate. Most commentators would put the latter figures at 10,000, and 15,000-20,000 for the whole country. The going rate for intercourse in 1996 was 10,000 riel or US$4, while a night with a prostitute cost 50,000 riel (US$20). But commercial sex workers providing services for cyclo drivers, for example, pare their rates to the bone: 500 riel, or less than US$0.25, for intercourse, according to the *Phnom Penh Post*. Many of the women and girls working in these establishments are from poor farming families and it seems that most intend to return home with their savings, some to set up small businesses. Most are also Vietnamese.

On paper at least, the prostitution industry in Phnom Penh should now be history: in Aug 1994 the Mayor of Phnom Penh banned brothels from operating in the city, threatening a fine of 1 million riel (US$200) to any brothel owners discovered ignoring the ban. However this edict has done little to stop prostitution, and many commentators saw it as just a wheeze so that the police could extort money from brothel owners, sex workers, and their clients. There were numerous reports of plainclothes policemen entering brothels, having sex, and then whipping out their police ID cards before demanding a payment. Other stories tell of prostitutes being arrested by the police for illegally plying their trade, and then being 'sold' to another brothel. The going rate for a girl starts at around US$40-60, but can be considerably more for an attractive girl. Health workers also fear that the banning of brothels will simply push the industry underground, creating an excellent environment for the unchecked spread of AIDS (see below). At the beginning of 1995 rumours were afoot in the capital that prostitution might be legalized such had been the failure of the 'crack down'.

Nor is prostitution just for the locals. The World Sex Guide on the internet breathlessly (of course) informs cyber-perverts "If you're looking for an adventure, Cambodia's IT right now". Child prostitution is rife and around a third of commercial prostitutes are thought to be under 18 years old. In

Modelling AIDS in Southeast Asia

There has been a tendency to assume that there is a single AIDS 'pandemic'. However, in reality it seems that there are possibly three different patterns to the spread of AIDS – one is characteristic of Europe and North America, the second of Sub-Saharan Africa, and a third of Asia. This third pattern, described by Tim Brown and Peter Xenos of the East-West Population Institute in Hawaii, is different in a number of important respects. Furthermore, they argue that these differences are likely to make the disease both more serious and more intractable. The pattern is based on the experience of Thailand, and it is assumed that the Thai experience will soon be seen reflected in other countries in Asia.

It seems that the possibility of transmission per exposure, whether that be through sexual relations or needle sharing, is higher in Asia than in Europe and North America because of the high incidence of other sexually transmitted diseases, especially among sex workers. Furthermore, a significant proportion of the male population of the countries of the region visit prostitutes for sex, meaning that the population 'at risk' is also very high. Therefore, in Thailand – and by implication also soon in many other countries of Asia – AIDS quickly made the cross-over from the homosexual and drug-using populations, to the heterosexual population. Thailand's first AIDS case was reported in 1984. By the end of 1988, 30% of addicts visiting methodone treatment centres were HIV positive. 5 years later, by the end of 1993, levels of infection among sex workers had also reached 30%. Now, nearly 2% of women visiting pre-natal clinics are testing HIV positive. Thus, in the space of less than 10 years – far faster than in Europe and North America, and faster even than in Africa – AIDS has spread from homosexuals and drug addicts to the wives and babies of heterosexual men.

In Aug 1994, at a major international conference on AIDS in Asia, James Allen of the American Medical Association likened – to considerable anger it should be added – AIDS to the Black Death in Europe. The costs to Asia of the disease are likely to be truly staggering: Scholars have put a figure of US$38-52bn on the social and economic costs of AIDS in the region.

Southeast Asia: potential for the spread of AIDS/HIV
Rapidly increasing: Burma; Cambodia; Thailand
Potential for rapid increase: Indonesia; Laos; Malaysia; Vietnam
Increasing: Singapore
Not classified: Brunei

Svey Paak, young girls who have been sold into prostitution for as little as US$300 by their destitute parents are paraded for clients from the Cambodian military and government, and for European and American paedophiles. A restricted Unicef report confirmed that 1,800 Vietnamese children had been sold into prostitution in Cambodia, though the real figure is thought to be higher.

Like other countries of Southeast Asia, Cambodia is thought to be on the verge of an **AIDS** epidemic. Although, the first AIDS case was only diagnosed in 1993 and even in Sep 1996 there were just 240 reported cases, the scale of HIV-infection is growing very rapidly. A study conducted in 1992 found that 9% of sex workers were HIV-infected, 3.5% of blood donors and 4% of those treated for other sexually transmitted diseases. But a more recent study conducted at the end of 1994 found that the rate of infection among sex workers had risen, alarmingly, to 69%. At the end of 1996 it was thought that between 70,000 and 120,000 people were HIV positive, with some scholars warning that there could be 40,000 cumulative deaths by 2000.

Most AIDS researchers believe that Cambodia is likely to follow the path that Thailand has already forged – towards an AIDS epidemic of exceedingly serious proportions. (The Cambodia-Thailand border is porous and the employment of Cambodian women in Thai brothels is helping Thailand 'export' its much more severe problem to Cambodia.) Though claims that 2 million Cambodians could die of AIDS seem highly excessive on current evidence and projections, sexual culture in Cambodia provides a fertile environment for rapid spread. A study recently completed by the Cambodian AIDS Social Research Project revealed that 80% of young men have had sex with a prostitute, and 10% with other men. Cambodia already has a very high dependency ratio – every 1,000 people of productive age in Cambodia must support 1,144 dependents (old, very young or infirm/disabled people). In the industrialized world the ratio is 1,000:616. AIDS will only further worsen this already high dependency rate. The challenge facing Dr Phalla, the unfortunately named head of Cambodia's AIDS programme, is the need to inform people of the dangers of unprotected sex and multiple partners when education levels and facilities are poor and resources comparatively paltry. He is hoping to meet the challenge through inter-personal communication – encouraging wives to tell their husbands, men to tell their friends, fathers their sons, and so on. In Khmer this is known much more descriptively as the 'one crow tells 10 crows' method.

RELIGION

The god-kings of Angkor

Up to the 14th century Buddhism and Hinduism existed side-by-side in Kambuja. In the pre-Angkor era, the Hindu gods Siva and Vishnu were worshipped as a single deity, *Harihara*. The statue of Harihara from Phnom Da (8th century) is divided in half: the 'stern' right half is Siva (with wild curly hair) and the 'sublime' left half, Vishnu (who wears a mitre). The first city at Angkor, built by Jayavarman II in the early 9th century, was called Hariharalaya after this god. Early Angkor kings promoted various Hindu sects, mainly dedicated to Siva and Vishnu. During the Angkor period, Siva was the most favoured deity but by the 12th century Vishnu replaced him. Jayavarman VII introduced Mahayana Buddhism as the official court religion at the end of the 12th century. The constant chopping, changing and refining of state religion helped sustain the power of the absolute monarch – each change ushered in a new style of rule and historians believe refinements and changes of religion were deliberately imported to consolidate the power of the kings.

One reason the Khmer Empire was so powerful was its basis on the Hindu concept of the **god-king or *devaraja***. Jayavarman II (802-850) crowned himself as a reincarnation of Siva and erected a Siva lingam (a phallic monument to the god) at Phnom Kulen, the source of power for the Khmer Dynasty. Siva-worship was not originally introduced by Jayavarman II however – it had been previously practised in the old kingdom of Funan (see page 57). The investiture of power was always performed by a Brahmin priest who also bestowed divinity on the king as a gift from Siva. This ceremony became an essential rite of kingship which was observed continuously – right into the 20th century. The king's spirit was said to reside in the lingam, which was enshrined in the centre of a monumental religious complex, representing the spiritual axis of the kingdom. Here, the people believed, their divinely ordained king communicated with the gods. Succeeding monarchs followed Jayavarman II's example and continued to install themselves as god-kings, evoking the loyalty of their subjects.

Funan (1st-6th centuries AD)

According to Chinese sources, Funan was a Hindu kingdom founded in the 1st century AD with its capital, Vyadhapura, close to the Mekong River near the border with Cambodia. A local legend records that Kaundinya, a great Indian Brahmin, acting on a dream, sailed to the coast of Vietnam carrying with him a bow and arrow. When he arrived, Kaundinya shot the arrow and where it landed he established the capital of Funan. Following this act, Kaundinya married the princess Soma, daughter of the local King of the Nagas (giant water serpents). The legend symbolizes the union between Indian and local cultural traditions – the *naga* representing indigenous fertility rites and customs (see page 112), and the arrow, the potency of the Hindu religion.

Funan built its wealth and power on its strategic location on the sea route between China and the islands to the S. Maritime technology at the time forced seafarers travelling between China and island Southeast Asia and India to stop and wait for the winds to change before they could continue on their way. This sometimes meant a stay of up to 5 months. The large port city of Oc-eo offered a safe harbour for merchant vessels and the revenues generated enabled the kings of the empire to expand rice cultivation, dominate a host of surrounding vassal states as far away as the Malay coast and S Burma, and build a series of impressive temples, cities and irrigation works. Although the Chinese chronicler K'ang T'ai records that the Funanese were barbarians – "ugly, black, and frizzy-haired" – it is clear from Chinese court annals that they were artistically and technologically accomplished. It is recorded for example that one Chinese emperor was so impressed by the skill of some visiting musicians in 263 AD that he ordered the establishment of an institute of Funanese music.

Funan reached the peak of its powers in the 4th century and went into decline during the 5th century AD when improving maritime technology made Oc-eo redundant as a haven for sailing vessels. No longer did merchants hug the coastline; ships were now large enough, and navigation skills sophisticated enough, to make the journey from S China to the Malacca Strait without landfall. By the mid-6th century, Funan, having suffered from a drawn out leadership crisis, was severely weakened. Neighbouring competing powers took advantage of this crisis, absorbing previously Funan-controlled lands. Irrigation works fell into disrepair as state control weakened, and peasants left the fields to seek more productive lands elsewhere. Funan, having lost both the economic wealth and the religious legitimacy on which its power had been based, was ultimately conquered by the Cham.

What is interesting about Funan is the degree to which it provided a model for future states in Southeast Asia. Funan's wealth was built on its links with the sea, and with its ability to exploit maritime trade. The later rulers of Champa, Langkasuka (Malaya), Srivijaya (Sumatra), and Malacca (Malaya) repeated this formula.

In Siddhartha's footsteps: a short history of Buddhism

Buddhism was founded by Siddhartha Gautama, a prince of the Sakya tribe of Nepal, who probably lived between 563 and 483 BC. He achieved enlightenment and the word *buddha* means 'fully enlightened one', or 'one who has woken up'. Siddhartha Gautama is known by a number of titles. In the W, he is usually referred to as *The Buddha*, ie the historic Buddha (but not just Buddha); more common in Southeast Asia is the title *Sakyamuni*, or Sage of the Sakyas (referring to his tribal origins).

Over the centuries, the life of the Buddha has become part legend, and the Jataka tales which recount his various lives are colourful and convoluted. But, central to any Buddhist's belief is that he was born under a *sal* tree (*Shorea robusta*), that he achieved enlightenment under a bodhi tree (*Ficus religiosa*) in the Bodh Gaya Gardens, that he preached the First Sermon at Sarnath, and that he died at Kusinagara (all in India or Nepal).

The Buddha was born at Lumbini (in present-day Nepal), as Queen Maya was on her way to her parents' home. She had had a very auspicious dream before the child's birth of being impregnated by an elephant, whereupon a sage prophesied that Siddhartha would become either a great king or a great spiritual leader. His father, being keen that the first option of the prophesy be fulfilled, brought him up in all the princely skills (at which Siddhartha excelled) and ensured that he only saw beautiful things, not the harsher elements of life.

Despite his father's efforts Siddhartha saw four things while travelling between palaces – a helpless old man, a very sick man, a corpse being carried by lamenting relatives, and an ascetic, calm and serene as he begged for food. These episodes made an enormous impact on the young prince, and he renounced his princely origins and left home to study under a series of spiritual teachers. He finally discovered the path to enlightenment at the Bodh Gaya Gardens in India. He then proclaimed his thoughts to a small group of disciples at Sarnath, near Benares, and continued to preach and attract followers until he died at the age of 81 at Kusinagara.

Very few of the statues of Vishnu and Siva and other gods left by the Khmer Empire were traditional representations of the deities. The great majority of the images were portraits of kings and princes and high dignitaries, each represented as the god into whom he would be absorbed at the end of his earthly existence. That the names given to the statues were usually a composite of the names of the man and the god, indicates that men were worshipped as gods.

The installation of the devaraja cult by Jayavarman II took place on the summit of Phnom Kulen. Under subsequent kings, it was transferred, in turn, to Bakong, Phnom Bakhen, Koh Ker and Phimeanakas. At the end of the 11th cen- tury, the Baphuon was constructed to house the golden lingam. The tradition of the god-king cult was so deeply rooted in the court that even Theravada Buddhism introduced in the 14th century bowed to its influence. Following the adoption of Buddhism in the second half of the 12th century, the god-king left his lingam to enter the statue of the Buddha. Jayavarman VII built the Bayon to shelter the statue of the Buddha-king in the centre of the city of Angkor.

Temple-mountains were built as microcosms of the universe, with Mt Meru, the home of the gods, at the centre, surrounded by oceans (followed most perfectly at Angkor Wat, see page 125). This concept was not invented by the

In the First Sermon at the deer park in Sarnath, the Buddha preached the Four Truths, which are still considered the root of Buddhist belief and practical experience. These are the 'Noble Truth' that suffering exists, the 'Noble Truth' that there is a cause of suffering, the 'Noble Truth' that suffering can be ended, and the 'Noble Truth' that to end suffering it is necessary to follow the 'Noble Eightfold Path' – namely, right speech, livelihood, action, effort, mindfulness, concentration, opinion and intention.

Soon after the Buddha began preaching, a monastic order – the *Sangha* – was established. As the monkhood evolved in India, it also began to fragment as different sects developed different interpretations of the life of the Buddha. An important change was the belief that the Buddha was transcendent: he had never been born, nor had he died; he had always existed and his life on earth had been mere illusion. The emergence of these new concepts helped to turn what up until then was an ethical code of conduct, into a religion. It eventually led to the appearance of a new Buddhist movement, Mahayana Buddhism which split from the more traditional Theravada 'sect'.

Despite the division of Buddhism into two sects, the central tenets of the religion are common to both. Specifically, the principles pertaining to the Four Noble Truths, the Noble Eightfold Path, the Dependent Origination, the Law of Karma and nirvana. In addition, the principles of non-violence and tolerance are also embraced by both sects. In essence, the differences between the two are of emphasis and interpretation. Theravada Buddhism is strictly based on the original Pali Canon, while the Mahayana tradition stems from later Sanskrit texts. Mahayana Buddhism also allows a broader and more varied interpretation of the doctrine. Other important differences are that while the Theravada tradition is more 'intellectual' and self-obsessed, with an emphasis upon the attaining of wisdom and insight for oneself, Mahayana Buddhism stresses devotion and compassion towards others.

Khmers but was part of an inherited tradition from India. At the summit of the cosmic mountain, located at the centre of the city, the king, embodied by his own sacred image, entered into contact with the world of gods. Each temple was the personal temple of an individual king, erected by him during his life. When, after his death, his ashes or remains were deposited there (to animate the statue and give the cult a living image), the temple became his mausoleum. His successor always built another sanctuary to house the image of the god-king. During the Angkor period the Khmers did not seem to question this system. It ordered their lives, regulating everything from agriculture to birth and death rites. But the temples were not the products of a popular faith, like Christian cathedrals – they were strictly the domain of royalty and high priests and were reserved for the worship of kings and members of the entourage deified in the form of one of the Hindu or Buddhist gods.

Theravada Buddhism

Despite the powerful devaraja cult, most Khmers also practised an amalgam of ancestor worship and animism. As Theravada Buddhism swept through Southeast Asia (well after the adoption of Mahayana Buddhism), propagated by missionary monks, its message of simplicity, austerity and humility began to undermine the cult of the god-king. As a popular religion, it held great attractions to a population which for so many centuries had been denied access to the élitist and extravagant devaraja cult. By the 15th century Theravada Buddhism was the dominant religion in Cambodia – and across mainland Southeast Asia.

Buddhism shares the belief, in common with Hinduism, in rebirth. A person goes through countless lives and the experience of one life is conditioned by the acts in a previous one. This is the Law of Karma (act or deed, from Pali *kamma*), the law of cause and effect. But, it is not, as commonly thought in the West, equivalent to fate.

For most people, nirvana is a distant goal, and they merely aim to accumulate merit by living good lives and performing good deeds such as giving alms to monks. In this way the layman embarks on the Path to Heaven. It is also common for a layman to become ordained, at some point in his life (usually as a young man) for a 3 month period during the Buddhist Rains Retreat.

Monks should endeavour to lead stringently ascetic lives. They must refrain from murder, theft, sexual intercourse, untruths, eating after noon, alcohol, entertainment, ornament, comfortable beds and wealth. They are allowed to own only a begging bowl, three pieces of clothing, a razor, needle, belt and water filter. They can only eat food that they have received through begging. Anyone who is male, over 20, and not a criminal can become a monk.

The 'Way of the Elders', is believed to be closest to Buddhism as it originally developed in India. It is often referred to by the term 'Hinayana' (Lesser Vehicle), a disparaging name foisted onto Theravadans by Mahayanists. This form of Buddhism is the dominant contemporary religion in the mainland Southeast Asian countries of Thailand, Cambodia, Laos and Burma.

In Theravadan Buddhism, the historic Buddha, Sakyamuni, is revered above all else and most images of the Buddha are of Sakyamuni. Importantly, and unlike Mahayana Buddhism, the Buddha image is only meant to serve as a meditation aid. In theory, it does not embody supernatural powers, and it is not supposed to be worshipped. But, the popular need for objects of veneration has meant that most images *are* worshipped. Pilgrims bring flowers and incense, and prostrate themselves in front of the image. This is a Mahayanist influence which has been embraced by Theravadans.

Buddhism in Cambodia

The Cambodian Buddhist clergy divided into two groups: the Mahanikay and Thommayuth (or Dhammayuttikanikay) orders. The latter was not introduced from Thailand until 1864, and was a reformist order with strong royal patronage. Theravada Buddhism remained the dominant and unchallenged faith until 1975.

It was a demonstration by Buddhist monks in Phnom Penh which first kindled Cambodian nationalism in the wake of WW2 (see page 35). According to historians, one of the reasons for this was the intensifying of the relationship between the king and the people, due to the founding of the Buddhist Institute in Phnom Penh in 1930. The Institute was under the joint patronage of the kings of Laos and Cambodia as well as the French. It began printing and disseminating Buddhist texts – in Pali and Khmer. American historian David P Chandler writes: "As the Institute's reputation grew, enhanced by frequent conferences, it became a rallying point for an emerging intelligentsia." The Institute's librarian founded a Khmer-language newspaper (*Nagaravatta* – or 'Angkor Wat') in 1936, which played a critical role in articulating and spreading the nationalist message.

Before 1975 and the arrival of the Khmers Rouges, there were 3,000 monasteries and 64,000 monks (*bonzes*) – many of these were young men who had become ordained to escape conscription – in Cambodia and rural life was centred around the *wat* (Buddhist monastery). Under Pol Pot, all monks were 'defrocked' and, according to some sources, as many as 62,000 were executed or died in the ricefields. Monasteries were torn down or converted to other uses, Pali – the language of Theravada Buddhism – was banned, and former monks were forced to marry. Ironically, Saloth Sar (Pol Pot) himself spent several years as a novice when he was a child. Buddhism was revived in 1979 with the ordination of monks by a visiting delegation of Buddhists from Vietnam; at the same time, many of the wats – which were defiled by the Khmers Rouges – were restored and reconsecrated. The two orders of Theravada Buddhism – the Thommayuth (aristocratic) and Mahanikay (common) – previously practised in Cambodia have now merged. The Hun Sen government softened the position on Buddhism to the degree that it was reintroduced as the national religion in 1989 and young men were allowed to be ordained (previously restricted to men over 45, ie no longer able to serve in the army).

Cambodian Buddhism is an easy-going faith and tolerates ancestor and territorial spirit worship, which is widely practised. There are often small rustic altars to the guardian spirits or *neak ta* in the corner of pagodas. Cambodians often wear *katha* – or charms – which are believed to control external magical forces. Many Khmer communities have *achars*, who share in the spiritual guidance of people but do not compete with the monks. Most important ceremonies – weddings, funerals, coming of age – have both Buddhist and animist elements.

Other religions

There are around 60,000 Roman Catholics in Cambodia, mainly Vietnamese, and about 2,000 Protestants. Islam, of the Sunni sect, is practised by many of the 200,000 (some commentators would say 500,000) Cham. During the Khmers Rouges period it has been reported that Chams were forced to eat pork while most Cham mosques were destroyed, and only now are they being slowly rebuilt. A new Internation Mosque in Phnom Penh, built with Saudi money, was opened in 1994. Almost all the Chinese in Cambodia are Taoist/Confucianist.

LANGUAGE AND LITERATURE

The Khmer Language

The Khmer language belongs to the Mon-Khmer family, enriched by the Indian Pali and Sanskrit languages and peppered with Thai and French influences. The use of Sanskrit in royal texts became more widespread after the introduction of Mahayana Buddhism in the 12th century (although there are inscriptions dating from the 6th century) and the Pali language spread into Cambodia via Siam with Theravada Buddhism. Khmer is related to languages spoken by hilltribe people of Laos, Vietnam and even Malaysia – but is very different to Thai or Lao. Khmer has no tones, no tenses, and words attached to the masculine or feminine genders. But Khmer does have 23 vowel-sounds and 33 consonants; it is also a very specific language – for instance, there are 100 different words for types of rice. The Khmer language is written from left to right with often no separation between words.

French was widely spoken by the intelligentsia before 1975 and is still spoken by a few elderly Cambodians. Today however, everyone seems to want to learn English, and there are informal pavement English schools setting up on Phnom Penh's streets. This has led to some Franco-Anglophone friction. Understandably, the French government – one of Cambodia's largest aid donors –

would like to see the French language sustained, perhaps even developed. In 1995 this led to the strange spectacle of language riots on the campus of Phnom Penh's Cambodian University of Technology as students burnt French text books in protest at being forced to learn a language which, they said, 'got them nowhere'.

Cambodian literature

Religious literature comprises works of religious instruction, derived from the Sanskrit and Pali texts of the Theravada Buddhist canon, the Tripitaka. The **Jataka tales** are well known in Cambodia and several modern adaptations have been made from these texts. The Jatakas recount the former lives of the historic Buddha and were probably first introduced to Cambodia from Laos. Most of the stories tell of how the Buddha – then a prince – managed to overcome some defect by the use of magic or the assis-

---

The Cambodian Ramayana: the Reamker

The *Reamker* – "The Story of Rama" – is an adaptation of the Indian Hindu classic, the Ramayana, which was written by the poet Valmiki about 2,000 years ago. This 48,000 line epic odyssey – often likened to the works of Homer – was introduced into mainland Southeast Asia in the early centuries of the first millennium. The heroes were simply transposed into a mythical, ancient, Southeast Asian landscape.

In Cambodia, the Reamker quickly became highly influential. The scenes carved in stone at Angkor, many of the murals painted on monastery walls, and the tales enacted in shadow theatre (*nang sbaek*) all derive inspiration from the Reamker. The Cambodian Ramayana dates back to the Angkor period, although the earliest existing written work only dates back to 1620.

In the first part of the story, Rama – who in the Cambodian version is depicted as the Buddha – renounces his throne following a long and convoluted court intrigue, and flees into exile. With his wife Sita and trusted companion Hanuman (the monkey god), they undertake a long and arduous journey. In the second part, his wife Sita is abducted by the evil king Ravana, forcing Rama to wage battle against the demons of Langka Island (Sri Lanka). He defeats the demons

with the help of Hanuman and his monkey army, and recovers his wife. In the third and final part of the story – and here it diverges sharply from the Indian original – Sita and Rama are reunited and reconciled with the help of the gods (in the Indian version there is no such reconciliation). Another difference to the Indian version is the significant role played by Hanuman – here an amorous adventurer who dominates much of the third part of the epic.

There are also numerous sub-plots which are original to the Reamker, many building upon events in Cambodian history and local myth and folklore. In tone and issues of morality, the Cambodian version is less puritanical than the Indian original. There are also, of course, differences in dress, ecology, location and custom.

Hanuman
Adapted from Hallet, Holt (1890)
A Thousand miles on an elephant in the Shan States,
William Blackwood: Edinburgh.

tance of some god, enabling him to be born higher up the scale of birth and re-birth on his long road to nirvana. The two Khmer epics are the poem of Angkor Wat and the **Reamker** (or *Ramakerti*), derived from the Indian **Ramayana**. Traditionally the literature was recorded by incising palm leaf manuscripts with a sharp stylus, the incisions then being blackened to make them easily visible. Such manuscripts, if stored in favourable conditions, can last for over 100 years.

From around the 17th century, *chap* poetry, an import from Thailand, became popular. The poetry took root in monasteries as a means by which monks could more easily teach the laity the lessons of the Buddhist texts. However, over time, they also took on a secular guise and became a means by which more everyday homilies were communicated.

Most of the early literature has been destroyed but there are surviving Sanskrit inscriptions on stone monuments dating from the 6th century and some early palm leaf manuscripts. Many of these are contained in the Bibliothèque Nationale in Paris – the Khmers Rouges managed to destroy most of those housed in monasteries and museums in Cambodia itself. Historical literature consists largely of inscriptions from Angkor Wat as well as the Cambodian royal chronicles. Fictional literature is diverse in Cambodia and includes the *Ipaen* folk stories written in prose. French literature has had a profound influence on modern Cambodian literature. The first modern Cambodian novel was *Sophat* published in 1938. It, and the novels and short stories that followed it, represented a break with the past. The authors wrote of ordinary people, used natural conversation, and wrote in prose, not poetry. Most of the recent Cambodian novels have been written by Cambodians living abroad – most writers and journalists were either killed by the Khmers Rouges or fled the country.

DANCE, DRAMA AND MUSIC

There is a strong tradition of dance in Cambodia which has its origins in the sacred dances of the apsaras, the mythological seductresses of ancient Cambodia. Classical dance reached its height during the Angkor period; it was based on interpretations of the Indian epics, particularly the Ramayana. Dance also became a religious tradition, designed to bring the king and his people divine blessing. Dancers, nearly all of whom were well born, were central to the royal court and were protected as a separate part of the king's harem; only the god-king could touch them. The dancers became legendary even outside Cambodia: when Thailand invaded, the Khmer classical ballet dancers were part of their war booty and were taken to the Thai court. The decline of Angkor brought the decline of classical dance, although it continued to survive as an art form through the patronage of the royal Thai court. When the French colonialists revived Khmer ballet in the 20th century they initially imported dancers from Thailand.

The dances are very symbolic. Court dances are subject to a precise order, a strict form and a prescribed language of movements and gestures. Most of the dancers are women and the male and female roles are distinguished by costume. All the dancers are barefoot as the unimpeded movement of the feet is very important. The national dance is called the lamthon which is characterized by slow graceful movements of the hands and arms. The most highly trained lamthon dancers wear elaborate, tight-fitting costumes of silk and velvet that have to be sewn onto them before each performance.

Due to their close association with the royal family (they were based at the royal palace and right up to 1970 and danced regularly for Prince Sihanouk), the once-famous and flourishing National Dance Group was a prime target for the Khmers Rouges regime of the mid-1970s. Many dancers were killed; others fled into exile. In 1981 the School of Fine Arts was reopened to train new recruits, 80% of whom were orphans. Today the National Dance Group performs for some tour groups and made its first tour to the West in 1990.

Folk dancing has managed to survive the 1970s intact, although as a form of regular village entertainment, it has been undermined by the arrival of radios, televisions and videos. Unlike the court dances, folk dances are less structured, with dancers responding to the rhythm of drums. The dancers act out tales from Cambodian folk stories; folk dancing can often be seen at local festivals.

Folk plays and **shadow plays** (*nang sbaek*) are also a popular form of entertainment in the countryside. The latter are based on stories from the Ramayana, embroidered with local legends. The characters are cut out of leather and often painted. Wandering shadow puppeteers perform at local festivals.

Because of the importance of dance to the ancient royal Khmer court, **music** – which always accompanied dance routines – was also central to Cambodian court and religious life. Singers and musicians were often attached to specific temples. Cambodian music has evolved from Indian and Indonesian influences and, more recently, Thai. The traditional orchestra consists of three xylophones, *khom thom* (a horseshoe-shaped arrangement with 16 flat gongs), violins, wind instruments including flutes, flageolets and a Khmer version of bagpipes, as well as drums of different shapes and sizes. There are three types of drum: the hand drum, the *cha ayam* drum and the *yike* drum. The drummer has the most important role in folk music as he sets the rhythm. In 1938 a musical scholar estimated that only 3,000 melodies were ever employed in Khmer music. There is no system of written notation so the tunes are transmitted orally from generation to generation. There are five tones (compared to seven in western music) and no real harmony – the melodies are always simple.

Modern Cambodia

POLITICS

Since the mid-1960s Cambodian politics has been chaotic, with warring and bickering factions, backed by different foreign powers and domestic cliques, and shifting alliances. The groups which battled for power following the Vietnamese invasion in 1979 are still in the political arena and although the country may have 'enjoyed' democratic elections in 1993 civil society remains poorly developed. Gangsterism, political terrorism and extra-judicial killings remain very much part of the political landscape despite the pretence of democracy. While there are many people who feel optimistic about Cambodia's future, there are probably just as many who are pessimistic.

The **Vietnamese withdrawal** in Sep 1989 resulted in an escalation of the civil war as the rebel factions – comprised of the Khmers Rouges, the Sihanoukists and Son Sann's KPNLF (see page 45) – tried to take advantage of the supposedly weakened Hun Sen regime in Phnom Penh. The government committed itself to liberalizing the economy and improving the infrastructure in order to undermine the political appeal of the rebels – particularly that of the Khmers Rouges. Peasant farmers were granted life tenancy and collective farms were substituted with agricultural co-operatives. But because nepotism and bribery were rife in Phnom Penh, the popularity of the Hun Sen regime declined. The rebel position was further strengthened as the disparities between living standards in Phnom Penh and those in the rest of the country widened. In the capital, the government became alarmed; in a radio broadcast in 1991 it announced a crackdown on corruption claiming it was causing a "loss of confidence in our superb regime... which is tantamount to paving the way for the return of the genocidal Pol Pot regime".

With the withdrawal of Vietnamese troops, the continuing civil war followed the familiar pattern of dry season government offensives, and consolidation of guerrilla positions during the monsoon rains. Much of the fighting focused on the potholed highways – particularly Highway 6 which connects the capital with Battambang – with the Khmers Rouges blowing up most of the bridges along the road. Their strategy involved cutting the roads in order to drain the government's limited resources. Other Khmers Rouges offensives were designed to serve their own economic ends – such as their capture of the gem-rich town of Pailin.

The Khmers Rouges ran extortion rackets throughout the country, even along the strategic Highway 4 which ferried military supplies, oil and consumer goods from the port of Kompong Som (Sihanoukville) to Phnom Penh. The State of Cambodia – or the government forces, known as SOC – was pressed to deploy troops to remote areas and allot scarce resources, settling refugees in more secure parts of the country. To add to their problems, Soviet and Eastern Bloc aid began to dry up.

Throughout 1991 the four warring factions were **repeatedly brought to the negotiating table** in an effort to hammer out a peace deal. Much of the argument centred on the word 'genocide'. The Prime Minister, Hun Sen, insisted that the wording of any agreement should explicitly condemn the former Khmers Rouges regime's 'genocidal acts'. But the Khmers Rouges refused to be party to any power-sharing deal which labelled them in such a way. Fighting intensified as hopes for a settlement increased – all sides wanted to consolidate their territory in advance of any agreement.

Rumours emerged that **China** was continuing to supply arms – including tanks, reportedly delivered through Thailand – to the Khmers Rouges. There were also accusations that the Phnom Penh government was using Vietnamese combat troops to stem Khmers Rouges advances – the first such reports since their official withdrawal in 1989. But finally, in Jun 1991, after several attempts, Sihanouk brokered a permanent ceasefire during a meeting of the Supreme National Council (SNC) in Pattaya, S Thailand. The SNC had been proposed by the United Nations Security Council in 1990 and formed in 1991, with an equal number of representatives from the Phnom Penh government and each of the resistance factions, with Sihanouk as its chairman. The following month he was elected chairman of the SNC, and resigned his presidency of the rebel coalition government in exile. Later in the year, the four factions agreed to reduce their armed guerrillas and militias by 70%. The remainder were to be placed under the supervision of the United Nations Transitional Authority in Cambodia (UNTAC), which supervised Cambodia's transition to multi-party democracy. Even more important was Heng Samrin's decision to drop his insistence that reference should be made to the former Khmers Rouges' "genocidal regime". It was also agreed that elections should be held in 1993 on the basis of proportional representation. Heng Samrin's Communist Party was promptly renamed the Cambodian People's Party, in an effort to persuade people that it sided with democracy and capitalism.

The Paris Peace Accord

On 23 October 1991, the four warring Cambodian factions signed a peace agreement in Paris which officially ended 13 years of civil war and more than 2 decades of warfare. The accord was co-signed by 15 other members of the International Peace Conference on Cambodia. There was an air of unreality about the whole event, which brought bitter enemies face to face after months of protracted negotiations. There was, however, a notable lack of enthusiasm on the part of the four warring factions. Hun Sen said that the treaty was far from perfect because it failed to contain the word 'genocide' to remind Cambodians of the atrocities of the former Khmers Rouges regime. Western powers obviously agreed. But in the knowledge that it was a fragile agreement, everyone remained diplomatically quiet. US Secretary of State James Baker was quoted as saying "I don't think anyone can tell you there will for sure be lasting peace, but there is great hope."

Political analysts ascribed the successful conclusion to the months of negotiations to improved relations between China and Vietnam – there were reports that the two had held secret summits at which the Cambodia situation was discussed. China put pressure on Prince Norodom Sihanouk to take a leading role in the peace process, and Hanoi's new understanding with Beijing prompted Hun Sen's participation. The easing of tensions between China and Moscow – particularly following the Soviet Union's demise – also helped apply pressure on the different factions. Finally, the United States had shifted its position: in Jul 1990 it had announced that it would not support the presence of the Khmers Rouges at the UN and by Sep US officials were talking to Hun Sen.

On 14 November 1991, **Prince Norodom Sihanouk returned** to Phnom Penh to an ecstatic welcome, followed, a few days later, by Son Sen, a Khmers

Rouges leader. On 27 Nov Khieu Samphan, who had represented the Khmers Rouges at all the peace negotiations, arrived on a flight from Bangkok. Within hours mayhem had broken out, and a lynch mob attacked him in his villa. Rumours circulated that Hun Sen had orchestrated the demonstration, and beating an undignified retreat down a ladder into a waiting armoured personnel carrier, the bloodied Khmers Rouges leader headed back to Pochentong Airport. The crowd had sent a clear signal that they, at least, were not happy to see him back. There were fears that this incident might derail the entire peace process – but in the event, the Khmers Rouges won a small public relations coup by playing the whole thing down. When the Supreme National Council (SNC) finally met in Phnom Penh at the end of Dec 1991, it was unanimously decided to rubberstamp the immediate deployment of UN troops to oversee the peace process in the run-up to a general election.

The UN peace-keeping mission

The UN mission "...conducted a brief, profound and very welcome social revolution [in Cambodia]" (William Shawcross (1994) *Cambodia's new deal: a report*).

The UN mission favoured "Phnom Penh's profiteers, the Khmers Rouges utopists, the Chinese businessmen of Southeast Asia, the annexationist neighbours..." (Marie Alexandrine Martin (1994) *Cambodia: a shattered society*).

Yasushi Akashi, a senior Japanese official in the United Nations, was assigned the daunting task of overseeing the biggest military and logistical operation in UN history. UNTAC, comprised an international team of 22,000 peacekeepers – including 16,000 soldiers from 22 countries, 6,000 officials as well as 3,500 police and 1,700 civilian employees and electoral volunteers. The first 'blue-be-

ret' UN troops began arriving in Nov 1991, even before the SNC had agreed to the full complement of peace-keepers. The UN Advance Mission to Cambodia (UNAMIC) was followed 4 months later by the first of the main peacekeeping battalions. The odds were stacked against them. Shortly after his arrival, Akashi commented: "If one was a masochist one could not wish for more."

UNTAC's task

UNTAC's central mission was to supervise free elections ... in a country where most of the population had never voted and had little idea of how democracy was meant to work. The UN was also given the task of resettling 360,000 refugees from camps in Thailand and of demobilizing more than a quarter of a million soldiers and militiamen from the four main factions. In addition, it was to ensure that no further arms shipments reached these factions, whose remaining forces were to be confined to cantonments. In the run-up to the elections, UNTAC also took over the administration of the country, taking over the defence, foreign affairs, finance, public security and information portfolios as well as ensuring respect for human rights.

By early 1993, UN electoral workers had successfully registered 4.7 million of roughly 9 million Cambodians – about 96% of the population above voting age. With a US$2bn price-tag, this huge operation was the most expensive mission ever undertaken by the UN. At the time, the UN was running 12 peacekeeping operations throughout the world, but two-thirds of its peacekeeping budget was earmarked for Cambodia. Over the months a steady stream of VIPs arrived to witness the operation – they included the UN Secretary-General, Boutros-Boutros Ghali, the Chinese Foreign Minister, Qian Qichen and President François Mitterrand of France.

Cambodia – the biggest minefield in the world

Thanks to free-flowing supplies of military hardware to rebel factions throughout the 1980s, Cambodia became the most heavily mined war zone in the world. Conservative estimates suggest that there are 4-8 million mines in the country, mostly concentrated in the NW province of Battambang (a Khmer Rouge stronghold) as well as countless thousands close to the main roads. The upper figure would mean almost one mine for every man, woman and child. But statistics on the likely number of mines are irrelevant. Far more meaningful is the total area of land which cannot be used for anything because of the threat of mines. One in every 236 Cambodians is an amputee, compared to one in 22,000 in the US, the highest proportion of any country in the world. Every month, another 300 to 700 new mine injuries are added to the list. In 1993, an Australian Red Cross doctor said Cambodia's most obvious characteristic of national identity is the one-legged man. There are thought to be around 40,000 amputees inside the country.

A number of charities have been set up, where Cambodian craftsmen are trained to make cheap and simple prostheses, and many amputees have now been fitted with artificial limbs. UN troops, as well as private companies – such as the British-based charity, the Halo Trust – have been involved in delicate mine-clearance operations since 1990. At the beginning of 1995 the first Mine Awareness Day was declared. But, lifting a single mine costs between US$300 and US$900 and in the 24 months to the beginning of 1995 only 40,000 mines had been cleared – less than 1% of the total. The most common mine in Cambodia is the plastic-encased, Soviet-made PMN-2 mine, which mine clearance experts say guarantees above-the-knee amputation if triggered.

In an attempt to speed up the de-mining process – which at the rate achieved up to mid-1996 would take 300 years – those involved are trying to introduce new technologies. The MV103C, for example, is a US$1 million Swedish-built, 45-tonne monster which rumbles a carbide steel roller along in front of it, gouging out mines in its path. Cheaper and nimbler is the Swedish-trained *Canis familiaris*: the domestic dog. These are trained to respond to the vapour that explosives give off, dropping prone to the ground with their noses – in theory – a foot or two away from the offending hardware. Though dogs are cheap, and unlike metal detectors don't get side-tracked by bits of scrap metal, deminers worry what would happen if an animal loses concentration on the job or just gets out on the wrong side of its basket.

Ba Bun Ra, a 29 year-old amputee and victim of a mine blast, is well aware of the challenges that face him: "I forgot my early dreams... I no longer have the capacity..." he was quoted as saying in 1994. Mines are the perfect weapon in a long war of attrition. They are designed not to kill, but to maim and thereby consume enemy resources in the evacuation, first aid, rehabilitaton and then support of the man, woman, girl or boy affected. They do not distinguish between men and women, children and the elderly, human beings and animals. Mines create dependents and, in turn, tend to create poverty. The civil war may end soon; the mine war will continue for years, perhaps decades to come – for mines do not respect the cessation of hostilities. To clear an area measuring just 50m by 50m is said to take 50 men one month. It does not bode well for a country where the average life expectancy has only just crept above 50.

UNTAC's job would have been easier if the different guerrilla factions and militias had stopped fighting once the Peace Accord was signed. In the months after their arrival UN troops had to broker successive ceasefires between government forces and the Khmers Rouges. During 1992, the Khmers Rouges refused to demobilize their fighters as required by the Accord and attempted to gain a foothold in the strategic central province of Kompong Thom in advance of the full deployment of UN peacekeeping forces. This prompted further scepticism among observers as to their commitment to the peace process. The Khmers Rouges – which was by then referred to (in politically neutral parlance) as the Party of Democratic Kampuchea, or the DK – made it as difficult as possible for the UN. It refused UN soldiers, officials and volunteers access to areas under its control. On a number of occasions in the months running up to the elections, UN military patrols were held hostage after entering Khmers Rouges-held territory.

The Khmers Rouges pulls out

At the beginning of 1993 it became apparent that the Khmers Rouges had no intention of playing ball, despite its claim of a solid rural support base. The DK failed to register for the election before the expiry of the UN deadline and its forces stepped up attacks on UN personnel. In Apr 1993 Khieu Samphan and his entire entourage at the Khmers Rouges compound in Phnom Penh left the city. It was at this stage that UN officials finally began expressing their exasperation and anxiety over the Khmers Rouges's avowed intention to disrupt the polls. The faction was well-known to have procured fresh supplies of Chinese weapons through Thailand – although there is no evidence that these came from Beijing – as well as their having large arms caches hidden all over the country.

By the time of the elections, the group was thought to be in control of between 10% and 15% of Cambodian territory. Khmers Rouges guerrillas launched attacks in Apr and May 1993. Having stoked racial antagonism, they started killing ethnic Vietnamese villagers and settlers, sending up to 20,000 of them fleeing into Vietnam. In one particularly vicious attack, 33 Vietnamese fishermen and their families were killed in a village on the Tonlé Sap. The Khmers Rouges also began ambushing and killing UN soldiers and electoral volunteers.

The UN remained determined that the elections should go ahead despite the Khmers Rouges threats and mounting political intimidation and violence between other factions, notably the Cambodian People's Party and Funcinpec. But, it did not take any chances: in the week before the elections, 6,000 flak jackets and helmets were flown into the country and security was tightened. In the event, however, there were remarkably few violent incidents and the feared coordinated effort to disrupt the voting failed to materialize. Voters took no notice of Khmers Rouges calls to boycott the election. In fact, reports came in from several provinces of large numbers of Khmers Rouges guerrillas and villagers from areas under their control, turning up at polling stations and casting their ballots.

The UN-supervised elections

The voting was by proportional representation, province by province. The election was conducted under the aegis of 1,400 International Polling Station Officers from more than 40 countries. The Cambodian people were voting for a 120-member Constituent Assembly to write a new constitution.

The days following the election saw a political farce – Cambodian style – which, as Nate Thayer wrote in the *Far Eastern Economic Review* "might have been comic if the implications were not so depressing for the country's future".

In just a handful of days, the Phnom Penh-based correspondent went on, Cambodia "witnessed an abortive secession, a failed attempt to establish a provisional government, a royal family feud and the manoeuvres of a prince [Sihanouk] obsessed with avenging his removal from power in a military coup more than 20 years [previously]". The elections gave Funcinpec 45% of the vote, the CPP 38% and the BLDP, 3% (see box, page 70). The CPP immediately claimed the results fraudulent, while Prince Norodom Chakrapong – one of Sihanouk's sons – announced the secession of the country's six eastern provinces. Fortunately, both attempts to undermine the election dissolved. The CPP agreed to join Funcinpec in a power sharing agreement while, remarkably, the Khmers Rouges were able to present themselves as defenders of democracy in the face of the CPP's claims of vote-rigging. The new Cambodian constitution was ratified in Sep 1993, marking the end of UNTAC's involvement in the country. Under the new constitution, Cambodia was to be a pluralistic liberal-democratic country. 70-year-old Sihanouk was crowned King of Cambodia, reclaiming the throne he relinquished in 1955. His son Norodom Ranariddh was appointed First Prime Minister and Hun Sen, Second Prime Minister, a situation intended to promote national unity but leading, inevitably, to internal bickering and dissent.

Politics and the military struggle since the elections, 1993-1996

Almost from day one of Cambodia's re-birth as an independent state espousing the principles of democracy and the market, cracks began to appear in the rickety structure that underlay these grand ideals. Rampant corruption, infighting among the coalition partners, political intrigue, murder and intimidation all became features of the political landscape. The Khmers Rouges spurned the offer of a role in government in return for a ceasefire; the civil war in the countryside began to gently simmer once more; and King Norodom Sihanouk continued to exasperate almost everyone.

In Jul 1994 there was another unsuccessful **coup attempt**, led by three former ministers: the troublesome Norodom Chakkrapong (a son of King Sihanouk), General Sin Song and Sin Sen. Sin Song and Norodom Chakkrapong had both been expelled from the government after alleged involvement in the attempted coup of Jun 1993. Norodom Chakkrapong managed to evade the authorities and fled the country while the two Sins – Sin Song

Party-time: Cambodia's new democrats

● **FUNCINPEC** (Front Uni National pour un Cambodge Independent Neutre, Pacifique et Cooperatif). Founded by Prince Norodom Sihanouk to oppose the CPP, and run by his son, Prince Norodom Ranariddh. 58 seats.

● The **Cambodian People's Party** (CPP – formerly the Communist Party). Headed by Hun Sen and originally installed by Vietnam in 1979. The CPP's main election ticket in the 1993 elections was the crushing of the Khmers Rouges. 51 seats.

● **Buddhist Liberal Democratic Party** (BDLP). Led by octogenarian Son Sann, the pre-1970 Finance Minister and ex-leader of the Khmer People's National Liberation Front (KPNLF) from 1993, replaced by Information Minister Ieng Mouly in Jul 1995. 10 seats.

● **Liberal Democratic Party** (LDP), formed from the old military wing of the KPNLF. 1 seat.

and Sin Sen – were arrested (Sin Song later escaped from prison, to be rearrested in Thailand – a country with which Cambodia does not have an extradition treaty). Just to add some international spice to the coup attempt, the government also arrested 14 Thai citizens at Phnom Penh Airport – allegedly weapons experts flown in to assist in the coup. Their arrest led to a further outbreak of bickering, accusation and counter-accusation between the Cambodian and Thai governments. Who, and what purpose, lay behind the plot seemed to grow murkier by the month. Allegations emerged, for example, that vice prime minister Sar Kheng and 42 others had been involved in the coup attempt. Commentators took this as indicating a split in the Cambodian People's Party (CPP). Another rumour circulating in the capital was that the entire coup was faked by Hun Sen to undermine his CPP colleagues in the government.

The intense friction that exists between the CPP and Funcinpec, the two key members of the ruling coalition, was brought to a head at the end of 1995 when **Prince Norodom Sirivudh was arrested** for plotting to kill Hun Sen. Hun Sen ordered troops and tanks on to the streets of Phnom Penh, and for a while the capital had the air of a city under siege. Sirivudh was secretary-general of Funcinpec and is King Norodom Sihanouk's half brother. He has also been a vocal critic of corruption in the government, and a supporter of Sam Rainsy, the country's most outspoken opposition politician and the bane of Hun Sen's life (see page 73). The National Assembly voted unanimously to suspend Sirivudh's immunity from prosecution. However few commentators really believed that Sirivudh had plotted to kill Hun Sen. Though he is certainly outspoken, and occasionally rather injudicious in his public remarks, Sirivudh is not seen to be someone who

would involve himself in such a serious conspiracy. The assumption, then, was that Hun Sen – a 'notorious bully' in the words of *The Economist* – was merely playing politics, albeit politics of a nature which most governments would find beyond the pale. But politics is never simple in Cambodia, even when it comes to setting someone up and although Hun Sen may have orchestrated the whole affair, even he didn't want a trial which would heighten criticism from foreign governments already concerned at human rights and other abuses in the country. So when the King requested an acquittal if his half-brother would agree to voluntary exile, Hun Sen jumped at the offer.

In 1996, **relations between the CPP and Funcinpec** reached an all time low. First Prime Minister Prince Norodom Ranariddh joined his two exiled brothers – princes Chakrapong (charged with involvement in a coup attempt in 1994, see above) and Sirivudh – along with Sam Rainsy, in France. Hun Sen, perhaps understandably, smelled a rat and when Ranariddh threatened in May to pull out of the coalition his worries seemed to be confirmed. Only pressure from the outside, it seemed, prevented a melt down. Foreign donors said that continuing aid was contingent on political harmony, and Asean sent the Malaysian foreign minister to knock a few heads together. A few months later relations became chillier still following the drive-by killing of Hun Sen's brother-in-law as he left a restaurant in Phnom Penh after eating breakfast.

The Cambodian government has had rather more success in confronting the Khmers Rouges. However, this has been more the result of political decisions than brilliance on the battlefield. In Jun 1994 the government closed Khmers Rouges offices in the capital – to the annoyance of King Norodom Sihanouk who continued to argue that the rebel group simply could not be ignored and

Whither the Khmers Rouges?

The Khmers Rouges may have refrained from its promised systematic disruption of the May 1993 elections because it feared that it would drive people to vote for its sworn enemy, the CPP, instead. At the time, analysts said the guerrillas were probably keeping their options open. But that Cambodian voters ignored Khmers Rouges calls to boycott the election – and that in many instances Khmers Rouges soldiers actually voted – was a slap in the face for the group's leaders.

There is no doubt that militarily, the Khmers Rouges remains a force to be reckoned with – even with the split in the organization in mid-1996. Latest estimates put the number of men under Pol Pot's control at around 3,000-5,000. That the Khmers Rouges is still a part of the Cambodian equation, western governments have themselves to blame. They did not intervene in 1979 when China began re-equipping the battered guerrillas – they wanted to signal their displeasure at the Vietnamese invasion. American policy reflected Washington's animosity towards Vietnam and, by extension, the Soviet Union. US opposition to Hanoi's occupation, led it to support the Khmers Rouges-dominated exiled Coalition Government of Democratic Kampuchea for over a decade. Other western countries joined the US in backing the CGDK's claim to a seat at the United Nations. During the 1980s the Khmers Rouges worked hard to consolidate its territorial support base so that it became impossible to exclude it from the eventual peace negotiations.

Any scenario which accommodates the possibility of a Khmers Rouges comeback is unthinkable to many foreign observers. To some Cambodians the concept of the Khmers Rouges returning to power would be like the Nazis returning to power in post-war Germany. But while the parallel is emotive, it is also misleading. Margaret Scott writes: "The Nazis killed Jews because they were Jews; but the Khmers Rouges was made up of Cambodians who killed other Cambodians."

What many westerners have found hard to understand is how the Khmers Rouges enjoyed considerable popular support among Cambodians – even after the massacres and the torture they have meted out. UN officials working in Phnom Penh in 1992 and 1993 noted this disquieting phenomenon. In Jun 1994, the retiring Australian ambassador to Cambodia, John Holloway, in a leaked account of his 2½ years in the country wrote:

"I was alarmed in a recent dialogue with about 100 students from different groups at the University of Phnom Penh to hear them espousing a return to government by the Khmers Rouges. ... They estimated that 60% of the student body favoured Khmers Rouges participation in government... It is necessary for outsiders to understand, that for most Cambodians, the Vietnamese are a far more traumatic issue than the Khmers Rouges."

Nonetheless, these are signs that the Khmers Rouges may, at long last, be in decline. Partly this is due to the amnesty declared in 1994 (see page 71) and the split between Ieng Sary and Pol Pot (see page 75). Partly because Beijing has stopped supplying and supporting the organization, while revenue from logging and gem mining is drying up. It is also partly due to a loss of support in rural areas following indiscriminate attacks on local officials. But most importantly, perhaps, it is because the Khmers Rouges has nothing to fight for, and stands for nothing. It is, as Nate Thayer put it in 1995 some 20 years after the Khmers Rouges took Phnom Penh, waging a 'war without issues'.

must be part of any political future. Shortly afterwards, the **National Assembly outlawed the KR** altogether, offering a 6 month **amnesty** to rank and file guerrillas. It was this latter act that seems to have most effectively undermined the Khmers Rouges' military strength. By the time the 6 months was up in Jan 1995, 7,000 Khmers Rouges had reportedly defected to the government, leaving at that time somewhere between 5,000 and 6,000 hardcore rebels still fighting. One of these defectors was Sar Kim Lemouth, a French-trained economist, who was, in effect, the Khmers Rouges' Finance Minister. It is hoped that he may be able to reveal where the millions earned by the Khmers Rouges from its gem and logging operations are stashed. This may, in turn, allow the Cambodian government to freeze their assets and seriously to undermine the group. The associated fear, though, is that if the Khmers Rouges does come under increasing pressure then it will turn its back on finding a political solution, and return to an all-out military strategy.

The war in Cambodia, though in many ways a rather unimportant footnote to the Cold War, occasionally reaches the front pages of western newspapers – when, that is, westerners are caught up in the maelstrom. In Apr 1994 two Britons and an Australian were **kidnapped** by the Khmers Rouges. 3 months later, three tourists (French, British and Australian) travelling on a train in Kompot province were also kidnapped. All were later reported murdered by the Khmers Rouges – for being 'spies'. The apparently cack-handed attempts on the part of the government to secure their release – the *Far Eastern Economic Review* called it a 'Theatre of the Absurd' – prompted harsh criticism from the British, French and Australian governments. The Australians even wanted to send their own special forces in – a plan which the British vetoed.

When Chhouk Rin, the commander of the Khmers Rouges forces involved in the seizure of the three tourists, defected to the government and received immunity from prosecution, anger turned to outrage. There were even rumours circulating that government forces had been involved in the train attack. Needless to say, the murder of 17 Thai loggers by the Khmers Rouges in Preah Vihear province in Nov 1994 did not make news in the West. Since these kidnappings, there has been the abduction of one other westerner by the KR – a mines expert working for the Mines Advisory Group (MAG), a NGO.

Politics in Cambodia, to put in mildly, remains 'tainted' by corruption, incompetence, nepotism and cronyism. In Oct 1994 one of the few respected men in the Cambodian cabinet, **Economy and Finance Minister Sam Rainsy**, resigned. Commentators interpreted this as a result of his tough anti-corruption stance, and significantly when the Minister for Foreign Affairs and International Cooperation, Prince Norodom Sirivudh, resigned in solidarity with Rainsy he explained his actions by saying that "we must show...there are some honest people [in the government]". Although Cambodia is still a democracy, there are those who see the government becoming increasingly authoritarian. Journalists are worried that their freedom to report the news will be jeopardized by a press law approved by the National Assembly in Jul 1995, and opposition politicians are becoming more circumspect in broadcasting their criticisms of the government in the face of continued – and apparently state-organized – thuggery. As one observer was quoted as saying in the *Far Eastern Economic Review* at the beginning of 1996, "many people's initial reactions in Cambodia are still violent". At times the sensitivity of politicians has descended into farce. In Mar 1995, Cambodian newspaper editor Chan Rottana was sentenced to a year in gaol for writing a 'false and defamatory statement' that First Prime Minister Prince Norodom Ranariddh was 'three times more stupid' than Second Prime Minister Hun Sen. In mid-1995 former foreign minister Sam Rainsy summed up the state of political affairs in the country when he said:

"If you are satisfied with cosmetics, everything is OK, like some Americans tell me. But if you scratch a little bit below the surface, there is nothing democratic about the government. The parliament is a rubber stamp. The press is being killed ... The judiciary is far from independent."

Sam Rainsy is far from being an unbiased commentator on Cambodian affairs. Following his resignation as foreign minister, he was expelled from the ruling Funcinpec party and then, at the end of Jun 1995, expelled from Parliament. As the international community responded critically to the announcement – which was reached without a vote or a debate – there was speculation that aid might be cut in response. One senior UN official observed that "this is the clearest signal that the honeymoon for democracy is over [in Cambodia]".

There is no doubt that newspaper editors face severe repercussions should they print stories derogatory of the government and key ministers. In May 1995, the *Khmer Ideal* newspaper was closed down and its publisher fined; in the same month, the editor of *New Liberty* was jailed for a year for penning an editorial entitled 'Nation of thieves', alluding to corruption in government ranks; a week later, the government began proceedings against the editor of the *Morning News* – a man who was jailed in 1994 for a previous offending article. Human Rights Watch Asia reported that this series of actions "represent one of the most serious assaults yet on freedom of expression". Yet the countries who bankrolled and supported the UN-administered move to democracy, namely Australia, France, Indonesia, and the US, are reluctant, apparently, to be too critical of the government. Partly, perhaps, this is because of the wish to present Cambodia as a UN 'success story' (there are notably few about), partly because they have invested considerable amounts of money and prestige in the country and fear that overt criticism might lead to instability. Whatever the reasoning, it does appear that Cambodia is becoming less democratic and less open as the government becomes increasingly defensive of its record.

Most commentators also see **King Norodom Sihanouk** as part of the problem, simply because he is so revered. He interferes in the political process, changes his mind constantly, and exasperates government ministers. Yet the respect held for him by his people means that he cannot be ignored, or easily contradicted or, for that matter, sacked. Nonetheless, the government does seem to be attempting to reduce his influence and role – perhaps with a view to permanently castrating the monarchy. At the beginning of 1995, police confiscated all copies of a booklet entitled *Only the King can save Cambodia* – reputed to call for a return of King Sihanouk to politics. Whether the monarchy can survive the buffeting is a moot point. The next King – Sihanouk turned 74 in 1996 and has cancer – must be nominated by the Royal Council to the Throne within 7 days of the death of his father. But this council consists of a myriad of competing factions. It seems that Hun Sen would like Prince Yuvancath crowned as the next king (until 1994 he was a factory hand in Boston, in the US). As King Sihanouk was reported as saying in the *Far Eastern Economic Review* at the beginning of 1995:

"You know, they [Hun Sen and the Cambodian People's Party] want someone very flexible, a lamb, a lamb! A small cat! Very obedient, or an obedient dog to use as a king. And it is not good. It is not good at all."

Politics by other means	
Aug 1994	The editor of *The Voice of Khmer Youth* is shot dead after publishing a story about drug smuggling.
May 1995	*Khmer Ideal* newspaper is closed down and its publisher fined.
May 1995	The editor of *New Liberty* is jailed for a year for penning an editorial entitled 'Nation of thieves'.
Aug 1995	A hand grenade is thrown into the house of the editor of the *Morning News* after an editorial is published accusing the military of complicity in drug smuggling.
Jan 1996	The offices of the opposition Khmer Nation Party are raided by police.
Feb 1996	Ek Mongkol, radio commentator and Funcinpec member, is shot and seriously injured.
May 1996	Anti-government newspaper editor Thun Bunly is gunned down and later dies.
Nov 1996	Kov Samuth, a senior government official and brother-in-law of Hun Sen is shot and killed

The Khmers Rouges Implodes?

On 8 August 1996 Khmers Rouges radio announced that former 'brother number two', **Ieng Sary**, had betrayed the revolution by embezzling money earned from mining and timber contracts and branded him a traitor. This was the first evidence available to western commentators that a significant split in the Khmers Rouges had occurred. In retrospect, it seems that the split has been brewing for some years – ever since the UN-sponsored elections had revealed a division between 'conservatives' and 'moderates'. The latter, apparently, wished to cooperate with the UN, while the former group desired to boycott the elections. As it turned out, while some Khmers Rouges fighters did vote, the majority toed the party line and stayed away from the polling booths. But now the moderate faction, headed by Ieng Sary, has finally broken away from the conservatives led by Pol Pot and hardman **General Ta Mok**. Hun Sen announced soon after that radio broadcast that two Khmers Rouges commanders, Ei Chhien and Sok Pheap had defected to the government and had been appointed generals within the Royal Cambodian Army. At the end of Sept Ieng Sary held a press conference to declare his defection from the Khmers Rouges, to the government. He told an incredulous audience that he "had nothing to do with ordering the execution of anyone, or even the suggestion of it". On 14 Sept King Norodom Sihanouk granted Ieng Sary a royal pardon.

The Cambodian government's conciliatory line towards Ieng Sary seems perplexing given the man's past. Although he has cast himself in the mould of 'misguided and ignorant revolutionary', there are few who doubt that he was fully cognizant, of what the Khmers Rouges under Pol Pot were doing even if, as Michael Vickery argues, he was not Brother Number Two, just Brother Number Four or Five. Indeed he has admitted as much in the past. Not only is he, as a man, thoroughly unpleasant – or so those who know him have said – but he was also a key figure in the leadership and was sentenced to death in absentia by the Phnom Penh government. Stephen Heder of London's School of Oriental & African Studies was quoted as saying after the Sept press conference: "It's totally implausible that Ieng Sary was unaware that people were being murdered [by the Khmers

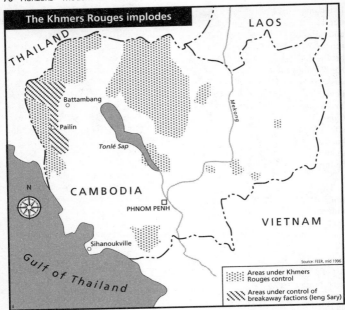

The Khmers Rouges implodes

Source: FEER, mid 1996

Areas under Khmers Rouges control

Areas under control of breakaway factions (Ieng Sary)

Rouges]". This was confirmed in Oct when Laurence Piq, formerly married to Suong Sikoeun an aide to Ieng Sary, wrote:

"As in *The Little Red Riding Hood*, the hand he [Ieng Sary] extends for photographs is the better to grab you with. The jovial demeanour he affixes to his mouth is the better to bite you with. The red carpet is laid out. Abominable crimes are being erased. All shame is swallowed. The world's nations accept this under the pretext of peace. What kind of peace? A peace *à la* Khmers Rouges, dripping with the blood of genocide."

It will take some convincing if western donors are to accept an amnesty for Ieng Sary on the basis that he did not know. More likely is that the West will simply recognize that if peace is to come to Cambodia, then it may be necessary to allow some people to get away with – well

– murder. As one western diplomat pondered: "Do you owe fealty to the dead for the living?" This pragmatic, albeit rather depressing, view on events in Cambodia seemed to be confirmed at the beginning of Nov when it was announced that Ieng Sary's troops would be integrated into the Royal Cambodian Armed Forces. (To begin with it was thought that Ieng Sary might keep control of his men and a period of internicine war would erupt across the Khmers Rouges controlled W of the country.) The government can argue that Cambodia's future is better served by integrating rather than alienating Ieng Sary, and they can also claim that no one, so far, has uncovered the 'smoking gun' that would irrefutably link Ieng Sary with the genocide.

What the split in the Khmers Rouges has done is scotched rumours that Pol Pot is dead. Ieng Sary reported that the Khmers Rouges' leader was alive and living in a village close to the Thai border. He is, though, nearly 70 years old and weak after living so long in the jungle. Who will take his place should he die has been confused with Ieng Sary's – long believed (perhaps erroneously) to be the Khmers Rouges' leader in waiting – defection. Some think that Ta (Grandfather) Mok is now in the frame. Ta Mok is one of Pol Pot's most effective field commanders. He is also known by the nickname 'the butcher', so any thoughts of a softer line should he take power can be safely put to one side.

The split has deprived Pol Pot of around 3,000-5,000 men, leaving him with a roughly equal force. So far as Pol Pot is concerned, not only has the defection halved his fighting force, but it has also deprived him of his main source of revenue. For Ieng Sary had control not just of 3,000 fighters but also of the key gem mining areas around Pailin and many of the richest forest concessions. On the surface, then, Ieng Sary's defection is nothing but bad news for Pol Pot. But there are those who suspect that it may be a ploy to allow Pol Pot to pursue his ends both through military action and through (legitimate) political means. This seems too conspiratorial even for Cambodia.

ECONOMY

With Cambodia's politics see-sawing between muddling through and melt down, it would be easy to assume that the country's economy is in similar turmoil. But in fact the economy is in remarkably good shape – at least for a place which has suffered on this scale and which continues to face the perils of economic mismanagement and corruption. Since the 1993 elections, the economy has grown by around 7-8% a year, inflation is under control, and foreign investment is buoyant. This could, of course, all change if the fragile coalition fragments, and certainly, as this book went to press, there were reports that foreign investors were turning away from the country as the domestic political scene became more unstable. In addition, 1996 saw a blossoming of labour unrest in Phnom Penh's small export-oriented industrial sector.

1989 was a turning point for Cambodia; when the Vietnamese troops pulled out in Sep that year, the economy was in a sorry state. Hanoi had done what it could to restore some semblance of order after the mess left by the Khmers Rouges in 1979. But with the collapse of the Soviet Union, aid from Moscow and its erstwhile Eastern Bloc allies dried up. This deprived Phnom Penh of about US$100mn a year. The Hun

Back on the tourist track

Between 1975, when the Khmers Rouges gained power, and the mid-1980s, Cambodia received virtually no tourists whatsoever. Since then, however, and linked with the peace settlement, numbers have picked up enormously, from 400 in 1986 to over 175,000 in 1994. In 1995, the Ministry of Tourism hopes to open offices in all of the country's 22 provinces (there are currently offices in 16) and the government clearly sees tourism as an easy way to generate foreign exchange. It was feared that the deaths in 1994 of a number of foreigners at the hands of the Khmers Rouges would deter travellers, although the effect seems to have been minimal.

Tourist arrivals

1986	400	1994	176,617
1991	4,500	2000	1 million (projected)
1993	118,183		

Sen government also faced a total aid and trade boycott from the W, while the civil war against the resistance factions further sapped the regime's scant resources. But the Phnom Penh regime gradually shifted away from orthodox Communist ideology and central planning towards market economics. At first this was nothing more than paper policy, but deregulation and reform began to spark an upsurge in business activity.

Before, during and immediately after the elections of 1993, the economy was in dire straits. The value of the riel collapsed against the US dollar, inflation reached 340%, provincial towns were crowded with people subsisting by recycling rubbish or begging, and foreign investors were shying away from a country so wracked by manifold problems.

Today, many of these problems have receded. In 1993 annual inflation stood at 100%. By the end of 1994 this had declined to a comparatively manageable 20%, and in mid-1996 was running at an annualized rate of around 4-5%. Furthermore, foreign investors have begun to pluck up courage and put their money in the country. Malaysian, Singaporean, Thai, Taiwanese and other Asian companies are in the vanguard of this investment tide. Between Aug 1994 and Apr 1995 US$625mn in foreign investment was approved. The role of Malaysian investors is particularly striking. Various explanations have been presented to account for this. First, the Malaysians are not the Thais, which is an advantage given the ever-present friction between Thailand and Cambodia. (Thai journalists refer to Siem Reap – which means 'Victory over Siam' – as Siem Rap – 'Plains of Siam', just one of many annoyances, small and big, which divide the two countries.) Second, Malaysia is just far enough away so the two countries have no lingering territorial disputes, and there is little chance that an army of Malaysian workers will arrive in Phnom Penh to take jobs away from deserving Cambodians. Third, of course, Malaysia is a successful economy, at the early stages of its own outward investment drive.

The intention is clearly to entice labour intensive manufacturing enterprises such as garment factories to set up shop, although to date most investment has been concentrated in the service sector. There has been speculation in land and property, and hotels, bars and restaurants have been going up or are being refurbished – mainly in Phnom Penh, but also in Sihanonkville and in Siem Reap. Grant Evans, writing in *The Far Eastern Economic Review* in Mar 1993 noted that businessmen "have descended on the country like locusts in the atmosphere of frontier, tax-free capitalism. A few dollars trickle down to the Khmer." In Aug 1994 the National Assembly passed a new investment law to make the country even more enticing, by providing foreign investors with tax exemption on profits for 8 years and allowing foreign investors to hold 100% equity.

Cambodia's future, to a considerable extent, rests in the hands of the **international aid community**, and especially the IMF and World Bank. Aid makes up around one half of all government spending, so without continuing generosity the country would collapse. Donors, operating through the International Conference for the Reconstruction of Cambodia, have dispersed (up to mid-1996) US$1.5 billion since the elections of 1992 and have been generally complimentary and upbeat about the country's economic progress. In a meeting in 1996, the donor nations promised another US$760 million in aid over the 3 years to 1999. The main areas of worry concern corruption – and especially the offering of logging concessions extended to politically well-connected businessmen (see page 22) – and what might be termed the lack of 'transparency' in public finances. At a wider level,

An Ambassador's view, circa 1994

In Jun 1994, the retiring Australian ambassador to Cambodia, John Holloway, wrote a concluding 3,500 word summary of his 2½ years sojourn in the country. Although the cable was supposed to be secret, it was leaked to the *Sydney Morning Herald* and provides a frank – and none too laudatory – assessment of Cambodia, its politicians and prospects. Unfortunately for him, Holloway then found himself accused in the Australian parliament of having sex with two underage Cambodian boys. He was charged under the new Australian Child Sex Tourism Act which allows people to be tried in Australia for crimes committed abroad. Two witnesses were flown to Canberra from Phnom Penh but the presiding magistrate threw out the case deciding that there was insufficient evidence to go to trial. Holloway hinted that there were those in Cambodia who wished to sully his name.

● **King Norodom Sihanouk**: "pathetically pursuing power although riddled with cancer, he has belittled the government, tried to cause splits in the ruling groups and thrown aside the government strategy to outlaw the Khmers Rouges ... He has strutted around his small stage, erratic and emotive, continuing the negative influence he has wielded over the last 2 years"

● **Prime ministers Hun Sen and Norodom Ranariddh**: are unable to "exercise leadership, even when they are in the country."

● **Government ministries**: "most government ministries are barely working."

● **Civil servants**: "are only motivated to attend their offices at all by the possibility of making some extra money."

● **Corruption**: "every business deal must have a cut for the relevant minister."

● **Khmers Rouges**: "well disciplined, committed, and not engaged in petty corruption."

● **Army**: "people join the army to use their uniforms and their weapons as a meal ticket. ...government forces move through the countryside, unpaid and out of control, looting and committing a wide range of crimes ...the [state of the army] is deplorable".

● **The economy**: "...inefficient government, massive corruption, a hemorrhage of Khmer wealth caused by an influx of skilled Vietnamese...and a concentration of all development funds on the cities."

● **The countryside**: "out in the Cambodian countryside, where 80% of Cambodians live, it is difficult to find any progress. Very little, if any, new money has percolated into the countryside, and the life of rural dwellers is as brutish as ever."

donors are also keeping an eye on political stability in the country. There have been veiled warnings that should the coalition partners fall out, then the country might see its aid drying up. Few people believe that the international community is getting a good return from its aid investment. Such vast quantities of money are siphoned off by the powerful and well-connected that, in developmental terms, Cambodia is not getting many bangs for its bucks.

Although Cambodia's economy might be in reasonable shape considering the turmoil of recent history, there is no getting away from the fact that it is not just poor, but one of the world's least developed nations. Cambodia's GDP is still estimated to be no higher than it was 25 years ago and per capita incomes in 1995 stood at just US$314. Roads are potholed, bridges destroyed, power cuts are commonplace and there is a shortage of skilled managers to oversee reconstruction of the war-shattered economy. Paddy fields are littered with landmines, and marketing and distribution systems continue to be hampered by the civil war. In the district of Rattanak Mondal in the W of Battambang province, comprising some of the country's richest farmland, one adult male in seven was killed or maimed by a mine between 1984 and 1994. The 1994/95 rice harvest was devastated by flood and drought and 1996 also saw extensive flooding. In short, there is a considerable gap between the macro-economic view from the windows of the Finance Ministry and that from the paddy field. (It needs to be remembered that 85% of the population still work on the land, and manufacturing accounts for just 17% of GDP.) Son Chhay, an MP representing Siem Reap, following the floods of 1994 said of the rescue efforts: "They [the government] probably spent three times more money on the reception for the prime minister than they are spending to help the flood victims."

The average monthly income of a medical officer in a Cambodian hospital – one of the busiest and most stressful jobs going – is about US$5 – plus a ration of rice and paraffin. These wages are paid 3 months late. Government soldiers earn a princely US$10 a month – but most of them have not been paid for 6 months. Most people consider themselves lucky to have jobs, however. It is hardly surprising that government soldiers, as well as Khmers Rouges rebels, commonly resort to highway robbery to top up their meagre earnings. Bandits regularly hold travellers at gunpoint as they point torches into the eyes of long-distance taxi-drivers – who now build the extortion money into the cost of a trip.

In the past, resentment due to the huge discrepancies in wealth between city and countryside have been responsible for much of the political upheaval. Rampant corruption and the creation of private monopolies of national resources – particularly timber, rubber and gemstones – made a few people very wealthy. Foreign investors are concerned by the lack of 'transparency' in government affairs and the control that individuals have over some sections of the bureaucracy. If historical precedent is anything to go by, future governments are unlikely to learn from past governments' mistakes. As in many Southeast Asian countries, politics is a sure way of getting rich quick. Gemstones and timber both offer Cambodia's most lucrative possibilities. Thai logging companies have long extracted timber from Khmers Rouges-controlled territory. In 1990 the Khmers Rouges built roads from their powerbase in W Cambodia into Thailand, to allow them to export timber and gemstones which help fund the organization. In the early 1990s these exports were thought to be worth around US$60mn a month, and the trade is likely to continue as long as the Khmers Rouges can maintain their hold on the borderlands with Thailand. The proceeds are said to be neatly divided between the Thai contractors (50%), the Thai military (5%) and the Khmers Rouges (45%).

Of all the plans for the Cambodian economy, none comes bigger than the plan to **build 17 dams** across the country. The Mekong River Commission has drawn up this slate of dams and while some people believe that they could play a critical role in the country's modernization and development, others are horrified at the environmental and human implications. Partly it is a response to dam-building plans upstream on the

Mekong: Laos has 56 on the drawing board and China 15. These will have implications for Cambodia and some experts consider that Cambodia has to get in on the act if it is not to lose out. The scale of some of the projects is awesome: the Sambor scheme, north of the town of Kratie, will flood an area of 800 sq km, will generate 3,300MW and will displace perhaps 60,000 people. The projected cost: US$4 billion, more than the cost of the UN operation in Cambodia.

Criticizing Cambodia's political system and the politicians and bureaucrats who are meant to be guiding it towards a bright new future is like shooting fish in a bucket. There is so much corruption, waste, intimidation and inefficiency that there's no fun in it. When foreign observers come to the country on fact-finding missions and are overtly critical tend to get rejected as 'unhelpful' or 'unconstructive'. The leadership fall back on the excuse that having experienced such horrors it will take time for the country to right itself. There is also no doubt that Cambodia and its people are in a better state today than at any time since 1975. And yet, as William Shawcross put it in an interview in Nov 1996, "There are lots of countries that are worse off than Cambodia...but the culture of victimhood has existed here for some years, and it's not a very healthy concept for Cambodia to indulge in forever."

Cambodia: fact file

Geographic

Land area	177,000 sq km
Arable land as % of total	13.6%
Average annual rate of deforestation	0.2%
Highest mountain Phnom Aoral	1,813m
Average rainfall in Phnom Penh	1,560mm
Average temperature in Phnom Penh	27.5°C

Economic

GNP/person (1995)	US$314
GDP/person (PPP*, 1992)	US$1,250
GNP growth (/capita, 1965-1980)	0.6%
% labour force in agriculture	74%
Total debt (% GDP)	n.a.
Debt service ratio (% exports)	n.a.
Military expenditure (% GNP)	n.a.

Social

Population	9.4 million
Population growth rate (1960-92)	1.7%
Adult literacy rate	37.8%
Mean years of schooling	2 years
Tertiary graduate as % of age group	n.a.
Population in absolute poverty	n.a.
Rural population as % of total	89%
Growth of urban population (1960-92)	1.8%/year
Urban population in largest city (%)	n.a.
Televisions per 1,000 people	10

Health

Life expectancy at birth	51.6 years
Population with access to clean water	36%
Calorie intake as % of requirements	96%
Malnourished children under 5 years old	522,000
Infant mortality rate/1,000 live births	116
Contraceptive prevalence rate†	na

*PPP = Purchasing Power Parity (based on what it costs to buy a similar basket of goods and services in different countries).

† % of women of childbearing age using contraception.

Source: UNDP (1995) *Human Development Report 1995*, OUP: New York; and other sources.

Phnom Penh
ភ្នំពេញ

LEGEND has it that Cambodia's capital is named after Penh, a rich Khmer lady, who lived on the banks of the Mekong River. Floodwaters are said to have washed a tree onto the riverbank and Penh found four statues of the Buddha hidden inside. In 1372 she built a monastery to house the statues on a nearby hill – or 'phnom' in Cambodian. The people of Cambodia believed the statues were a sign from the gods that they wanted a new home. When the Thais invaded in 1431 and after the kingdom of Angkor later collapsed, the capital duly moved to Ondong and then to a site near the important temple of Phnom Penh. The city lies at the confluence of the Sap, Mekong and Bassac rivers and it quickly grew into an important commercial centre. The French called the junction 'Les Quatre Bras'; in Khmer it is known as the Chamean Mon.

Before 1970, the capital was the beguiling beauty of Indochina with its wide boulevards – laid out by the French – elegant colonial villas and Art Deco town houses. Only now, 25 years on, is the Phnom Penh of 1970 re-emerging. Energetic landscaping of the boulevards and promenades alongside the Tonlé Sap has much to do with this. Many of the buildings survive, although most are in a serious state of disrepair: the best-preserved colonial architecture is around Victory Monument.

Phnom Penh is more like a country town, than a capital city. The newest buildings still fail to top 10 storeys and Phnom Penh exudes a provincial charm, in stark contrast to its near neighbour, Bangkok. Rickety bamboo scaffolding is going up all over the city now that the country is more stable: residential and office properties are in heavy demand. Rents have come down from the UNTAC – inflated era of 1992/93 but are still surprisingly high – a result of foreign businesses clamouring for a share in the new free market climate. Phnom

Penh faces a housing crisis – two-thirds of its houses were damaged by the Khmers Rouges between 1975 and 1979. Apart from the sheer cost of building new ones and renovating the crumbling colonial mansions, there is a severe shortage of skilled workers in Cambodia: under Pol Pot 20,000 engineers were killed as well as nearly all the country's architects (three students survived within Cambodia).

The years of war have also taken a heavy toll on the city's inhabitants: Phnom Penh's population fluctuations in recent decades give some indication of the scale of social disruption. Refugees first began to flood in from the countryside in the early 1950s during the First Indochina War – the population grew from 100,000 to 600,000 by the late 1960s. In the early 1970s there was another surge as people streamed in from the countryside again, this time to escape US bombing and guerrilla warfare: on the eve of the Khmers Rouges takeover in 1975, the capital had a population of 2 million. Phnom Penh then became a ghost town; on Pol Pot's orders it was forcibly emptied and the townspeople frog-marched into the country-

side to work as labourers. Only 45,000 inhabitants were left in the city in 1975 and a large number were soldiers. In 1979, after 4 years of virtual abandonment, Phnom Penh had a population of a few thousand. People began to drift back following the Vietnamese invasion (1978/79) and as hopes for peace rose in 1991, the floodgates opened yet again: today the population is approaching 1 million. Most of the original population of Phnom Penh died during the Pol Pot era or are in exile and the population of the city is now more rural in character. In fact the population of the city tends to vary from season to season: in the dry season people pour into the capital when there is little work in the countryside but go back to their farms in the wet season when the rice has to be planted and the population drops to 750,000-800,000.

Public health facilities are woefully inadequate – the city's services are overstretched and there are problems with everything from water and electricity supplies to sewage and refuse disposal. The Khmers Rouges saw to it that the plumbing network was completely destroyed before they left. The capital's streets are potholed and in bad need of repair. Mao Tse Tung St is a notable exception having, in 1996, been entirely resurfaced – courtesy of the Chinese Embassy and the owner of a major hotel. Even if the main thoroughfares are newly metalled every sidestreet remains ample justification for the capital's fleets of 4WD. A British newspaper correspondent, visiting the city in late 1991 noted that Phnom Penh boasted of the new urban phenomenon of traffic jams, regarding them as an indicator of economic development. By 1996 traffic jams on Monivong had become a serious twice-daily problem.

Phnom Penh has undergone an economic revival since the Paris Peace Accord was signed in 1991; there has been a frenzy of business deals in real estate (one of the most serious problems for

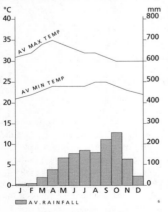

Climate: Phnom Penh

Mean streets and how to avoid them

From April 1996 the night time streets of Phnom Penh were once more dangerous places for foreigners to go. A spate of armed hold-ups in which money and jewellery were stolen had the effect of a dusk to dawn curfew and only those with cars (there being no taxis) were able to venture out with any degree of confidence. Expatriate security officers said "the best advice to avoid armed robbery is not to go out" or "tuck yourself up in bed early" – hardly the sort of suggestion hardened hedonists are likely to heed, the more so given that Phnom Penh's nightlife is, for many, its chief attraction.

Kidnapping too is far more prevalent than the few headline cases of Europeans abducted by the Khmers Rouges would suggest. Tens of thousands of Thai labourers, scores of Chinese market traders and businessmen have all been held to ransom, sometimes by the Khmers Rouges at other times by opportunists taking advantage of the vacuum normally occupied by moral behaviour and the forces of law and order. Although not yet on the scale of Manila, kidnapping looks set to become a major growth industry.

NGOs operating in Cambodia have issued the following guidelines:

- Whenever possible avoid walking alone at night
- Carry your bag in a secure manner to prevent 'grab and runs'
- Be alert and aware of your surroundings
- Do not travel with your passport or a large amount of money
- Divide and conceal your money, do not carry it all in your wallet
- Do not carry your address in your bag as it is also likely to contain your house keys
- Try to use a moto driver you trust; ask him to come back at an appointed time
- Try to travel in the company of friends
- Explain clearly, exactly where you want to go; if the driver continues in the wrong direction demand he stop
- Don't argue about the price – fix it before travelling

residents is land disputes and expulsion as many do not possess title deeds to their property). Small businesses are springing up, Phnom Penh's river port which has recently been the recipient of a US$30mn investment programme to renovate it by the Japanese – is bustling with traders from throughout the region – especially Singapore. Venture capitalists and aid organizations are homing in as evidenced by the presence of over 100 international non-governmental organizations. Thai investors have capitalized on their geographical proximity and linguistic advantage to develop a commanding position in the capital's reviving economy, and the Phnom Penh of 1996 is growing daily in manner and

appearance, more like Bangkok. The Thai look is underscored by growing volumes of cars and pick-up trucks, lent added authenticity by their Thai registration plates; the majority of vehicles are smuggled over the border, many stolen. Other vices (not *necessarily* the preserve of Bangkok) are flourishing and Thai-style massage parlours are springing up, despite the departure of UN-TAC. Monks' saffron robes are once again lending a splash of colour to the capital's streets, following the reinstatement of Buddhism as the national religion in 1989. But the amputees on street corners are a constant reminder of Cambodia's tragic story.

The Cambodian capital relies on the

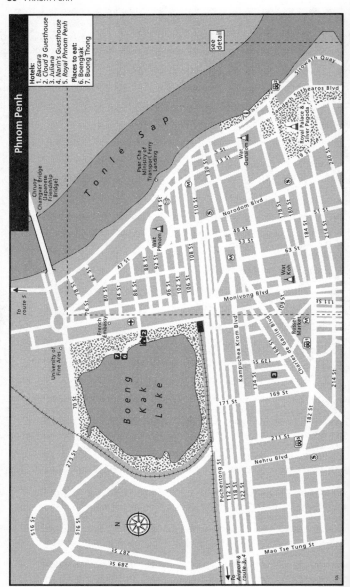

Phnom Penh

Hotels:
1. Baccara
2. Cloud 9 Guesthouse
3. Juliana
4. Narin's Guesthouse
5. Royal Phnom Penh

Places to eat:
6. Boengkak
7. Buong Thong

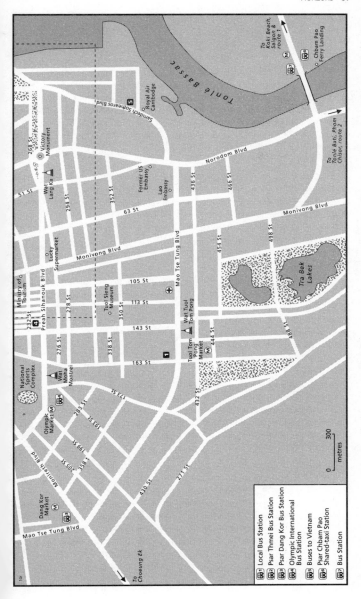

Legend:

- 1 Local Bus Station
- 2 Psar Thmei Bus Station
- 3 Psar Dang Kor Bus Station
- 4 Olympic International Bus Station
- 5 Buses to Vietnam
- 6 Psar Chbam Pao Shared-taxi Station
- 7 Bus Station

river. The Mekong provides the city's water supply. It is the only significant port on the Mekong above the delta and is navigable by ships of about 5,000-8,000 tons.

Finding your way around Phnom Penh can be very confusing. Most of the street names were changed in 1979 by the Vietnamese who decided that even urban nomenclature should be ideologically sound. However, since the elections of 1993 the street names have reverted to those used in the Sangkum era (1955-69): That said, street names have changed so many times in recent history that it is sometimes hard to establish the prevailing official name for a road. Maps and street signs commonly contradict each other. The majority of larger streets are named and the smaller streets numbered: as a rule, even numbered streets run E-W, odd numbered streets run N-S. The S is the royal quarter and the Khmer area; the N is the colonial quarter with the *Grand Hotel* and several large and dilapidated French buildings. Chinatown, the commercial quarter, surrounds the central covered market. The modern area, built after independence, is to the W of Monivong St.

PLACES OF INTEREST

One of the main sights in Phnom Penh is the Royal Palace, which, along with the Silver Pagoda, was closed to the public since its reinstatement as Prince Sihanouk's main residence. The Silver Pagoda is now open again, pay at the gate.

The **Royal Palace**, between 184 and 240 sts, was mainly built by the French in 1866 on the site of the old town. The entrance is on Samdech Sothearos Blvd via the Pavilion of Dancers (or Chan Chaya Pavilion). Opposite the entrance are the walls of the royal residence (closed to the public) and the stable of the white elephant (a highly auspicious and sacred animal treasured as a symbol of royal beneficence). The pagoda-style compound was built by the French, and since Nov 1991, has been home, once again, to Prince Norodom Sihanouk. In the weeks leading up to his return, there was a flurry of activity behind the royal residence's orange walls as decorators strove to give it as much regal opulence as Cambodia could muster – despite the abolition of the monarchy in 1970.

The **Throne Room**, the main building to the left of the entrance, was built in 1917 in Khmer style; it has a tiered roof and a 59m tower, influenced by Angkor's Bayon Temple (see page 116). It was used for coronations and other official occasions such as the reception of foreign ambassadors when they presented their official credentials: scenes from the Ramayana adorn the walls. Inside stand the sacred gong and French-style thrones only used by the sovereign. There are two chambers for the king and queen at the back of the hall, which were used only in the week before a coronation when the royal couple were barred from sleeping together. The other adjoining room is used to house the ashes of dead monarchs before they are placed in a royal stupa. There are Buddha images in the left nave, at which the kings would pray before each day. Returning to his former abode in Nov 1991, Sihanouk must have found it much as he had left it – although many of the state gifts from the display cases have sadly been smashed or stolen. The chairs closest to the entrance were reserved for high officials and the others were for visiting ambassadors. The yellow chairs were used by visiting heads of state.

The **royal treasury** and the **Napoleon III villa** – or summerhouse – built in 1866, are to the S of the Throne Room. It is currently closed to the public. The latter was presented by Napoleon III to his Empress Eugenie as accommodation for the princess during the Suez Canal opening celebrations who later had it dismantled and dispatched it to Phnom Penh as a gift to the king. The prefabricated folly was renovated and refurbished in 1990 and its ersatz marble walls remarbled – all with French money. Next to the villa are rooms built in 1959 by Sihanouk to accommodate his cabinet. Beyond is the N gate and the Silver Pagoda enclosure.

The **Silver Pagoda** is often called the Pagoda of the Emerald Buddha or Wat Preah Kaeo after the statue housed here. The wooden temple was originally built by King Norodom in 1892 to enshrine royal ashes and then rebuilt by Sihanouk in 1962. The pagoda's steps are of Italian marble, and inside, its floor is comprised of more than 5,000 silver blocks which together weigh nearly 6 tonnes. All around are cabinets filled with presents from foreign dignitaries – the pagoda is remarkably intact, having been granted special dispensation by the Khmers Rouges, although 60% of the Khmer treasures were stolen from here. It is a magpie-style collection, as the writer Norman Lewis said in 1957: "One imagined the Queen, or perhaps a succession of queens, making a periodic clear out of their cupboards and then tripping down to the Silver Pagoda with all the attractive useless things that had to be found a home somewhere". In the centre of the pagoda is a magnificent 17th century emerald Buddha statue made of Baccarat crystal. In front is a 90 kg golden Buddha studded with 9,584 diamonds, dating from 1906. It was made from the jewellery of King Norodom and its vital statistics conform exactly to his – a tradition that can be traced back to the god-kings of Angkor. The gold Buddha image is flanked by bronze and silver statues of the Buddha. Under a glass cover is a golden lotus – a Buddhist relic from India. At the back of the room there is a marble Buddha (from Burma) and a litter used for coronations which required 12 porters to carry it.

Useful place names	
Choeung Ek	ជើងឯក
Koki Beach	ព្រែកគី
Oudong	ឧត្តុង
Phnom Chet Ath Roeus	ភ្នំចិត្តអត្តរុស់
Phnom Chisor	ភ្នំជីសូ
Preah Sakyamoni Chedi	ព្រះសក្យមុនីចេតិ
Royal Palace	ព្រះបរមរាជវាំង
Tonle Bati	ទន្លេបាទី
Tuol Sleng Museum	សារមន្ទីរទួលស្លែង
Wat Lang Ka	វត្តលង្កា
Wat Ounalom	វត្តឧណ្ណាលោម
Wat Phnom	វត្តភ្នំ
Wat Tuol Tom Pong	វត្តទួលតពូង

The 600m-long wall enclosing the Silver Pagoda is galleried; its inward face is covered in frescoes, painted at the turn of the century, which depict epic scenes from the Ramayana – the story starts by the E gate. To the E of the Silver Pagoda is a **statue of King Norodom** on horseback (it is in fact a statue of Napoleon III with the head replaced with that of the Cambodian monarch) and a **stupa** containing the ashes of King Ang Duong (1845-59). Beyond the stupa, on the S wall, are **pavilions** containing a footprint of the Buddha (to the E) and a pavilion for royal celebrations (to the W). Next to **Phnom Mondap**, an artificial hill with a building covering the Buddha's footprint, in the centre of the S wall is a **stupa** dedicated to Sihanouk's favourite daughter who died of leukaemia in 1953. On the W wall is a stupa of King Norodom Suramarit with a bell tower in the NW corner. Beyond the bell tower on the N wall is the **mondap** or library, originally containing precious Buddhist texts. Admission US$2. Camera US$2, video US$5. Open 0800-1100, 1400-1700, 7 days a week.

The **National Museum of Arts** (also called Musée des Beaux Arts) is the terracotta building just N of the palace (on 13 St between 178 and 184 sts). It was designed by a French archeologist and painter, George Groslier, in Khmer style in 1920 to exhibit works scattered throughout the country. The museum contains a collection of Khmer art – notably sculpture – throughout the ages (although some periods are not represented). Most of the exhibits date from the Angkor period but there are several examples from the pre-Angkor era (ie from the kingdoms of Funan, Chenla and Cham). The collection of Buddhas from the 6th and 7th centuries, includes a statue of Krishna Bovardhana found at Angkor Borei showing the freedom and grace of early Khmer sculpture. The chief attraction is probably the pre-Angkorian statue of Harihara, found at Prasat Andat near Kompong Thom. There is a fragment from a beautiful bronze statue of Vishnu found in the West Baray at Angkor, as well as frescoes and engraved doors. The library at the museum was one of the largest of its type in Southeast Asia but has now been dismantled and sold.

The shop attached to the museum sells reproductions of works from Angkor and a good selection of books, maps and cards. The Fine Arts School, *École des Beaux Arts*, is behind the main building. French-speaking and English-speaking guides are available and most are excellent. Admission US$2. Camera US$2. Open 0700-1130, 1400-1730 Tues-Sun. Photographs only permitted in the garden.

Phnom Penh's most important wat, **Wat Ounalom**, is N of the museum, at the junction of 154 St and Samdech Sothearos Blvd, facing the Tonlé Sap. The first building on this site was a monastery, built in 1443 to house a hair of the Buddha. Before 1975, more than 500 monks lived at the wat but the Khmers Rouges murdered the Patriarch and did their best to demolish the capital's principal temple. Nonetheless it remains Cambodian Buddhism's headquarters. The complex has been restored since 1979 although its famous library was completely destroyed. The stupa behind the main sanctuary is the oldest part of the wat. The main sanctuary, which dates from 1952, now contains only the poorly-assembled fragments of a Burmese marble Buddha. On the first level there is a fine bust of the Buddha; frescoes on the second level represent scenes from the Buddha's life, painted in 1952.

Wat Phnom stands on a small hill at the end of Blvd Tou Samouth (in the N end of town, where it intersects 96 St) and is the temple from which the city takes its name. It was built by a wealthy Khmer lady called Penh (see page 83) in 1372. The sanctuary was rebuilt in 1434, 1890, 1894 and 1926. The main entrance is to the E, the steps are guarded by nagas and lions. The principal sanctuary is decorated inside with frescoes depicting scenes from Buddha's life and the Ramayana. At the front, on a pedestal, is a statue of the Buddha with four faces. There is a statue of Penh inside a small pavilion between the vihara and the stupa; the latter contains the ashes of King Ponhea Yat (1405-67).

Wat Phnom is a favourite with the Phnom Penhois and is often teeming with worshippers praying for a dose of good fortune. Vietnamese devotees flock to the shrine of the spirit Preah Chau, N of the main sanctuary. To the left of the image of Preah Chau is a statue of the Hindu god, Vishnu, 'the preserver', and the shrine is guarded by spirits wielding clubs. The summit affords nice views down Phnom Penh's tree-lined avenues, and there are plans to replant the hill with hundreds of trees to recall how it looked in former times. On the slope behind the wat is an overgrown royal stupa.

King Sihanouk chose this wat to be the site of a new chedi – the **Preah Sakyamoni Chedei**. The chedi was to be built to house a bone of the Buddha himself, which is currently contained in the small, rather nondescript, Sakyamoni Chedei in front of the city's railway station. King Sihanouk no doubt thought that this was a far too insignificant, not to say noisy, shrine for such a relic and that the comparatively peaceful Wat Phnom a short way NE would be much more fitting. Construction of the new 50m-high chedi was begun on 14 July 1992 and was scheduled to have been completed within 18 months. The architects came up with a design which might be described as Art Deco Meets Angkor. Innovative perhaps, but the purists cannot be jumping for joy and the concrete piles already in place do not bode well for the finished product. However, and like many things Cambodian, funds dried up. Apparently, donations were dripping in at the princely sum of between US$1 and US$2 a day, hardly a king's ransom. But even this might be thought remarkable in a country as poor as Cambodia. Fearing his chedi might not be built in his lifetime, King Sihanouk donated US$900,000 in Oct 1994 from his own royal fund, arguing that his country would not see peace, unity and national reconciliation if the edifice was not completed. In Jun 1995 however, the building programme was curtailed, apparently because the foundations were too shallow to take the weight of the proposed 150-tonne structure. Instead, the chedi was to be converted into a museum housing Buddhist scriptures or *prey tray bedah*. How Cambodia happens to have a bone of the Buddha, is because at the death of the sage his bones were divided up and shipped to all Buddhist quarters of the world. Today there are far more bones housed in assorted shrines than even the Buddha is likely to have been endowed with.

The **French Embassy**, recently rebuilt as a low concrete whitewashed complex for the French to occupy once again, was the building into which 800 expatriates and 600 Cambodians crowded when the Khmers Rouges first occupied the city in mid-Apr 1975, is on the intersection of Monivong Blvd and 76 St, N of Wat Phnom. Within 48 hrs of Pol Pot's troops arrival in Phnom Penh, the French vice-consul was informed that the new regime did not recognize diplomatic privilege. Cambodian women married to foreigners were allowed to stay in the Embassy, but all Cambodian men were ordered to leave. In *Sideshow*, William Shawcross says marriages were hastily arranged to safeguard the women. The foreigners were finally escorted out of Cambodia; everyone else was marched out of the compound. Many met their deaths in the killing fields. The scale of the new building is testimony to the importance France attaches to its former Indochinese colonies.

South of the Royal Palace and Silver Pagoda between 268 St and Preah Sihanouk Blvd is **Victory Monument**. It was built in 1958 to commemorate independence but has now assumed the role of a cenotaph. The best colonial architecture is on roads 114 and 53, 178, Norodom Blvd and Samdech Sothearos Blvd.

Wat Lang Ka, just off Norodom Blvd (close to the Victory Monument), was another beautiful pagoda that fell victim to Pol Pot's architectural holocaust. Like Wat Ounalom, it was restored in Khmer style on the direction of the Hanoi-backed government in the 1980s.

Further SW, on 103 St (close to 350 St), is the **Tuol Sleng Museum** (or Museum of Genocide). After 17 April 1975 the classrooms of Tuol Svay Prey High School became the Khmers Rouges main torture and interrogation centre, known as Security Prison 21 – or just S-21. More than 20,000 people were taken from S-21 to their executions at Choeung Ek extermination camp. Countless others died under torture and were thrown into mass graves in the school grounds. Only seven prisoners survived because they were sculptors and could turn out countless busts of Pol Pot. The school was converted into a 'museum of genocide' by the Vietnamese (with help from the East Germans who had experience in setting up the Auschwitz Museum) and exhibits, through the display of torture implements, photographs and paintings, the scale of the Khmers Rouges' atrocities. All their victims were methodically numbered and photographed; these pictures now cover the museum's walls. Admission US$2. Open 0800-1100, 1400-1700, closed Mon. Open Public Holidays 0800-1800.

Wat Tuol Tom Pong, next to a market of the same name (just off Mao Tse Tung Blvd – the entrance is on 135 St) is a modern pagoda – very bright, almost kitsch. Surrounded by a high wall, it has entrances with mythical animals associated with the Buddha.

There are several other wats worthy of a visit: **Wat Koh**, on Monivong Blvd (between 174 and 178 sts), is popular for its lake. **Wat Moha Montrei** on Preah Sihanouk Blvd (between 173 and 163 sts) was used as a rice storage depot by the Pol Pot regime. A second brick mosque on Chraing Chamres II, called **An-Nur an-Na'im Mosque**, is much smaller than the one which previously occupied the site: the original building, built in 1901 was destroyed by the Khmers Rouges.

The former **US Embassy**, now home to the Ministry of Fisheries, is at the intersection of Norodom and Mao Tse Tung blvds. As the Khmers Rouges closed on the city from the N and the S in Apr 1975, US Ambassador John Gunther Dean pleaded with Secretary of State Henry Kissinger for an urgent airlift of embassy staff. But it was not until the very last minute, just after 1000 on 12 April 1975, with the Khmers Rouges firing mortars from across the Bassac River onto the football pitch near the compound that served as a landing zone, that the last US Marine helicopter left the city. Flight 462, a convoy of military transport helicopters, evacuated the 82 remaining Americans, 159 Cambodians and 35 other foreigners to a US aircraft carrier in the Gulf of Thailand. Their departure was overseen by 360 heavily armed marines. Despite letters to all senior government figures from the ambassador, offering them places on the helicopters, only one, Acting President Saukham Khoy, fled the country. The American airlift was a deathblow to Cambodian morale. Within 5 days, the Khmers Rouges had taken the city and within hours all senior officials of the former Lon Nol government were executed on the tennis courts of the embassy.

The **Defence Museum**, on Norodom Blvd, traces the phases of Cambodian history, notably the war against the USA and the Khmer revolution. Closed at the moment.

EXCURSIONS

It is often easier to hire your own transport (see page 102). Travel agents will also organize trips to surrounding sights.

Boat trips on the Mekong *Phnom Penh Tourism* own a boat which visitors can book to cruise the Mekong and see Mekong Island (famous for its silk production) fishing villages and 'river life'. A relaxing trip, includes lunch and cultural show although some visitors consider the trip expensive and disappointing. The boat is moored next to *Cambodiana Hotel* daily, depart 0930, return 1500. (Four French tourists drowned on one such boat earlier this year.) Contact Phnom Penh Tourism for more details (see below) US$28. Better value are the boats moored alongside Sisowath Quay. Stock up with food and drink and set off for a picnic, US$10/hr.

NORTH

Nur ul-Ihsan Mosque, 7 km N of Phnom Penh on Route 5, was desecrated by the Khmers Rouges, who used it as a pig sty; it was reconsecrated in 1980. *Getting there*: take buses from the Olympic International bus station N towards Battambang or hire transport.

Oudong, 35 km N of Phnom Penh, was the royal capital between 1618 and 1866 – only the foundations of the ancient palace remain. At the top of the larger of two ridges, just S of Oudong itself, are the ruins of **Phnom Chet Ath Roeus**. The vihara was built in 1911 by King Sisowath to house a large Buddha image, but was destroyed by the Khmers Rouges. Excellent views of surrounding country from the summit. Beyond the wat to the NW is a string of viharas – now in ruins – and beyond them several stupas, including one (the middle one) intended to house the ashes of King Ang Douong (1845-1859) by his son, King Norodom. On the other side of the ridge stands a **memorial** to those murdered by the Khmers Rouges, whose remains were unearthed from mass graves on the site in the early 1980s. *Getting there*: N from Phnom Penh on Route 5, approximately 5 km after the Prek Kdam ferry, turn left (S) to Psar Dek Krom. Take buses from Olympic International bus station heading for Battambang or hire transport. **NB** This area is supposed to be mined – keep to well-trodden paths. Drink stalls at the foot of the hill.

SOUTH

Choeung Ek, now in a peaceful setting surrounded by orchards and rice fields – was the execution ground for the torture victims of Tuol Sleng – the Khmers Rouges extermination centre, S-21 (see page 91). Today a huge **glass tower** stands on the site, filled with the cracked skulls of men, women and children exhumed from 129 mass graves in the area (which were not discovered until 1980). It is estimated that around 40,000 Cambodians were murdered at Choeung Ek between 1975 and 1978. The haunting memorial is often featured in Western TV documentaries and newspaper articles, as its mountains of skulls have a forceful impact, and serve as a graphic reminder of the scale of the Khmers Rouges' atrocities. *Getting there*: SW on Pokambor Blvd, about 9 km from the bridge. Hire transport from Phnom Penh – informal motorbike taxis are willing to make the return trip for between US$2-5. Like many places, officially 'closed' on Mon but is 'open' for the exchange of a couple of dollars.

Tonle Bati, 42 km S of Phnom Penh, is a popular weekend picnic site and beside the lake there is the added attraction of the temple of **Ta Phrom**. The temple dates from Jayavarman VII's reign (1181-1201) and, unusually, it is consecrated to both Brahma and the Buddha. There is a smaller temple, **Yeay Peau**, just N of Ta Phrom. Both temples have a number of fine bas-reliefs. The modern Wat Tonle Bati is nearby – it is another of the Khmers Rouge's architectural victims and a site of remembrance for the thousands who were murdered during the Pol Pot era. 10 km from Tonle Bati is a house belonging to Khmer royalty; locals climb the hill on Sun to make donations to the monks. *Getting there*: 33 km S of Phnom Penh on Route 2 and about 2.5 km from the main road. Take buses from Psar Dang Kor bus station heading for Takeo or hire transport.

Phnom Chisor, 62 km S of Phnom Penh, this phnom (or hill) is topped by a large rock platform on which many buildings from different eras have been built and from which are tremendous views over the surrounding plains. The principal remaining sanctuary (originally called Suryagiri, literally meaning 'Sun Mountain') is dedicated to Brahma and dates from the 11th century. *Getting there*: 55 km S of Phnom Penh on Route

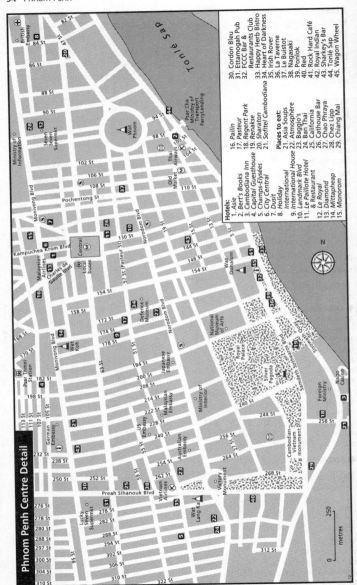

Phnom Penh Centre Detail

Hotels:
1. Asie
2. Bert's Books
3. Cambodiana Inn
4. Capital Guesthouse
5. Champs-Elysees
6. City Central
7. Dusit
8. Holiday International
9. International House
10. Landmark Blvd
11. Le Paillote Hotel & Restaurant
12. Le Royal
13. Diamond
14. Mittapheap
15. Monorom
16. Pailin
17. Pasteur Park
18. Regent Park
19. Renakse
20. Sharaton
21. Sofitel Cambodiana

Places to eat:
22. Asia Soups
22. Atmosphere
23. Baggio's
24. Ban Thai
25. California
26. Cathouse Bar
27. Chao Phraya
28. Chez Lipp
29. Chiang Mai
30. Cordon Bleu
31. Ettamogah Pub
32. FCCC Bar & Restaurants Club
33. Happy Herb Bistro
34. Heart of Darkness
35. Irish Rover
36. La Taverne
37. Le Buistot
38. Nagasaki
39. Ponlok
40. Red
41. Rock Hard Café
42. Royal Indian
43. Sharkey's Bar
44. Tonlé Sap
45. Wagon Wheel

2, the turn off is marked by Prasat Neang Khmau (the temple of the Black Virgin); Phnom Chisor is approximately 4 km from the main road. Take buses from Psar Dang Kor bus station heading for Takeo or hire transport. Busier at weekends which may confer a degree of security.

WEST

Koki Beach is a riverside resort popular at weekends. Families bring picnics but there are several food stalls. Wooden huts on stilts over the river are for hire to shelter from the midday sun. There's an interesting wat close by and the surrounding villages are very traditional. *Getting there*: 12 km from Phnom Penh, turn off Route 1. Taxis leave from Chbam Pao shared taxi station or hire your own transport.

TOURS

Most agents offer tours to surrounding sights, leaving early in the morning.

LOCAL INFORMATION

● **Orientation**

Monivong and Norodom blvds are the main roads running N-S, and E-W is Kampuchea Krom Blvd. Sisowath Quay and Samdech Sothearos Blvd run parallel to the river, on the E side of the city. Most streets have numbers, rather than names. As a general rule even numbers run E-W, and low even numbers are in the N. Only main streets are signposted. Shops tend to have three numbers, a) number of the area, b) number of the street, c) number of the shop. These are not always presented in this order so look for similar numbers to work out which street you are in.

● **Accommodation**

Price guide

L	over US$200	**C**	US$15-25
A+	US$100-200	**D**	US$8-15
A	US$50-100	**E**	US$4-8
B	US$25-50	**F**	under US$4

Visitors to Phnom Penh currently have a choice of accommodation at reasonable rates. A number of old hotels were renovated and new ones hurriedly put together to meet the needs of UNTAC. With the departure of the Blue Berets, space is relatively plentiful but the cheaper hotels tend to fill up astonishingly quickly. Most hotels are along Monivong Blvd. The more expensive hotels add 10% tax and 10% service charge.

L *Sofitel Cambodiana*, 313 Sisowath Quay, T 426288, F 426392, a/c, 2 restaurants, pool, also has tennis courts, health centre, boutique, US travel office (*Sunrise*) and business centre, originally built for Prince Sihanouk's guests (construction stopped in 1970), it was completed with funds from Cambodians living in Hong Kong and Singapore, and has well-maintained chalet-style accommodation overlooking the confluence of the Mekong, Sap and Bassac rivers; the *Cambodiana* is the best Phnom Penh has to offer, and is used by many tour groups, it is equivalent to any first class hotel in Bangkok, with the opening of newer hotels getting a room here is not as hard as it was, satellite TV, numerous restaurants incl *L'Amboise* (French), *Dragon Court* (Chinese), *Burgermania*, and an excellent deli, good afternoon teas, served in the *Lobby Bar*, rec. Overseas reservations at: *Bangkok Vacation Planners (Thailand) Ltd*, T 2451897, F 2462821; *Singapore Cambodiana Investment*, T 2980733, T 2987022; *Hong Kong Express Holidays*, T 3678083, F 3113278.

A+ *City Central* (formerly *Allson*), Monivong Blvd (128 St), T 722022, F 722021, a/c, new management, central, restaurant: excellent Sun, buffet lunches (US$7 for all you can eat), renovation programme underway through 1997, rec; **A+** *Diamond*, 172-184 Monivong Blvd, T 427325, F 426635, a/c, nr central market, restaurant, change TCs, a second *Diamond Hotel* is at 132 Monivong; **A+** *Juliana*, 16, 152 St, T 366070-2, bungalow style accommodation, attractive and efficient, popular haircut and Thai massage centre, hotel and restaurant rec; **A+** *Landmark Boulevard*, 63 Norodom Blvd, T 426943, F 428506, new '4-star' hotel with rooftop garden restaurant and bar, said to be 'soulless'; **A+** *Royal Palace*, 95 Monireth St, T 720002-7, F 720008, newly opened Thai run hotel, restaurants, pool, massage, karaoke and all the other touches necessary for the survival of a Thai businessman overseas; **A+** *Royal Phnom Penh*, Old 26 August Site, Tonle Bassac, Samdech Sothearos Blvd, adjacent to Russian Embassy, T 360026, F 360036 (or book in Bangkok T 5892021), a/c, restaurant, deluxe hotel opened 1993 under Thai management;

A+ Sharaton, 47 St (behind Wat Phnom), T/F 361199, a/c, restaurant, pool, business centre, the Sharaton opened in Nov 1994 with 112 rm in glitzy marble luxury, this is not a Sheraton, but is owned and operated by one of Cambodia's Sino-Khmer tycoons, the single lift means reaching the rooftop pool can be either a long wait, or an exhausting business, reports suggest-over charging on food is not uncommon; **A+-A Le Royal**, 92 St/Monivong Blvd (next to the library), a colonial style hotel built in 1910, used to be the *Hotel le Phnom* which was the journalists' headquarters during the war, undergoing renovation by Raffles Group – should be completed by end 1997; **A Cambodiana Inn**, Sisowath Quay, T 425059, F 426139, a/c, restaurant, next door to the *Cambodiana* but not under the same management, Cambodian style bungalows looking out onto the river, peaceful location, rec; **A Holiday International**, 84 St, T 427402, F 427401, a/c, restaurant, pool, new international-style hotel; **A Regent Park**, 58 Samdech Sotheoros Blvd, T 427674, F 361999, serviced apartments, comfortable; **A-B La Paillote**, 234 St (nr central market), T 722151, F 426513, a/c, restaurant, good middle range hotel; **A-B Monorom**, 89 Monivong Blvd (corner of 118 St, nr the main railway station), T 4426073, F 426149, a/c, restaurants, large rather shabby rooms, boutiques, noisy, run by *Phnom Penh Tourism*, the *Monorom* is the third main hotel for tour groups, journalists and aid workers, central location and helpful staff, business centre behind reception, IDD calls can be made from the manager's office, rooftop disco; **A-B Orchidée**, 262 Monivong Blvd, T 722659, F 426576, a/c, restaurant, modern hotel in the centre of town (built early 1990s), overflow for *Cambodiana* but not nearly as nice; **A-B Pailin**, 219B and C Monivong Blvd/Charles de Gaulle Blvd (next door to the *International Restaurant*), T 426375, F 426376, restaurant, newly renovated, best rooms on the upper floors (with views over city), good location, 81 comfortable rm with satellite TV, friendly welcome, 2 (Vietnamese and Chinese) good restaurants.

B Asie, 113-119 Monivong Blvd, T 427674, F 361999, serviced apartments, comfortable; **B Champs-Elysées**, 185 63 St, T 427268, French-speaking, helpful staff; **B Dusit**, 2, 118 St, T 427483, large and popular place with range of rooms, some of them very acceptable and good value; **B Mittapheap**, 262

Monivong Blvd, T 423464, restaurant, average; **B Rama Inn East**, 17, 9 St, T 428381, F 427948, charming, tranquil hotel with tropical garden, rec; **B Renakse**, opp the Royal Palace, T (IDD) 2326036 (local) 722457, F 426100, a/c, restaurant, splendid French colonial building in large but overgrown grounds, own bathrooms and fridge, spectacular location and good atmosphere, even though the rooms are not in great condition, well run, *Naga Diva Travel Tours* based here, accepts Visa, rec; **B The International House**, 35, 178 St, T/F 426246, restaurant, reasonably priced, simple but clean; **B-C Baccara**, 85A 163 St (a few steps from the corner of Mao Tse Tung St), T 720755, a/c, hot water, attached bathroom, TV and fridge, international dialling, friendly and helpful manager, quiet area of town, good value; **B-C L'Imprévu**, Route 1 (7 km out of the city), restaurant, pool, run by a French couple and their son and daughter who have escaped from Nice, charming wooden bungalows and good restaurant, peaceful, bicycles for hire, note that rates double over the weekend.

C Asie, 136 St, T 427825; **C Pasteur**, 60 51 St, a/c, small, family-run hotel, clean; **C Santepheap**, Monivong Blvd/136 St, T 423227, a/c, restaurant; **C-D Beauty Inn Hotel**, 537 Monivong Blvd, T/F 464505, a/c, clean rooms with attached bathrooms and fridge.

D Cathay, 123-125 110 St (not far from Wat Phnom), T 427188, F 26303, a/c, big clean rooms, minibar, laundry service, satellite TV, friendly and helpful staff, one of the best for its price, rec; **D Timorda Guesthouse**, 128 St, a/c, restaurant.

E Capitol Guesthouse I and II, 182 St/107 St, T 364104, restaurant, centre for budget travellers and a good centre for information, bicycle hire (US$1/day), organizes trips to "Killing Fields" (US$5) and Siem Reap, IDD telephone service; **E Guesthouse No 50 (aka Narin's)**, 50 125 St, good value rooms, shared facilities, bicycle hire (US$1/day), good, cheap food and a wide 1st flr balcony to sit out on; **E Happy Guesthouse**, nr the *Capitol*, is run by the same owners and has similar facilities; **E Lotus Guesthouse**, 121 St, nr *La Paillote* restaurant and Central Market, some a/c, restaurant (good Indian food); **E Seng Sokhom's Guesthouse**, 111 St, motorbikes for hire, friendly management; **E Sok Sin's Guesthouse**, on small dirt road between the old French Embassy and Calmette Hospital,

Monivong Blvd, the owner is a fountain of knowledge on Cambodia; fan rooms, bikes and motorbikes for hire, restaurant. Other budget hotels close by; **E-F** *Bert's Books*, 79 Sisowath Quay, T 360806, a few rooms for rent, Mr Bert serves good coffee and croissants. **F** Several new guesthouses W of Monivong Blvd on 86 St. There are signposts on 86 St to some small but popular guesthouses, they usually have no name but are referred to as No 9 and No 8, wooden in nature and overlooking the lake, they are cheap and cheerful and offer a place to relax. **F** *Cloud 9* (was known as No 9) is one of the more popular ones, good food.

● **Places to eat**

Price guide

✦✦✦✦	over US$10	(27,000 riel)
✦✦✦	US$5-10	(13,500-27,000 riel)
✦✦	US$2-5	(5,400-13,500 riel)
✦	under US$2	(5,400 riel)

Most places are relatively inexpensive – US$2-6/head. There are several cheaper cafés along Monivong Blvd, Kampuchea Krom Blvd (128 St) in the city centre and along the river as well as stalls by the main markets (see below). Generally the food in Phnom Penh is excellent and the restaurants surprisingly refined. One of the most remarkable assemblages of restaurants in Indochina is to be found over the Japanese Bridge. From late afternoon until early evening the road is packed with cars with customers looking out for a place to eat. The newer establishments are embellished with strings of fairy lights, fountains and wedding cake architecture; others are more modest. Dancing, live and piped music may be regarded as irritants or attractions. All are pretty much of a muchness and offer great value, but *Hang Neak* and *Big Mangoes* (sic) have received particular acclaim.

Khmer

✦✦✦*Apsara*, 361 Sisowath Quay, T 427081, underneath FCCC, known for its delicious *amok* and other Khmer dishes; peaceful setting and engaging owner; ✦✦✦*Ponlok*, 323 Sisowath Quay, big and brash, overlooking Tonlé Sap, popular; ✦✦*Little Boeng Kak*, Boeng Kak Lake and amusement park off Monivong Blvd N of the city centre; ✦✦*Paksupieabal*, 40 Monivong Blvd/84 St, rec by locals; ✦✦*Sereipheap*, 76 Monivong Blvd/Kampuchea Krom Blvd (not far from the Monorom), serves almost every alcoholic drink as well as a mixture of Cambodian, Vietnamese and French dishes; ✦✦*Tesphea Tonlé Sap Café*, Sisowath Quay/106 St; ✦✦*Tonlé Sap* is at the junction of Sisowath Quay and 94 St, open air restaurant, reasonable; ✦✦✦*Thmor Da*, Kampuchea Krom Blvd, opp. Siam City Bank, popular, Khmer and Vietnamese dishes; *Calmette*, Monivong Blvd, nr hospital, good soups; ✦*Asia Soups*, Monivong Blvd/204 St, excellent soups, roof terrace, rec.

Asian

✦✦✦✦*Dragon Court*, *Cambodiana Hotel*, expensive Chinese restaurant overseen by Chinese-Singaporean Chef Lee Yan Hai, wide range of Chinese cuisine prepared incl Szechuan, Cantonese, Peking and 'Singaporean', stylish; ✦✦✦*Ban Thai*, 306 St, Thai, good menu and excellent service, try the delicious prawn and vegetable tempura, garden setting; ✦✦✦*Boung Thong*, Boeng Kak Lake, Thai food but some Khmer, Chinese and western, lovely outdoor setting on wooden jetties over the lake, however, despite the quantity of food, it is not up to much and the waiters are rather over-attentive; ✦✦✦*Chao Phraya*, 67 Norodom Blvd, attractive setting in the forecourt of a colonial French building (despite green galvanized sheeting), Thai cuisine (the restaurant is Thai-owned) but also serves Japanese and some western dishes, quality of food is a little disappointing but quantity is more than adequate, Thai buffet available; ✦✦✦*Chiang Mai*, 110 Samdech Sothearos Blvd, T 015 916805, a pavement café with, as the name suggests, an emphasis on Thai food – from simple one plate dishes like *phat thai* (fried noodles with prawns, lime and nuts) to the famous fiery prawn soup *tom yang kung*, this restaurant and bar are run by a Thai, Madame Nui, from Surat Thani in S Thailand, opens 1100, happy hour 1600-1900, best Thai food in town; ✦✦✦*Coca*, Monivong Blvd/240 St, Thai and Chinese dishes; ✦✦✦*Hua Nam*, 753 Monivong Blvd, Thai, known for its shark soup; ✦✦✦*Kababeesh*, 58 128 St, T 723205, range of Indian food, rec; ✦✦✦*Midori*, 145 Norodom Blvd, authentic Japanese cuisine; ✦✦✦*Nagasaki*, 39 Sihanouk Blvd, T 428394, no English on the menu so all bar the Japanese reader chooses blind!; ✦✦✦*New Wishing Well*, 9A, 163 St, Malay food and BBQ steaks, happy hours 1700-2100; ✦✦✦*Royal Bassac*, Phnom Penh Hotel, serves mainly Thai food but also other Asian and European cuisines, live music and dancing; ◆◆◆*Royal Indian*, 310 Monivong Blvd, T 725605, vies with Kabbeesh, each doing their best to outclass each other; ◆◆◆*Taj Mahal*, Norodom Blvd (S of Independence Monument), N Indian dishes; ◆*Asian International*, 118 St, cheap Malaysian cuisine.

International

Several of the international restaurants are of a similar standard and offer Cambodian, Chinese, French and European dishes. Expect to pay US$3-5, some restaurants even stock champagne. ◆◆◆◆*L'Amboise*, Sofitel Cambodiana, top French cuisine, a little large and impersonal at times; ◆◆◆◆*La Paillote*, 234 St, rated as the best restaurant in town because of its excellent predominantly French fare, good wines, elegant restaurant with good range of excellent cuisine (incl breakfast), rather over-attentive service, rec; ◆◆◆*Atmosphère*, 141C Norodom Blvd, T 363222, French style brasserie and wine bar curiously lacking in 'ambience'; ◆◆◆*Foreign Correspondents Club (FCCC)*, 363 Sisowath Quay, T 427757, superb colonial building, 2nd floor bar and restaurant overlooks the Tonlé Sap, open to non-members, friendly service and great food, new roof-top bar makes a perfect location for watching Khmer festivals; ◆◆◆*La Casa*, 4, 261 St, T 366184, French and Khmer food, lovely atmosphere, rec; ◆◆◆*La Taverne*, 373 Sisowath Quay, T 360780, next to *FCCC*, good spot for a beer with a pleasant terrace on the Tonle Sap River, French cuisine is rec; ◆◆◆*Le Buistot*, 76 108 St, Mediterranean flavour menu with Provençal and Italian specialities, rec; ◆◆◆*Le Cordon Bleu*, Sihanouk Blvd, range of meat dishes, pasta and salad, delicious creme caramel, said to be 'a bit starchy atmosphere wise'; ◆◆◆*L'Imprévu*, Route 1 (7 km out of the city), hotel and restaurant, run by a French couple and their son and daughter, this place consists of bungalows, pool, and restaurant serving good bistro food from pasta to salads to fish, non-residents use the pool for US$3 (weekdays) or US$5 (weekends), a great place to escape to; ◆◆◆*Red*, 56E1 Sihanouk Blvd, T 360676, European food, European prices; ◆◆◆*Trattoria del Gecko*, 114/61 St, decent pasta; ◆◆◆*Wagon Wheel*, 353 Sisowath Quay, popular for the breakfasts; ◆◆◆–◆◆*Golden Eagle*, 144 St (just off Norodom Blvd), known for its bar but also has good menu; ◆◆◆–◆◆*Monorom Hotel Restaurant*, 89 Monivong Blvd (corner of 118 St), 6th flr restaurant with good views of the city; ◆◆◆–◆◆*Pailin Hotel*, 1st flr, Monivong Blvd (nr

central market), quiet, good atmosphere, Vietnamese food; ◆◆*Baggios Pizza*, 14 51 St, sidestreet restaurant, tasty pizzas, take away, rec; ◆◆*Bayon*, corner of Monivong Blvd/130 St; ◆◆*California*, 55 Preah Sihanouk Blvd, trad American fare, open for breakfast; ◆◆*Capitol*, 14 182 St, cheap and cheerful; ◆◆*Chez Lipp*, Monivong Blvd, French fare, rec for steak; ◆◆*Faculty of Medicine Restaurant*, Monivong Blvd/106 St, Asian and French; ◆◆*Happy Herb Bistro*, 345 Sisowath Quay, T 426051, watch out for the 'happy' pizza full of hash – it has a nasty kick; ◆◆*La Pagode*, behind the *Monorom Hotel*, in a traditional Khmer building; ◆◆*Lotus*, nr Central Market, pizzas, vegetarian and Indian dishes, popular; ◆◆*McSam Burgers*, 13 St, opp Post Office; ◆◆*Oasis*, 139 Monireth Blvd, home cooked European dishes.

Seafood:

Floating restaurants moored to the bank opp the old Royal Palace, nr the broken bridge: ◆◆*Chaktomuk* and *Kong Kea* floating restaurants at Sisowath Quay; *Boengkak*, on Boeng Kak Lake, open air restaurant best known for its seafood, European and Asian dishes. (There is a second seafood restaurant here but it's not nearly as good.)

Boulangerie

Boucherie de Paris, 243 51 St; *Cambodiana Hotel*, more expensive than the *Chefs Deli*, but as good a selection; *Chefs Deli*, 87 St, a/c café with excellent breakfasts (newspapers provided) and a very good selection of patiserries, cakes, breads and biscuits.

Foodstalls

According to a recent survey by the Ministry of Health, 75% of the street food tested contained high levels of bacteria. If locals with money avoid such places there is no good reason for visitors to patronize them. Those wishing to try should ensure their hepatitis antibody count is high. There are many Vietnamese stalls along Kampuchea Krom Blvd, Monivong Blvd and 117 St. Also some stalls between the railway station and Puchentong Blvd at night. *Central Market*, just off Monivong Blvd (at the intersection of 118 St and Charles de Gaulle Blvd); *O Russei Market*, 182 St; *Olympic Market*, 286 St; also good foodstalls around the *Capitol Hotel* on 182 St; *The Old Market*, between 13, 106 and 110 sts; *Tuol Tum Pong Market*, between 163, 432 and 450 sts, stalls in the centre of the market. Several Vietnamese stalls on 242 St.

● **Bars**

Ettamogah Pub, 154 Preah Sihanouk Blvd (next door to the Lucky Market), opened in Aug 1994 and popular with expat residents of Phnom Penh who maintain it serves the coldest beer in the capital, and the finest chips (fries), run by two Aussies, there is a small menu with the emphasis on things like steak and chicken served in baskets, opens 0700 for breakfast and closes late; *Heart of Darkness*, 51 St, value for money, good Bloody Mary's, run by the same owners as *Apocalypse Now* in Vietnam; bar at the *Hotel Royal*, 92 St, is a popular hangout; *Cathouse*, 51/81 St, good pool table (serves food until 1 am), satellite TV; *Foreign Correspondents Club (FCCC)*, 363 Sisowath Quay, satellite TV, pool, *Bangkok Post* and *The Nation* both available for reading here, new roof top bar is good location festival-watching; *Le Bar*, Preah Sihanouk, has a nice terrace; *Martini Pub*, 402 Mao Tse Tung St, girls, dancing, barbecue, video, fun, open till late; *Rock Hard Cafe* (nr *Foreign Correspondents Club*), backgammon sets kept behind the bar; *San Miguel*, Sisowath Quay, Filipino bands, lively atmosphere; *Irish Rover*, 79 Sihanouk Blvd, Irish pub with a real Irishman running the place. Several restaurants also have good bars (see above).

● **Airline offices**

Aeroflot, *City Central Hotel*, Monivong Blvd, T 722022; **Air France**, *Cambodiana Hotel*, T 426426; **Dragon Air**, 19 106 St, T 427665; **Lao Aviation**, 206 Norodom Blvd, T 725887; **Malaysian Airlines**, *Diamond Hotel*, 172-184 Monivong Blvd, T 426688; **Royal Air Cambodge**, 206 Norodom Blvd, T 428891-4, F 427910; **Silk Air**, *Pailin Hotel*, Monivong Blvd, T 422236; **Thai**, 19 106 St, T 722335; **Transindo**, 16 Monivong Blvd, T 426298, represents **Bangkok Airways**; **Vietnam Airlines**, 537 Monivong, in *Beauty Inn Mini Hotel*, T 427426.

● **Banks & money changers**

There are several money changers at the central market. **Bangkok Bank**, 26 Norodom Blvd, T/F 26593; **Bank of Commerce of Kampuchea**, 26 Monivong Blvd; **Banque du Commerce Exterior du Cambodge**, 24 Norodom Blvd, **Foreign exchange bureau** changes TCs and accepts Visa; **Banque Indosuez**, 70 Norodom Blvd; **Banque Municipal de Phnom Penh**, 102 St/13 St; **Cambodian Commercial Bank**, Monivong Blvd, 118 St; **National Bank**, Norodom/118 St; **Silver/gold bazaar**, Grand Market is the best area for changing US dollars.

● **Embassies & consulates**

Australia, 11 254 St, T 426001, F 426003; **Canada**, 11 254 St, T 426000, F 426003; **China**, 156 Mao Tse Tung Blvd, T 426971; **Cuba**, 98 214 St, T 427428; **France**, 1 Monivong Blvd, T 430020, F 430037; **Germany**, 76 214 St, T 426381, F 427746; **Hungary**, 771 Monivong Blvd, T 721401; **India**, 777 Monivong Blvd, T 725582; **Indonesia**, 179 51 St, T 426148; **Japan**, 21 Ho Chi Minh Blvd, T 427161, F 426162; **Laos**, 15 Mao Tse Tung Blvd, T 426441, F 427454; **Malaysia**, 161 51 St, T 426177, F 426004; **Russia**, 213 Samdech Sothearos Blvd, T 722081, F 426776; **Singapore**, *Sofitel Cambodiana*, T 426288; **Thailand**, 4 Monivong Blvd, T 426182, F 426182; **UK**, 27 75 St, T 427124, F 427125; **USA**, 27 240 St, T 426436, F 426437; **Vietnam**, Monivong Blvd/436 St (consular section on Monivong Blvd S of Mao Tse Tung Blvd), T 725481, F 427385.

● **Entertainment**

Casino: Singaporean-owned *Holiday International Hotel* (84 St) opened the only casino in town in Nov 1994 – the first to begin operating since 1970. Roulette, black jack and usual entertainments provided. *Naga*, floating casino moored nr *Sofitel Cambodiana Hotel* but may be forced to leave.

Dance: folk and national dances are performed by the National Dance group at the National Museum of Arts, on 70 St in the N of the city. (Open to some tour groups.) Contact the National Museum of Arts directly or the Ministry of Information and Culture, 395 Monivong Blvd. Royal Pavilion, *Sofitel Cambodiana Hotel*, has classical Khmer dancing every Fri 1900 (if it's not raining). It is possible to watch trainee classical Khmer dancers at the University of Fine Arts, 70 St, opp Boeng Kak Lake.

Discos: *Fantazia*, nr Olympic Stadium, disco owned by 2 Los Angelinos, entrance is free; *New Wishing Well*, 9A, 163 St, new disco; *Sharky's Bar*, 126 130 St, bar and disco; *Le Saint Tropez*, 46 214 St, T 015 916502, piano bar and disco, closes 0300.

Films: *Foreign Correspondents Club (FCCC)*, 363 Sisowath Quay, T 427757, F 427758, shows films Tues (2000) and Sun (1730 and 2000), US$2, programme of lectures, films and discussions – expatriate visitors from Vietnam (where such meetings and screenings are highly illegal), envy the Phnom Penois their level of freedom.

Music: the Lounge Bar at the *Cambodiana* is known for the Phnom Penh Blues Band – best avoided. The *Rock Hard Café* (nr *Foreign Correspondents Club*) 315 Sisowath Quay, has live music on Thur, Fri and Sat, plus a jam session on Sun afternoons. The *Cyclo Bar* has a band.

Nightclubs: the *Cambodiana Nightclub* (*Sofitel Cambodiana Hotel*) tops the list – otherwise there are a plethora of seedy discos and bars which periodically open and close; the 7th flr of the *Monorom Hotel* is a popular spot with its balcony overlooking the city and a band which plays every night until 2300; *Royal Hotel*, 92 St has a restaurant with dancing, popular with Vietnamese 'taxi girls', ie prostitutes (closes 2300); *Martini Pub*, 402 Mao Tse Tung St, bar, food, disco, favourite haunt of ex-pats and local and Vietnamese girls (closes 0300).

● **Hospitals & medical services**
Dentist: *European Dental Clinic*, 195A Norodom Blvd, T 018 812055, 362656, French-run.

Hospital: *Access Medical Services*, 4 St 432, T 364877, T 015 831405, open 0800-1700 Mon-Fri, 0800-1200 Sat; *Calmette Hospital*, Monivong Blvd, T 723173, is generally considered the best, 24 hrs emergency. There is also a western clinic at *SOS International Medical Centre*, 83 Mao Tse Tung Blvd, T 9129645; *Polyclinic 'Angkor'*, 75 St 242, English speaking doctors, 5 mins walk from *Hotel Capitol*.

Opticians: *Royal Optic*, 220 Monivong Blvd (opp *Pailin Hotel*) and 136, 52 St.

● **Libraries**
National Library, 92 St. Most of the books were destroyed by the Khmers Rouges in the 1970s and the building was used as a pigpen for several years, open 0700-1130 and 1400-1730 Tues Sun.

● **Post & telecommunications**
Post Office: 13 St, it is possible to place international telephone calls from here.

Shipping/courier services: *DHL*, Monivong Blvd, T 427726; *OCS* (express courier service), *Cambodiana Hotel*; *TNT*, 28 47 St, T 426694; *Transpeed Cargo*, 19 108 St, T 427633; *UPS*, 8 134 St, T 366324, F 366324.

Telephone: easiest to make international calls from top hotels. Note that Phnom Pneh has mobile phone companies which have the following prefixes: 015, 017, and 018, and soon, probably, 012. All land line numbers begin with either a 4 or 7. Finally, Shinawatra radio phone (a service operated by a Thai company) numbers all begin 36. Simple!

● **Shopping**
Art Galleries: *Happy Cambodia Gallery*, *Sofitel Cambodiana Hotel*, gallery owned by French Canadian artist Stéphane Delaprée, his work is colourful, witty and full of life, depicting rural life, monks, dancers and cyclos in his distinctive naïf style, the Cambodian royal family and many others have bought his charming work; *New Art Gallery*, 9 20 St, local artists.

Books/maps: *Central Market*, *Tuol Tum Pong Market* and shops in some of the top hotels. *Berts Books*, 79 Sisowath Quay, T 360806, said to have the largest selection of books in English, sells second-hand books and magazines, also offers e-mail and fax service, and some tour services incl rooms for rent; *Bookazine*, 228 Monivong Blvd, extensive collection of SE Asian books and Western magazines; *Sofitel Cambodiana* has a selection of travel books. *International Stationery and Book Centre*, Monivong Blvd.

Buddha images: the area on the E side of Norodom Blvd (not far from the Victory Monument) is packed with workshops making images to replace those destroyed between 1975 and 1979. There's also a shop opposite the museum selling reproduction statues.

Handicrafts: many of the hotels have small boutiques selling local crafts; the National Museum of Arts, 19 St/184 St (behind the National Museum) also sells reproductions of Khmer statues, prints and frescoes of Angkor. Other recommended shops: *Banteay Srei*, 108 Monivong Blvd; *Ratana*, 118 St; *Vicheth Sal*, 121 Monivong Blvd, T 723137. *Kramas* (checked scarves) can be found in the Central Market. *Tabitha*, 26 297 St, elephants of all types, fabrics and other handicrafts.

Markets: *Tuol Tum Pong* (in the middle of 155, 163, 440 and 450 sts, close to the pagoda of the same name) sells antiques (genuine articles and fakes) and jewellery – nearby is an antique furniture market as well as clothing and an immense variety of tobacco. There are also several foodstalls here. The *Central Covered Market*, just off Monivong Blvd, distinguished by its central dome (built 1937), is mostly full of stalls selling silver and gold jewellery, old coins and assorted fake antiques. Around the main building more mundane items are for sale, incl kramas. The *Old Market* or *Psar Cha* is between 13, 106 and 110 sts, and also sells jewellery. *O Russei Market* (Russian Market), 182 St, has a good selection of antiques – bargain hard. The 'new' *Olympic*

Market is located in a large 2-storey building adjacent to the Olympic Stadium. It stocks reasonably priced electrical goods incl hi-fi's, there are no taxes to pay in Cambodia.

Rice paper prints: rubbings of bas reliefs from temples at Angkor, sold in museum shop and markets.

Silk: Koh Doch, a large island in the Mekong N of Phnom Penh is renowned for its silk.

Silverware & jewellery: old silver boxes, belts, antique jewellery along Monivong Blvd (the main thoroughfare), Samdech Sothearos Blvd, or *Tuol Tum Pong Market*, where Hoen Sareth (384) is rec for gold and setting gems. The state jewellery shop, *Bijouterie d'Etat*, 13 St/106 St and the *Silver Shop*, 1 Monivong Blvd, are rec by tourists, also the 2 shops in *Sofitel Cambodiana Hotel*. There are plenty of jewellery stalls in the central covered market. Most modern silverware is no more than 80% silver.

Supermarkets: *Lucky Supermarket*, Preah Sihanouk Blvd, opp Standard Chartered Bank, excellent French and Australian wine starting at US$5/bottle. (Cambodia has the cheapest wine in SE Asia.) *Lucky* sells *The European* and various English newspapers' weekly international editions. Also *Seven Seven Supermarket* 13 90 St, open 0700-2200. *McSam's*, 20-22 13 St and *International Supermarket*, 35 178 St.

● **Sports**

Aerobics: *Sofitel Cambodiana*, US$2 Mon-Fri, 1800-1900.

Badminton/squash: *Sofitel Cambodiana*, US$10/hr for court hire. *International Youth Club*, 51/96 St.

Gym: *Sofitel Cambodiana*, US$10/day.

Running: Cinder track at the Olympic Stadium. Hash House Harriers meet 1500 Sun at the railway station.

Spectator sports: The 1960s Olympic Stadium is the centre of sport in Phnom Penh. Basketball (ablebodied and wheelchaired), volleyball and training sessions of Tai-kwondo can be watched. University and schools football league play from Nov-Apr. A semi-professional league plays Jan-Jun. The standard is good. Crowds reach several thousand for the big games.

Swimming: *Sofitel Cambodiana*, 20m pool, US$4 Mon-Fri, US$8 Sat, Sun. *International Youth Club*, 51/96 St, 50m pool, US$10.

Tennis: *Hotel Sofitel Cambodiana*, US$5-

15/hr. *International Youth Club*, US$10/hr.

'Touch' rugby: Phnom Penh University every Sat from 1530.

● **Tour companies & travel agents**

Apsara Tours, 8 254 St, T/F 426705; *Aroon Tours*, 99 136 St, T 426300; *Cambodian-Australian Travel*, 6 222 St, T/F 426225; *Cams-Air Travel*, 187 Mao Tse Tung Blvd, T 426739, F 426740; *Diethelm Travel*, 8 Samdech Sothearos Blvd, T 426648, F 426676, the most reliable of the lot, rec; *East-West*, 17 114 St, T/F 426189; *Eurasie Travel*, 97 Monivong Blvd, T 423620; *Explotra*, 43 105 St, T/F 427973; *International Travel & Tours*, 339 Monivong Blvd, T/F 427248; *Khemara Travel*, 134 Preah Sihanouk Blvd, T/F 427434; *Naga*, Renakse Hotel, Samdech Sothearos Blvd, T 426288; *Orient Express Tour Company*, 19 106 St, T 426248, F 426313; *Peace Travel Agency*, 246 Monivong Blvd, T 424640, F 426533; *Preferred Indochina Travel*, *Monorom Hotel*, Monivong Blvd, T 725350, F 426625; *Royal Phnom Penh Travel* (Japanese management), 32 Novodom Blvd, T 360546; *Skylink Travel*, 124 Tou Samouth Blvd, T 427010; *Sunrise Travel*, opp *Cambodiana Hotel*, Sisowath Quay, T/F 426762; *Suraya Voyages*, 17 294 St, T 360105; *Transair Cambodia Travel*, 63 Norodom Blvd (ground floor of *Landmark Boulevard Hotel*), T 428323, F 426981; *Transindo*, 16 Monivong Blvd/84 St, T 426298, F 427119; *Transpeed Travel*, 19, 106 St, T/F 427633.

● **Tourist offices**

General Directorate of Tourism (Angkor Tourism or Cambodia Tourism), Monivong Blvd (at the junction with 232 St), T 725607, organizes tours and hires cars (US$25-30/day), friendly and helpful. **Phnom Penh Tourism**, 313 Sisawath Quay (nr the junction with Samdech Sithearos Blvd), T 723949/725349, open 0700-1100, 1400-1700 Mon-Sat, organizes tours, trips around Phnom Penh as well as trips to Saigon. The 2 tourist offices don't communicate, which can be confusing for visitors.

● **Useful addresses**

Emergency numbers: **Ambulance**: T 119; **Fire**: T 118; **Police**: T 117.

Bureau d'Immigration: 5 Oknha Men St, T 723893.

Business centre: *Foreign Correspondents Club*, 363 Sisowath Quay; *Global*, 378 Preah Sihanouk Blvd, T 427397.

Ministry of Culture: Monivong Blvd, T 362647; **Ministry of Information**,

Monivong Blvd, T/F 426059; **Ministry of the Interior**: 214 St/Norodom Blvd, T 724237, issues internal travel permits; **Ministry of Tourism**: 3 Monivong Blvd, T 726107.
Press Office of the Foreign Ministry: Sisowath Quay (at the intersection of 240 St), T 422241.

Visa extensions: Foreign Ministry, Sisowath Quay (at the intersection of 240 St), T 426146, takes 3 days, administration fee of US$10 is charged.

● **Transport**
Local Bicycle hire: from shops nr O Russei market or guesthouses. Bicycling is probably the best way to explore the city: it is mostly flat, so not too exhausting. **Bus**: most local buses leave from 182 St (next to O Russei market). Buses from here go to the Olympic Intercity bus station, the long distance terminal. Buses S leave from the Psar Thmei terminal, Charles de Gaulle Blvd/136 St (not far from central market). There are inexpensive buses around town. **Car**: chauffeur-driven cars are available at major hotels from US$30/day upwards, eg *Cambodiana*. Several travel agents will also hire cars. Prices increase if you're venturing out of town. **Cyclo** (French name for bicycle rickshaws): are plentiful but slow; fares are bargainable but cheap – Monorom to Cambodiana should be no more than 500CR. A few cyclo drivers speak English or French – they are most likely to be found loitering around the big hotels (US$0.25-0.35/hr), can also be hired for the day. **Motorcycle hire**: from 413 Monivong Blvd (US$5-15/day). **Motorbike taxi**: 'motos' are 50-100cc motorbikes; the fastest way to get around Phnom Penh. The moto driver is easily recognized by his sunglasses and baseball cap and will automatically approach anyone walking or standing by the road. Standard cost per journey is 500 Riel (short) 1,000 Riel (long) and 2,000 Riel after 2200. **Taxi**: from Psar Chbam Pao Shared-Taxi Station over Monivong Bridge on Route 1, nr the market of the same name (approx US$25/day, depending on where you want to go).

Air All domestic flights are with **Royal Air Cambodge**. See page 231 for details on flights and page 214 in Information for travellers for details on arrival at the airport and entry formalities. There are 7 flights a day to Siem Reap. Flights should be booked in advance, particularly at busy times of the year (ie Khmer New Year). **Transport to town**: a taxi from the airport costs US$5.

Train Station is between 106 and 108 Sts. Two main lines: one goes S to Kompong Som and the other N to Battambang. Travelling by train was forbidden as this book went to press. Three tourists were kidnapped and later killed travelling from Phnom Penh to Sihanoukville by train in late 1994. In addition to the dangers of Khmers Rouges kidnapping, the track is frequently blown up.

Road Bus: times and destinations of buses are in Khmer, so the only sure way to get the right bus is to ask. Most buses leave from the Olympic International bus station, 199 St (next to the Olympic Market). Those going S and SW of Phnom Penh leave from Psar Dang Kor bus station, Mao Tse Tung Blvd (next to Dang Kor market). Travelling out of Phnom Penh by bus is hazardous – both because of extreme overloading (people and luggage) and because of your vulnerability to attack from Khmers Rouges or bandits. It is not recommended. New bus services to Kompong Son and Kompong Chhang, twice daily, a/c, video (US$7 one way), non-stop, comfortable and considered relatively safe. **Shared taxi**: Psar Chbam Pao, nr Chbam Pao market on Route 1.

Boat Ferries leave from Psar Cha Ministry of Transport Ferry Landing on Samdech Sotheavos Blvd (between 102 and 104 Sts). Connections to Siem Reap (Angkor), Kratie, Stung Treng, Kompong Cham and Kompong Chhnang. Other ferries leave from Psar Cha Municipal Ferry Landing. Fast boat connections (5 hrs) with Siem Reap, US$25 one way, details and tickets from *Bert's Books* and FCCC. Apart from the security risk and the boredom factor, and the break downs, it halves the cost of flying. Many NGOs prohibit their staff from travelling by any form of public transport incl the ferry due to the security risk.

International connections NB If travelling to Vietnam by road, ensure that your visa is appropriately stamped (*Moc Bai*), otherwise you may be turned back at the border, although it may be possible to offer a bribe (about US$50). Curiously the Vietnamese side tends to adopt an uncharacteristically high minded attitude in this regard. **NB**: at the beginning of 1997, as this book went to press, the border crossing between Cambodia and Vietnam at Moc Bai was closed. Check on the status of the crossing border before embarking from Phnom Penh or Saigon/ Ho Chi Minh City. **Road Bus**: buses to Saigon leave from the junction of 211 and 182 sts. The office is open 0700-1100, 1400-1900 Mon-Sun, US$5 (same price for a shared taxi), a/c bus Thur, Fri and Sat, US$15.

Angkor
អង្គរ

NGKOR, the ancient capital of the powerful Khmer Empire, is one of the archaeological gems of Asia and the spiritual and cultural heart of Cambodia. Henri Mouhot, the Frenchman, wrote that "it is grander than anything of Greece or Rome". Its mystical grandeur and architectural wonders are on a par with Peru's 'lost' Inca city of Machu Picchu. The huge complex of palaces and temples was built on the sprawling alluvial plain to the North of the Tonlé Sap.

Under Jayavarman VII (1181-1218), the Angkor complex stretched more than 25 km E to W and nearly 10 km N to S. For 5 centuries (9th-13th), the court of Angkor held sway over a vast territory. At its height, according to a 12th century Chinese account, Khmer influence spanned half of Southeast Asia, from Burma to the southernmost tip of Indochina and from the borders of Yunnan to the Malay peninsula. Khmer monuments can be found in the S of Laos and East Thailand as well as in Cambodia. The only threat to this great empire was a riverborne invasion in 1177, when the Chams used a Chinese navigator to pilot their war canoes up the Mekong. Scenes are depicted in bas reliefs of the Bayon temple.

Thai ascendency, and their eventual occupation of Angkor in 1431 led to the city's abandonment and the subsequent invasion of the jungle. 4 centuries later, in 1860, Henri Mouhot – a French naturalist – stumbled across the forgotten city, its monumental temple towers enmeshed in the forest canopy. Locals told him they were the work of a race of giant gods. Only the stone temples remained; all the wooden secular buildings had decomposed in the intervening centuries. Mouhot's diaries, published in the 1860s, with his accounts of 'the lost city in the jungle' fired the imagination of archaeologists, adventurers and treasure-hunters in Europe. In 1873 French archaeologist Louis Delaporte removed many of Angkor's finest statues for 'the cultural enrichment of France'.

In 1898, the École Française d'Extrême Orient started clearing the jungle, restoring the temples, mapping the complex and making an inventory of the site. Delaporte was later to write the two-volume *Les Monuments du Cambodge*, the most comprehensive Angkorian inventory of its time, and his

From souvenir-hunting to antiquities-smuggling

An article in the *Far Eastern Economic Review* in March 1993 noted that the feeling of cultural disintegration that pervades Cambodia is epitomized by the hundreds of headless and limbless statues. Khmers Rouges guerrillas moved into Angkor Wat in 1971, lit fires in the galleries, installed rocket-launchers on Phnom Bakheng, looted temples and sliced the heads off sculptures. Like other guerrilla groups after them, they sold them on the black market in neighbouring Thailand to help finance their war efforts. From the mid-1970s, ancient Khmer sculptures began to resurface in private art collections in the West, and on the floors of leading auction houses. But much of the looting occurred during the year before the May 1993 elections.

In 1992 and 1993 there were reported thefts from many of the temples and from the conservation office in Siem Reap, where about 7,000 of the most valuable artifacts have been stored. Between February and April 1993, there was a series of carefully organized break-ins into the conservation office; many priceless statues were stolen. In the most dramatic raid, in February, thieves used machine guns to enter the conservation centre, shot one of the guards, fired a rocket-propelled grenade at the storeroom door and left with 11 of the most valuable statues. UN and local officials said they had been smuggled into Thailand. They also alleged that all four political factions were behind the thefts as well as soldiers "from a neighbouring country". And there was strong evidence that some of the thefts were orchestrated by the conservation office staff.

Today Angkorian antiquities can be viewed and purchased in the air-conditioned antique shops of Bangkok's River City complex or Singapore's Tanglin Shopping Centre. There has been growing evidence that wealthy, but unethical, Western art buyers have been able to place orders for busts and sculptures of their choice through some of these shops. There are persistent rumours pointing

---

earlier sketches, plans and reconstructions, published in *Voyage au Cambodge* in 1880 are without parallel. Henri Parmentier was chief of the School's archaeological service in Cambodia until 1930. Public interest was rekindled in the 1920s when French adventurer and novelist André Malraux was imprisoned in Phnom Penh, charged with stealing sculptures from one of the temples, Banteay Srei at Angkor. He published a thriller, *The Royal Way*, based on his experiences. Today around 400 sandstone, laterite and brick-built temples, walls, tombs and other structures remain scattered around the site.

Colonial souvenir-hunters were not the first – or the last – to get their hands on Angkor's treasures. The great city's monuments were all subjected, at one time or another, to systematic plundering, mainly by the warring Chams (from S Vietnam) and Thais. Many temple pedestals were smashed to afford access to the treasure, hidden deep in pits under the central sanctuaries. Other looters knocked the tops off towers to reach the carefully concealed treasure chambers.

Centuries of entanglement in the jungle also took their toll on the buildings – strangler figs caused much structural damage and roots and vines rent roofs and walls asunder. In 1912, French writer Pierre Loti noted: "The fig tree is the ruler of Angkor today... Over the temples which it has patiently prised (presumably) apart, everywhere its dome of foliage triumphantly unfolds its sleek pale branches speckled like a serpent's skin." Even today, some roots and trees remain stubbornly tangled in the ancient masonry – affording visitors a

to the existence of 'catalogues', containing detailed photographs of Angkorian statues and bas-reliefs. River City shopkeepers will surreptitiously offer to 'organize' the acquisition of specific pieces.

Dealers in the antiquities-smuggling racket are reported to have links with organized crime. The underworld's labyrinthine networks – used in the trafficking of narcotics – facilitate the movement of statues around the world. 'Licences' for the illegal export of ancient works of art can be readily procured in Bangkok by dealers with good connections. Although Thailand does its best to prevent the smuggling of its own cultural treasures, it has refused to sign the UN's 1970 convention for preventing antiquities trafficking. This allows Bangkok dealers to trade Burmese and Cambodian pieces with impunity.

While many of the genuine pieces – there are plenty of fakes on the market – in Bangkok (and Singapore) are from Myanmar, Khmer sculpture is not uncommon. Having survived a thousand years of warfare and weather, many of Angkor's remaining statues are doomed to decapitation. The heads of the dancing Apsaras – the most famous motif of Angkor's temples – have disappeared, as have many of the heads from the western gate. As recently as July 1996 art historian and archaeologist Nancy Dowling reported the systematic pillage of works of art from the pre-Angkorian site of Angkor Borei. This ancient city is pock-marked with clandestine diggings, some 7m deep. In the case of one temple, the entire upper structure has been removed and spirited away. Growing cultural consciousness – combined with uneasy consciences of some Western collectors – may allow for some of this invaluable loot to be returned in the years to come. But for the present, Cambodia is losing tonnes of its cultural and artistic heritage of unscrupulous dealers and collectors.

Mouhot-style glimpse of the forgotten city. Between 1953 and 1970, the Angkor Conservancy – set up jointly by the French and Cambodian governments – maintained and restored the ruins. But when war broke out, the destructive forces of the Khmers Rouges – and other guerrilla factions – were unleashed on what the jungle had spared and the French archaeologists, such as Bernard Grosslier, had restored.

As if the conservation and protection of the complex was not already fraught with difficulties, a threat emerged in the mid-1980s, from the most unlikely of sources. The Vietnamese-backed administration enlisted the services of Indian archaeologists to begin where the Angkor Conservancy had left off. They were given a 6-year contract to clean and restore the galleries and towers of Angkor Wat itself. Prince Sihanouk is reported to have burst into tears when he heard that the Indians, using unskilled Cambodian workmen, had begun their concrete and chemical-assisted restoration effort.

The powerful cleaning agents stripped off the patina which for a millennium had protected the sandstone from erosion by the elements. Bas-reliefs depicting scenes from the Ramayana were scrubbed, scratched and scraped until some were barely discernable. Cement was used with abandon. Archaeologists around the world, who, since 1970, have only been dimly aware of the rape of Angkor, now consider the gimcrack restoration programme the last straw after 2 decades of pillage and destruction. A British journalist, visiting the complex in late 1990 wrote that after several centuries of abandonment in the jungle, "What is 20 years of neglect? The answer is: a lot."

However, whether the Indian team of archaeologists and conservators have really caused untold damage to the monuments of Angkor through insensitive restoration and the use of untested solvents is a source of some dispute. Generally, press reports in the W, as described above, have taken the latter line – that their work, rather than helping to restore and preserve the monuments, has helped to further ruin it. Cement has been used to fill in cracks, where western archaeologists would probably have left well alone. New stone have been cut and fitted where, again, other specialists might have been happy merely to have done sufficient restoration to prevent further degeneration. The Indian team also used chemical cleaning agents – an unorthodox and contentious approach to restoration. Although some of the methods used by the Indian team do seem rather crude and insensitive to the atmosphere of the place, the carping of some western archaeologists seems to have been motivated as much by professional envy as anything else. The Indians were called in by the government in Phnom Penh at a time when most western countries were boycotting the country, in protest at the Vietnamese occupation of the country. French archaeologists particularly, must have been pacing their offices in indignation and pique as a country with such 'primitive' skills took all the glory. Now, though, the French and the Japanese are back with their brushes and hammers, contributing to the preservation of Angkor.

In 1989 UNESCO commissioned a Japanese art historian to draw up an Angkor plan of action. The top priority in its restoration, he said, was to underpin the foundations of Angkor Wat, Bayon, Baphoun, Preah Khan, Neak Khan and Pre Rup. Once the Paris Peace agreements had been signed in 1991, the Ecole Française, the New York based World Monuments Fund and the Japanese started work. UNESCO is co-ordinating the activities of the various teams and Angkor was declared a world heritage sight. Some temples are closed for restoration work, check with guides. The agency has trained up police in order to counteract the greatest scourge, the organized theft of carvings. Many believe prompt action is the only way to protect Angkor from a post-peace settlement souvenir-hunters' free-for-all. Today however, would-be treasure hunters have to contend with horrors that even Mouhot could never have dreamt – minefields. Thousands of anti-personnel mines, the lethal legacy of the years of civil war, lie primed and buried in the undergrowth surrounding some temples – particularly the outer ones. **NB** Visitors are strongly advised to stick to the well-beaten track.

DOCUMENTATION OF ANGKOR

About 900 inscriptions have been found in Indochina that give a jigsaw set of clues to Angkor civilization. Those written in Sanskrit are largely poetic praises dedicated to gods and kings; Khmer-language ones give a much more focused insight into life and customs under the great kings. Some give a remarkably detailed picture of everyday life: one documents a ruling that pigs had the right to forage in ricefields, another dictates that ginger and honey should be used in the preparation of ritual foods. Most of the inscriptions have now been deciphered. Contemporary palm-leaf and paper documents which would have added to this knowledge have long since rotted away in the humid climate.

Bas-reliefs, carved in perpetuity into Angkor's temple walls also give a fascinating pictorial impression of life in the great city. Its citizens are shown, warring, hunting, playing and partying, and the reliefs present a picture which is often reassuringly normal in its detail... men played chess, old women read palms and people ate and drank and gossiped while local musicians provided live entertainment. Young men went hunting and young women evidently spent hours at the Angkorian equivalent of the hairdressers and boutiques.

The most complete eyewitness account of Angkor was written by Chou Ta-kuan, an envoy from the Chinese court, who visited Cambodia in 1296, around 75 years after the death of Jayavarman VII, the last great conqueror of the Angkor period. Chou Ta-Kuan wrote detailed accounts of his observations and impressions, and cast Angkor as a grand and highly sophisticated civilization, despite the fact that it was, by then, well past its heyday.

What the French archaeologists managed to do, with brilliance, was to apply scientific principles to deciphering the mysteries of Angkor. The French, and by extension the West, nonetheless managed to 'invent' Angkor for its own interests, moulding the Angkorian Empire and its art so that it fitted in with the accepted image of the Orient. (This notion that Europeans invented the Orient is most effectively argued in Edward Said's seminal book *Orientalism*, first published in 1978 and now widely available in paperback. It is a book that does not deal specifically with Angkor but much of the argument can be applied to the French appropriation of Angkor and the Khmers.) Much that has been written about the ruins at Angkor and the empire and people that built them says as much about what the French were trying to do in Indochina, as about the place and people themselves. What is perhaps ironic is that educated Cambodians then reappropriated the French vision and made it their own. Today, French invention and Cambodian 'tradition' are one and the same. Cambodia, lacking the cultural integrity to resist the influence of the French, became French; in so doing they took on board the French image of themselves and made it their own.

ART AND ARCHITECTURE

The Angkor period (9th-13th centuries) encapsulated the greatest and best of Cambodia's art and architecture. Much of it shows strong Indian influence. The so-called 'Indianization' of Cambodia was more a product of trade than Hindu proselytism; there was no attempt made at formal conquest, and no great emigration of Indians to the region. In order to meet the Romans' demand for exotic oriental merchandise and commodities, Indian traders ventured into the South China Sea – well before the 1st century AD, it was discovered that monsoon winds could carry them to the Malay peninsula and on to Indochina and Cambodia. Because of their reliance on seasonal winds, Indian navigators were obliged to while away many months in countries with which they traded and the influence of their sophisticated culture spread.

But although Khmer art and architecture was rooted in Indian prototypes, the expression and content was distinctively Cambodian. Most of the art from the Angkor period is Hindu although Mahayana Buddhism took hold in the late 12th century. Some Buddhist figures have been dated to as early as the 6th century – the standing Buddhas were carved in the same style as the Hindu deities, minus the sensuous voluptuousness.

The ancient kingdoms of Funan (the Chinese name for the mercantile state encompassing the area SW of the Mekong Delta, in what is now S Vietnam and S Cambodia) and Chenla (a mountain kingdom centred on N Cambodia and S Laos) were the first to be artistically and culturally influenced by India. In his book *The Art of Southeast Asia*, Philip Rawson writes that the art-styles of Funan and Chenla were "the greatest phase of pre-Angkor Khmer art, and... we can treat the evolution under these two kingdoms together as a stylistic unity. It was the foundation of classic

Khmer art, just as archaic Greek sculpture was the foundation of later classical Greek art."

The only remaining traces of the kingdom of Funan – whose influence is thought to have spread as far afield as S Burma and Indonesia – are limited to four Sanskrit inscriptions on stelae and a few sculptures. The earliest surviving Funanese statues were found at Angkor Borei (see page 150) and have been dated to the 6th century. Most represent the Hindu god, Vishnu (patron of King Rudravarman) and their faces are distinctly Angkorian in style. Scattered remains of these pre-Angkorian periods are all over S Cambodia – especially between the Mekong and the Tonlé Sap. Most of the earliest buildings would

have been made of wood and have consequently rotted away – there being a paucity of stone in the delta region.

The kingdom of Chenla, based at Sambor and later at Sambor Prei Kuk (see page 146), expanded at the expense of Funan, which gradually became a vassal state. Chenla inherited Funan's Indianized art and architectural traditions. Some buildings were built of brick and stone and typical architectural relics are brick towers with a square (or sometimes octagonal) plan: a shrine set atop a pedestal comprised of mounting tiers of decreasing size – a style which may have been structurally patterned on early Pallava temples in SE India. The sculptural work was strongly rooted in Indian ideas but carved in a unique style

The Churning of the Sea

The Hindu legend, the Churning of the Sea, relates how the gods and demons resolved matters in the turbulent days when the world was being created. The elixir of immortality was one of 13 precious things lost in the churning of the cosmic sea. It took a thousand years before the gods and demons, in a joint dredging operation – aided by Sesha, the sea snake, and Vishnu – recovered them all.

The design of the temples of Angkor was based on this ancient legend. The moat represents the ocean and the gods use the top of Mount Meru – represented by the tower – as their churning stick. The cosmic serpent offered himself as a rope to enable the gods and demons to twirl the stick. Paul Mus, a French archaeologist, suggests that the bridge with the naga balustrades which went over the moat from the world of men to the royal city was an image of the rainbow. Throughout Southeast Asia and India, the rainbow is alluded to as a multi-coloured serpent rearing its head in the sky.

Vishnu churning the sea
Source: Aymonier, Etoenne (1901) *Cambodge*, Paris

– many of the statues from this era are in the museum at Phnom Penh (see page 90). Rawson writes: "Among the few great stone icons which have survived are some of the world's outstanding masterpieces, while the smaller bronzes reflect the same sophisticated and profound style."

In the late 8th century the Chenla Kingdom collapsed and contact with India came to an end. Chenla is thought to have been eclipsed by the increasingly important Sumatran-based Srivijayan Empire. Jayavarman II, who had lived most of his life in the Sailendra court in Java, but who was of royal lineage, returned to Cambodia in about 790 AD. Jayavarman II's reign marked the transition period between pre-Angkorian and Angkorian styles – by the 9th century the larger images were recognizably Khmer in style. From Jayavarman II onwards, the kings of Cambodia were regarded as god-kings – or devaraja (see page 27).

Jayavarman II established a royal Siva-lingam (phallic) cult which was to prove the inspiration for successive generations of Khmer kings. "He summoned a Brahmin learned in the appropriate texts, and erected a lingam... with all the correct Indian ritual," Rawson says. "This lingam, in which the king's own soul was held to reside, became the source and centre of power for the Khmer Dynasty. At the same time – and by that act – he severed all ties of dependence upon Indonesia." To house the sacred lingam each king in turn built a new temple, some of the mightiest and finest of the monuments of the Khmer civilization.

The temples at Angkor were modelled on those of the kingdom of Chenla, which in turn were modelled on Indian temples. They represent Mt Meru – the home of the gods of Indian cosmology. The central towers symbolize the peaks of Mt Meru, surrounded by a wall – representing the earth – and moats and basins – the oceans. The devaraja, or god-king, was enshrined in the centre of

Khmer-style Prang

the religious complex, which acted as the spiritual axis of the kingdom. The people believed their apotheosized king communicated directly with the gods.

The central tower sanctuaries housed the images of the Hindu gods to whom the temples were dedicated. Dead members of the royal and priestly families were accorded a status on a par with these gods. Libraries to store the sacred scriptures were also built within the ceremonial centre. The temples were mainly built to shelter the images of the gods – unlike Christian churches, Moslem mosques and some Buddhist pagodas, they were not intended to accommodate worshippers. Only priests, the servants of the god, were allowed into the interiors. The 'congregation' would mill around outside in open courtyards or wooden pavilions.

The first temples were of a very simple design, but with time they became more grandiose and doors and galleries were added. Most of Angkor's buildings are made from a soft sandstone which is easy to work. It was transported to the site from Phnom Kulen, about 30 km to the NE. Laterite was used for foundations, core material, and enclosure walls, as it was widely available and could be easily cut into blocks (see box). The Khmer sandstone architecture has echoes of earlier wooden structures: gallery roofs are sculpted with false tiles, while balustred windows imitate wooden ones. A common feature of Khmer temples were false doors and windows on the sides and backs of sanctuaries and other buildings. In most cases there was no need for well-lit rooms and corridors as hardly anyone ever went into them. That said, the galleries round the central towers in later temples, such as Angkor Wat, indicate that worshippers did use the

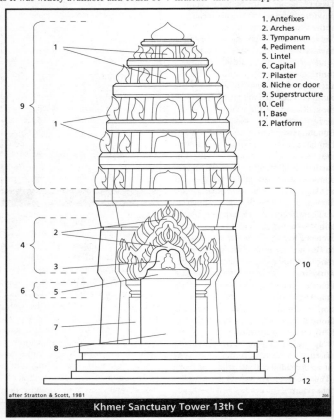

1. Antefixes
2. Arches
3. Tympanum
4. Pediment
5. Lintel
6. Capital
7. Pilaster
8. Niche or door
9. Superstructure
10. Cell
11. Base
12. Platform

after Stratton & Scott, 1981

Khmer Sanctuary Tower 13th C

temples for ceremonial circumambulation when they would contemplate the inspiring bas-reliefs from the *Ramayana* and *Mahabharata*.

In Europe and the Middle East, the arch and vault were used in contemporary buildings but at Angkor, architects used the false vault – known as a corbel stone. It was a fairly primitive vaulting system so the interiors of sanctuaries could never be very large. The stones were often laid without staggering the vertical joints and mortar was not used. The builders relied on the weight of the structure, gravity and a good fit between the stones to hold their buildings together. This is why so many of the temples have collapsed.

Despite the court's conversion to Mahayana Buddhism in the 12th century (under Jayavarman VII) the architectural ground-plans of temples did not alter much – even though they were based on Hindu cosmology. The idea of the god-king was simply grafted onto the new state religion and statues of the Buddha rather than the gods of the Hindu pantheon were used to represent the god-king (see Bayon, page 119). One particular image of the Buddha predominated at Angkor in which he wears an Angkor-style crown, with a conical top which is encrusted with jewellery.

There are some scholars who maintain that Angkor has, perhaps, been over-praised. The label of 'genius' that has been attached to the architects that conceived the edifices, the builders that worked on them, and the empire that financed their construction, demands that Angkor be put in the highest division of human artistic achievement. Anthony Barnett in the *New Left Review* in 1990, for example, wrote:

"...to measure [Angkor's] greatness by the fact that it is nearly a mile square is to deny it a proper admiration through hyperbole. Thus the Church of Saint Sophia, to take one example, was for nearly a millennium the largest domed space in the world until St Peter's was constructed. Saint Sophia still stands in Istanbul. It was built 600 years before Angkor Wat, while Khmer architects never managed to discover the principles of the arch" (1990: 103).

SCULPTURE

The sculpture of the early temples at Angkor is rather stiff and plain, but forms the basis for the ornate bas-reliefs of the later Angkor Wat. Lintel-carving became a highly developed art form at an early stage in the evolution of Khmer architecture. The use of columns around doorways was another distinctive feature – they too had their antecedents in the earlier Chenla period. Frontons – the masonry covering originally used to conceal the corbeled end gables – were elaborate at Angkor. They were intricately carved and conveyed stories from the Ramayana and other great Hindu epics. The carved fronton is still used in temples throughout modern Thailand, Laos and Cambodia. Sanctuary doorways, through which priests would pass to enter the sacred heart of the temple, were an important site for icons. Ornately carved sandstone blocks were placed in front of and above the true lintel.

Angkor's most impressive carvings are its bas-reliefs, which, like the fronton, were devoted to allegorical depictions and mostly illustrate stories from the Hindu classics, the Mahabharata and Ramayana. The latter is best exemplified at the Baphuon (11th century) – see page 118. Details of the everyday lives of the Angkor civilization can be pieced together thanks to these bas-reliefs. Those on the Bayon illustrate the weaponry and armour used in battle, market scenes, fishing and cockfighting – probably the Khmers' favourite excuse for gambling. In contrast to the highly sculpted outer walls of the temples, the interiors were typically bare; this has led to speculation that they may originally have been decorated with murals.

Laterite, which is a coarse soft stone, found widely across Southeast Asia, was excavated to form many of the moats and

Motifs in Khmer sculpture

● The **kala** – a jawless monster commanded by the gods to devour his own body – made its first appearance in lintels at Roluos. The monster represented devouring time and was an early import from Java.

● **Singhas** or lions appeared in stylized forms and are often guardians to temples. The lions lack realism probably because the carvers had never seen one.

● The **makara** was a mythical water-monster with a scaley body, eagles' talons and an elephantine trunk.

● The sacred snakes, or **nagas**, play an important part in Hindu mythology and the Khmers drew on them for architectural inspiration. Possibly more than any other single symbol or motif, the naga is characteristic of Southeast Asia. The naga is an aquatic serpent, the word being Sanskrit for snake, and is intimately associated with water (a key component of Khmer prosperity). In Hindu mythology, the naga coils beneath and supports Vishnu on the cosmic ocean. The snake also swallows the waters of life, these only being set free to reinvigorate the world after Indra ruptures the serpent with a bolt of lightning. Another version has Vishnu's servants pulling at the serpent to squeeze the waters of life from it (the so-called churning of the sea, see page 108).

The naga permeates Southeast Asian life from royalty to villager. The bridge across the Bayon to Angkor Wat features nagas churning the oceans; men in Vietnam, Laos and Thailand used to tattoo their bodies with nagas for protection; water, the gift of life in a region where wet rice is the staple crop, is measured in Thailand in terms of numbers of nagas; while objects throughout Southeast Asia are decorated with the naga motif from boats, to water storage jars, to temples (gable ends, barge boards, finials), to musical instruments.

● The **garuda** appeared relatively late in Khmer architecture. This mythical creature – half-man, half-bird – was the vehicle of the Hindu god, Vishnu, and the sworn enemy of the nagas.

● The **apsaras** are regarded as one of the greatest invention of the Khmers. The gorgeous temptresses – born, according to legend, 'during the churning of the Sea of Milk' – were Angkor's equivalent of pin-up girls and represented the ultimate ideal of feminine beauty. They lived in heaven where their sole *raison d'être* was to have eternal sex with Khmer heroes and holy men. The apsaras are carved with splendidly ornate jewellery and, clothed in the latest Angkor fashion, they strike seductive poses and seemingly compete with each other like models on a cat-walk. Different facial features suggest the existence of several races at Angkor – it is possible that they might be modelled on women captured in war. Together with the 5 towers of Angkor Wat they have become the symbol of Khmer culture. The god-king himself possessed an apsara-like retinue of court dancers – who obviously impressed Chinese envoy Chou Ta-kuan sufficiently for him to write home about it in 1296.

Apsaras: celestial nymphs.

Naga: mythical serpent of Southeast Asia.

Garuda: half man, half bird.

Singha: guardian lion.

ZVL204

barays at Angkor. Early structures such as those at Preah Ko in the Roluos group were built in brick. The brickwork was often laid with dry joints and the only mortar used was a type of vegetable-based adhesive. Bricks were sometimes carved in situ and occasionally plastered. In the early temples sandstone was only used for architectural embellishments. But nearly all of the later temples were built entirely of sandstone – with some blocks weighing over 4 tonnes. Most of the sandstone is thought to have been quarried from the northern hills around Kulen and brought by barge to Angkor.

The post-Angkor period was characterized by wooden buildings and fastidiously carved and decorated sculptures, but the humid climate has allowed little to survive. The contemporary art of 1990s Cambodia is still redolent of the grandeur of the Angkor era and today, Khmer craftsmen retain their inherent skills, and are renowned for their refined carvings. Art historians believe that the richness of Cambodia's heritage, and its incorporation into the modern artistic psyche, has enabled Khmer artists to produce work which is reckoned to be aesthetically superior to contemporary carving and sculpture in Thailand.

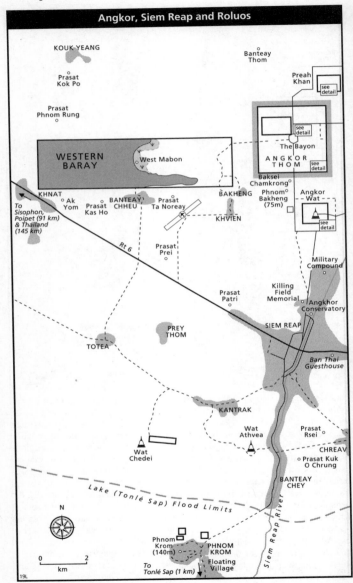

Angkor, Siem Reap and Roluos

KOUK YEANG

Prasat Kok Po

Prasat Phnom Rung

Banteay Thom

Preah Khan

see detail

WESTERN BARAY

West Mabon

The Bayon

see detail

ANGKOR THOM

see detail

Baksei Chamkrong

Phnom Bakheng (75m)

Angkor Wat

see detail

KHNAT

Ak Yom

Prasat Kas Ho

BANTEAY CHHEU

Prasat Ta Noreay

BAKHENG

To Sisophon, Poipet (91 km) & Thailand (145 km)

Rt 6

KHVIEN

Prasat Prei

Military Compound

Prasat Patri

Killing Field Memorial

Angkhor Conservatory

PREY THOM

SIEM REAP

TOTEA

Ban Thai Guesthouse

KANTRAK

Wat Athvea

Prasat Rsei

CHREAV

Prasat Kuk O Chrung

Wat Chedei

BANTEAY CHEY

Lake (Tonlé Sap) Flood Limits

Siem Reap River

N

0   2
km

Phnom Krom (140m)

PHNOM KROM

To Tonlé Sap (1 km)

Floating Village

19L

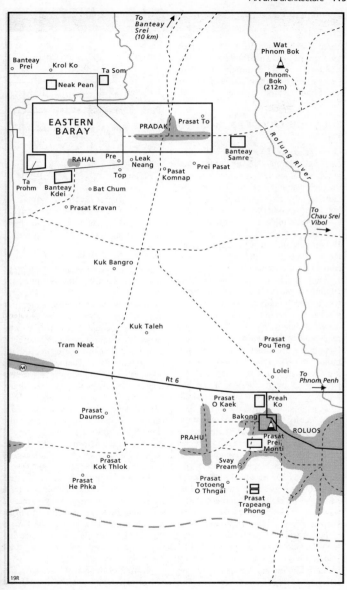

Banteay
Prei
Krol Ko
Ta Som

Neak Pean

*To Banteay
Srei
(10 km)*

Wat
Phnom Bok
Phnom
Bok
(212m)

EASTERN
BARAY

PRADAK
Prasat To

Rolung River

RAHAL
Pre
Leak
Neang
Pasat
Komnap
Prei Pasat

Banteay
Samre

Ta
Prohm
Top
Banteay
Kdei
Bat Chum

Prasat Kravan

*To Chau Srei
Vibol*

Kuk Bangro

Kuk Taleh

Prasat
Pou Teng

Tram Neak
(M)

Lolei

*To
Phnom Penh*

Rt 6

Prasat
Daunso

Prasat
O Kaek

Bakong

Preah
Ko

ROLUOS

PRAHU

Prasat
Prei
Monti

Prasat
Kok Thlok

Svay
Pream

Prasat
He Phka

Prasat
Totoeng
O Thngai

Prasat
Trapeang
Phong

19R

PLACES OF INTEREST

The main cluster of monuments are about 7 km N of Siem Reap. The temples are scattered over an area in excess of 160 sq km. Two hills dominate the plain: Phnom Bakeng to the NW of Angkor Wat and Phnom Khrom at the N end of the Tonlé Sap.

THE ROYAL CITY OF ANGKOR THOM

Construction of Jayavarman VII's spacious walled capital, **Angkor Thom**, began at the end of the 12th century: he rebuilt the capital after it had been captured and destroyed by the Chams. Some stone buildings survived the sacking of the city, such as the temples of Phimeanakas and Baphuon, and these were incorporated by Jayavarman in his new plan. He adopted the general layout of the royal centre conceived by Suryavarman II.

Angkor Thom was colossal: the 100m-wide moat surrounding the city – which was probably stocked with crocodiles as a protection against the enemy – extended more than 12 km. Inside the moat was an 8m-high stone wall, buttressed on the inner side by a high mound of earth along the top of which ran a terrace for troops to man the ramparts. Four great gateways in the city wall face N, S, E and W and lead to the city's geometric centre, the Bayon. The fifth, Victory Gate, leads from the royal palace (within the Royal Enclosure) to the E Baray. The height of the gates was determined by the headroom needed to accommodate an elephant and howdah, complete with parasols. The flanks of each gateway are decorated with three-headed stone elephants, and each gateway tower has four giant faces, which keep an eye on all four cardinal points.

Five causeways traverse the moat, each bordered by sculptured balustrades of nagas gripped, on one side, by 54 stern-looking giant gods and on the other by 54 fierce-faced demons. The

Useful place names	
Angkor Thom	អង្គរធំ
Bayon	បាយ័ន
Kleangs, North	ឃ្លាំងខាងជើង
Kleangs, South	ឃ្លាំងខាងត្បូង
Phimeanakas	ភិមានអាកាស
Prasat Suor Prat	ប្រាសាទសួរព្រ័ត
Sras Srei	ស្រះ ស្រី
Terrace of the Elephants	រោងដំរី
Terrace of the Leper King	ព្រលានព្រះគិលង់

balustrade depicts the Hindu legend of the churning sea (see page 108).

INSIDE THE WALLED CITY

The **Bayon**, Jayavarman VII's temple-mountain, stands at the centre of the royal city of Angkor Thom. The area within the walls was more spacious than that of any walled city in medieval Europe – it could easily have encompassed the whole of ancient Rome. Yet it is believed that this enclosure, like the Forbidden City in Peking, was only a royal, religious and administrative centre accommodating the court and dignitaries. The rest of the population lived outside the walls between the two artificial lakes – the E and W barays – and along the Siem Reap River.

The **Royal Enclosure**, to the N of the Bayon, had already been laid out by Suryavarman I: the official palace was in the front with the domestic quarters behind, its gardens surrounded by a laterite wall and moat. Suryavarman I also beautified the royal city with ornamental pools. Jayavarman VII simply improved his designs. The jungle has now taken over where the royal landscapers left off.

In front of the Royal Enclosure, Suryavarman I laid out the first Grand

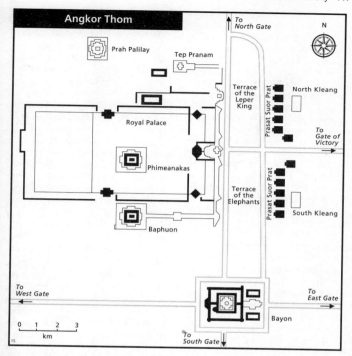

Angkor Thom

Prah Palilay

Tep Pranam

Royal Palace

Phimeanakas

Baphuon

To North Gate

N

Terrace of the Leper King

North Kleang

Prasat Suor Prat

To Gate of Victory

Terrace of the Elephants

Prasat Suor Prat

South Kleang

To West Gate

To East Gate

Bayon

To South Gate

0 1 2 3
km

15

Plaza with the recently renovated **Terrace of the Elephants** (also called the Royal Terrace) and the stately **North and South Kleangs** on the E side of the central square, which are thought to have provided accommodation for foreign envoys. The North Kleang was started by Jayavarman V; Jayavarman VII later added 12 laterite victory towers, called the **Prasat Suor Prat**. The Royal Terrace (also called the Terrace of the Elephants) was built by Suryavarman I and was originally the raised base of a hall of the palace complex. It is decorated with a bas-relief of elephants – depicting a hunting scene – and at the centre, where kings once sat in gold-topped pavilions, are rows of garudas, their wings lifted as if in flight. They were intended to give the impression that the god-king's palace was floating in the heavens, like the imagined flying celestial palaces of the gods.

At the NE corner of the 'central square' is the 12th century **Terrace of the Leper King**, which may have been a cremation platform for the aristocracy of Angkor. Now rebuilt and a little too fresh and contemporary for some tastes. The practice of some places of rebuilding as opposed to preservation has been questioned. The 7m-high terrace has bands of bas-reliefs, one on top of the other, with intricately sculptured scenes of royal pageantry and seated apsaras as well as nagas and garudas which frequented the slopes of Mt Meru. Above is a strange statue of an earlier date, which probably depicts the god of death, Yama, and once held a staff in its right hand. It is unusual because, unlike most Khmer statues, it is sexless. It does not represent a king as it does not wear a crown. The statue's naked, lichen-covered body gives the terrace its name – the lichen gives the uncanny impression of leprosy. Jayavarman VII may have suffered from leprosy, but this statue is not a representation of him.

Opposite the Terrace of the Elephants, on the S side of the Terrace of the Leper King are the remains of an earlier wall, carved with bas-reliefs of demons. These reliefs were found by French archaeologists and had been intentionally concealed. This illustrates the lengths to which the Khmers went to recreate Mt Meru (the home of the Gods) as faithfully as possible. According to Hindu mythology, Mt Meru extended into the bowels of the earth; the bas-relief section below ground level was carved with weird and wonderful creatures to symbolize the mystical hidden depths of the underworld. The second layer of carving is the base of Mt Meru on earth. Flights of steps led through these to the lawns and pavilions of the royal gardens and Suryavarman's palace.

The **Phimeanakas** (meaning Celestial or Flying Palace in Sanskrit) inside the Royal Enclosure was started by Rajendravarman and used by all the later kings. Suryavarman I rebuilt this pyramidal temple when he was renovating the Royal Enclosure. It rises from the centre of the former royal palace. Lions guard all four stairways to the central tower. It is now ruined but was originally covered in gold, as the Chinese envoy, Chou Ta-kuan related in 1296:

"The king sleeps in the summit of the palace's golden tower. All the people believe that the tower is also inhabited by the Lord of the Sun, who is a nine-headed serpent. Every night the serpent appears in the form of a woman with whom the king sleeps during the first watch. None of the royal wives are allowed in the tower. The king leaves at the second watch to go to his wives and concubines. If the naga spirit does not appear one night, it is a sign that the king's death is imminent. Should the king fail to visit the naga for a single night, the welfare of the kingdom will suffer dire consequences."

The Phimeanakas represented a genuine architectural revolution: it was not square, but rectangular and on the upper terrace, surrounding the central tower, there was a gallery with corbelled vaults, used as a passageway. The **Celestial Palace** is now in a bad state of repair. The **Sras Srei**, or the women's bath, to the N of the Celestial Palace is also within the walled enclosure. Chou Ta-kuan, whose Chinese delegation appears to have enjoyed watching Angkor's womenfolk bathe, noted that women, even of noble families, would shamelessly take off their clothes to bathe in public. "To enter the water, the women simply hide their sex with their left hand," he wrote. The Phimeanakas is linked by the **Avenue of Victory** to the Eastern Baray.

South of the Royal Enclosure and near the Terrace of the Elephants is the **Baphuon**, built by Udayadityavarman II. The temple was approached by a 200m-long causeway, raised on pillars, which was probably constructed after the temple was built. The Baphuon is not well preserved as it was erected on an artificial hill which weakened its foundations. Only the three massive terraces of its pyramidal, Mt Meru-style form remain and these afford little indication of its former glory: it was second only to the Bayon in size. Chou Ta-kuan, the Chinese envoy, reported that its great tower was made of bronze and that it was "truly marvellous to behold". Most of the bas-reliefs were carved in panels and refer to the Hindu epics, in particular the stories of Rama and Krishna. Some archaeologists believe the sculptors were trying to tell stories in the same way as the shadow plays.

South of the Baphuon is one of Angkor's most famous sights, the **Bayon**. This was Jayavarman VII's own temple mountain, built right in the middle of Angkor Thom. Unlike other Khmer monuments, the Bayon has no protective wall immediately enclosing it. The central tower, at the intersection of the diagonals of the perfect square of the city walls, indicates that the city walls and the temple were built at the same time.

It is a pyramid temple with a 45m-high tower topped by four gigantic carved heads – images of Jayavarman VII as a Bodhisattra, facing the four compass points. They are crowned with lotus flowers, symbol of enlightenment, and are surrounded by 51 smaller towers each with heads facing N, S, E and W. When Pierre Loti, the French writer, first saw these towers in 1912 he was astounded: "I looked up at the tree-covered towers which dwarfed me, when all of a sudden my blood curdled as I saw an enormous smile looking down on me, and then another smile on another wall, then three, then five, then 10, appearing in every direction". The facial features are striking and the full lips, curling upwards at the corners, are known as 'the smile of Angkor'.

Even the archaeologists of the École Française d'Extrême Orient were not able to decide immediately whether the heads on the Bayon represented Brahma, Siva or the Buddha. There are many theories. One of the most plausable ones was conceived in 1934 by George Coedès – an archaeologist who spent many years studying the temples at Angkor. He postulated that the sculptures represented King Jayavarman VII in the form of Avaloketsvara, the Universal Buddha. If true, this would have meant that the Hindu concept of the god-king had been appended to Buddhist cosmology. Jayavarman VII, once

a humble monk who twice renounced the throne and then became the mightiest of all the Khmer rulers, may be the smiling face, cast in stone, at the centre of his kingdom. The multiplication of faces, all looking out to the four cardinal points, may symbolize Jayavarman blessing the four quarters of the kingdom. After Jayavarman's death, the Brahmin priests turned the Bayon into a place of Hindu worship (confusing the archaeologists).

The Bayon underwent a series of reconstructions, a point first observed by Henri Parmentier – a French archaeologist who worked for the L'École Français d'Extrême Orient – in 1924 and later excavations revealed vestiges of a former building. It is thought that the first temple was planned as a two-tiered structure dedicated to Siva, which was then altered to its present form. As a result, it gives the impression of crowding – the towers rise right next to each other and the courtyards are narrow without much air or light. When Henri Mouhot rediscovered Angkor, local villagers had dubbed the Bayon 'the hide and seek sanctuary' because of its complex layout.

The bas-reliefs which decorate the walls of the Bayon all seem to tell a story but are much less imposing than those at Angkor Wat. The Bayon reliefs vary greatly in quality; this may have been because the sculptors' skills were being overstretched by Jayavarman's ambitious building programme. The reliefs on the outer wall and on the inner gallery differ completely and seem to belong to two different worlds: the relief on the outside depicts historical events; those on the inside are drawn from the epic world of gods and legends, representing the creatures who were supposed to haunt the subterranean depths of Mt Meru.

Two recurring themes in Angkor's bas-reliefs are the king and his might and the Hindu epics. Jayavarman is depicted in the throes of battle with the

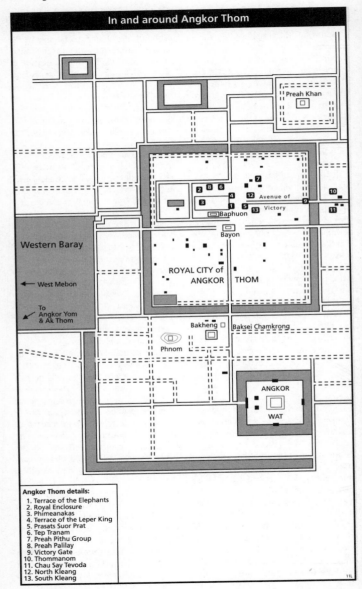

In and around Angkor Thom

Preah Khan

Avenue of
Victory

Baphuon

Bayon

Western Baray

West Mebon

To
Angkor Yom
& Ak Thom

ROYAL CITY of
ANGKOR   THOM

Bakheng   Baksei Chamkrong

Phnom

ANGKOR

WAT

Angkor Thom details:
1. Terrace of the Elephants
2. Royal Enclosure
3. Phimeanakas
4. Terrace of the Leper King
5. Prasats Suor Prat
6. Tep Tranam
7. Preah Pithu Group
8. Preah Palilay
9. Victory Gate
10. Thommanom
11. Chau Say Tevoda
12. North Kleang
13. South Kleang

11L

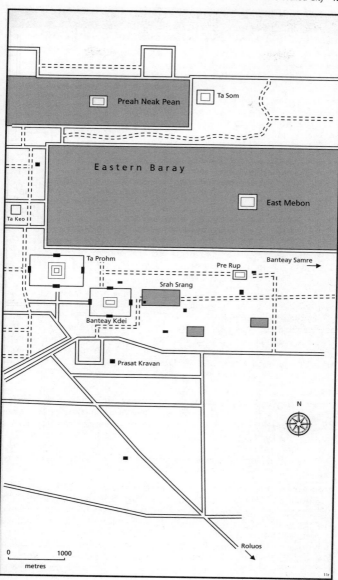

Barays and the Jayavarman Conundrum: The case for irrigation

By founding his capital at Roluos, just SE of Angkor, in the middle of an arid plain annually plagued by drought and flash floods, Jayavarman II bequeathed to archaeologists and other scholars a geo-climatic conundrum. What possessed him to site the nerve-centre of Khmer civilization at such an environmentally unfriendly spot and how did the great city sustain itself through the centuries? Archaeologists have postulated that the Khmers engineered a complex irrigation system to grow enough rice to feed the city's population. In this view, Angkor was a classic hydraulic society.

In *The Art of Southeast Asia*, Philip Rawson writes: "Angkor was a capital, filled with temples and supporting many inhabitants. But its nucleus was a splendid irrigation project, based on a number of huge artificial reservoirs fed by the local rivers and linked to each other by means of a rectangular grid system of canals." The *barays*, or man-made lakes, associated with the famous temples were used to feed an intricate network of irrigation channels. The first *baray* was Lolei, built by Indravarman at the city of Rolous. "The engineering involved at Angkor," Rawson says, "...was vaster and far more sophisticated than anything seen before in that part of the world." Lolei was more than 3.5 km long and 800m wide. The E Baray was twice the size of Lolei and the W Baray, built during Udayadityavarman II's reign, is thought to have held about 4 million cubic metres of water when full.

The barays were constructed by building up dykes above the level of the land, and waiting for the monsoon flood. Because the resultant reservoirs were higher than the surrounding agricultural lands, there was no need to pump the water to flood the paddy fields: a gap was simply cut in the dyke. The water stored in the barays would have been replenished by each monsoon, making it possible to irrigate the ricelands – even during the dry season. With their land being watered year-round, the Khmers would have been able to grow three crops of rice a year.

The barays were central to the health and vigour of Khmer civilization but because they were sitting targets for enemy saboteurs, they may also have played a part in its downfall. During successive Siamese invasions the fragile irrigation system would have been irreparably damaged and essential maintenance of the hydraulic works was neglected through a lack of manpower. The precarious – and artificial – balance between man and nature was disturbed and as the irrigation channels cracked and dried up, so did the mighty Khmer Empire.

Why Angkor should have gone into decline from about the 13th century has exercised the minds of historians for years. Apart from the destruction of the fragile irrigation system, several other explanations as to Angkor's downfall have been suggested: climatic change, the shift of trade from land to sea-based empires and the corruption of a system which, like the Roman emperors, made the king a demi-god. Some think the builder King Jayavarman VII bankrupted the empire with his vast building schemes.

Barays and the Jayavarman Conundrum: the case against irrigation

🐾 When the first Westerners stumbled upon the Khmer ruins at Angkor – the lost city in the jungle – in the middle of the 19th century, they judged it to be the finest example of a civilization based upon the massive control of water for irrigation. The sheer size of the monuments, the vast *barays* storing millions of gallons of water, all seemed to lend force to the notion that here was the finest example of state-controlled irrigation. In Karl Marx's words, the Khmer Kingdom was a society based upon the Asiatic mode of production. The upshot of this was that, by necessity, there needed to be a centralized state and an all-powerful king – leading, in Karl Wittfogel's famous phrase, to a system of 'Oriental Despotism'. Such a view seemed hard to refute – how could such enormous expanses of water in the baray be used for anything but irrigation?

But, in the past decade, archaeologists, irrigation engineers and geographers have challenged the view of the Khmer Kingdom as the hydraulic civilization *par excellence*. Their challenge rests on 4 main pillars of evidence. First, they point out that if irrigation was so central to life in Angkor, why is it not mentioned once in over 1,000 inscriptions? Second, they question the usual interpretation of Angkorian agriculture contained in the Chinese emissary Chou Ta-Kouan's account – *Notes on the customs of Cambodia* – written in 1312. This account talks of "three or four rice harvests a year" – which scholars have assumed means irrigated rice agriculture. However, the detractors put a different interpretation on Chou Ta-Kouan's words, arguing they in fact describe a system of flood retreat agriculture in which rice was sown as the waters of the Great Lake, the Tonlé Sap, receded at the end of the rainy season. Third, they note that aerial photographs show none of the feeder canals needed to carry water from the barays to the fields, nor any of the other irrigation structures needed to control water. Finally, the sceptics draw upon engineering evidence to support their case. They have calculated that the combined storage capacity of all the barays and reservoirs is sufficient to irrigate only 400 ha of riceland – hardly the stuff on which great civilizations are built.

The geographer Philip Stott maintains that flood retreat agriculture would have produced the surplus needed to feed the soldiers, priests and the court of the Khmer god-king, while postulating that the barays were only for urban use. He writes that they were "just like the temple mountains, essentially a part of the urban scene, providing urban symbolism, beauty, water for bathing and drinking, a means of transport, and perhaps a supply of fish as well. Yet, not one drop of their water is likely to have fed the rice fields of Angkor."

Today the E Baray is dry whereas the W Baray has been excavated for fish cultivation.

Chams – who are recognizable thanks to their unusual and distinctive headdress, which looks like an inverted lotus flower. The naval battle pictured on the walls of Banteay Chmar is almost identical. The bas-reliefs give a good idea of Khmer life at the time – the warrior elephants, ox-carts, fishing with nets, cockfights and skewered fish drying on racks. Other vignettes show musicians, hunters, chess-players, palm-readers and reassuringly down-to-earth scenes of Angkor citizens enjoying drinking sessions. In the naval battle scenes, the water around the war-canoes is depicted by the presence of fish, crocodiles and

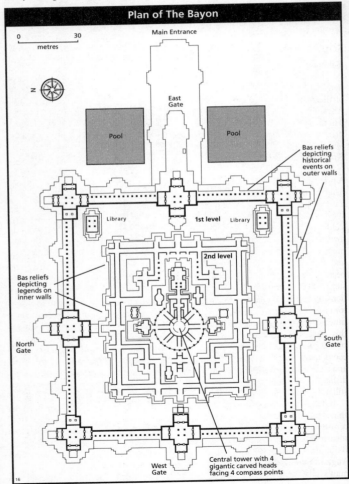

Plan of The Bayon

0   30
metres

N

Main Entrance

East Gate

Pool

Pool

Bas reliefs depicting historical events on outer walls

Library   **1st level**   Library

2nd level

Bas reliefs depicting legends on inner walls

North Gate

South Gate

West Gate

Central tower with 4 gigantic carved heads facing 4 compass points

16

floating corpses. The sculpture work at the Bayon is, however, more naive and less sophisticated than the bas reliefs at Angkor Wat.

Preah Palilay, just outside the N wall of the Royal Enclosure was also built by Jayavarman VII. Just to the E of this temple is **Tep Tranam**, the base of a pagoda, with a pool in front of it. To the E of Tep Tranam and the other side of the Northern Ave is the **Preah Pithu Group**, a cluster of five temples.

SOUTH OF ANGKOR THOM

Bakheng, Yasovarman's temple-mountain, stands on a natural hill (Phnom Bakheng, 60m high) which affords good views of the plain of Angkor and particularly Angkor Wat – beautiful sunrises and sets. There is also a roped off Buddha's footprint to see. It is just outside the S gate of Angkor Thom and was the centre of King Yasovarman's city, Yasodharapura – the 'City Endowed with Splendour'. A pyramid-temple dedicated to Siva, Bakheng was the home of the royal lingam and Yasovarman's mausoleum after his death. It is composed of five towers built on a sandstone platform. There are 108 smaller towers scattered around the terraces. The main tower has been partially demolished and the others have completely disappeared. It was entered via a steep flight of steps which were guarded by squatting lions. The steps have deteriorated with the towers. Foliate scroll relief carving covers much of the main shrine – the first time this style was used. This strategically placed hill served as a camp for various combatants, including the Vietnamese, and suffered accordingly. Today the hill is disfigured by a radio mast and the area is still not clear of mines.

Baksei Chamkrong was built by Harshavarman I at the beginning of the 10th century and dedicated to his father, Yasovarman I. It lies at the foot of Phnom Bakheng (between Bakheng and Angkor Thom), the centre of Yasovarman's city, and was one of the first temples to be built in durable material: brick on a stepped laterite base. An inscription tells of a golden image of Siva inside the temple.

ANGKOR WAT

To the S of Angkor Thom is the most famous of all the temples on the plain of Angkor: **Angkor Wat**. Angkor literally means 'city' or 'capital'. Probably the biggest religious monument ever built; it is certainly one of the most spectacular. The temple complex covers 81 ha and is comparable in size to the Imperial Palace in Beijing. Its distinctive five towers are emblazoned on the Cambodian flag and the 12th century masterpiece is considered by art historians to be the prime example of Classical Khmer art and architecture. It took over 30 years to build and is contemporary with Notre Dame in Paris and Durham Cathedral in England. The temple is dedicated to the Hindu god Vishnu, personified in earthly form by its builder, the god-king Suryavarman II, and is aligned E to W, as it is a funeral monument.

Like other Khmer temple mountains, Angkor Wat is an architectural allegory, depicting in stone the epic tales of Hindu mythology. The central sanctuary of the temple complex represents the sacred Mt Meru, the centre of the Hindu universe, on whose summit the gods reside. Angkor Wat's five towers symbolize Meru's five peaks; the enclosing wall represents the mountains at the edge of the world and the surrounding moat, the ocean beyond.

Angkor Wat was found in much better condition than most of the other temples in the complex because it seems to have been continuously inhabited by Buddhist monks after the Thais invaded. They were able to keep back the encroaching jungle. A giant stone Buddha was placed in the hall of the highest central tower, formerly sacred to the Hindu god, Vishnu. Three modern Buddhist monasteries flank the wat.

The temple complex is enclosed by a

The Kings of Angkor and their creations

KING	MONUMENTS
JAYAVARMAN II (802-850) Founder of the Khmer Empire, he established his capital at Roluos. Instituted the linga cult of the god-king.	Ak Thom, Phnom Kulen, Banteay Chmar
JAYAVARMAN III (850-877)	
INDRAVARMAN I (877-889) Credited with presiding over the emergence of classical Khmer art. He also built the first baray (Lolei).	Bakong, Preah Ko
YASOVARMAN I (889-900) Built a new capital at Angkor called Yashodharapura.	Bakheng, Eastern Baray, Lolei
HARSHAVARMAN I (900-921)	Baksei Chamkrong, Prasat Kraven
ISHANAVARMAN II (c.921)	
JAYAVARMAN IV (921-941) Established his capital at Koh Ker, N of Angkor.	Prasat Thom
HASHAVARMAN II (941-944)	
RAJENDRAVARMAN (944-968) Moved the capital back to Angkor.	East Mebon, Pre Rup, started the Phimeanakas
JAYAVARMAN V (968-1001) **UDAYADITYAVARMAN I** (1001-1002)	Continued building the Phimeanakas

square moat – more than 5 km in length – and a high, galleried wall, which is covered in epic bas-reliefs and has four ceremonial tower gateways. The main gateway faces W and the temple is approached by a 475m-long road, built along a causeway, which is lined with naga balustrades (representing the rainbow bridge between heaven and earth). There are small rectangular barays on either side of the roadway. To either side of the balustrades are two isolated buildings, thought to have been libraries – there are two more pairs of them within the temple precincts on the first and second terraces.

At the far end of the causeway stands a **cruciform platform**, guarded by stone lions, from which the devaraja may have held audiences; his backdrop being the three-tiered central sanctuary. It is entered through the colonnaded processional gateway of the outer gallery. The transitional enclosure beyond it is again cruciform in shape. Its four quadrants formed galleries, once stocked full of statues of the Buddha. Only a handful of the original 1,000-odd images remain. Each gallery also had a basin which would originally have contained water for priests' ritual ablution. The second terrace, which is also square, rises from behind the Gallery of a Thousand Buddhas. It has a tower at each corner.

The cluster of central towers, 12m above the second terrace, is reached by 12 steep stairways, which represent the precipitous slopes of Mt Meru. The five lotus flower-shaped sandstone towers – the first appearance of these

SURYAVARMAN I (1002-1050) The influence of Mahayana Buddhism spread; Buddhist sculpture became more common at Angkor.	Added to the Phimeanakas, Grand Plaza, N and S Kleangs, Ta Keo, Royal Enclosure, Terrace of the Elephants, Western Baray
UDAYADITAVARMAN II (1050-1066)	Baphuon, finished the Western Baray
HARSHAVARMAN III (1066-1080),	
JAYAVARMAN VI (1080-1107)	Phimai (Thailand), Preah Vihear, Wat Phou (Laos)
DHARANINDRAVARMAN I (1107-1113)	
SURYAVARMAN II (1131-1150)	Angkor Wat, Chan Say Tevoda, Banteay Samre, Thommanon
DHARANINDRAVARMAN II (c 1160)	
YASOVARMAN II (1160-1165)	
TRIBHUVANADITYAVARMAN (1165-1177)	
JAYAVARMAN VII (1181-1218)	Angkor Thom, Bayon, Banteay Kdei, Preah Neak Pean, Preah Khan, Preah Palilay, Ta Prohm, Terrace of the Leper King, Sras Srang, Sras Srei, Ta Som, added to Banteay Chmar
INDRAVARMAN II (c.1200-1243)	
JAYAVARMAN VIII (1243-1295)	

features in Khmer architecture – are believed to have once been covered in gold. The eight-storey towers are square, although they appear octagonal, and give the impression of a sprouting bud. Above the ascending tiers of roofs – each jutting gable has an elaborately carved pediment – the tower tapers into a circular roof. The towers are dominated by the central one, the Siva shrine and principal sanctuary, whose pinnacle rises more than 30m above the third level; 55m above ground level. This sanctuary would have contained an image of Siva in the likeness of King Suryavarman II, as it was his temple-mountain. But it is now a Buddhist shrine and contains statues of the Buddha. The steps leading up to the third level are worn and very steep. On the S side the steps have a hand rail.

The temple's greatest sculptural treasure is its 2m high **bas-reliefs**, around the walls of the outer gallery. It is the longest continuous bas-relief in the world. In some areas traces of the paint and gilt that once covered the carvings can still be seen. Most famous are the hundreds of figures of devatas and apsaras in niches along the walls. The apsaras – the celestial women – are modelled on the god-king's own bevy of bare-breasted beauties, and the sculptors' attention to detail provides an insight into the world of 12th century haute couture. Their hair is often knotted on the crown and bejewelled – although all manner of wild and exotic coiffures are depicted. Jewelled collars and hip-girdles also are common and bracelets worn on the upper arms. Sadly many of the apsaras have been removed in recent years.

The bas-reliefs narrate stories from the Ramayana and Mahabharata, as well as legends of Vishnu, and are reminiscent of Pallava and Chola art in SE India. Pious artisans and peasants were probably only allowed as far as Angkor Wat's outer gallery, where they could admire the bas-reliefs and pay hommage to the god-king. In the open courtyards, statues of animals enliven the walls. Lions stand on guard beside the staircases. There were supposed to be 300 of them in the original building. Part of the bas-reliefs were hit by shrapnel in 1972, and some of its apsaras were used for target practice.

Anti-clockwise round Angkor Wat's bas reliefs

1. West gallery, southern half represents a scene from the Mahabharata of a battle between the Pandavas (with pointed headdresses, attacking from the right) and the Kauravas. The 2 armies come from the 2 ends of the panel and meet in the middle. **NB:** The larger the figure the more important the person. The SW corner has been badly damaged – some say by the Khmer Rouge – but shows scenes from Vishnu's life.

2. South gallery, western half depicts Suryavarman II (builder of Angkor Wat) leading a procession. He is riding a royal elephant, giving orders to his army before leading them into battle against the Chams. The rank of the army officers is indicated by the number of umbrellas. The undisciplined, outlandishly dressed figures are the Thais helping the Khmers in battle against the Chams.

3. South gallery, eastern half was restored in 1946, it depicts the punishments and rewards one can expect in the after life. The damned, depicted in the bottom row, are in for a rough ride: the chances of their being savaged by wild animals, seized by demons or having their tongues pulled out (or any combination thereof) are quite high. The blessed, depicted in the upper two rows, are borne along in palanquins surrounded by large numbers of bare breasted apsaras.

4. Eastern gallery, southern half is the best-known part of the bas-relief – the churning of the sea of milk by gods and demons to make ambrosia (the nectar of the gods which gives immortality). In the centre, Vishnu commands the operation. Below are sea animals (cut in half by the churning close to the pivot) and above, apsaras. Shortly before Cambodia collapsed into civil war in 1970, French archaeologists, who were repairing the roof and columns of the E gallery dismantled the structure. Because they were unable to finish the job, the finest bas-reliefs have been left open to the elements.

5. Eastern gallery, northern half – this unfinished section represents a war between the gods for the possession of the ambrosia. The gate in the centre of the E gallery was used by Khmer royalty and dignitaries for mounting and dismounting elephants.

6. North gallery represents a war between gods and demons. Siva is shown in meditation with Ganesh, Brahma and Krishna. Most of the other scenes are from the Ramayana, notably the visit of Hanuman (the monkey god) to Sita.

7. Western gallery, northern half has another scene from the Ramayana depicting a battle between Rama and Ravana who rides on a chariot pulled by monsters and commands an army of giants.

In *Angkor Wat: Time, Space and Kingship*, University of Hawaii Press, 1996, Eleanor Mannikka suggests that in the original cubit units used in the construction of Angkor Wat the temple's dimensions embody a surprising amount of information. This includes the dates of King Suryavarman II's birth, his accession and important dates in the construction of the temple. In addition the buildings and statues are aligned with the solar equinox and solstice so as ritually to fuse Angkor with the movement of the heavenly bodies and harmonize this edifice with the revolving universe.

One of the great delights of Angkor,

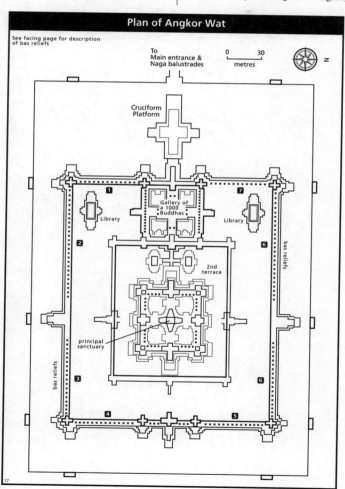

Plan of Angkor Wat

See facing page for description of bas reliefs

To Main entrance & Naga balustrades

0   30
metres

N

Cruciform Platform

1   7

Gallery of a 1000 Buddhas

Library   Library

2   6

bas reliefs

2nd terrace

principal sanctuary

bas reliefs

3   6

4   5

17

Angkor Wat
Source: Keane, AH (1909) *Asia*, volume 2, London: Edward Stanford

particularly at Angkor Wat, is the glorious trees. Huge tropical trees grow in Angkor's forests – a reminder of how much of Cambodia used to look. Driving in from town, the flat landscape is bare of trees but once inside the protected area wildlife flourishes. Arguably local fauna and flora have benefited more from the temple's protection than the antiquities have.

Outside the entrance to Angkor Wat is a selection of cafés and restaurants including the *Angkor Wat Restaurant* (rec) and souvenir shops.

EAST OF ANGKOR THOM

There are a close group of temples just outside the E gate of Angkor Thom. **Chau Say Tevoda**, built by Suryavarman II is the first temple outside the E gate and is dwarfed by Ta Keo. The temple is dedicated to Siva but many of the carvings are of Vishnu. It is similar in plan to **Thommanon**, next door, whose surrounding walls have completely disappeared, leaving only the gateways on the E and W ends and a ruined central tower. Originally both temples would have had a hall linked to the central tower, and enclosing walls with elaborate gateways. A library, to the S-E, is the only other building in the complex. There are repeated pediments above the doorways, which are more elaborate than those at Angkor Wat.

Ta Keo, begun during Jayavarman V's reign and left unfinished, stands E of the Royal Palace and just off the Avenue of Victory. The pyramid-temple rises over 50m: its five tower shrines are supported on a five-tiered pyramid. This temple was one of the first to be entirely built of sandstone. Previous tower sanctuaries had entrances only on the E side, but Ta Keo has openings on all four sides. It was originally surrounded by a moat.

The temple of **Ta Prohm**, to the S of Ta Keo, was consecrated in 1186 – 5 years after Jayavarman VII seized power. It

Useful place names	
Banteay Kdei	បន្ទាយក្ដី
East Mebon	មេបុណ្យខាងកើត
Eastern Baray	ប្រាយខាងកើត
Preah Khan	ព្រះខ័ន
Preah Neak Pean	ព្រះនាគព័ន្ធ
Srah Srang	ស្រះស្រង់
Ta Prohm	តាព្រហ្ម
Ta Som	តាសោម
West Mebon	មេបុណ្យខាងលិច
Western Baray	ប្រាយខាងលិច

was built to house the divine image of the Queen Mother. It underwent many transformations and an inscription gives detailed information on the complex. It contained 39 sanctuaries or prasats, 566 stone dwellings and 288 brick dwellings. Ta Prohm functioned as a monastery which was home to 18 abbots and 2,740 monks. By the 12th century, temples were no longer exclusively places of worship – they also had to accommodate monks, so roofed halls were increasingly built within the complexes. According to contemporary inscriptions, the temple required 79,365 people for its upkeep and relied on the income of 3,140 villages. The list of property it owned was on an equally impressive scale: it included 523 parasols, 35 diamonds, and 40,620 pearls. Ta Prohm is one of the most beautiful temples in the area, as it has been relatively untouched since it was discovered and retains much of its mystery.

For all would-be Mouhots and closet Indiana Joneses, Ta Prohm is the perfect lost-temple-in-the-jungle: unlike most of the other monuments at Angkor, it has been only minimally cleared of its undergrowth, fig trees and creepers. It is widely regarded as one of Angkor's most enchanting temples. The French writer Elie Lauré wrote: "With its millions of knotted limbs, the forest embraces the ruins with a violent love".

The massive complex of **Banteay Kdei** is 3 km E of Angkor Thom and just to the SE of Ta Prohm. Some archaeologists think it may be dedicated to Jayavarman VII's religious teacher. It is a crowded collection of towers and connecting galleries on a flat plan, surrounded by a galleried enclosure. No inscriptions have been found here to indicate either its name or purpose, but it is almost certainly a Buddhist temple built in the 12th century, about the same time as Ta Prohm. The central tower was never finished. The artificial lake next to Banteay Kdei is called **Srah Srang** – 'the Pool of Ablutions' – which was doubtless used for ritual bathing. The steps down to the water face the rising sun and are flanked with lions and nagas.

Prasat Kravan, built in 921, means 'Cardamom Sanctuary' and is unusual in that it is built of brick. By that time brick had been replaced by laterite and sandstone. It consists of a row of five brick towers arranged in a line. In the central sanctuary is a bas-relief portrait of Vishnu and on the inner wall of the N tower his consort Lakshmi. In the early 10th century temples were commissioned by individuals other than the king; Prasat Kravan is one of the earliest examples.

Pre Rup, constructed in laterite with brick prasats, marks the centre of the royal city built by Rajendravarman (just NE of Srah Srang). Built in 961, it is larger and higher than its predecessor, the East Mebon, which it closely resembles. An important innovation at Pre Rup and East Mebon is that the sanctuary at the top is no longer a single tower – it is a group of five towers and is surrounded by smaller towers on the outer, lower levels. This more complicated plan reached its final development at Angkor Wat 150 years later. The group of five brick towers were originally elaborately decorated with plaster, but most of it has now fallen off. The shrine has fine lintels and columns on its doorways. Its modern name means 'turning the body' and, according to local legend, it is named after a cremation ritual in which the outline of a body was traced in the cinders one way and then the other.

The **Eastern Baray** – or Baray Orientale – was built by Yasovarman I and fed by the Siem Reap River. The four corners are marked by stelae. In the middle of the Eastern Baray, the flamboyant five towers of the **East Mebon** were finished in 952. Rajendravarman seems to have followed the Roluos trend and dedicated East Mebon to his parents. The East Mebon and Pre Rup were the last monuments in plaster and brick; they mark the end of a Khmer architectural epoch. The Siem Reap River is said to have been diverted while the temple was built: it is now dry.

NORTH OF ANGKOR THOM

Northeast of the walled city of Angkor Thom, about 3.5 km from the Bayon, is the rambling 12th century complex of **Preah Khan**. It was Jayavarman VII's first capital before Angkor Thom was completed and means 'Fortunate City of Victory'. It is similar in ground-plan to Ta Prohm (see page 131) but great attention was paid to the approaches: its E and W entrance avenues leading to ornamental causeways are lined with carved-stone boundary posts.

Holes in the inner walls of the central sanctuary of Preah Khan, suggest they may once have been decorated with brass plates – an obvious target for looters. The temple was built to shelter the statue of Jayavarman VII's father, Dharanindravarman II, in the likeness of Bodhisattva Avatokitsvara. The complex includes a 2-storey columnar pavilion and a generously sized hall built to accommodate the king's dancers – unusual Khmer architectural extras. A stele was discovered at the site glorifying the builder, Jayavarman VII and detailing what it took to keep the place ticking over. The inventory mentions

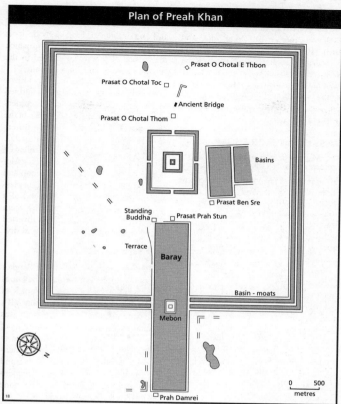

Plan of Preah Khan

Prasat O Chotal E Thbon

Prasat O Chotal Toc

Ancient Bridge

Prasat O Chotal Thom

Basins

Prasat Ben Sre

Standing Buddha

Prasat Prah Stun

Terrace

Baray

Basin - moats

Mebon

0   500
metres

Prah Damrei

that for Preah Khan's upkeep, it required the services of 97,840 men and women, 444 chefs, 4,606 footmen and 2,298 servants. A dharmasala (or resting house for monks) has been recently discovered at the site. The World Monuments Fund (WMF) has built a vernacular-style reception centre inside the W entrance of Preah Khan. Brochures and some guide books to Angkor are available. During the dry season, the WMF, based in New York, undertakes archaeological site conservation activities here.

To the E of Preah Khan and N of the Eastern Baray are two more Buddhist temples built by Jayavarman VII: **Preah Neak Pean** (the westernmost one) and the ruins of **Ta Som**. The exquisite temple of Neak Pean is also a fountain, built in the middle of a pool and representing the paradisiacal Himalayan mountain-lake, Anaavatapta, from Hindu mythology. It is a small sanctuary on an island in the baray of Preah Khan. Two nagas form the edge of the island, and their tails join at the back. In modern Khmer it is known as the *Prea-sat neac pon* – the 'tower of the intertwined dragons'. The colossal image of the horse is the compassionate Bodhisattva who is supposed to save sailors from drowning. The temple pools were an important part of the aesthetic experience of Preah Khan and Neak Pean – the ornate stone carving of both doubly visible by reflection. Such basins within a temple complex were used for religious ritual, while the larger moats and barays were used for practical purposes of bathing, transport and possibly for irrigation.

WEST OF ANGKOR THOM

The **Western Baray** was built by Udayadi-tavarman II, possibly to increase the size of the irrigated farmlands. In the centre, on an island, is the **West Mebon**, where the famous bronze statue of Vishnu was discovered (now in the National Museum at Phnom Penh, see page 90). Today, the eastern end of the Western Baray is dry but the scale remains astonishing, more than 2 km across and 9 km long. Boats can be hired from the beach on the S of the Weston Baray. *Getting there*: take Highway 6 W, about 3 km W of the airport turning a track leads N. 4 km from Highway 6 to Western Baray.

Just S of the Western Baray is **Ak Thom**, which marks the site of Jayavarman II's earlier city. It is the oldest surviving temple in the Angkor region and although little remains, it is worth a visit. The central towers are constructed mostly of brick, with some stone features. The bricks were cemented together with a mortar of vegetable sap, palm sugar and termite soil.

OUTLYING TEMPLES

Depending on the political situation, transport availability and the state of the roads, it is possible to visit some of the other ancient Khmer sites dotted around the main temples at Angkor. Most of these temples can be reached by motos (motorbike taxi). It is reported that the years of war took a heavy toll on many of these monuments. **Beware** These areas tend to be mined.

Useful place names	
Bakong	ប្រាគង់
Banteay Chmar	បន្ទាយឆ្មា
Banteay Samre	បន្ទាយសំរែ
Banteay Srei	បន្ទាយស្រី
Beng Mealea	បឹងមាលា
Koh Ker	កោះកែរ
Kompong Chhnang	កំពង់ឆ្នាំង
Lolei	លលៃ
Phnom Krom	ភ្នំក្រោម
Phnom Kulen	ភ្នំគូលេន
Prasat Thom	ប្រាសាទធំ
Preah Ko	ព្រះគោ
Preah Vihear	ព្រះវិហារ
Siem Reap	សៀមរាប
Tonle Sap	ទន្លេសាប

SOUTH-EAST

The **Roluos Group**, some 16 km E, is worth visiting if time permits. Jayavarman II built several capitals including one at Roluos, at that time called Hari-haralaya. This was the site of his last city and remained the capital during the reigns of his three successors. The three remaining Hindu sanctuaries at Roluos are **Preah Ko**, **Bakong** and **Lolei**. They were finished in 879, 881 and 893 respectively by Indravarman I and his son Yashovarman I and are the best-preserved of the early temples.

All three temples are built of brick, with sandstone doorways and niches. The use of human figures as sculptural decoration in religious architecture developed around this time – examples of these guardian spirits can be seen in the niches of Preah Ko and Lolei. Other sculptured figures which appear in the

Roluos group are the crouching lion, the reclining bull (Nandi – Siva's mount) and the naga (snake). The gopura – an arched gateway leading to the temple courtyards – was also a contemporary innovation in Roluos. Libraries – used for the storage of sacred manuscripts – also appeared for the first time, as did the concentric enclosures surrounding the central group of towers. Preah Ko and Lolei have characteristics in common: for example, both were dedicated to the parents and grandparents of the kings who built them. Neither temple has a pyramid centre like Bakhong as the pyramid temples were built exclusively for kings.

Preah Ko, meaning 'sacred ox', was named after the three statues of Nandi (the mount of the Hindu god, Siva) which stand in front of the temple. Orientated E-W, there is a cluster of six towers arranged in two rows on a low platform. The front row of towers was devoted to Indravarman's male ancestors and the second row to the female. The ancestors were represented in the image of a Hindu god. Only patches remain of the once-magnificent stucco relief work, including a remnant of a kala – a motif also found on contemporary monuments in Java.

Indravarman's temple-mountain, **Bakong**, is a royal five-stepped pyramid temple with a sandstone central tower built on a series of successively receding terraces with surrounding brick towers. It may have been inspired by Borobudur in Java. Indravarman himself was buried in the temple. The central tower was built to replace the original one when the monument was restored in the 12th century and is probably larger than the original. The Bakong denotes the true beginning of classical Khmer architecture and contained the god-king's Siva lingam. The most important innovations of Indravarman's artists are the free-standing sandstone statues – such as the group of three figures, probably depicting the king with his two wives, who are represented as Siva with Uma and Ganga. The heads of all the figures are now missing but the simplicity of the sculpture is nonetheless distinctive; it is a good example of early Khmer craftsmanship. The statues are more static and stockier than the earlier statues of Chenla. There is now a Buddhist monastery in the grounds – originally it was dedicated to Siva.

Lolei was built by Yashovarman I in the middle of Indravarman's baray. The brick towers were dedicated to the king's ancestors, but over the centuries they have largely disintegrated; hardly any of the decoration remains.

SOUTH

On top of **Phnom Krom**, 12 km S of Siem Reap, is an 11th century temple overlooking the Tonlé Sap. Many of the statues have disappeared.

The **Tonlé Sap**, the Great Lake of Cambodia, is one of the natural wonders of Asia. Uniquely, the 100 km-long Tonlé Sap River, a tributary of the mighty Mekong, reverses its flow and runs uphill for 6 months of the year. Spring meltwaters in the Himalayas, coupled with seasonal rains, increase the flow of the Mekong to such an extent that some is deflected up the Tonlé Sap River. From Jun the lake begins to expand until, by the end of the rainy season, it has increased in area ten-fold and in depth by some 12m. At its greatest extent, the lake occupies nearly a seventh of Cambodia's land area, around 1.5 million ha, making it the largest freshwater lake in Southeast Asia. From Nov, with the onset of the dry season, the Tonlé Sap River reverses its flow once more and begins to act like a regular tributary – flowing downhill into the Mekong. By Feb the lake has shrunk to a fraction of its wet season size and covers 'just' 300,000 ha.

This pattern of expansion and contraction has three major benefits. First, it helps to restrict flooding in the Mekong Delta in Vietnam. Second, it forms the basis for a substantial part of Cambodia's rice production. And third, it supports perhaps the world's largest and richest inland fisheries, yielding as much as 10 tonnes of fish per sq km. It is thought that 4 million people depend on the lake for their subsistence and 3 out of every 4 kg of fish caught in the country come from the Tonlé Sap.

Because of the dramatic changes in the size of the lake some of the fish, such as the 'walking catfish', have evolved to survive several hours out of water, flopping overland to find deeper pools. These *hok yue* – or elephant fish – are renowned as a delicacy well beyond Cambodia's borders. Large-scale commercial fishing is a major occupation during Feb to May and the fishing grounds are divided into plots and leased out. Although recent lack of dredging means the lake is not as deep as it was and fish are tending to swim downstream into the Mekong and Tonlé Sap rivers. The annual flooding covers the surrounding countryside with a layer of moist, nutrient-rich mud – which is ideal for rice-growing. Farmers grow a deepwater rice, long-stalked and fast growing – it grows with the rising lake to keep the grain above water and the stem can be up to 6m long. The lake also houses people and communities live in floating villages close to the shore. **Kompong Chhnang**, near the lake, is an important fishing village and a local hub for water transport, also known for its pottery. Boats for trips around the lake

---

The survival of the Tonlé Sap

The Tonlé Sap is not just any lake. It is, in many respects, the heart of Cambodia. It controls the flow of the Mekong, it is the largest body of freshwater in Southeast Asia, a large slice of the Cambodian rice crop depends on its unique annual cycle of flood and retreat, and it is thought to contribute three out of every four kilograms of fish caught in the country. So when scientists start to warn of an environmental catastrophe in the making, people sit up and take notice.

Some scholars maintain that the lake is silting up at an unprecedented rate, that fish stocks are declining as it is exploited at an unsustainable rate, and that the banks of the lake are eroding due to uncontrolled deforestation. King Sihanouk and many environmentalists would like it designated a World Heritage Site. This would protect it from development and also prevent many of the planned dams on the rivers that feed the lake from going ahead. This, of course, is why many people in the government oppose putting it forward for World Heritage Site status. They fear that it would hobble attempts at modernizing Cambodia's economy. They say that the doom-mongers have exaggerated the threat facing the lake. In particular they point to claims that the lake is silting up at a rate of 4 cm a year. This is based on a 10-year French study and report on the lake by Carbonnel published in 1963. In the report, Carbonnel stated that the lake was silting up at a rate of 0.04 cm a year. Misunderstanding the French use of the comma in place of the decimal point, this was taken to mean 4 cm a year. Apparently no one really knows what is happening in the lake. They can only guess at the rate of siltation, and as for what would be a sustainable fish yield, this is open to a huge margin of error. Cautious environmentalists might say that this is all the more reason to be careful; modernizers use it as a pretext to go ahead with their grandiose plans.

can be hired from fisheries police (fee negotiable) and from Chong Khneas (see page 141) US$5 per hr.

The Tonlé Sap is said by some scientists to be facing an ecological calamity. Excessive forest clearance has undermined the annual cycle of renewal described above. The lake's level is lower than it has been for decades, and the life-giving inflow of silt which is so critical to the success of the fishing industry and rice cultivation, is much reduced due to excessive logging upstream.

EAST

Banteay Samre, further to the E, around ½ km past the E end of the East Baray.

It is a Hindu temple dedicated to Vishnu, although reliefs decorating some of the frontons (the triangular areas above arches) portray Buddhist scenes. It is thought to have been built by Suryavarman II and has many characteristics of Angkor Wat such as stone-vaulted galleries and a high central tower. The bas reliefs are in fine condition.

NORTH

Banteay Srei is further away, about 25 km N of Angkor, but is well worth the trip. It was built by the Brahmin tutor to King Rajendravarman, Yajnavaraha, grandson of Harshavarman (900-921), and founded in 967. Covered terraces, of

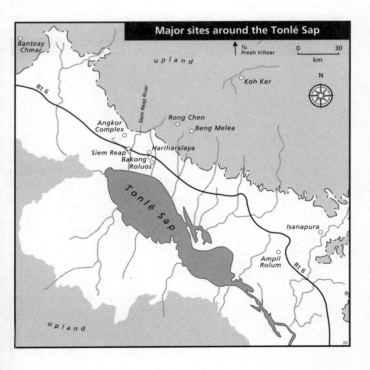

Major sites around the Tonlé Sap

which only the columns remain, once lined both sides of the primary entrance (East). The layout was inspired by Prasat Thom at Koh Ker (see below). Three beautifully carved tower-shrines stand side by side on a low terrace in the middle of a quadrangle, with a pair of libraries on either side enclosed by a wall. Two of the shrines were dedicated to Vishnu and Siva, and both had libraries close by, with carvings depicting appropriate legends. The whole temple is dedicated to Brahma. Beyond this inner group of buildings was a monastery surrounded by a moat. One of the best-known statues from this site is a sculpture of Siva, sitting down and holding his wife, Uma, on his knee: it is in the National Museum of Arts in Phnom Penh (see page 90).

Having been built by a Brahmin priest, the temple was never intended for use by a king, which goes some way towards explaining its small size – you have to duck to get through the doorways to the sanctuary towers. Surprisingly, though, it contains some of the finest examples of Khmer sculpture. Finely carved and rare pink sandstone replaces the plaster-coated carved-brick decoration, typical of earlier temples. All the buildings are covered in carvings: the jambs, the lintels, the balustered windows. Banteay Srei's ornamentation is exceptional – its roofs, pediments and lintels are magnificently carved with tongues of flame, coiling serpents' tails, gods, demons and floral garlands. **NB** It was at Banteay Srei that an American tourist was killed at the end of 1994 by the Khmers Rouges. Visitors wishing to see Banteay Srei must first contact the Governor's office in Siem Reap for permission. The police will probably insist upon sending an armed guard, sadly no guarantee of safety. Several illegal visits to Banteay Srei have been made: without untoward consequences, but it is definitely **not** recommended.

Andre Malraux, who wrote the novel *The royal way* (1930) attempted to pillage Banteay Srei of its treasures. He apparently read in an issue of the *Bulletin de l'Ecole Francaise d'Extreme Orient* that the temple not only contained a series of brilliant carvings in excellent condition but also that the temple was unexcavated. Taking 'unexcavated' to mean 'abandoned', and assuming that it was then also unclaimed, he set out for Cambodia with a friend to loot the temple. He arrived in Cambodia, travelled to Angkor and proceeded to cut out one tonne of the finest statues and bas reliefs. Fortunately, he was arrested trying to leave the country with the treasures and was sentenced to 3 years in prison (a term that he did not serve).

Phnom Kulen – or Mt Mohendrapura – 28 km NE of Angkor and 48 km from Siem Reap, is a sandstone plateau considered sacred by the Khmers. The site is the mythical birthplace of the Cambodian Kingdom. At the hill's summit is the largest reclining Buddha in the country – over 900 years old. Jayavarman II built his first brick pyramid temple mountain – to house the sacred golden Siva-lingam – here at the beginning of the 9th century. Today the temple is only visible in fragments although, over a millennium later, the phallic emblem is said to be still on display in the Phnom Kulen complex. The temple is best known for its elaborately carved lintels and bas reliefs. There are also some remains of 9th century Cham temples in the area. Today the hill is clothed in forest, and the nights here are cold and the days fresh and invigorating. Given that the area, until recently, was under Khmers Rouges control (see below) it is likely that the remains have suffered accordingly. Cutting through the area is the holy **River of a Thousand Lingas**. Cut into the sandstone bed of this river are some 1,000 lingas. Finnish journalist Teppo Turkki who visited the site for the *Phnom Penh Post* wrote at the beginning of 1995: "The lingas, some of which date back to the 9th century, are about 25 cm square and 10 cm deep and lined in a perfect grid pattern. The river runs over them, covering them with about 5 cm of pristine water." He continues: "The holy objects are designed to create a 'power path' for the Khmer kings." Further downstream, larger blocks of stone, also under water, are carved with apsaras, vishnus, and other figures. Altogether a wondrous and magical place. Note that until the beginning of 1995, Phnom Kulen was under the control of the Khmers Rouges and there are still occasional skirmishes in the area, so whether the site is open to visitors is far from clear. However, in Feb, a group of reporters were allowed to visit the area, and it is said to be being made ready for a pilgrimage trip by King Sihanouk.

Beng Mealea, a huge 12th century temple complex, 40 km E of the Bayon and about 7 km SE of Phnom Kulen, is completely ruined even though it was built at about the same time as Angkor Wat. Its dimensions are similar, but Beng Mealea has no central pyramid. Most of the Buddhist temples built under Jayavarman VII – Preah Khan, Banteay Kdei, Ta Som and Ta Prohm – were modelled after this complex.

Well over 100 km to the NE of Angkor, on the Thai border, is **Preah Vihear** (or Prasat Phra Viharn), which dates from the beginning of the 11th century but was added to by Suryavarman II. The temple dominates the plain from its prominent position in the Dangrek Mountains at an altitude of more than 700m and was only returned to Cambodia by a ruling of the International Court of Justice in the Hague in 1963 (previously it was occupied by the Thais). It is only possible to reach this temple from Thailand.

At the beginning of 1995 the Cambodian government appeared to be preparing to take the Preah Vihear temple complex from the Khmers Rouges. The temple's position at the summit of an escarpment means that it is most easily approached from Thai territory. The slopes of the escarpment are also strewn with mines. Whether the Thais will allow the Cambodian government to mount an assault through Thai territory is unclear. Many in Cambodia still feel that the Thai government and army offer support to the Khmers Rouges. In any case, the Khmers Rouges commander defending the capital is likely to be the feared, one-legged warrior, Ta Mok. The preferred option appears to be to starve the rebels into surrender or defection: in Mar about 3,000 Cambodian army men were dug in around the temple complex facing perhaps just 100 Khmers Rouges fighters.

Also to the NE, but closer to Angkor, is **Koh Ker**, the site of the old capital of Jayavarman IV. The main ruin here is **Prasat Thom**. Its surrounding land was irrigated by baray, similar to but smaller than, the ones at Angkor.

Banteay Chmar, 61 km from Sisophon and to the NW of Angkor was one of the capitals of Jayavarman II. It was rebuilt by Jayavarman VII and dedicated to his son and four generals who were killed in battle repelling a Cham invasion in 1177. Banteay Chmar, because of its secluded location, is rarely visited. This remoteness has made the temple particularly vulnerable to looting, and in Jul 1994 valuable 12th century carvings were stolen from the site. Local officials say that Cambodian army units were involved in the looting, using trucks to pull statues from their pedestals and then transport them the short 30 mins journey across the Thai border for sale.

SITE INFORMATION

● **Tours**

Tours can be organized in Cambodia through **Phnom Penh Tourism**, **General Directorate of Tourism (GDT)**, **Diethelm Travel**, and **Apsara** (see page 223 for details). Diethelm inclusive tours cost US$315 for 2 days. There are 6 flights daily to Siem Reap (US$110 return plus US$10 aiport tax) the first flight leaves at 0645 and one or two others follow at 10-min

Angkor and Siem Reap and the forces of Modernity

Over the last year or two, control of Angkor has been the subject of a power struggle. In 1995 the Ministry of Culture and Arts lost control of the temples in favour of a newly constituted conservation and tourism agency, APSARA. Headed by the two deputy prime ministers, APSARA is responsible not only for the antiquities but also for the creation of a 1,000 ha 'tourism zone' designed to accommodate the projected 1 million annual visitors that are expected in the new century.

Given Angkor's tourist potential the authorities have decided to create a tourist town away from Siem Reap in order to prevent the latter from being 'destroyed completely' by tourism. Large international style hotels are planned and the Vice President of APSARA, Vanh Moulyvann, flew to Bali to see how the authorities there had managed to corral tourists within the Nusa Dua complex. On his return he announced that the anodyne Balinese experiment had been a 'beautiful success'. Whether Malaysian investors YTL Corp are the right people for the job is subject to debate. Eleanor Mannikka, who has spent 20 years researching Angkor, is alarmed at YTL's proposals for a nightly sound and light entertainment within the precincts of Angkor Wat. The developer trumpets that it will be 'the greatest show on earth' while Mannikka is concerned about the selling of Angkor by entrepreneurs whose main aim is to make as much money as they can. She condemns the project as the 'prostitution' of Angkor Wat. Others have argued that while damage to the stones may be minimal, the monumental themes of dynastic and popular history that have been played out in this setting for hundreds of years would be trivialized in a Hollywood-style entertainment. Whatever the outcome of this debate Angkor is increasingly accessible to foreign visitors and will no doubt see changes over the coming few years as dramatic as any in the past few centuries.

intervals, but day tours allow only 3 hrs sightseeing before the return flight leaves for Phnom Penh. It takes at least 2 days to see Angkor's temples properly, preferably three. **Angkor Tourism** hires out cars and drivers. The larger the group the cheaper the tour pp. Tours ask for a single room surcharge. Tour agencies in Siem Reap offer tours to outlying temples, eg *Eurasie* (opposite Pra Chea Chun Hospital).

● **Guides**

Guides are generally well trained by *Angkor Conservation*. Guides will explain the history of the temples as well as the best way to get around them. Numerous self-appointed, but generally knowledgeable, guides meet all the flights from Phnom Penh. Similarly, every hotel has its own collection of guides. An English speaking moto driver with a good knowledge of Angkor normally costs US$7/day. For car and guide expect to pay US$20/day. At each temple there are numerous children who will escort you around for a small fee.

● **Cost**

Temple fees: 1 day pass US$20, 2 or 3-day pass US$40, 4-7 days US$60. Entry is free after 1715. A number of local guides and hotels are running a scam whereby tickets are being recycled. Needless to say none of the proceeds go to the upkeep of the monuments. Visitors should insist on buying their tickets from the official office leading into the temples not from a hotel in Siem Reap. Keep your ticket after you leave so that it is not recycled (your guide may ask for the ticket). It should be said that some people believe more benefit accrues to the local area through these fraudulent tickets than through the real thing. As one guide put it, "At least the money is going here and not into some Swiss bank account". The assumption is that a large hunk of the entrance fees are syphoned off.

● **Local transport**

There is no public transport around the sights. All transport for day trips is organized through **Phnom Penh Tourism** and organized tour companies and is usually included in the tour price. **Car hire**: from **Angkor Tourism** US$40/day with driver, plus US$20 for guide. Independent car and guide US$20/day. Moped taxis are also available. **Motorbikes**: from guesthouses (US$5-7/day). **NB** It is illegal to hire a motorbike without a driver.

● **Circuits of the Temples**
There are 3 so-called 'circuits'. The **Petit Circuit** takes in the main, central temples including Angkor Wat, Bayon, Baphuon and the Terrace of the Elephants. The **Grand Circuit** takes a wider route, including smaller temples like Ta Prohm, East Mebon and Neak Pean. The **Roluos Group Circuit** ventures further afield still, taking in the temples near Roluos – Lolei, Preah Ko and Bakong.

● **Safety**
All the temples are guarded. However, though obvious, the security presence is not oppressive. Land mines have been planted on some outlying paths to prevent Khmers Rouges guerrillas from infiltrating the temples. They are more likely to be buried in the environs of the outer temples. The guides know which areas are dangerous. **Stick to well used paths**.

● **Snakes**
Be especially wary of snakes in the dry season. The very poisonous *Hanuman snake* – which is a lurid green colour – is fairly common in the area. There are also certain varieties of *centipede* which can give a nasty bite.

● **Angkor Conservation**
Angkor Conservation is a specialist research institution, just off the main road to Angkor and about 1 km from the *Grand Hotel* (signed *Conservation d' Angkor*). Many statues, stelae and linga found at Angkor are stored here to prevent theft. Accessible by special appointment only. Contact the Ministry of Culture in Phnom Penh (see page 101) for a written invitation which needs to describe the research objectives of the visitor.

SIEM REAP

Before Cambodia's civil war, Siem Reap was a bustling town but it has been considerably damaged by the constant fighting. This area was strategic to both sides and was a battle ground for 20 years. However, the growth of tourism to Angkor may yet put Siem Reap back on its feet – certainly many new hotels have sprung up in the past year or so.

Siem Reap is seldom considered as anything other than a service centre for Angkor and it is true that without the temples, few people would ever find themselves here. But visitors exhausted by the temple trail might care to while away a morning or afternoon in Siem Reap itself.

Siem Reap is laid out formally and because there was ample land on which to build, the town is pleasantly airy. Buildings are often set in large overgrown grounds resembling mini-wildernesses. A fair proportion of the buildings, particularly on the road S to Tonlé Sap, are built of wood and raised off the ground on stilts. The distance from Siem Reap to the water's edge fluctuates by many kilometres; the highest water levels occur towards the end of Oct at the end of the wet season (see page 136).

Excursions

Siem Reap's **Crocodile Farm** is a few kilometres from town and the reptiles are bred for their skins. Once they have reached a certain size they are sold to agents in Thailand for around US$2,000 each. A rather sinister feature of this farm is that the Khmers Rouges are reputed to have fed their victims alive to the beasts. Admission 1,000 Riel. *Getting there*: by moto, a few km S of the centre of Siem Reap on the Tonlé Sap road.

Chong Khneas is 10 km S of Siem Reap. It consists of some permanent buildings but is a largely floating settlement. The majority of the population live in houseboats and most services, including police, health, international aid agency, retail and karaoke are all provided on water. Boats can be hired and trips to floating villages are offered. Expect to pay about US$5/hr. *Getting there*: moto from Siem Reap (US$1). Boats from Phnom Penh berth at Chong Khneas.

Local information
● Accommodation

Most hotels around Angkor did not survive the war intact but since 1991, some new hotels have been built whilst others have been upgraded. At the end of 1995 *Le Meridien* and *Four Seasons* both signed contracts to build large hotels but only the sites have been cleared so far. A plan mooted at around the same time was to create a special tourist enclave a few kilometres from town (rather like Nusa Dua on Bali, on which the idea is modelled) to protect local people from the corrosive effects of international tourism.

Many hotels are run by Thais. Most serve Thai, Khmer and European food and sometimes Vietnamese. There is a concentration of cheaper guesthouses near the *Bayon Restaurant*. The electricity supply is available 24 hrs a day, water supplies are similarly reliable. **NB** Telephone numbers listed here beginning 9 or 6 are for mobile phones and need 015 prefix.

A *Banteay Srei*, on the road on the way in from the airport, 2 km from town, T 913839, new, a/c, one of the most professionally managed places with reliable water and electricity supplies, restaurant with reasonably priced menu, rec; **A** *Ta Prohm*, T 911783, a/c, restaurant, satellite TV, pleasant aspect, overlooking small park and river, attracts groups from Angkor Tourism and Phnom Penh Tourism, upmarket for Siem Reap but plastic and modern, Bangkok Post available in lobby; **A-B** *Grand Hotel d'Angkor*, this used to be the place to stay, 1920s colonial splendour, it is now under renovation by the Raffles group of Singapore – at a reputed cost of US$30mn, given their work elsewhere – on the *Raffles* in Singapore and the *Strand* in Yangon – it will be very slick, very expensive, and rather charmless. The renovation programme began in Mar 1996, starting with the garden. A sign now reads "if you like our gardens wait until you see the hotel".

B *Angkor Village*, resort-style hotel with traditional wooden houses on stilts set in tropical gardens, French/Khmer restaurant, run by French/Khmer couple, rec; **B** *Baray*, Sangkat I (past *Grand Hotel* on right, on road to temples, before *Solid Rock Bar*), a/c, restaurant, 12 rm, prices negotiable; **B** *Bayon*, T 911769, further along the riverside road from *Bopha Angkor*, a/c, restaurant, room prices negotiable; **B** *Bopha Angkor*, situated next to river in fairly quiet street, T 911710, a/c, restaurant, rather tacky and overpriced, old rooms cheaper; **B** *Diamond*, Vithei Achasva Rd, T 910020, a/c, makeshift restaurant (serves breakfast in front of your villa), if no tourists in town half-price deals negotiable, opened '93, looks rather like motel with small villas; **B** *Golden Apsara*, Sivutha St, T 911292, a/c, clean; **B** *Hotel de La Paix*, Sivutha St, T 912322, a/c, restaurant, prices negotiable; **B** *Or Kan Sap* (behind *Grand*), a/c, no restaurant, fridge, mosquito net and big clean towels in every room, no English spoken, good bet as cheaper option; **B** *Prasat Sour*, Sivutha St, a/c, restaurant; **B-C** *Stung Siem Reap*, Wat Prom Rath St, T 914058, a/c, restaurant (even serves pizza and spaghetti), difficult to find, up a side street, but attractive old building, renovated but retains its character, nr a temple and in interesting part of town, rec.

C *Bakheng*, Sivutha St, a/c, 12 rm.

E *Apsara*, next to *Green House Kitchen*, clean and friendly, rooms with bathrooms, fans and mosquito nets; **E** *260 Guesthouse*, clean; **E** *Mom's Guesthouse*, 99 Wath Bo St (next to the *Bayon Restaurant*), T 914494, comes highly rec as a cheap place to stay, now has 10 rm, fan only; **E** *Smiley Guesthouse*, 19 Krom 1, T 631365, good food and advice, rec; **E** *Sun Rise Guesthouse*, 54 Sivutha St, rooms simple and clean, mosquito nets provided, clean bathrooms. Many travellers also rec **E** *Mahogany*, 593 Wat Bo St, T 630086, fan only, an attractive wooden building, friendly and helpful, car rental US$20/day, motorbike US$6/day.

● Places to eat

Menus translated into English may not be much more informative than the Khmer version: 'stomach cow ox pork water' is likely to remain a mystery.

Asian: ◆◆◆*Ta Prohm*, in *Ta Prohm Hotel*; ◆◆*Bayon*, nr guesthouses on Wath Bo St, serves excellent Thai food in a garden strung with fairy lights, welcoming, friendly service, delicious chicken curry and fish and seafood cooked in coconut; ◆◆*Green House Kitchen*, 6 St, on road to the airport, Khmer and Thai curries and soups; ◆*Arun*, opp bank of the river to tourist information, good Cambodian food; ◆*Bayon Chinese Restaurant*, Route 6 (E of the river on the road to the Roluos Group before the central market); *Diamond Hotel*, by the river, Thai dishes. ◆◆*Banteay Srei* (not the hotel of the same name) Airport Rd, 2 km from Siem Reap, good food.

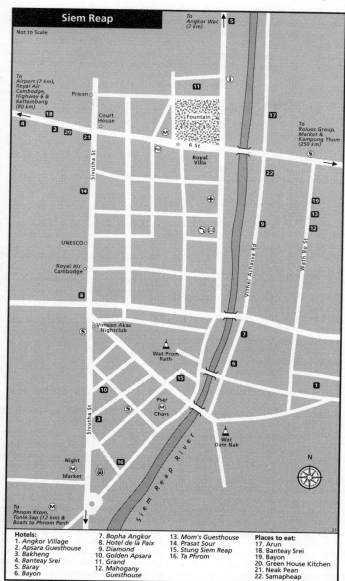

Siem Reap

Not to Scale

To Angkor Wat (7 km)

To Airport (7 km), Royal Air Cambodge, Highway 6 & Battambang (80 km)

Prison

Court House

Fountain

6 St

Royal Villa

To Roluos Group, Market & Kampong Thom (250 km)

UNESCO

Royal Air Cambodge

Sivutha St

Vimean Akas Nightclub

Wat Prom Rath

Vithei Achasva Rd

Wath Bo St

Psar Chars

Sivutha St

Night Market

Wat Dam Nak

Siem Reap River

N

To Phnom Krom, Tonlé Sap (12 km) & Boats to Phnom Penh

Hotels:
1. Angkor Village
2. Apsara Guesthouse
3. Bakheng
4. Banteay Srei
5. Baray
6. Bayon
7. Bopha Angkor
8. Hotel de la Paix
9. Diamond
10. Golden Apsara
11. Grand
12. Mahogany Guesthouse
13. Mom's Guesthouse
14. Prasat Sour
15. Stung Siem Reap
16. Ta Phrom

Places to eat:
17. Arun
18. Banteay Srei
19. Bayon
20. Green House Kitchen
21. Neak Pean
22. Samapheap

International: **Samapheap**, S of the *Grand Hotel* (just past the bridge), European, Chinese and Cambodian dishes; *Neak Pean*, opp courthouse, basic but cheap.

Foodstalls: on the main road S of the *Hotel de la Paix*, and on E bank of the river just N of the bridge on 6 St.

● **Airline offices**

Royal Air Cambodge, 362 6 St, on the right hand side of the road in from the airport, 0800-1200, 1400-1800 closed Sat pm and Sun, return flights need reconfirming but hotels will usually do this.

● **Entertainment**

Prassat Sonr, live music and dancing; *Nannow*, Taiwanese-owned karaoke bar.

● **Post & telecommunications**

Post Office and **Telephone**: (*Samart*), satellite telephone service, W side of Siem Reap River (between bridges – across from *Samapheap Restaurant*). A number of hotels and offices offer international telephone and fax services.

● **Shopping**

Gifts: there are small stalls at many of the main temples selling souvenirs.

Handicrafts: there are small stalls selling crafts at the main temple complexes and a good choice in the Psar Chars.

Markets: central market is approximately 1.5 km E of Siem Reap on Route 6 (towards the Roluos Group). It is now mainly oriented towards the Khmer housewife. Of greater interest to the overseas visitor is the new *Psar Chars* at the southern end of Siem Reap. Here a wide variety of Cambodian handicrafts is available. The surrounding streets are well provided with silver shops. The night market further S is interesting after dark.

● **Tour companies & travel agents**

Diethelm, 4 6 St, T 632888, F 963694; *Eurasie*, opp Pra Chea Chun hospital, organize day trips to Banteay Srei (US$80); *Paradise Angkor Wat Tours*, a short way N of 6 St E of the bridge, T 634128, F 963692.

● **Tourist offices**

Angkor Tourism, opp *Grand Hotel*.

● **Transport**

314 km N of Phnom Penh.

Local Cars with driver/guides: available from major hotels, US$25/day. Depending on the political climate, it may soon be possible to visit the Angkor temples directly from Thailand – just 150 km to the W – without going via Phnom Penh. **Minibus and car tours**: arranged by Angkor Tourism. **Motorbikes & bicycle hire**: US$5/day from guesthouses nr the market and *Grand Hotel*. **Pillion tours on bikes**: around the temples US$5-10/day (prices negotiable).

Air Airport is 7 km from Siem Reap and 4 km from Angkor. Round trips 7-8 times daily between Phnom Penh and Siem Reap (US$110 return). See domestic flight schedules on page 231 for details. Booking as early as possible during the tourist season is recommended. Military airport is next to the civilian one. Some visitors have hitched rides back to Phnom Penh on military transports – helicopters etc, US$40 one way. No regular schedule – just ask. **Transport to town**: motorbike taxis (US$1) or cars (US$8-10).

Train Forbidden.

Road Shared taxi: in the dry season only, 10 hrs (US$6), but start early.

Boat: boats upriver from Phnom Penh. Ask at **Ministry of Tourism** in Phnom Penh, **Bert's Books**, *Capitol Hotel*, or *FCCC*, 4-5 hrs in dry season 6 hrs in wet, US$25 one way. Daily departures. From the boat landing at Chong Khneas (Siem Reap), free (but long) rides on motos are provided by enterprising hotels keen for custom – otherwise US$1. Slow boats, 8-9 hrs, US$14, every other day and even slower boats which take 2 days. **NB** Boat travel is **not** recommended by western embassies or the Cambodian government and forbidden by most aid agencies. For those determined to go by boat take the biggest and fastest one going. "We took the boat in Jul 1996. We almost sank. The Tonlé Sap had a high water level and the weather was bad. Our boat was full of people and luggage. It was a nightmare for everybody. The boat had two 200 hp engines but it was an old boat, overloaded and too weak for the stormy sea. All the time we crashed against the waves. Suddenly water came into the boat. Engines cut out. Panic broke out. Children crying. We got life vests, but there wasn't enough for everybody and they were in poor condition. There were two holes in the boat where water came in. We made it to land about 50 km from Siem Reap".

North of Phnom Penh

KOMPONG CHAM

Kompong Cham is a lively port on the banks of the Mekong, and has some good examples of colonial architecture. **Wat Nokor**, not far from town, is a well preserved 13th century monument. At **Phnom Pros** and **Phnom Srei**, to the N are the foundations of two early temples, as well as five mass graves in which thousands of victims of the Khmers Rouges are buried.

South of Kompong Cham is **Preah Theat Preah Srei**, the former capital of the Chenla kingdom in the 8th century. **Preah Nokor** to the SE was another ancient Khmer capital in the 7th century.

● **Accommodation** D *Hotel Mekong*, on the river, some a/c, large rooms with bathrooms attached, pleasant balcony for watching life on the river. Several cheaper guesthouses (**E-F**), among them **D-E** *Monorom*, nr *Mekong Hotel*, a/c rooms and several fan rooms.

● **Transport Road Shared taxi**: regular connections with Phnom Penh from Olympic Market, 3 hrs (8,000 riel). **Sea Boat**: connections with Phnom Penh, 2 hrs for the express boat (US$8), 5/6 hrs for infrequent slow boat. Boats leave Phnom Penh from Sisowath Quay/106 St. Daily boats to Kratie leave at 0930, 2 hrs (US$8).

KRATIE AND AREA

Around the town of Kratie is the ancient capital of **Sambor**. The monuments are spread over an area of 1 sq km and were visited, in the mid-17th century, by Gerrit Van Wusthoff, the Dutch merchant-adventurer who also visited Laos. The most renowned stupa was built over the ashes of Princess Nucheat Khatr Vorpheak (who was killed by a crocodile in 1834) and the stupa became a pilgrimage site. Prince Sihanouk is supposed to have consulted a medium on matters of state here. Crocodiles are still supposed to inhabit the Mekong around Sambor. Below Sambor is the French colonial style town of Kratie and Kompong Cham, Cambodia's third largest city. It has

Useful place names	
Battambang	ព្រាត់ដំបង
Kompong Cham	កំពង់ចាម
Kompong Thom	កំពង់ធំ
Kratie	ក្រចេះ
Phnom Pros	ភ្នំប្រុស
Phnom Srei	ភ្នំស្រី
Prasat Sneng	ប្រាសាទស្នែង
Preah Nokor	ព្រះនគរ
Preah Srei	ព្រះ ស្រី
Sambor	សម្បូរណ៌
Sambor Preo Kuk	សម្បូរណ៌ ព្រៃគុក
Stung Treng	ស្ទឹងត្រែង
Wat Ek	វត្តឯក
Wat Nokor	វត្តនគរ

some good examples of shophouse architecture common in Cambodian riverside towns. Tobacco and rubber, introduced by the French, are important local crops. **Transport Road Shared taxi:** regular connections with Phnom Penh from Olympic Market, 8 hrs (US$5). **Sea Boat:** express connections with Phnom Penh, 5 hrs (US$14) or slower boats overnight (US$6), every 5-6 days.

STUNG TRENG

Stung Treng is a pretty town on the Mekong, only 40 km from Laos and a convenient stop-off on the way to Rattanakiri. The town has two busy, and interesting markets right next door to each other.

Excursions The area is renowned for its tribal people, the Montagnards.

- **Accommodation** E *Sekong*, a/c, hot water. There are also a couple of cheaper but more basic options.

- **Transport Local** It is possible to hire boats for trips along the Mekong (about US$5/hr). **Air** Connections 3 times a week with Phnom Penh (US$45). **Road Shared taxi:** regular connections with Phnom Penh, via Kratie where you can pick up shared taxis to Stung Treng 6 hrs, (US$4). **Sea Boat:** connections with Phnom Penh via Kratie, 4 days (US$15).

KOMPONG THOM and area

Approximately 35 km N of Kompong Thom is the important archaeological site of **Sambor Prei Kuk**, an ancient Chenla capital dating from the 7th century. The main temples are square or octagonal brick tower-shrines on high brick terraces with wonderful ornamentation in sandstone, especially the lintel stones. The idea of the jewel strings carved here is believed to be Indian in origin, as Indian donors used to literally hang their wealth on sacred trees or shrines. The temple in the group to the

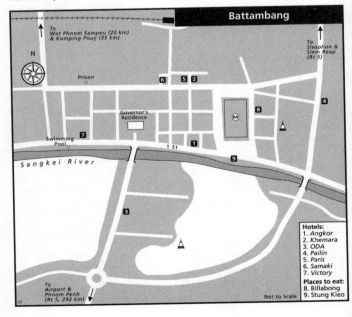

Battambang

To Wat Phnom Sampeu (20 km) & Komping Pouy (35 km)

To Sisophon & Siem Reap (Rt 5)

N

Prison

6 5 2

Governor's Residence

4

8

M

Swimming Pool

7

1 St

1

Sangkei River

9

3

To Airport & Phnom Penh (Rt 5, 292 km)

Not to Scale

Hotels:
1. Angkor
2. Khemara
3. ODA
4. Pailin
5. Paris
6. Samaki
7. Victory

Places to eat:
8. Billabong
9. Stung Kieo

S is supposed to have contained a golden lingam.

● **Accommodation** Guesthouse on the lake, contact Mrs Kao Cheng Hour.

● **Transport Road Shared taxi**: regular connections with Phnom Penh.

BATTAMBANG

Cambodia's second city, lies 40 km W of the Tonlé Sap, on the route to Bangkok. Since 1979 Battambang has profited enormously from contraband trade with Thailand; it was also heavily fought-over during the civil war. In the past, it was a bread-basket – or, more accurately, a rice-basket – but it is now better known for its fishing industry (run by the Chinese), jute sack factory, industry making fishing nets as well as its rubber and sulphur processing plants. Rice production has been severely disrupted by the civil war.

Wat Ek, 8 km N of Battambang, is an 11th century temple, built by Suryavar-man. Having been used by the Khmers Rouges as a prison, the temple has fallen into disrepair. The **Prasat Sneng** temples, 22 km S of Battambang, were also ruined by the Khmers Rouges, who used the stones for the construction of their own buildings.

● **Accommodation** A number of new hotels were built to accommodate UNTAC, now possible to bargain on price. **B** *Angkor*, 1 St, a/c, hot water; **B-C** *ODA*, a better option; **C** *Khemara*, 3 St, nr railway station, a/c, hot water; **C** *Paris*, 3 St, nr *Khemara*, a/c, hot water; **C-D** *Victory* is also close to the railway station and has a small swimming pool, no a/c.

● **Transport Air** Connections 5 times a week with Phnom Penh (US$90 return). **Road** It is a difficult trip from Phnom Penh and should definitely not be attempted between Feb and May, when guerrilla warfare is at its height.

South of Phnom Penh

SIHANOUKVILLE (KOMPONG SOM)

Sihanoukville, or Kompong Som as it was previously called, has been rebuilt with Soviet aid and is now an important port. Opened in 1964 by Prince Sihanouk, its glory has somewhat faded but the beaches are good. Of the three beaches (from N to S), Independence, Sokha and Ochateal, the latter is the better. Sihanoukville's fortunes may be revived by the expansion of the airport to accept international flights and the opening of a US$100 million casino on the nearby Naga Island, all due to open in 1997 with Malaysian backing. Club Med have also signed a deal to open a resort here.

Excursions

Boat trips to nearby islands, organized by Claude of *Claude's Restaurant*.

Local information
● **Accommodation**

Plenty of middle-range accommodation here.

B *Bungalow Sokha*, Sokha Beach; **B** *Hong Kong Motel*, Sokha Beach, a/c, hot water; **B-C** *Seaside*, Ochateal Beach, attractive rooms, satellite TV, hot water and baths, large terrace.

C *Eagles Nest*, Ochateal Beach, c/o PO Box 974, Phnom Penh, T 015 914657, F 015 913864, was formerly named the *Villa Rendezvous* and run by Dominic Chappell and Kellie Wilkinson who were murdered by the Khmers Rouges in 1994, it was the warmest place in town. Kellie is said to have acted as foster parent and the café was a refuge for most of the local street children. Colin Jerram now runs the guesthouse, it has a rooftop bar, rooms with hot water bathrooms attached, satellite TV, Cambodian and Australian dishes incl an excellent cooked breakfast, and access to the beach and sea.

E *Sam's Hostel*, Sokha beach, run by an Englishman, Vic, an ex UN volunteer and Sam, a Cambodian.

● **Places to eat**

♦♦♦*Koh Pos*, Sokha beach, renowned for its deliciously fresh fish and seafood dishes, good Khmer salads with unusual leaves and fresh herbs, charming owner, very popular restaurant, rec; **♦♦***Sam's*, Sokha Beach, on the hill overlooking the beach, excellent fresh fish dishes and salads; *Crocodile Café* on the adjoining beach is run by the owners of *Koh Pos*.

● **Transport**

232 km from Phnom Penh.

Local Motos cost about US$1 for most longer trips. **Motorbike hire**: at some guesthouses. Fishermen will take visitors out to the islands (fee negotiable).

Air 10 km from town on Route 4, 4 flights a week (US$75 return).

Useful place names	
Angkor Borei	អង្គរបុរី
Bokor	បូកគោរ
Elephant Mountains	ភ្នំដំរី
Kirirom	គីរីរម្យ
Sihanoukville	ក្រុងព្រះសីហនុ
(Kompong Som)	(កំពង់សោម)
Takeo	តាកែវ

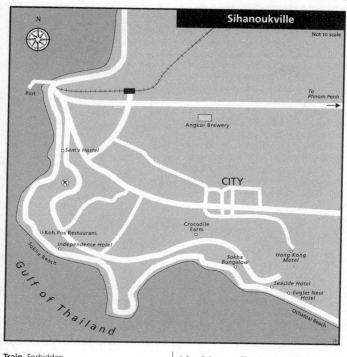

Sihanoukville

Not to scale

N

Port

To Phnom Penh

Angkor Brewery

Sam's Hostel

CITY

Koh Pos Restaurant

Crocodile Farm

Independence Hotel

Sokha Beach

Sokha Bungalow

Hong Kong Motel

Seaside Hotel

Eagles Nest Hotel

Ochateal Beach

G u l f   o f   T h a i l a n d

Train Forbidden.

Road Route 4 to the coast should be OK but check with your embassy on safety of road before attempting the journey. **Bus**: a/c bus 3 times a day from Phnom Penh, US$5. **Shared taxi**: connections with Phnom Penh, 3-3½ hrs on new USAID tarmacadam road (US$25 for whole taxi).

THE SOUTH COAST

There are plans to develop the S coast beaches like **Kep**. 'Kep-sur-Mer' was once a fashionable French colonial resort, founded in 1908, just 90 km W of Sihanoukville. The Khmers Rouges razed the resort to the ground in 1975. It was known as La Perle de la Cote d'Agathe and has beautiful offshore islands, including Ile du Pic and Ile Tonsay. In the past Sihanouk had his own private island here – Ile des Ambassadeurs – where he entertained guests. Kep has no town centre as such but the town follows a beautiful bay. The bay lacks the white sands of Sihanoukville *Best time to visit*: Nov-Jul.

Kampot is a pretty riverine town, only 5 km from the sea, and is also on the hit list for tourism development.

● **Accommodation** It is possible to stay with locals in Kep and Kampot. **Kep**: there's a hotel behind the hospital (**D**) and a guesthouse on the main road (**D**). **Kampot**: **B** *Phnom Khiew*; **D** *Kamchay*; **D** *Restaurant Hotel*, on riverside, popular with travellers.

● **Entertainment** *Hotel Kamchay* has live bands and dancing in the evening.

● **Transport Road Shared taxi**: from Kompong Som.

TAKEO

Takeo is a small, relaxed town even though it is capital of the province of the same name. About 20 km E of Takeo is **Angkor Borei**, a 6th century monument. It was built in laterite by King Rudravarman of Funan (see page 107). His patron deity was Vishnu and many Hindu statues survive from this site. The images are carved from the front and back and have distinctly Indochinese faces (some are in the National Museum of Arts in Phnom Penh, see page 90). **Phnom Bayang**, 40 km from Takeo, is a 6th century monument, now badly damaged. **Transport Road Shared taxi**: regular connections with Phnom Penh.

ELEPHANT MOUNTAINS

There are hill resorts in the Elephant Mountains, such as **Bokor** and **Kiriom**, which have been untouched for decades. There are plans to develop them for tourism.

● **Accommodation** *Bokor Mountain Club*, run by the owners of the Foreign Correspondents Club in Phnom Penh.

● **Transport** There's no direct transport from Phnom Penh. The easiest route is to go to Kompong Som and take a shared taxi from there.

Bangkok

MANY people visiting Cambodia pass through Thailand en route. Bangkok has the greatest concentration of companies offering tours to Cambodia and it is also the best place to obtain a visa. There are regular air connections between Bangkok's Don Muang and Phnom Penh's Pochentong airports. This section of the book provides a basic guide to Bangkok. There is also a short **Information for travellers** section providing some general practical background. The information has been condensed from the *Thailand Handbook* also published by Footprint Handbooks. Please note that the information here is not comprehensive: much of the background material, details on the more obscure sights, and practicalities have been either omitted or substantially edited. Those wishing to spend any length of time in Thailand are strongly advised to buy a dedicated guide to the country. We, naturally enough, would recommend the *Thailand Handbook*.

BANGKOK

Bangkok is not a city to be trifled with: a population of 11 million struggle to make their living in a conurbation with perhaps the worst traffic in the world; a level of pollution which causes some children, so it is (rather improbably) said, to lose four intelligence points by the time they are seven; and a climate which can take one's breath away. (The *Guinness Book of Records* credits Bangkok as the world's hottest city because of the limited seasonal and day-night temperature variations.) As journalist Hugo Gurdon wrote at the end of 1992: "One would have to describe Bangkok as unliveable were it not for the fact that more and more people live here". But, Bangkok is not just a perfect case study for academics studying the strains of rapid urban growth. There is charm and fun beneath the grime, and Bangkokians live life with a *joie de vivre* which belies the congestion. There are also numerous sights, including the spectacular Grand Palace, glittering wats (monasteries) and the breezy river, along with excellent food and good shopping.

The official name for Thailand's capital city begins Krungthep – phramaha – nakhonbawon – rathanakosin – mahinthara – yutthayaa – mahadilok – phiphobnobpharaat – raatchathaanii – buriiromudomsantisuk. It is not hard to see why Thais prefer the shortened version – Krungthep, or the 'City of Angels'. The name used by the rest of the world – Bangkok – is derived from 17th century Western maps, which referred to the city (or town as it then was) as Bancok, the 'village of the wild plum'. This name was only superseded by Krungthep in 1782, and so the Western name has deeper historical roots.

In 1767, Ayutthaya, then the capital of Siam, fell to the marauding Burmese for the second time and it was imperative that the remnants of the court and army find a more defensible site for a new capital. Taksin, the Lord of Tak, chose Thonburi, on the western banks of the Chao Phraya River, far from the Burmese and from Phitsanulok, where a rival to the throne had become ensconsed. In 3 years, Taksin had established a kingdom and crowned himself king. His reign was short-lived, however; the pressure of thwarting the Burmese over three arduous years caused him to go mad and in 1782 he was forced to abdicate. General Phraya Chakri was recalled from Cambodia and invited to accept the throne. This marked the beginning of the present Chakri Dynasty.

Bangkok highlights

Temples Bangkok's best known sight is the temple of *Wat Phra Kaeo*, situated within the grounds of the *Grand Palace* (page 159). Other notable temples include *Wat Pho* (page 157), *Wat Arun* (page 167), *Wat Suthat* (page 163) and *Wat Traimitr* (page 166).

Museums Bangkok's extensive *National Museum* houses the best collection in the country (page 161); other notable collections include those in *Jim Thompson's House* (page 171), the *Suan Pakkard Palace* (page 170) and *Vimanmek Palace* (page 170).

Markets The sprawling *Chatuchak Weekend market* (page 172), *Nakhon Kasem* or Thieves' market (page 164), *Pahurat Indian market* (page 164) and Chinatown's *Sampeng Lane* (page 166).

Boat trip On *Bangkok's canals* (page 166).

Excursions Day trips to the *floating market at Damnoen Saduak* (page 173).

In 1782, Chakri (now known as Rama I) moved his capital across the river to Bangkok (an even more defensible site) anticipating trouble from King Bodawpaya who had seized the throne of Burma. The river that flows between Thonburi and Bangkok and on which many of the luxury hotels – such as *The Oriental* – are now located, began life not as a river at all, but as a canal (or *khlong*). The canal was dug in the 16th century to reduce the distance between Ayutthaya and the sea by shortcutting a number of bends in the river. Since then, the canal has become the main channel of the Chao Phraya River. Its original course has shrunk in size, and is now represented by two khlongs, Bangkok Yai and Bangkok Noi.

This new capital of Siam grew in size and influence. Symbolically, many of the new buildings were constructed using bricks from the palaces and temples of the ruined former capital of Ayutthaya. But population growth was hardly spectacular – it appears that outbreaks of cholera sometimes reduced the population by a fifth or more in a matter of a few weeks. An almanac from 1820 records that "on the 7th month of the waxing moon, a little past 2100 in the evening, a shining light was seen in the N-W and multitudes of people purged, vomited and died". In 1900 Bangkok had a population of approximately 200,000. By 1950 it had surpassed 1 million, and in 1992 it was, officially, 5,562,141. Most people believe that the official figure considerably understates the true population of the city – 10-11 million would be more realistic. By 2010, analysts believe Bangkok will have a population of 20 million. As the population of the city has expanded, so has the area that it encompasses: in 1900 it covered a mere 13.3 sq km; in 1958, 96.4 sq km; while today the Bangkok Metropolitan region extends over 1,600 sq km and the outskirts of the city sprawl into neighbouring provinces. Such is the physical size of the capital that analysts talk of Bangkok as an EMR or Extended Metropolitan Region.

In terms of size, Bangkok is at least 23 times larger than the country's second city, Chiang Mai – 40 times bigger, using the unofficial population estimates. It also dominates Thailand in cultural, political and economic terms. All Thai civil servants have the ambition of serving in Bangkok, while many regard a posting to the poor NE as (almost) the kiss of death. Most of the country's industry is located in and around the city (the area contributes 45% of national GDP), and Bangkok supports a far wider array of services than other towns in the country. Although the city contains only 10% of the kingdom's population, its colleges of higher education graduate 71% of degree students, it contains 83% of pharmacists, and has 69% of Thailand's telephone lines. It is because of Bangkok's dominance that people often, and inaccurately, say 'Bangkok is Thailand'.

The immediate impression of the city to a first-time visitor is bedlam. The heat, noise, traffic, pollution – the general chaos – can be overwhelming. This was obviously the impression of Somerset Maugham, following his visit in 1930:

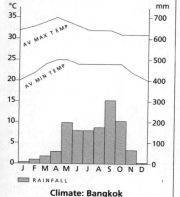

Climate: Bangkok

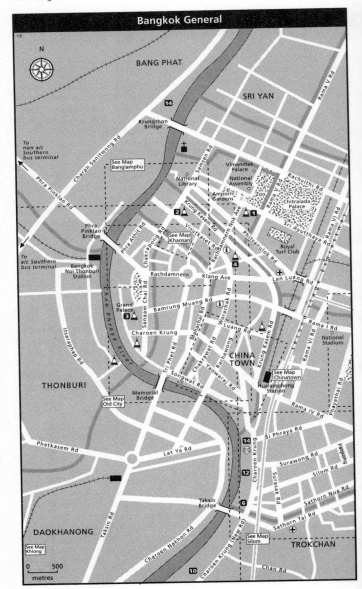

Bangkok General

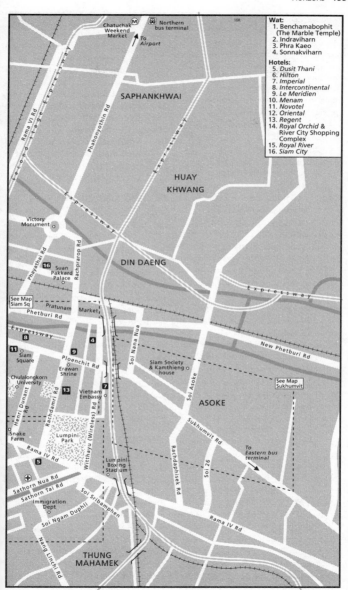

Wat:
1. Benchamabophit (The Marble Temple)
2. Indraviharn
3. Phra Kaeo
4. Sonnakviharn

Hotels:
5. *Dusit Thani*
6. *Hilton*
7. *Imperial*
8. *Intercontinental*
9. *Le Meridien*
10. *Menam*
11. *Novotel*
12. *Oriental*
13. *Regent*
14. *Royal Orchid & River City Shopping Complex*
15. *Royal River*
16. *Siam City*

'I do not know why the insipid Eastern food sickened me. The heat of Bangkok was overwhelming. The wats oppressed me by their garish magnificence, making my head ache, and their fantastic ornaments filled me with malaise. All I saw looked too bright, the crowds in the street tired me, and the incessant din jangled my nerves. I felt very unwell ...'

It is estimated that over 1 million Bangkokians live in slum or squatter communities, while average traffic speeds can be less than 10 km/hour. During peak periods the traffic congestion is such that 'gridlock' seems inevitable. The figures are sometimes hard to believe: US$500mn of petrol is consumed each year while cars wait at traffic lights; one day in Jul 1992 it took 11 hrs for some motorists to get home after a monsoon storm; and the number of cars on the capital's streets increases by 800 each day (the figure for the country is 1,300); while traffic speeds are snail pace – and expected to fall further. For those in Bangkok who are concerned about their city and the environment, the worst aspect is that things will undoubtedly get worse before they get any better – despite the plethora of road building programmes the car and truck population is growing faster than the roads to accommodate them. The government of former Prime Minister Anand did give the go-ahead to a number of important infrastructural projects, but many would say a decade too late. As one analyst has observed: "Bangkok is only just beginning to happen". Even editorial writers at the *Bangkok Post* who, one might imagine, are used to the traffic find it a constant topic for comment. At the end of 1993 the newspaper stated: "Bangkok's traffic congestion and pollution are just about the worst in the world – ever. Never in history have people had to live in the conditions we endure each day".

PLACES OF INTEREST

This section is divided into five main areas: the Old City, around the Grand Palace; the Golden Mount, to the E of the Old City; Chinatown, which lies to the S of the Golden Mount; the Dusit area, which is to the N and contains the present day parliament buildings and the King's residence; and Wat Arun and the khlongs, which are to the W, on the other bank of the Chao Phraya River in Thonburi. Other miscellaneous sights, not in these areas, are at the end of the section, under Other places of interest.

GETTING AROUND THE SIGHTS

Buses, both a/c and non-a/c, travel to all city sights (see Local transport, page 194). A taxi or tuk-tuk for a centre of town trip should cost ฿50-100. Now that taxis are almost all metered visitors may find it easier, and more comfortable (they have a/c) – not to mention safer – than the venerable tuk-tuk, although a ride on one of these three-wheeled machines is a tourist experience in itself. If travelling by bus, a bus map of the city – and there are several, available from most bookshops and hotel gift shops – is an invaluable aid. The express river taxi is a far more pleasant way to get around town and is also often quicker than going by road (see map page 169 for piers, and box page 168).

THE OLD CITY

The Old City contains the largest concentration of sights in Bangkok, and for visitors with only one day in the capital, this is the area to concentrate on. It is possible to walk around all the sights mentioned below quite easily in a single day. For the energetic, it would also be possible to visit the sights in and around the Golden Mount. If intending to walk around all the sights in the old city start from Wat Pho; if you have less time or less energy, begin with the Grand Palace.

Wat Phra Chetuphon

(Temple of the Reclining Buddha) or **Wat Pho**, as it is known to Westerners (a contraction of its original name Wat Potaram), has its entrance on Chetuphon Rd on the S side of the complex. It is 200 years old and the largest wat in Bangkok, now most famous for its 46m long, 15m high gold-plated reclining Buddha, with beautiful mother-of-pearl soles (showing the 108 auspicious signs). The reclining Buddha is contained in a large viharn built during the reign of Rama III (1832).

The grounds of the wat contain more than 1,000 bronze images, rescued from the ruins of Ayutthaya and Sukhothai

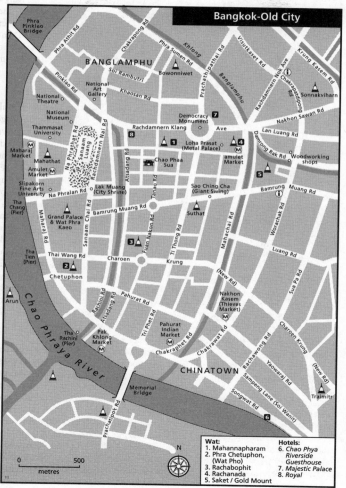

Bangkok-Old City

Wat:
1. Mahannapharam
2. Phra Chetuphon, (Wat Pho)
3. Rachabophit
4. Rachanada
5. Saket / Gold Mount

Hotels:
6. *Chao Phya Riverside Guesthouse*
7. *Majestic Palace*
8. *Royal*

0   500
metres

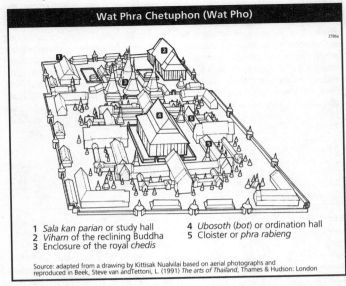

Wat Phra Chetuphon (Wat Pho)

1 *Sala kan parian* or study hall
2 *Viharn* of the reclining Buddha
3 Enclosure of the royal *chedis*

4 *Ubosoth* (*bot*) or ordination hall
5 Cloister or *phra rabieng*

Source: adapted from a drawing by Kittisak Nualvilai based on aerial photographs and reproduced in Beek, Steve van and Tettoni, L. (1991) *The arts of Thailand*, Thames & Hudson: London

by Rama I's brother. The bot, or ubosoth, houses a bronze Ayutthayan Buddha in an attitude of meditation and the pedestal of this image contains the ashes of Rama I. Also notable is the 11-piece altar table set in front of the Buddha, and the magnificent mother-of-pearl inlaid doors which are possibly the best examples of this art from the Bangkok Period (depicting episodes from the Ramakien). The bot is enclosed by two galleries which house 394 seated bronze Buddha images. They were brought from the N during Rama I's reign and are of assorted periods and styles. Around the exterior base of the bot are marble reliefs telling the story of the Ramakien as adapted in the Thai poem the *Maxims of King Ruang* (formerly these reliefs were much copied by making rubbings onto rice paper). The 152 panels are the finest of their type in Bangkok. They recount only the second section of the Ramakien: the abduction and recovery of Ram's wife Seeda. The rather – to Western eyes – unsatisfactory conclusion to the story as told here has led some art historians to argue they were originally taken from Ayutthaya. Thai scholars argue otherwise.

A particular feature of the wat are the 95 chedis of various sizes which are scattered across the 20-acre complex. To the left of the bot are four large chedis, memorials to the first four Bangkok kings. The library nearby is richly decorated with broken pieces of porcelain. The large top-hatted stone figures, the stone animals and the Chinese pagodas scattered throughout the compound came to Bangkok as ballast on the royal rice boats returning from China. Rama III, whose rice barges dominated the trade, is said to have had a particular penchant for these figures, as well as for other works of Chinese art. The Chinese merchants who served the King – and who are said to have called him *Chao Sua* or millionaire – loaded the empty barges with the carvings to please their lord.

The Emerald Buddha

Wat Phra Kaeo was specifically built to house the Emerald Buddha, the most venerated Buddha image in Thailand, carved from green jade (the emerald in the name referring only to its colour), a mere 75 cm high, and seated in an attitude of meditation. It is believed to have been found in 1434 in Chiang Rai, and stylistically belongs to the Late Chiang Saen or Chiang Mai schools. Since then, it has been moved on a number of occasions – to Lampang, Chiang Mai and Laos (both Luang Prabang and Vientiane). It stayed in Vientiane for 214 years before being recaptured by the Thai army in 1778 and placed in Wat Phra Kaeo on 22 March, 1784. The image wears seasonal costumes of gold and jewellery; one each for the hot, cool and the rainy seasons. The changing ceremony occurs 3 times a year in the presence of the King.

Buddha images are often thought to have personalities. The Phra Kaeo is no exception. It is said, for example, that such is the antipathy between the Phra Bang in Luang Prabang (Laos) and the Phra Kaeo that they can never reside in the same town.

Rama III wanted Wat Pho to become known as a place of learning, a kind of exhibition of all the knowledge of the time and it is regarded as Thailand's first university. Admission ฿20. Open 0900-1700 Mon-Sun. **NB** From Tha Tien pier at the end of Thai Wang Rd, close to Wat Pho, it is possible to get boats to Wat Arun (see page 166). Wat Pho is also probably Bangkok's most respected centre of traditional Thai massage, and politicians, businessmen and military officers go there to seek relief from the tensions of modern life. Most medical texts were destroyed when the Burmese sacked the former capital, Ayutthaya, in 1776 and in 1832 Rama III had what was known about Thai massage inscribed on stone and then had those stones set into the walls of Wat Pho to guide and teach. For Westerners wishing to learn the art, special 30-hrs courses can be taken for ฿3,000, stretching over either 15 days (2 hrs/day) or 10 days (3 hrs/day). The centre is located at the back of the Wat, on the opposite side from the entrance. A massage costs ฿100 for 30 mins, ฿180 for 1 hr. With herbal treatment, the fee is ฿260 for 1.30 hr. For other centres of Thai Traditional massage see page 194.

Grand Palace and Wat Phra Kaeo
About 10-15 mins walk from Wat Pho northwards along Sanaam Chai Rd is the entrance to the **Grand Palace** and **Wat Phra Kaeo**. (**NB** The main entrance is the Viseschaisri Gate on Na Phralan Rd.) The Grand Palace is situated on the banks of the Chao Phraya River and is the most spectacular – some might say 'gaudy' – collection of buildings in Bangkok. The complex covers an area of over 1.5 sq km and the architectural plan is almost identical to that of the Royal Palace in the former capital of Ayutthaya. It was started in 1782 and was subsequently added to. Initially, the palace was the city, the seat of power, surrounded by high walls and built to be self-sufficient.

The buildings of greatest interest are clustered around **Wat Phra Kaeo**, or the 'Temple of the Emerald Buddha'. On entering the compound, the impression is one of glittering brilliance, as the outside is covered by a mosaic of coloured glass. The buildings were last restored for Bangkok's bicentenary in 1982 (the Wat Phra Kaeo Museum shows the methods used in the restoration process). Wat Phra Kaeo was built by Rama I in imitation of the royal chapel in Ayutthaya and was the first of the buildings within the Grand Palace

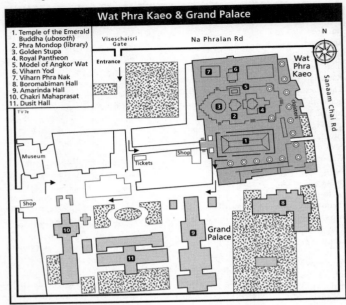

Wat Phra Kaeo & Grand Palace

1. Temple of the Emerald Buddha (ubosoth)
2. Phra Mondop (library)
3. Golden Stupa
4. Royal Pantheon
5. Model of Angkor Wat
6. Viharn Yod
7. Viharn Phra Nak
8. Boromabiman Hall
9. Amarinda Hall
10. Chakri Mahaprasat
11. Dusit Hall

complex to be constructed. While it was being erected the king lived in a small wooden building in one corner of the palace compound.

The ubosoth is raised on a marble platform with a frieze of gilded figures of garudas holding nagas running round the base. Bronze singhas act as door guardians. The door panels are of inlaid mother-of-pearl and date from Rama I's reign (late 18th century). Flanking the door posts are Chinese door guardians riding on lions. Inside the temple, the Emerald Buddha (see box) sits high up, illuminated above a large golden altar. In addition, there are many other gilded Buddha images, mostly in the attitude of dispelling fear, and a series of mural paintings depicting the jataka stories. Those facing the Emerald Buddha show the enlightenment of the Buddha when he subdues the evil demon Mara. Mara is underneath, wringing out his hair, while on either side, the Buddha is surrounded by evil spirits. Those on one side have been subjugated; those on the other have not. The water from the wringing out of Mara's hair drowns the evil army, and the Buddha is shown 'touching ground' calling the earth goddess Thoranee up to witness his enlightenment. No photography is allowed inside the ubosoth.

Around the walls of the shaded cloister that encompasses Wat Phra Kaeo, is a continuous mural depicting the Ramakien – the Thai version of the Indian Ramayana. There are 178 sections in all, which were first painted during the reign of King Rama I but have since been restored on a number of occasions.

To the N of the ubosoth on a raised platform, are the Royal Pantheon, the Phra Mondop (the library), two gilt stupas, a model of Angkor Wat and the Golden Stupa. At the entrance to the

Royal Pantheon are gilded kinarees. The Royal Pantheon is only open to the public once a year on Chakri Day, 6 Apr (the anniversary of the founding of the present Royal Dynasty). On the same terrace there are two gilt stupas built by King Rama I in commemoration of his parents. The Mondop was also built by Rama I to house the first revised Buddhist scriptural canon. To the W of the mondop is the large Golden Stupa or chedi, with its circular base, in Ceylonese style. To the N of the mondop is a model of Angkor Wat constructed during the reign of King Mongkut (1851-1868) when Cambodia was under Thai suzerainty.

To the N again from the Royal Pantheon is the Supplementary Library and two viharns – Viharn Yod and Phra Nak. The former is encrusted in pieces of Chinese porcelain.

To the S of Wat Phra Kaeo are the buildings of the Grand Palace. These are interesting for the contrast that they make with those of Wat Phra Kaeo. Walk out through the cloisters. On your left can be seen Boromabiman Hall, which is French in style and was completed during the reign of Rama VI. His three successors lived here at one time or another. The Amarinda Hall has an impressive airy interior, with chunky pillars and gilded thrones. The Chakri Mahaprasart (the Palace Reception Hall) stands in front of a carefully manicured garden with topiary. It was built and lived in by Rama V shortly after he had returned from a trip to Java and Singapore in 1876, and it shows: the building is a rather unhappy amalgam of colonial and traditional Thai styles of architecture. Initially the intention was to top the structure with a Western dome, but the architects settled for a Thai-style roof. The building was completed in time for Bangkok's first centenary in 1882. King Chulalongkorn (Rama V) found the overcrowded Grand Palace oppressive and after a visit to Europe in 1897, built himself a new

home at Vimanmek (see page 170) in the area to the N, known as Dusit. The present King Bhumibol lives in the Chitralada Palace, built by Rama VI, also in the Dusit area. The Grand Palace is now only used for state occasions. Next to the Chakri Mahaprasart is the raised Dusit Hall; a cool, airy building containing mother-of-pearl thrones. Near the Dusit Hall is a museum, which has information on the restoration of the Grand Palace, models of the Palace and many Buddha statues. There is a collection of old cannon, mainly supplied by London gun foundries. Close by is a small café selling refreshing coconut drinks. All labels in Thai, but there are free guided tours in English throughout the day. Admission ฿50. Open: Mon-Sun 0900-1600.

ADMISSION to the Grand Palace complex ฿125, ticket office open 0830-1130, 1300-1530 Mon-Sun except Buddhist holidays when Wat Phra Kaeo is free but the rest of the palace is closed. The cost of the admission includes a free guidebook to the palace (with plan) as well as a ticket to the *Coin Pavilion*, with its collection of medals and 'honours' presented to members of the Royal Family and to the Vimanmek Palace in the Dusit area (see page 170). **NB** Decorum of dress is required (trousers can be hired for ฿10 near the entrance to the Grand Palace) which means no shorts, and no singlets or sleeveless shirts.

The National Museum

On the N edge of Sanamm Luang is the National Museum, reputedly the largest museum in Southeast Asia. It is an excellent place to view the full range of Thai art before visiting the ancient Thai capitals, Ayutthaya and Sukhothai.

Gallery No 1, the gallery of Thai history, is interesting and informative, as well as being air-conditioned, so it is a good place to cool-off. The gallery clearly shows Kings Mongkut and Chulalongkorn's fascination with Western technology. The other 22 galleries and 19 rooms contain a vast assortment of arts and artefacts divided according to period and style. If you are interested in Thai art, the museum alone might take a day to browse around. A shortcoming for those with no background knowledge is the lack of information in some of the galleries and it is recommended that interested visitors buy the 'Guide to the National Museum, Bangkok' for ฿50 or join one of the tours. Admission ฿20, together with a skimpy leaflet outlining the galleries. Open 0900-1600, Wed-Sun, tickets on sale until 1530. For English, French, German, Spanish and Portuguese-speaking tour information call T 2241333. They are free, and start at 0930, lasting 2 hrs (usually on Wed and Thur).

The Buddhaisawan Chapel, to the right of the ticket office for the National Museum, contains some of the finest Bangkok period murals in Thailand. The chapel was built in 1795 to house the famous Phra Sihing Buddha. Folklore has it that this image originated in Ceylon and when the boat carrying it to Thailand sank, it floated off on a plank to be washed ashore in Southern Thailand, near the town of Nakhon Si Thammarat. This, believe it or not, is probably untrue: the image is early Sukhothai in style (1250), admittedly showing Ceylonese influences, and almost certainly Northern Thai in origin. There are two other images that claim to be the magical Phra Buddha Sihing, one in Nakhon Si Thammarat and another in Chiang Mai. The chapel's magnificent murals were painted between 1795 and 1797 and depict stories from the Buddha's life. They are classical in style, without any sense of perspective, and the narrative of the Buddha's life begins to the right of the rear door behind the principal image, and progresses clockwise through 28 panels. German-speaking tours of the chapel are held on the third Tues of the month (0930).

THE GOLDEN MOUNT, GIANT SWING AND SURROUNDING WATS

From the Democracy Monument, across Mahachai Rd, at the point where Rachdamnern Klang Ave crosses Khlong Banglamphu can be seen the **Golden Mount** (also known as the Royal Mount), an impressive artificial hill nearly 80m high. The climb to the top is exhausting but worth it for the fabulous views of Bangkok. On the way up, the path passes holy trees, memorial plaques and Chinese shrines. The construction of the mount was begun during the reign of Rama III who intended to build the greatest chedi in his kingdom. The structure collapsed before completion, and Rama IV decided merely to pile up the rubble in a heap and place a far smaller golden chedi on its summit. The chedi contains a relic of the Buddha placed there by the present king after the structure had been most recently repaired in 1966. Admission ฿5. Open 0800-1800 Mon-Sun.

Wat Saket

This lies at the bottom of the mount, between it and Damrong Rak Rd – the mount actually lies within the wat's compound. Saket means 'washing of hair' – Rama I is reputed to have stopped here and ceremoniously washed himself before being crowned King in Thonburi (see Festivals, Nov). The only building of real note is the *library* (hor trai) which is Ayutthayan in style. The door panels and lower windows are decorated with woodcarvings depicting everyday Ayutthayan life, while the window panels show Persian and French soldiers from Louis XIV's reign. Open 0800-1800 Mon-Sun.

Also in the shadow of the Golden Mount but to the W and on the corner of Rachdamnern Klang Ave and Mahachai Rd lies Wat Rachanada and the Loha Prasat. Until 1989 these buildings were obscured by the Chalerm Thai movie theatre, a landmark which Bangkok's taxi and tuk-tuk drivers still refer to. In the place of the theatre there is now a neat garden, with an elaborate gilded **sala**, which is used to receive visiting dignitaries. Behind the garden the strange looking **Loha Prasat** or Metal Palace, with its 37 spires, is easily recognizable. This palace was built by Rama III in 1846, and is said to be modelled on the first Loha Prasat built in India 2,500 years ago. A second was constructed in Ceylon in 160 BC, although Bangkok's Loha Prasat is the only one still standing. The palace was built by Rama III as a memorial to his beloved niece Princess Soammanas Vadhanavadi. The 37 spires represent the 37 Dharma of the Bodhipakya. The building, which contains Buddha images and numerous meditation cells, has been closed to visitors for many years, although it is possible to walk around the outside.

Next to the Loha Prasat is the much more traditional **Wat Rachanada**. Wat Rachanada was built by Rama III for his niece who later became Rama IV's queen. The main Buddha image is made of copper mined in Nakhon Ratchasima province to the NE of Bangkok, and the ordination hall also has some fine doors. Open 0600-1800 Mon-Sun. What makes the wat particularly worth visiting is the **Amulet market** to be found close by, between the Golden Mount and the wat. The sign, in English, below the covered part of the market reads 'Buddha and Antiques Centre'. The market also contains Buddha images and other religious artefacts and is open every day.

Wat Suthat

A 5 min walk S of Wat Rachanada, on Bamrung Muang Rd, is the **Sao Ching Cha** or **Giant Swing**, consisting of two tall red pillars linked by an elaborate cross piece, set in the centre of a square. The Giant Swing was the original centre for a Brahmanic festival in honour of Siva. Young men, on a giant 'raft', would be swung high into the air to grab pouches of coins, hung from bamboo poles, between their teeth. Because the swinging was from E to W, it has been said that it symbolized the rising and setting of the sun. The festival was banned in the 1930s because of the injuries that occurred; prior to its banning, thousands would congregate around the Giant Swing for 2 days of dancing and music. The magnificent **Wat Suthat** faces the Giant Swing. The wat was begun by Rama I in 1807, and his intention was to build a temple that would equal the most glorious in Ayutthaya. The wat was not finished until the end of the reign of Rama III in 1851.

The viharn is in early-Bangkok style and is surrounded by Chinese pagodas. Its six pairs of doors, each made from a single piece of teak, are deeply carved with animals and celestial beings from the Himavanta forest. The central doors are said to have been carved by Rama II himself, and are considered some of the most important works of art of the period. Inside the viharn is the bronze Phra Sri Sakyamuni Buddha in an attitude of subduing Mara. This image was previously contained in Wat Mahathat in Sukhothai, established in 1362. Behind the Buddha is a very fine gilded stone carving from the Dvaravati Period (2nd-11th centuries AD), 2.5m in height and showing the miracle at Sravasti and the Buddha preaching in the Tavatimsa heaven.

The bot is the tallest in Bangkok and one of the largest in Thailand. The murals in the bot painted during the reign of Rama III are interesting in that they are traditional Thai in style, largely unaffected by Western artistic influences. They use flat colours and lack perspective. The bot also contains a particularly large cast Buddha image. Open 0900-1700; the viharn is only open on weekends and Buddhist holidays 0900-1700.

Wat Rachabophit

The little visited Wat Rachabophit is

close to the Ministry of the Interior on Rachabophit Rd, a few minutes walk S of Wat Suthat down Ti Thong Rd. It is recognizable by its distinctive doors carved in high relief with jaunty looking soldiers wearing European-style uniforms. The temple was started in 1869, took 20 years to complete, and is a rich blend of Western and Thai art forms (carried further in Wat Benchamabophit 40 years later, see page 170). Wat Rachabophit is peculiar in that it follows the ancient temple plan of placing the Phra Chedi in the centre of the complex, surrounded by the other buildings. It later became the fashion to place the ordination hall at the centre.

The 43m high gilded chedi's most striking feature are the five-coloured Chinese glass tiles which richly encrust the lower section. The ordination hall has 10 door panels and 28 window panels each decorated with gilded black lacquer on the inside and mother-of-pearl inlay on the outside showing the various royal insignia. They are felt to be among the masterpieces of the Rattanakosin Period (1782-present). The principal Buddha image in the ordination hall, in an attitude of meditation, sits on a base of Italian marble and is covered by the umbrella that protected the urn and ashes of Rama V. It also has a surprising interior – an oriental version of Italian Gothic, more like Versailles than Bangkok. Admission ¢10. Open 0800-1700 Mon-Sun.

From Wat Rachabophit, it is only a short distance to the **Pahurat Indian Market** on Pahurat Rd, where Indian, Malaysian and Thai textiles are sold. To get there, walk S on Ti Thong Rd which quickly becomes Tri Phet Rd. After a few blocks, Pahurat Rd crosses Tri Phet Rd. **Pak Khlong Market** is to be found a little further S on Tri Phet Rd at the foot of the Memorial Bridge. It is a huge wholesale market for fresh produce, and a photographer's paradise. It begins very early in the morning and has ended by 1000. The closest pier to the Pak Khlong Market is Tha Rachini, which is remembered for a particularly nasty episode in Thai history. It is said that in the 1840s a troublemaking upcountry *chao* or lord was brought to Bangkok and sentenced to death. His eyes were burnt out with heated irons and then the unfortunate man was suspended above the river at Tha Rachini in a cage. The cage was so positioned that the *chao* could touch the water with his finger tips but could not cup water to drink. He died of thirst and sunstroke after 3 days and for years afterwards people would not live near the spot where he died.

CHINATOWN AND THE GOLDEN BUDDHA

Chinatown covers the area from Charoen Krung (or New Rd) down to the river and leads on from Pahurat Rd Market; cross over Chakraphet Rd and immediately opposite is the entrance to Sampeng Lane. A trip through **Chinatown** can either begin with the Thieves Market to the NW, or at Wat Traimitr, the Golden Buddha, to the SE. An easy stroll between the two should not take more than 2 hrs. This part of Bangkok has a different atmosphere from elsewhere. Roads become narrower, buildings smaller, and there is a continuous bustle of activity. There remain some attractive, weathered examples of early 20th century shophouses. The industrious Sino-Thais of the area make everything from offertory candles and gold jewellery to metalwork, gravestones and light machinery.

Nakhon Kasem, or the Thieves Market, lies between Charoen Krung and Yaowaraj Rd, to the E of the khlong that runs parallel to Mahachai Rd. Its boundaries are marked by archways. As its name suggests, this market used to be the centre for the fencing of stolen goods. It is not quite so colourful today, but there remain a number of second-hand and antique shops which are worth a browse – such as the *Good Luck Antique*

Shop. Amongst other things, musical instruments, brass ornaments, antique (and not so antique) coffee grinders are all on sale here.

Just to the SE of the Thieves Market are two interesting roads that run next to and parallel with one another:

Yaowaraj Road and Sampeng Lane. **Yaowaraj Road**, a busy thoroughfare, is the centre of the country's gold trade. The trade is run by a cartel of seven shops, the Gold Traders Association, and the price is fixed by the government. Sino-Thais often convert their cash into

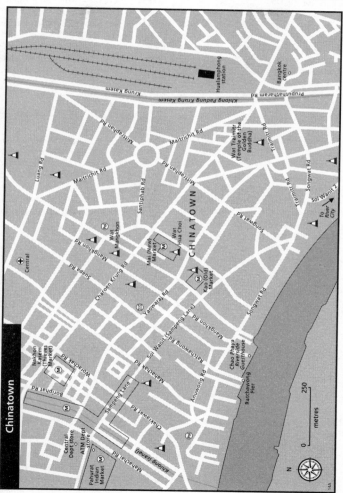

gold jewellery, usually bracelets and necklaces. The jewellery is bought by its 'baht weight' which fluctuates daily with the price of gold (most shops post the price daily). Should the owner need to convert their necklace or bracelet back into cash it is again weighed to determine its value. The narrower, almost pedestrian **Sampeng Lane**, also called **Soi Wanit**, is just to the S of Yaowaraj Rd. This road's history is shrouded in murder and intrigue. It used to be populated by prostitutes and opium addicts and was fought over by Chinese gangs. Today, it remains a commercial centre, but rather less illicit. It is still interesting (and cool, being shaded by awnings) to walk down, but there is not much to buy here – it is primarily a wholesale centre specializing in cloth and textiles although it is a good place to go for odd lengths of material, buttons of any shape and size, and things like costume jewellery.

The most celebrated example of the goldsmiths' art in Thailand sits within **Wat Traimitr**, or the **Temple of the Golden Buddha**, which is located at the E edge of Chinatown, squashed between Charoen Krung, Yaowaraj Rd and Traimitr Rd (just to the S of Bangkok's Hualamphong railway station). The Golden Buddha is housed in a small, rather gaudy and unimpressive room. Although the leaflet offered to visitors says the 3m-high, 700 year-old image is 'unrivalled in beauty', be prepared to be disappointed. It is in fact rather featureless, showing the Buddha in an attitude of subduing Mara. What makes it special, drawing large numbers of visitors each day, is that it is made of 5.5 tonnes of solid gold. Apparently, when the East Asiatic Company was extending the port of Bangkok, they came across a huge stucco Buddha image which they obtained permission to move. However, whilst being moved by crane in 1957, it fell and the stucco cracked open to reveal a solid gold image. During the Ayut-

thayan Period it was the custom to cover valuable Buddha images in plaster to protect them from the Burmese, and this particular example stayed that way for several 100 years. In the grounds of the wat there is a school, crematorium, food-stalls and, inappropriately, a money changer. Admission ฿10. Open 0900-1700 Mon-Sun. Gold beaters can still be seen at work behind Suksaphan store.

Between the river and Soi Wanit 2 there is a warren of lanes, too small for traffic – this is the Chinatown of old. From here it is possible to thread your way through to the River City shopping complex which is air-conditioned and a good place to cool-off.

RECOMMENDED READING Visitors wishing to explore the wonders of China-town more thoroughly, should buy Nancy Chandler's *Map of Bangkok*, a lively, detailed (but not altogether accurate) map of all the shops, restaurants and out of the way wats and shrines. ฿70 from most book-stores.

WAT ARUN AND THE KHLONGS

One of the most enjoyable ways to see Bangkok is by boat – and particularly by the fast and noisy *hang yaaws* (**long-tailed boats**). You will know them when you see them; these powerful, lean machines roar around the river and the khlongs at break-neck speed, as though they are involved in a race to the death. There are innumerable tours around the khlongs of Thonburi taking in a number of sights which include the floating market, snake farm and Wat Arun. Boats go from the various piers located along the E banks of the Chao Phraya River. The journey begins by travelling downstream along the Chao Phraya, before turning 'inland' after passing underneath the Krungthep Bridge. The route skirts past laden rice-barges, squatter communities on public land and houses overhanging the canals. This is a very popular route with tourists, and boats are intercepted by salesmen and women marketing everything from cold beer to straw hats. You may also get caught in a boat jam; traffic snarl-ups are not confined to the capital's roads. Nevertheless, the trip is a fascinating insight into what Bangkok must have been like when it was still the 'Venice of the East', and around every bend there seems to be yet another wat – some of them very beautiful. On private tours the first stop is usually the **Floating market** (*Talaat Nam*). This is now an artificial, ersatz gathering which exists purely for the tourist industry. It is worth only a brief visit – unless the so-called 'post-tourist' is looking for just this sort of sight. The nearest functioning floating market is at Damnoen Saduak (see excursions from Bangkok, page 173). The **Snake Farm** is the next stop where man fights snake in an epic battle of wills. Visitors can even pose with a python. The poisonous snakes are incited, to burst balloon with their fangs, 'proving' how dangerous they are. There is also a rather motley zoo with a collection of crocodiles and sad-looking animals in small cages. The other snake farm in Central Bangkok is (appropriately) attached to the Thai Red Cross and is more professional and cheaper (see page 172). Admission ฿70, shows every 20 mins. Refreshments available. On leaving the snake farm, the boat will join up with Khlong Bangkok Yai at the site of the large **Wat Paknam**. Just before re-entering the Chao Phraya itself, the route passes by the impressive **Wat Kalaya Nimit**.

Wat Arun

North on the Chao Phraya River is the famous Wat Arun, or the Temple of the Dawn, facing Wat Pho across the river. Wat Arun stands 81m high, making it the highest prang (tower) in Thailand. It was built in the early 19th century on the site of Wat Chaeng, the Royal Palace complex when Thonburi was briefly the capital of Thailand. The wat housed the Emerald Buddha before the image was transferred to Bangkok and it is said that King Taksin vowed to restore the wat after passing it one dawn. The prang is completely covered with pieces of Chinese porcelain and includes some delicate gold and black lacquered doors. The temple is really meant to be viewed from across the river; its scale and beauty can only be appreciated from a distance. Young, a European visitor to the capital, wrote in 1898: 'Thousands upon thousands of pieces of cheap china must have been smashed to bits in order to furnish sufficient material to decorate this curious structure ... though the material is tawdry, the effect is indescribably wonderful'.

Energetic visitors can climb up to the halfway point and view the city. This is not recommended for people suffering from vertigo; the steps are very steep – be prepared for jelly-like legs after descending. Admission ฿10. Open 0830-1730 Mon-Sun. The men at the pier may demand ฿10 to help 'in the maintenance of the pier'. **NB** It is possible to get to Wat Arun by water-taxi from Tha Tien pier (at the end of Thai Wang Rd near Wat Pho), or from Tha Chang (at the end of Na Phralan near Wat Phra Kaeo) (฿1). The best view of Wat Arun is in the evening from the Bangkok side of the river when the sun sets behind the prang.

After visiting Wat Arun, some tours then go further upstream to the mouth of Khlong Bangkok Noi where the **Royal Barges** are housed in a hangar-like boathouse. These ornately carved boats, winched out of the water in cradles, were used by the king at 'krathin' (see OK Phansa festival, page 205) to present robes to the monks in Wat Arun at the end of the rainy season. The ceremony ceased in 1967 but the Royal Thai Navy restored the barges for the revival of the spectacle, as part of the Chakri Dynasty's bicentennial celebrations in 1982. The oldest and most beautiful barge is the Sri Supannahong, built during the reign of Rama I (1782-1809) and repaired during that of Rama

VI (1910-1925). It measures 45m long and 3m wide, weighs 15 tonnes and was created from a single piece of teak. It required a crew of 50 oarsmen, and two coxwains, along with such assorted crew members as a flagman, a rhythm-keeper and singer. Its gilded prow was carved in the form of a *hamsa* (or goose) and its stern, in the shape of a *naga*. Admission ₿10. Open 0830-1630 Mon-Sun (see Festivals, Sep, page 174).

Arranging a boat tour

Either book a tour at your hotel, or go to one of the piers and organize your own customized trip. The most frequented piers are located between the Oriental Hotel and the Grand Palace (see map, or ask at your hotel). The pier just to the S of the

---

The Chao Phraya River Express

One of the most relaxing – and one of the cheapest – ways to see Bangkok is by taking the Chao Phraya River Express. These boats (or *rua duan*) link almost 40 piers (or *tha*) along the Chao Phraya River from Tha Wat Rajsingkorn in the S to Tha Nonthaburi in the N. The entire route entails a journey of about $1\frac{1}{4}$-$1\frac{1}{2}$ hr, and fares are ₿4, ₿6 or ₿8. Adjacent to many of the piers are excellent riverside restaurants. At peak periods, boats leave every 10 mins, off-peak about every 15-25 mins. Note that boats flying red or green pennants do not stop at every pier; they also exact a ₿1 surcharge. Also, boats will only stop if passengers wish to board or alight, so make your destination known.

Selected piers and places of interest, travelling upstream

Tha Orienten By the *Oriental Hotel*; access to *Silom Road*.

Tha River City In the shadow of the *Royal Orchid Hotel*, on the S side and close to *River City* shopping centre.

Tha Ratchawong *Rabieng Ratchawong Restaurant*; access to *Chinatown* and *Sampeng Lane*.

Tha Saphan Phut Under the *Memorial Bridge* and close to *Pahurat Indian market*.

Tha Rachini *Pak Khlong Market*; just upstream, the *Catholic seminary* surrounded by high walls.

Tha Tien Close to *Wat Pho*; *Wat Arun* on the opposite bank; and just downstream from Wat Arun the *Vichaiprasit fort* headquarters of the Thai navy), lurking behind crenellated ramparts.

Tha Chang Just downstream is the *Grand Palace* peeking out above white-washed walls; *Wat Rakhang* with its white corn-cob prang lies opposite.

Tha Maharat *Lan The Restaurant*; access to *Wat Mahathat* and *Sanaam Luang*.

Tha Phra Arthit *Yen Jai Restaurant*; access to *Khaosan Road*.

Tha Visutkasat *Yok Yor Restaurant*; just upstream the elegant central *Bank of Thailand*.

Tha Thewes *Son Ngen Restaurant*; just upstream are *boatsheds* with royal barges; close to the *National Library*.

Tha Wat Chan Just upstream is the *Singha Beer* Samoson brewery.

Tha Wat Khema *Wat Khema* in large, tree-filled compound.

Tha Wat Khian *Wat Kien*, semi-submerged.

Tha Nonthaburi Last stop on the express boat route .

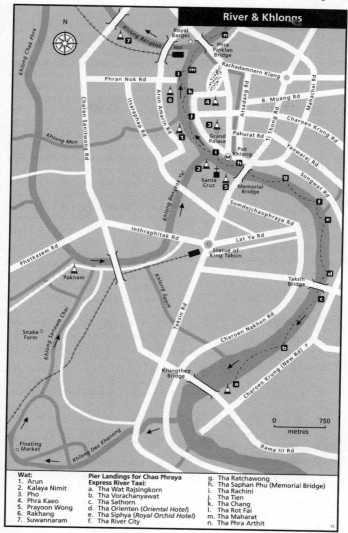

River & Khlongs

Wat:
1. Arun
2. Kalaya Nimit
3. Pho
4. Phra Kaeo
5. Prayoon Wong
6. Rakhang
7. Suwannaram

Pier Landings for Chao Phraya Express River Taxi:
a. Tha Wat Rajsingkorn
b. Tha Vorachanyawat
c. Tha Sathorn
d. Tha Orienten (*Oriental Hotel*)
e. Tha Siphya (*Royal Orchid Hotel*)
f. Tha River City
g. Tha Ratchawong
h. Tha Saphan Phu (Memorial Bridge)
i. Tha Rachini
j. Tha Tien
k. Tha Chang
l. Tha Rot Fai
m. Tha Maharat
n. Tha Phra Arthit

Royal Orchid Sheraton Hotel is recommended. Organizing your own trip gives greater freedom to stop and start when the mood takes you. It is best to go in the morning (0700). For the trip given above (excluding Wat Rakhang and Wat Suwannaram), the cost for a hang yaaw which can sit 10 people should be about

฿600 for the boat for a half-day. If visiting Rakhang and Suwannaram as well as the other sights, expect to pay about another ฿200-300 for the hire of a boat. Be sure to settle the route and cost before setting out.

THE DUSIT AREA

The Dusit area of Bangkok lies N of the Old City. The area is intersected by wide tree-lined avenues, and has an almost European flavour. The **Vimanmek Palace** lies off Rachvithi Rd, just to the N of the National Assembly. Vimanmek is the largest golden teakwood mansion in the world. It was built by Rama V in 1901 and designed by one of his brothers. The palace makes an interesting contrast to Jim Thompson's House (see page 171) or Suan Pakkard (page 170). While Jim Thompson was enchanted by Thai arts, King Rama V was clearly taken with Western arts. It seems like a large Victorian hunting lodge – but raised off the ground – and is filled with china, silver and paintings from all over the world (as well as some gruesome hunting trophies). The photographs are fascinating – one shows the last time elephants were used in warfare in Thailand. Behind the palace is the Audience Hall which houses a fine exhibition of crafts made by the Support Foundation, an organization set up and funded by Queen Sirikit. Support, rather clumsily perhaps, is the acronym for the Foundation for the Promotion of Supplementary Occupations and Related Techniques. Also worth seeing is the exhibition of the king's own photographs, and the clock museum. Dance shows are held twice a day. Visitors are not free to wander, but must be shown around by one of the charming guides who demonstrate the continued deep reverence for King Rama V (tour approx 1hr). Admission ฿50, ฿20 for children. Note that tickets to the Grand Palace include entrance to Vimanmek Palace. Open 0930-1600 (last tickets sold at 1500) Mon-Sun. Refreshments available. **NB** Visitors to the palace are required to wear long trousers or a skirt; sarongs available for hire (฿100, refundable). Buses do go past the palace, but from the centre of town it is easier to get a tuk-tuk or taxi (฿50-60).

Wat Benchamabophit

Or the **Marble Temple**, is the most modern of the royal temples and was only finished in 1911. It is of unusual architectural design (the architect was the king's half brother, Prince Naris), with carrara marble pillars, a marble courtyard and two large singhas guarding the entrance to the bot. Rama V was so pleased with the marble-faced ordination hall that he wrote to his brother: 'I never flatter anyone but I cannot help saying that you have captured my heart in accomplishing such beauty as this'. The interior is magnificently decorated with crossbeams of lacquer and gold, and in shallow niches in the walls are paintings of important stupas from all over the kingdom. The door panels are faced with bronze sculptures and the windows are of stained-glass, painted with angels. The cloisters around the assembly hall house 52 figures (both original and imitation) – a display of the evolution of the Buddha image in India, China and Japan. The Walking Buddha from the Sukhothai Period is particularly worth a look. The rear courtyard houses a large 80-year-old bodhi tree and a pond filled with turtles, released by people hoping to gain merit. The best time to visit this temple complex is early morning, when monks can be heard chanting inside the chapel. Admission ฿10. Open 0800-1700 Mon-Sun.

OTHER PLACES OF INTEREST

In addition to the Vimanmek Palace, Bangkok also has a number of other beautiful Thai-style houses that are open to the public. **Suan Pakkard Palace** or Lettuce Garden Palace is at 352-354 Sri Ayutthaya Rd, S of the Victory Monument. The five raised traditional Thai houses (domestic rather than royal) were built by Princess Chumbhot, a great-grand-daughter of King Rama IV. They contain her fine collection of antiquities, both historic and prehistoric (the latter are particularly rare). Like the artefacts in the National Museum, those in Suan Pakkard are also poorly labelled. The rear pavilion is particularly lovely, decorated in black and gold lacquerwork panels. Prince Chumbhot discovered this temple near Ayutthaya and reassembled and restored it here for his wife's 50th birthday. The grounds are very peaceful. Admission ø80 – including a fan to ward off the heat. Open 0900-1600, Mon-Sat. All receipts go to a fund for artists.

Jim Thompson's House is on the quiet Soi Kasemsan Song (2), opposite the National Stadium on Rama I Rd. It is an assemblage of traditional teak Northern Thai houses, some more than 200 years old, transported here and reassembled (these houses were designed to be transportable, consisting of five parts – the floor, posts, roof, walls and decorative elements constructed without the use of nails). Jim Thompson arrived in Bangkok as an intelligence officer attached to the United States' OSS (Office of Strategic Services) and then made his name by reinvigorating the Thai silk industry after WW2. He disappeared mysteriously in the Malaysian jungle on 27 March 1967, but his silk industry continues to thrive. (The *Jim Thompson Silk Company*, selling fine Thai silk, is at the NE end of Surawong Rd. This shop is a tourist attraction in itself. Shoppers can buy high-quality bolts of silk and silk clothing here – anything from a pocket handkerchief to a silk suit. Prices are top of the scale.) Jim Thompson chose this site for his house partly because a collection of silk weavers lived nearby on Khlong Saensaep. The house contains an eclectic collection of antiques from Thailand and China, with work displayed as though it was still his home. Shoes must be removed before entering; walking barefoot around the house adds to the appreciation of the cool teak floor-

boards. Bustling Bangkok only intrudes in the form of the stench from the khlong that runs behind the house. Compulsory guided tours around the house and no photography allowed. Admission ø100 (profits to charity). Open 0900-1630, Mon-Sat. **Getting there:** bus along Rama I Rd, taxi or tuk-tuk.

A 10 mins' walk E along Rama I Rd is the shopping area known as **Siam Square** (or *Siam Sa-quare*). This has the greatest concentration of fast food restaurants, boutiques and cinemas in the city. Needless to say, it is patronized by young Thais sporting the latest fashions and doing the sorts of things their parents would never have dreamed of doing – girls smoking and couples holding hands, for instance. For Thais worried about the direction their country is taking, Siam Square encapsulates all their fears in just a few *rai*. This is crude materalism; this is Thais aping the West; this is the erosion of Thai values and culture with scarcely a thought to the future. Because of the tourists and wealthy Thais who congregate around Siam Square it is also a popular patch for beggars. It seems that over the last few years the number of beggars has increased – which may seem odd given Thailands's rapid economic growth. It may be that this economic expansion hasn't reached the poor in rural areas (Thailand has become a more unequal society over the last decade or so); or it maybe that with greater wealth, begging has become a more attractive – in terms of economic return – occupation.

East of Siam Square is the **Erawan Shrine** on the corner of Ploenchit and Rachdamri rds, at the Rachparasong intersection. This is Bangkok's most popular shrine, attracting not just Thais but also large numbers of other Asian visitors. The spirit of the shrine, the Hindu god Thao Maha Brahma, is reputed to grant people's wishes – it certainly has little artistic worth. In thanks, visitors offer garlands, wooden elephants and pay to have dances performed for them accompanied by the resident Thai orchestra. The popular *Thai Rath* newspaper reported in 1991 that some female devotees show their thanks by covorting naked at the shrine in the middle of the night. Others, rather more coy about exposing themselves in this way, have taken to giving the god pornographic videos instead. Although it is unlikely that visitors will be rewarded with the sight of naked bodies, the shrine is a hive of activity at most hours, incongruously set on a noisy, polluted intersection tucked into a corner, and in the shadow of the Sogo Department Store.

One other traditional house worth visiting is the home of the **Siam Society**, off Sukhumvit Rd, at 131 Soi Asoke. The Siam Society is a learned society established in 1904 and has benefited from almost continual royal patronage. The **Kamthieng House** is a 120-year-old N Thai house from Chiang Mai. It was donated to the society in 1963, transported to Bangkok and then reassembled a few years later. It now serves as an ethnological museum, devoted to preserving the traditional technologies and folk arts of Northern Thailand. It makes an interesting contrast to the fine arts displayed in Suan Pakkard Palace and Jim Thompson's house. The Siam Society houses a library, organizes lectures and tours and publishes books, magazines and pamphlets. Admission ฿25, ฿10 for children. Open 0900-1200, 1300-1700, Tues-Sat, T 2583491 for information on lectures.

For those with a penchant for snakes, the **Snake Farm** of the Thai Red Cross is very central and easy to reach from Silom or Surawong rds. It was established in 1923, and raises snakes for serum production, which is distributed worldwide. The farm also has a collection of non-venomous snakes. During showtime (which lasts 30 mins) various snakes are exhibited, and venom extracted. Visitors can fondle a python. The farm is well maintained and professional. Admission ฿70. Open 0830-1630 Mon-Fri (shows at 1100 and 1430), 0830-1200 Sat/Sun and holidays (show at 1100). The farm is within the Science Division of the Thai Red Cross Society at the corner of Rama IV and Henri Dunant rds.

Slightly further out of the centre of Bangkok is the **Chatuchak Weekend Market** which is off Phahonyothin Rd, opposite the Northern bus terminal. Until 1982 this market was held at Sanaam Luang, but was moved because it had outgrown its original home and also because the authorities wanted to clean up the area for the Bangkok bicentenary celebrations. It is a huge conglomeration of 8,672 stallholders spread over an area of 28 acres, selling virtually everything under the sun, and an estimated 200,000 people visit the market

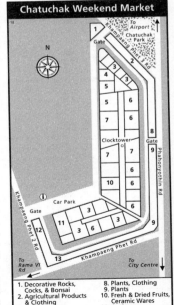

Chatuchak Weekend Market

1. Decorative Rocks, Cocks, & Bonsai
2. Agricultural Products & Clothing
3. Miscellaneous
4. Pets, Handicrafts
5. Pets
6. Clothing
7. Fresh & Dried Fruits
8. Plants, Clothing
9. Plants
10. Fresh & Dried Fruits, Ceramic Wares
11. Antiques
12. Buddha's Image, Plants & Books
13. Paintings, Plants

over a weekend. It is probably the best place to buy handicrafts and all things Thai in the whole Kingdom. There are antique stalls, basket stalls, textile sellers, shirt vendors, carvers, painters ... along with the usual array of fish sellers, vegetable hawkers, butchers and candlestick makers. In the last couple of years a number of bars and food stalls geared to tourists and Thai yuppies have also opened so it is possible to rest and recharge before foraging once more. Definitely worth a visit – and allocate half a day at least. In addition to the map below, Nancy Chandler's Map of Bangkok has an inset map of the market to help you get around. Believe it or not, the market is open on weekends, officially from 0900-1800 (although in fact it begins earlier around 0700). It's best to go early in the day. In 1994 plans were announced to transform the market by building a three-storey purpose-built structure with car parking and various other amenities. Such has been the outcry that the planners have retired to think again. But the fear is that this gem of shopping chaos will be re-organized, sanitized, bureaucratized and, in the process, ruined. **Beware pickpockets**. There is a tourist information centre at the entrance gate off Kamphaeng Phet 2 Rd, and the Clock tower serves as a good reference point should visitors become disoriented. **Getting there:** a/c buses 2 (from Silom Rd), 3, 10, 13 and 29 go past the market, and non-a/c buses 8, 24, 26, 27, 29, 34, 39, 44, 59, and 96. Or take a taxi or tuk-tuk.

EXCURSIONS

FLOATING MARKET AT DAMNOEN SADUAK

Ratchaburi Province, 109 km W of

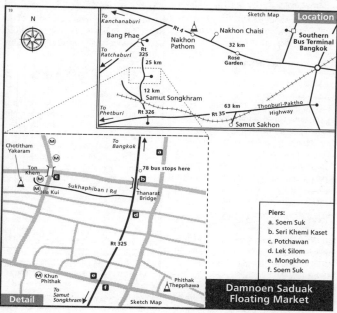

Damnoen Saduak Floating Market

Piers:
a. Soem Suk
b. Seri Khemi Kaset
c. Potchawan
d. Lek Silom
e. Mongkhon
f. Soem Suk

Bangkok. Sadly, it is becoming increasingly like the Floating Market in Thonburi, although it does still function as a legitimate market. **Getting there**: catch an early morning bus (No 78) from the Southern bus terminal in Thonburi – aim to get to Damnoen Saduak between 0800-1000, as the market winds down after 1000, leaving only trinket stalls. The trip takes about 1½ hrs. A/c and non-a/c buses leave every 40 mins from 0600 (฿30-49) (T 4355031 for booking). The bus travels via Nakhon Pathom (where it is possible to stop on the way back and see the great chedi – see Nakhon Pathom). Ask the conductor to drop you at Thanarat Bridge in Damnoen Saduak. Then either walk down the lane (1.5 km) that leads to the market and follows the canal, or take a river taxi for ฿10, or a mini-bus (฿2). There are a number of floating markets in the maze of khlongs – Ton Khem, Hia Kui and Khun Phithak – and it is best to hire a hang yaaw to explore the back-waters and roam around the markets, about ฿300/hour (agree the price before setting out). Tour companies also visit the floating market.

TOURS

Bangkok has innumerable tour companies that can take visitors virtually anywhere. If there is not a tour to fit your bill – most run the same range of tours – many companies will organize one for you, for a price. Most top hotels have their own tour desk and it is probably easiest to book there (arrange to be picked up from your hotel as part of the deal). Prices per person are about ฿250-500 for a half day tour, ฿600-1,000 for a full day (incl lunch).

FESTIVALS AND MAJOR EVENTS

Jan: *Red Cross Fair* (movable), held in Amporn Gardens next to the Parliament. Stalls, classical dancing, folk performances etc.

Feb: *Chinese New Year* (movable), Chinatown closes down, but Chinese temples are packed. *Handicraft Fair* (mid-month), all the handicrafts are made by Thai prisoners.

Mar-Apr: *Kite Flying* (movable, for 1 month), every afternoon/evening at Sanaam Luang there is kite fighting. An *International Kite Festival* is held in late Mar at Sanaam Luang when kite fighting and demonstrations by kite-flyers from across the globe take place.

May: *Royal Ploughing Ceremony* (movable), this celebrates the official start of the rice-planting season and is held at Sanaam Luang. It is an ancient Brahman ritual and is attended by the king.

Sep: *Swan-boat races* (movable), on the Chao Phraya River.

Nov: *Golden Mount Fair* (movable), stalls and theatres set-up all around the Golden Mount and Wat Saket. Candles are carried in procession to the top of the mount. *Marathon* road race, fortunately at one of the coolest times of year.

Dec: *Trooping of the Colour* (movable), the élite Royal Guards swear allegiance to the king and march past members of the Royal Family. It is held in the Royal Plaza near the equestrian statue of King Chulalongkorn.

LOCAL INFORMATION

● **Accommodation**

Bangkok offers a vast range of accommodation at all levels of luxury. There are a number of hotel areas in the city, each with its own character and locational advantages. Accommodation has been divided into five such areas with a sixth – 'other' – for the handful situated elsewhere. A new type of hotel which has emerged in Bangkok in recent years is the 'boutique' hotel. These are small, with immaculate service, and represent an attempt to emulate the philosophy of 'small is beautiful'.

For the last few years Bangkok has had a glut of hotel rooms – especially 5-star – as hotels planned during the heady days of the late 1980s and early 1990s have opened. Room rates at the top end fell around 50% between 1991 and 1996, so there are bargains to be had.

NB For business women travelling alone, the *Oriental, Dusit Thani* and *Amari Airport* hotels allocate a floor to women travellers, with all-female staff.

Many of the more expensive places to stay are on the Chao Phraya River with its views, good shopping and access to the old city. Running eastwards from the river are Silom and Surawong rds, in the heart of Bangkok's business district and close to many embassies. The bars of Patpong link the two roads. This is a good area to stay for shopping and bars, but transport to the tourist sights can be problematic. A more recently developed area is along Sukhumvit Rd running E from Soi Nana Nua (Soi 3). The bulk of the accommodation here is in the A-B range, and within easy reach is a wide range of restaurants, 'girlie' bars, and reasonable shopping. But, the hotels are a long taxi or tuk-tuk ride from the sights of the old city and most of the places of interest to the tourist in Bangkok. In the vicinity of Siam Square are two deluxe hotels and several 'budget' class establishments (especially along Rama 1 Soi Kasemsan Nung). Siam Square is central, a good shopping area, with easy bus and taxi access to Silom and Sukhumvit rds and the sights of the old city. Guesthouses are to be found along and around Khaosan Rd (an area known as Banglamphu); or just to the N, at the NW end of Sri Ayutthaya Rd there is a small cluster of rather friendly places. Soi Ngam Duphli, off Rama IV Rd, is the other big area for cheap places to stay. These hotel areas encompass about 90% of Bangkok's accommodation, although there are other places to stay scattered across the city; these are listed under Other.

● **Silom, Surawong and the River**

L *Dusit Thani*, 946 Rama IV Rd, T 2360450, F 2366400, a/c, restaurants, pool, when it was built it was the tallest building in Bangkok, refurbished, still excellent and has been continually refurbished and upgraded, though disappointing pool, rec; L *Montien*, 54 Surawong Rd, T 2348060, F 2365219, a/c, restaurants, pool, one of the first high-rise hotels (opened 1967) with good location for business, shopping and bars, slick service, and continuing good reputation with loyal patrons; L *Oriental*, 48 Soi Oriental, Charoen Krung, T 2360400, F 2361939, a/c, restaurants, pool, one of the best hotels in the world, beautiful position overlooking the river, superb personal service despite its size (400 rm). The hotel claims that Joseph Conrad, Somerset Maugham and Noel Coward all stayed here at one time or another, although the first of these

probably did not – he lived aboard his ship or, perhaps, stayed in the now defunct *Universal Hotel*. Good shopping arcade, good programme of 'cultural' events, and 6 excellent restaurants, some of the equipment and bathrooms could be said to be a little old, however it still comes highly rec; L *Royal Orchid Sheraton*, 2 Captain Bush Lane, Si Phraya Rd, T 2345599, F 2368320, a/c, restaurants, pool, at times strong and rather unpleasant smell from nearby khlong, lovely views over the river, close to River City shopping centre (good for antiques), rooms are average at this price but service is very slick; L *Shangri-La*, 89 Soi Wat Suan Plu, Charoen Krung, T 2367777, F 2368570, a/c, restaurants, lovely pool, great location overlooking river, sometimes preferred to *Oriental* but some consider it dull and impersonal, recently upgraded and extended, rec; L *The Western Banyan Tree*, 21/100 Sathorn Tai Rd, T 6791200, F 6791199, a/c, restaurant, pool, new hotel and the tallest in Bangkok. It is targeting the business traveller, all rooms are suites with working area, in room fax and copier, computer port and voice mail, good position for many offices; L-A+ *Sukhothai*, 13/3 Sathorn Tai Rd, T 2870222, F 2874980, a/c, restaurants (especially good poolside Italian restaurant), beautiful rooms and excellent service, in Thai postmodern style, clean and elegant, there are those who say it is even better than such established hotels as *The Regent*, even *The Oriental*, rec; L-A+ *Holiday Inn Crowne Plaza*, 981 Silom Rd, T 2384300, F 2385289, a/c, restaurants, pool, vast, pristine marble-filled hotel, all amenities, immensely comfortable, minimum atmosphere and character.

A+ *Marriott Royal Garden Riverside Hotel*, 257/1-3 Charoen Nakorn Rd, T 4760021, F 4761120, a/c, restaurant, large pool, situated on the river but on the Thonburi bank,

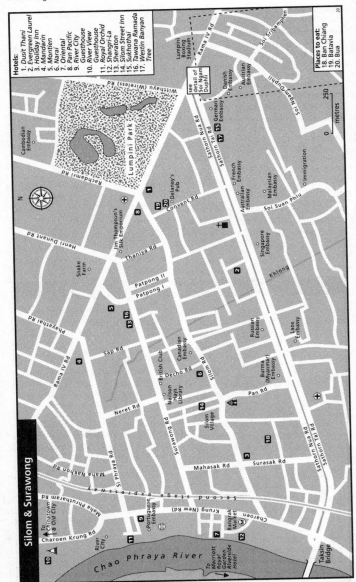

Silom & Surawong

Hotels:
1. Dusit Thani
2. Evergreen Laurel
3. Holiday Inn
4. Mandarin
5. Montien
6. Narai
7. Oriental
8. Pan Pacific
9. River City Guesthouse
10. River View Guesthouse
11. Royal Orchid
12. Shangri-La
13. Sheraton
14. Silom Street Inn
15. Sukhothai
16. Tawana Ramada
17. Westin Banyan Tree

Places to eat:
18. Ban Chiang
19. Batavia
20. Bua

0 — 250 metres

see detail of Soi Ngam Duphli

Lumpini Boxing Stadium

Lumpini Park

Cambodian Embassy
Danish Embassy
Austrian Embassy
German Embassy
French Embassy
Australian Embassy
Malaysian Embassy
Immigration
Singapore Embassy
Russian Embassy
Laos Embassy
Burma (Myanmar) Embassy
Canadian Embassy
British Club
Neilson Hays Library
Snake Farm
Jim Thompson's Silk Emporium
Delaney's Pub
Portuguese Embassy
Bangkok Market
Silom Village
River City

Wittayu (Wireless) Rd
Rachadamri Rd
Henri Dunant Rd
Phayathai Rd
Rama IV Rd
Sathorn Nua Rd
Sathorn Tai Rd
Soi Ngam Duphli
Soi Sribamphen
Soi Suan Phlu
Convent Rd
Thaniya Rd
Patpong II
Patpong I
Sap Rd
Silom Rd
Decho Rd
Pan Rd
Neret Rd
Surawong Rd
Mahasak Rd
Surasak Rd
Maha Nakhon Rd
Si Phraya Rd
Maha Phruttharam Rd
Charoen Krung Rd
Krung (New Rd)
Khlong
Second stage expressway

Chao phraya River

Taksin Bridge

To Marriott Royal Garden Riverside Hotel

To Chinatown & Old City

attractive low rise hotel with some attempt to create Thai-style and ambience; **A+ *Monarch Lee Gardens***, 188 Silom Rd, T 2381991, F 2381999, a/c, restaurants, pool, opened 1992, stark and gleaming high-tech high-rise, all facilities, still trying hard to attract custom, discounts available; **A+ *Pan Pacific Hotel***, 952 Rama IV Rd, T 6329000, F 6329001, a/c, restaurant, pool, 235 rm hotel, good central position for business and shopping.

A *Mandarin*, 662 Rama IV Rd, T 2380230, F 2371620, a/c, restaurant, small pool, friendly atmosphere, comfortable rooms, popular nightclub; **A *Silom Street Inn***, 284/11-13 Silom Rd, opp the junction with Pan Rd (between sois 22 and 24), T 2384680, F 2384689, a/c, restaurant, pool, small new hotel, small, comfortable, 30 well-equipped rm with CNN News, grubby rather seedy lobby, set back from road; **A *Tower Inn***, 533 Silom Rd, T 2344051, F 2344051, a/c, restaurant, pool, simple but comfortable hotel, with large rooms and an excellent roof terrace, good value.

B *River City Guesthouse*, 11/4 Charoen Krung Soi Rong Nam Khang 1, T 2351429, F 2373127, a/c, not very welcoming but rooms are a good size and clean, good bathrooms, short walk to River City and the river; **B *Rose***, 118 Surawong Rd, T 2337695, F 2346381, a/c, restaurant, pool, opp Patpong, favourite among single male visitors, but getting seedier by the month; **B *Swan***, 31 Charoen Krung Soi 36, T 2348594, some a/c, great position, clean but scruffy rooms.

C *Chao Phya Riverside*, 1128 Songward Rd (opp the Chinese school), T 2226344, F 2231696, some a/c, old style house overlooking river, clean rooms, atmospheric, unusual location in commercial Chinatown with *sip lors* (ten-wheelers) loading rice, and metal workers fashioning steel, seems to be a little more run-down than a few years back and characteristically brusque management but worth considering for its position and character; **C *River View Guesthouse***, 768 Songwad Soi Panurangsri, T 2345429, F 2375771, some a/c, the restaurant/bar is on the top floor and overlooks the river, food is mediocre, but the atmosphere is friendly, rooms are large, clean, some with balconies, some hot water,

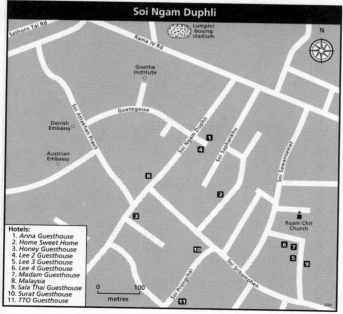

Soi Ngam Duphli

Hotels:
1. Anna Guesthouse
2. Home Sweet Home
3. Honey Guesthouse
4. Lee 2 Guesthouse
5. Lee 3 Guesthouse
6. Lee 4 Guesthouse
7. Madam Guesthouse
8. Malaysia
9. Sala Thai Guesthouse
10. Surat Guesthouse
11. TTO Guesthouse

difficult to find but in a central position in Chinatown and overlooking (as the name suggests) the river, professional management, Khun Phi Yai, the owner, is a pharmacist, so can even prescribe pills.

● **Soi Ngam Duphli**

Soi Ngam Duphli is much the smaller of Bangkok's two centres of guesthouse accommodation. Locationally, the area is good for the shopping and bars of Silom Rd but inconvenient for most of the city's main places of interest in the old city. Guesthouses tend to be quieter and more refined than those of Khaosan Rd – and therefore more expensive too. See the Soi Ngam Duphli map for locations.

B *Malaysia*, 54 Rama IV Soi Ngam Duphli, T 2863582, F 2493120, a/c, restaurant, pool, once a Bangkok favourite for travellers.

C *TTO*, 2/48 Soi Sribamphen, T 2866783, F 2871571, a/c, well-run and popular, homely atmosphere, rooms a little small; **C-D** *Honey*, 35/2-4 Soi Ngam Duphli, T 2863460, some a/c, large rooms, in a rather rambling block, clean and good value, service can be rather surly, no hot water.

D *Sala Thai Guesthouse*, 15 Soi Sribamphen, T 2871436, at end of peaceful, almost leafy,

soi, clean rooms, family run, good food, but shared bathroom, rec; **D-E** *Anna*, 21/30 Soi Ngam Duphli, clean rooms, some with bathrooms; **D-E** *Home Sweet Home*, 27/7 Soi Sribamphen (opp Boston Inn, down small soi, so relatively quiet, average rooms with attached bathrooms; **D-E** *Lee 3*, 13 Soi Saphan Khu, T 2863042, some a/c, wooden house with character, down quiet soi, rooms are clean but with shared bathrooms, rec; **D-E** *Madam*, 11 Soi Saphan Khu, T 2869289, wooden house, friendly atmosphere, attached bathrooms, no hot water, quiet, rec.

E *Lee 2*, 21/38-39 Soi Ngam Duphli, T 2862069, clean, friendly, rec; **E** *Lee 4*, 9 Soi Saphan Khu, T 2867874, spotless rooms and bathrooms, some with balconies and views over city, rec; **E** *Surat*, 2/18-20 Sribumphen Rd, T 2867919, some a/c, own bathroom, no hot water, clean and well-run, rec.

● **Siam Square, Rama I, Ploenchit and Phetburi roads**

L *Grand Hyatt Erawan*, 494 Rachdamri Rd, T 2541234, F 2535856, the replacement hotel for the much-loved old *Erawan Hotel*, towering structure with grandiose entrance and a plastic tree-filled atrium plus sumptuous rooms and every

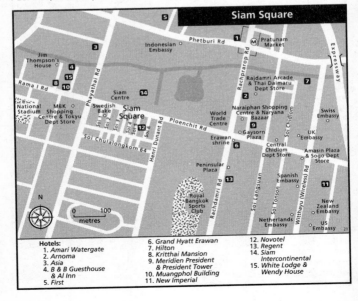

Siam Square

Hotels:
1. *Amari Watergate*
2. *Arnoma*
3. *Asia*
4. *B & B Guesthouse & Al Inn*
5. *First*
6. *Grand Hyatt Erawan*
7. *Hilton*
8. *Kritthai Mansion*
9. *Meridien President & President Tower*
10. *Muangphol Building*
11. *New Imperial*
12. *Novotel*
13. *Regent*
14. *Siam Intercontinental*
15. *White Lodge & Wendy House*

facility but has lost atmosphere in the process; **L** *Hilton*, 2 Witthayu Rd, T 2530123, F 2536509, a/c, restaurants, attractive pool, excellent hotel set in lovely grounds with a remarkable garden feel for a hotel that is so central, comparatively small for such a large plot and first class service; **L** *Novotel*, Siam Sq Soi 6, T 2556888, F 2551824, a/c, restaurant, pool, undistinguished but commendably comfortable; **L** *Siam Intercontinental*, 967 Rama I Rd, T 2530355, F 2532275, a/c, restaurants, small pool, relatively low-key hotel, set in 26 acres of grounds, good sports facilities, excellent service; **L-A+** *Imperial*, 6-10 Witthayu Rd, (on the edge of Siam Sq area), T 2540023, F 2533190, a/c, restaurants, pool, lovely grounds but hotel seems rather jaded next to Bangkok's newer upstarts, 370 rm and numerous bars and restaurants where, apparently, it is possible to rub shoulders with the city's 'beautiful people', walls are very thin and recent visitors have been disappointed at how this hotel has declined in quality; **L-A+** *Regent Bangkok*, 155 Rachdamri Rd, T 2516127, F 2539195, a/c, restaurants (see Thai Restaurants, page 187), pool (although rather noisy, set above a busy road), excellent reputation amongst frequent visitors who insist on staying here, stylish and postmodern in atmosphere with arguably the best range of cuisine in Bangkok. It is also perhaps the most impressive piece of modern hotel architecture in Bangkok – which admittedly isn't saying much, rec.

A+ *Amari Atrium Hotel*, 1880 Phetburi Rd, T 7182000, F 7182002, a/c, restaurant, pool, Clark Hatch fitness centre, opened early 1996, 600 rm, all facilities, reasonably accessible for airport but not particularly well placed for the sights of the old city, nor for the central business district for that matter; **A+** *Amari Watergate*, 847 Phetburi Rd, T 6539000, F 6539045, a/c, restaurants, pool, fitness centre, squash court, situated close to the Pratunam market, great curvey pool (which makes swimming lengths a little tricky), but close to 600 rm makes this a hotel on a grand scale, lots of marble and plastic trees, uninspired block, good facilities; **A+** *Le Meridien President*, 971 Ploenchit Rd, T 2530444, F 2549988, pool, health club, 400 rm in this, one of the older but still excellent luxury hotels in Bangkok (it opened in 1966), tranquil atmosphere, good service, excellent French food, a new sister hotel, *The President Tower* is due for completion in late 1996 and will tower 36 storeys skywards, the original hotel is still rec; **A+** *Siam City*, 477 Sri Ayutthaya Rd, T 2470120,

F 2470178, a/c, restaurants, pool, stylish hotel with attentive staff, large rooms with in-house movies, all facilities (gym etc) and well managed, good Mediterranean restaurant and bakery, rec.

B *Florida*, 43 Phayathai Rd, T 2470990, a/c, restaurant, pool, one of Thailand's first international hotels and it shows, average even at this price.

C *A-1 Inn*, 25/13 Soi Kasemsan Nung (1), Rama I Rd, T 2153029, a/c, well run, intimate hotel, rec; **C** *Bed and Breakfast*, 36/42 Soi Kasemsan Nung (1), Rama 1 Rd, T 2153004, F 2152493, a/c, friendly efficient staff, clean but small rooms, good security, bright 'lobby', price includes breakfast, rec; **C** *Muangphol Building*, 931/9 Rama I Rd, T 2150033, F 2168053, a/c, pool, hot water, good sized rooms, reasonable rates; **C** *Wendy House*, 36/2 Soi Kasemsan Nung (1), Rama I Rd, T 2162436, F 2168053, a/c, spotless, but small rooms with eating area downstairs, hot water; **C** *White Lodge*, 36/8 Soi Kasemsan Nung (1), Rama I Rd, T 2168867, F 2168228, a/c, hot water, airy, light reasonably sized rooms, rec; **C-E** *Alternative Tour Guesthouse*, 14/1 Rachaprarop Soi Rachatapan, T 2452963, F 2467020, friendly, excellent source of information, attached to *Alternative Tour Company*, promoting culturally and environmentally sensitive tourism, clean.

● **Sukhumvit Road**

L *Imperial Queen's Park*, Sukhumvit Soi 22, T 2619000, F 2619530, massive new 37-storey hotel with a mind boggling 1,400 rm, how service can, in any sense, be personal is hard to imagine, but all possible facilities, location is away from most sights and the main business district so means guests have to battle with the traffic to do most things; **L** *Windsor Plaza Embassy Suites*, 8 Sukhumvit Soi 20, T 2580160, F 2581491, a/c, restaurants, pool, next door to the *Windsor Hotel*, 460 suites, health centre.

A+ *Delta Grand Pacific*, 259 Sukhumvit Rd, T 2544998, F 2552441, a/c, restaurants, pool, almost 400 rm in this large high-rise hotel, all facilities but characterless for the price; **A+** *Rembrandt*, 15-15/1 Sukhumvit Soi 20, T 2617040, F 2617017, a/c, restaurants, pool, new hotel with lots of marble and limited ambience; **A+-A** *Somerset*, 10 Sukhumvit Soi 15, T 2548500, F 2548534, a/c, restaurant, tiny enclosed pool, small hotel, rather ostentatious, rooms are nondescript but comfortable, baths are designed for people of small stature.

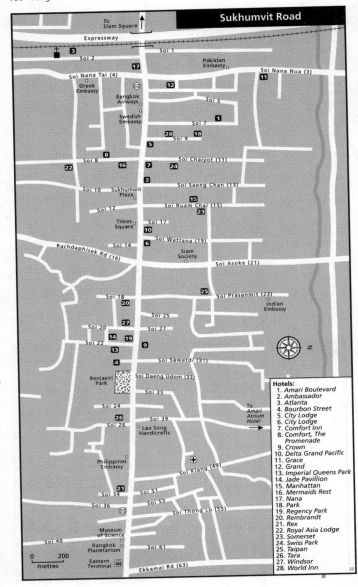

Sukhumvit Road

Hotels:
1. Amari Boulevard
2. Ambassador
3. Atlanta
4. Bourbon Street
5. City Lodge
6. City Lodge
7. Comfort Inn
8. Comfort, The Promenade
9. Crown
10. Delta Grand Pacific
11. Grace
12. Grand
13. Imperial Queens Park
14. Jade Pavillion
15. Manhattan
16. Mermaids Rest
17. Nana
18. Park
19. Regency Park
20. Rembrandt
21. Rex
22. Royal Asia Lodge
23. Somerset
24. Swiss Park
25. Taipan
26. Tara
27. Windsor
28. World Inn

A *Amari Boulevard*, 2 Sukhumvit Soi 5, T 2552930, F 2552950, a/c, restauarant, roof top, pool, good mid-range hotel, over 300 rm, fitness centre, nothing to mark it out as particularly Thai – generic tropical feel; **A** *Ambassador*, 171 Sukhumvit Rd, T 2540444, F 2534123, a/c, restaurants, pool, large, impersonal rather characterless hotel, with great food hall (see restaurants); **A** *Manhattan*, 13 Sukhumvit Soi 15, T 2550166, F 2553481, a/c, restaurant, pool, recently renovated high-rise, lacks character but rooms are comfortable and competitively priced although some are rather shabby so ask to inspect; **A** *Tai-pan*, 25 Sukhumvit Soi 23, T 2609888, F 2597908, a/c, restaurant, pool, tasteful new hotel; **A** *Windsor*, 8 Sukhumvit Soi 20, T 2580160, F 2581491, a/c, restaurant, pool, tennis.

B *Bourbon Street*, 29/4-6 Sukhumvit Soi 22 (behind Washington Theatre), T 2590328, F 2594318, a/c, small number of rooms attached to this Cajun restaurant, well run and good value, rec; **B** *China*, 19/27-28 Sukhumvit Soi 19, T 2557571, F 2541333, a/c, restaurant, a small hotel masquerading as a large one, but rooms are up to the standard of more expensive places, so good value; **B** *Comfort Inn*, 153/11 Sukhumvit Soi 11, T 2519250, F 2543562, a/c, restaurant, small hotel, friendly management, rec; **B** *Crown*, 503 Sukhumvit Soi 29, T 2580318, F 2584438, a/c, clean, good service; **B** *Grand*, 2/7-8 Sukhumvit Soi Nana Nua (Soi 3), T 2533380, F 2549020, a/c, restaurant, small hotel with friendly staff, good value.

C *Atlanta*, 78 Sukhumvit Soi 2, T 2521650, a/c, restaurant, large pool, left-luggage facility, poste restante, daily video-shows, good tour company in foyer, rec.

D *Chu's*, 35 Sukhumvit Soi 19, T 2544683, restaurant, one of the cheapest in the area, good food, rec; **D** *Happy Inn*, 20/1 Sukhumvit Soi 4, T 2526508, some a/c, basic rooms, cheerful management; **D** *SV*, 19/35-36 Sukhumvit Soi 19, T 2544724, some a/c, another cheap hotel in this area, musty rooms, shared bathrooms and poor service; **D-E** *Disra House*, 593/28 Sukhumvit Soi 33-33/1, T 2585102, some a/c, friendly and well run place which comes highly recommended, rather out-of-the-way but good value a/c rooms.

● **Banglamphu (Khaosan Road) and surrounds**

Khaosan Rd lies NE of Sanaam Luang, just off Rachdamnern Klang Ave, close to the Democracy Monument. It is continually expanding into new roads and sois, in particular the area W of Chakrapong Rd. The sois off the main road are often quieter, such as Soi Chana Songkhran or Soi Rambutri. Note that rooms facing on to Khaosan Rd tend to be very noisy.

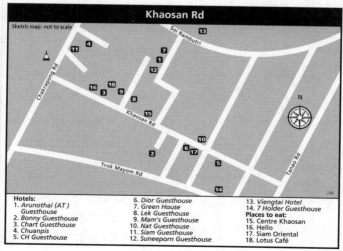

Khaosan Rd

Sketch map: not to scale

Soi Rambutri

Chakrapong Rd

Khaosan Rd

Trok Mayom Rd

Tanao Rd

N

23A

Hotels:
1. Arunothai (AT) Guesthouse
2. Bonny Guesthouse
3. Chart Guesthouse
4. Chuanpis
5. CH Guesthouse
6. Dior Guesthouse
7. Green House
8. Lek Guesthouse
9. Mam's Guesthouse
10. Nat Guesthouse
11. Siam Guesthouse
12. Suneeporn Guesthouse
13. *Viengtai Hotel*
14. *7 Holder Guesthouse*
Places to eat:
15. Centre Khaosan
16. Hello
17. Siam Oriental
18. Lotus Café

Khaosan Rd is not just a place to spend the night. Also here are multitudes of restaurants, travel and tour agents, shops, stalls, tattoo artists, bars, bus companies – almost any and every service a traveller might need. They are geared to budget visitors' needs and more than a few have dubious reputations, in general the guesthouses of Khaosan Rd itself have been eclipsed in terms of quality and cleanliness by those to the N, closer to the river. The useful little post office that used to be at the top of Khaosan Rd and operated a poste restante service and a fax facility has recently closed. Whether it will re-open is not certain.

A+ *Royal Princess*, 269 Lan Luang Rd, T 2813088, F 2801314, a/c, restaurants, pool, newish addition to Dusit chain of hotels, good facilities.

A *Majestic Palace*, 97 Rachdamnern Klang Ave (opp Democracy Monument), T 2805610, F 2800965, a/c, restaurant, pool, old hotel given half-hearted face-lift, good location but rooms overpriced and limited facilities; **A** *Royal*, 2 Rachdamnern Klang Ave, T 2229111, F 2242083, a/c, restaurant, pool, old (by Bangkok standards) hotel which acted as a refuge for demonstrators during the 1991 riots, rooms are dated and featureless; **A** *Vi-*

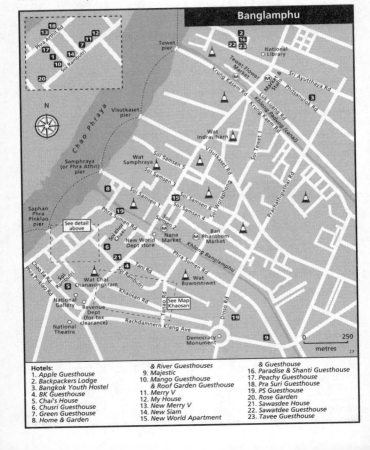

Banglamphu

Hotels:
1. Apple Guesthouse
2. Backpackers Lodge
3. Bangkok Youth Hostel
4. BK Guesthouse
5. Chai's House
6. Chusri Guesthouse
7. Green Guesthouse
8. Home & Garden

& River Guesthouses
9. Majestic
10. Mango Guesthouse & Roof Garden Guesthouse
11. Merry V
12. My House
13. New Merry V
14. New Siam
15. New World Apartment

& Guesthouse
16. Paradise & Shanti Guesthouse
17. Peachy Guesthouse
18. Pra Suri Guesthouse
19. PS Guesthouse
20. Rose Garden
21. Sawasdee House
22. Sawatdee Guesthouse
23. Tavee Guesthouse

engtai, 42 Tanee Rd, Banglamphu, T 2815788, a/c, restaurant, pool, rooms are very good, clean relatively spacious, with all the advantages of this area in terms of proximity to the Old City.

B *Trang Hotel*, 99/1 Visutkaset Rd, T 2811402, F 2803160, a/c, restaurant, pool, clean and friendly mid-range hotel which comes rec by regular visitors to Bangkok, discount voucher available from *Vieng Travel* in the same building.

C *New World Apartment and Guesthouse*, 2 Samsen Rd, T 2815596, F 2815596, some a/c, good location for the Old City yet away from the hurly-burly of Khaosan Rd, rooms are clean and good value even if the overall atmosphere is rather institutional; **C** *Pia Arthit Mansion*, 22 Phra Arthit Rd, comfortable rooms, hot water, a/c, carpeted, bath tubs, pleasant communal sitting area; **C-D** *7 Holder*, 216/2-3 Khaosan Rd, T 2813682, some a/c, clean, friendly, located on the narrow soi behind Khaosan Rd, so quieter than those places situated right on the street; **C-D** *New Siam*, Phra Athit 21 Soi Chana Songkram, T 2824554, F 2817461, some a/c, good restaurant, modern and clean, friendly helpful staff, airy rooms, but featureless block, tickets and tour information, fax facilities, lockers available, overpriced; **C-E** *Chart*, 58 Khaosan Rd, T 2803785, restaurant, some a/c, small but clean rooms, some have no windows; **C-E** *Green House*, 88/1 Khaosan Soi Rambutri, T 2819572, some a/c, ask for rooms away from street, for an extra ฿100 they will flip the switch for a/c, rec; **C-E** *Peachy*, 10 Phra Athit Rd, T 2816659, some a/c and more expensive rooms with hot water, recent visitors have reported a deterioration in quality and cleanliness, but still has pleasant restaurant area.

D *My House*, 37 Phra Athit Soi Chana Songkram, T 2829263, management are a little off-hand but the rooms are well maintained and loos are kept clean, remains popular; **D** *Pra Suri*, 85/1 Soi Pra Suri (off Dinso Rd), 5 mins E from Khaosan Rd not far from the Democracy Monument, fan, restaurant, own bathrooms (no hot water), clean and quiet, very friendly and helpful family-run guesthouse, rec; **D-E** *BK*, 11/1 Chakrapong Soi Sulaow, T 2815278, some a/c, in busy area of Banglamphu, but guesthouse is set back from road, so not too noisy, clean but dark rooms, shared bathrooms, good information; **D-E** *Buddy*, 137/1 Khaosan Rd, T 2824351, off main street, some a/c, rooms are small and dingy but it remains popular, large open restaurant area

bustles with people exchanging information; **D-E** *CH*, 216/1 Khaosan Rd, T 2822023, some a/c, good reputation, left luggage (฿5/day, ฿30/week); **D-E** *Chai's House*, 49/4-8 Chao Fa Soi Rongmai, T 2814901, F 2818686, some a/c, friendly atmosphere, clean and colourful with borgainvillea growing from the balconies and bamboos and orchids in the restaurant, last house down Soi Rambutri, so away from the others, rec; **D-E** *Hello*, 63-65 Khaosan Rd, T 2818579, some a/c, popular; **D-E** *Privacy Tourist House*, 69 Tanow Rd, T 2827028, popular, quiet, rec; **D-E** *Sawasdee House*, 147 Chakrapong Soi Rambutri, T 2818138, bit of a warren of a place and feels like a cross between a guesthouse and a hotel, shared loos and showers are kept clean, and rooms though box-like are fine. Out the front is a sitting area and what is rather optimistically called a beer 'garden'.

E *Apple 2*, 11 Phra Sumen Rd, T 2811219, old-time favourite, very small rooms, basic, but friendly and characterful; **E** *Arunothai (AT)*, 90/1, 5, 12 Khaosan Soi Rambutri, T 2826979, friendly owner, situated in a quiet little courtyard with 4 or 5 other guesthouses, good place to start looking for a room as it is easy to check them all out; **E** *Bonny*, 132 Khaosan Rd, T 2819877, quiet, situated down a narrow alley off Khaosan itself, reports of bed bugs; **E** *Chuanpis*, 86 Chakrapong Rd (nr intersection with Khaosan Rd, down small soi opp Wat Chanasongkhram), popular, geared particularly to Israeli visitors, good food, average rooms, often full; **E** *Democratic*, 211/8 Rachdamnern Ave, T 2826035, F 2249149, set back, opp the Democracy Monument, 4-storey concrete house with friendly management but small rooms and grubby stairwell; **E** *Dior*, 146-158 Khaosan Rd, T 2829142, small but clean rooms and bathrooms, quiet, as set back from road, 'family' atmosphere, rec; **E** *Green Guesthouse*, 27 Phra Athit Soi Chana Songkram, T 2828994, not to be confused with the *Green House*, rooms are fine and competively priced; **E** *Home and Garden*, 16 Samphraya Rd (Samsen 3), T 2801475, away from main concentration of guesthouses, down quiet soi (quite difficult to find), good location for river taxi, rooms are small and basic but clean, well run and friendly, rec; **E** *Lek*, 90/9 Khaosan Soi Rambutri, T 2812775, popular; **E** *Mam's*, 119 Khaosan Rd, friendly, homely atmosphere, rec; **E** *Merry V*, 33-35 Phra Athit Soi Chana Songkram, T 2829267, some a/c, large place, some rooms with balconies although interior rooms have no outside windows and are dark, lockers available, friendly and well run with good information; **E** *Nat*, 217 Khaosan Rd, brusque management but clean, larger than average rooms with fan, rec; **E** *New Merry V*, 18-20 Phra Athit Rd, T 2803315, new guesthouse with clean but very small rooms, pleasant place to stay, friendly, with a good travel service; **E** *PS*, 9 Phra Sumen Rd, T 2823932, spotlessly clean, rooms with no windows, but satellite TV and free tea and coffee, rec; **E** The River Guest House, 18/1 Samphraya Rd (Samsen 3), T 2800876, next to the *Home and Garden* and very similar, good location, quiet but accessible by express boat, friendly, rec. (**NB** There is a third guesthouse on Samphraya Rd, *The Clean and Calm* about which we have received disturbing reports.) **E** *Rose Garden*, 28/6 Phra Athit Soi Trok Rongmai, T 2818366, friendly although rooms are a bit dark; **E** *Siam*, 76 Chakrapong Rd, T 2810930, rooms facing onto the street are noisy, small rooms but good clean bathrooms; **E** *Suneeporn*, 90/10 Khaosan Soi Rambutri, T 2826887, popular; **E** *Sweety*, 49 Thani Rd, clean, rec; **E-F** *Uimol Guesthouse*, Soi 2 Samsen Rd, home relaxing and friendly guesthouse, good eating places in vicinity.

F *KC*, 60-64 Phra Sumen Rd Soi Khai Chae, T 2820618, friendly management, clean rooms, rec.

● **Sri Ayutthaya Road**
Sri Ayutthaya is emerging as an 'alternative' area for budget travellers. It is a central location with restaurants and foodstalls nearby, but does not suffer the over-crowding and sheer pandemonium of Khaosan Rd and so is considerably quieter and more peaceful. It is also close to the Tewet Pier for the express river boats (see the Banglamphu map). The guesthouses are perhaps a little more expensive but the rooms are better and the places seem to be generally better managed. One family runs four of the guesthouses which means if one is full you will probably be moved on to another.

D *Shanti Lodge*, 37 Sri Ayutthaya Rd, T 2812497, restaurant with extensive menu, very popular, rooms nicely done up, rec.

E *Backpackers Lodge*, 85 Sir Ayutthaya Rd, Soi 14, T 2823231, restaurant, rooms with fans, small patio, quiet and friendly, large python (*ngulaam*) keeps watch at the bottom of the stairs, fortunately caged, rec; **E** *Paradise*, 57 Sri Ayutthaya Rd, T 2828673, some fans, small guesthouse, rooms with no outward-looking windows, friendly management; **E** *Sawatdee*, 71 Sri Ayutthaya Rd, T 2810757, Western menu, pokey rooms, popular with German travellers, management rather brusque and off-hand; **E** *Tavee*, 83 Sri Ayutthaya Rd, Soi 14, T 2801447, restaurant, fan, small garden, clean and pleasant, rooms and shared showers and loos are kept spotless, down a quiet little soi, has been operating since 1985 and has managed to maintain a very high standard, rec; **E-F** *Bangkok Youth Hostel*, 25/2 Phitsanulok Rd (off Samsen Rd), T 2820950, N of Khaosan Rd, away from the bustle, dorms available.

● **Others**
A+ *Central Hotel*, 1695 Phahonyothin Rd, T 5411234, F 5411087, a/c, restaurant, pool, out of town, close to w/e market, efficiently run, but inconveniently located and recently taken over by the Central Department Store group.

A+ *Marriot Royal Garden*, Riverside Resort, 257/1-3 Charoen Nakrom Rd, T 4760021, F 4761120, a/c, restaurant, excellent swimming pool, almost resort-like, very spacious surrounding, opp the *Oriental*, nr the Krung Thep Bridge, free shuttle-boat service every 30 mins between hotel and the *Oriental* and River City piers.

A *Sunroute Bangkok*, 288 Rama IX Rd, T 2480011, F 2485990, a/c, restaurants, pool, part of a Japanese chain, markets itself as the 'route to satisfaction', located away from most sights and shopping; Dusit Riverside, over Sathorn Bridge in Thonburi (opening late 1992); **A-B** *Ramada Renaissance Bridgeview*, 3999 Rama III Rd, T 2923160, F 2923164, a/c, numerous restaurants, pools, tennis, squash, new 476 room high-rise overlooking Chao Phraya River, all facilities, poor location for sights, shopping and business.

C-E *The Artists Club*, 61 Soi Tiem Boon Yang, T 4389653, some a/c, run by an artist, this is a guesthouse cum studio cum gallery in Thonburi (ie the other side of the river), clean rooms and a real alternative place to stay with concerts and drawing lessons, away from the centre of guesthouse activity.

● **Places to eat**
Bangkok has the largest and widest selection of restaurants in Thailand – everyone eats out, so the number of places is vast. Food is generally very good and cheap – this applies not just to Thai restaurants but also to places serving other Asian cuisines, and Western dishes. Roadside food is good value – many Thais eat on the street, businessmen and civil servants rubbing shoulders with factory workers and truck drivers. **NB** Most restaurants close be-

tween 2200 and 2230. For a fuller listing of places to eat see *Bangkok Metro Magazine*, published monthly. The magazine is also good for bars, music venues, shopping etc.

Afternoon tea: *The Authors Lounge*, *Oriental Hotel*; the *Bakery Shop*, *Siam Intercontinental Hotel*; *The Cup*, second floor of Peninsula Plaza, Rachdamri Rd; *The Regent Hotel* lobby (music accompaniment), Rachdamri Rd; the *Dusit Thani Hotel* library, Rama IV Rd.

Bakeries: Bangkok has a large selection of fine bakeries, many attached to hotels like the *Landmark*, *Dusit Thani* and *Oriental*. There are also the generic 'donut' fast food places although few lovers of bread and pastries would want to lump the two together. *The Bakery Landmark Hotel*, 138 Sukhumvit Rd, many cakes and pastry connoiseurs argue that this is the best of the hotel places, popular with expats, wide range of breads and cakes; *Basket of Plenty*, Peninsula Plaza, Rachdamri Rd (another branch at 66-67 Sukhumvit Soi 33), bakery, deli and trendy restaurant, very good things baked and a classy (though expensive) place for lunch; *Bei Otto*, Sukhumvit Soi 20, a German bakery and deli, makes really very good pastries, breads and cakes; *Cheesecake House*, 69/2 Ekamai Soi 22, rather out of town for most tourists but patronized enthusiastically by the city's large Sukhumvit-based expat population, as the name suggests cheescakes of all descriptions are a speciality – and are excellent; *Folies*, 309/3 Soi Nang Linchee (Yannawa), T 2869786, French expats and bake-o-philes maintain this bakery makes the most authentic pastries and breads in town, coffee available, a great place to sit, eat and read; *Jimmy*, 1270-2, nr Oriental Lane, Charoen Krung, a/c, cakes and ice creams, very little else around here, so it's a good stopping place; *La Brioche*, ground flr of Novotel Hotel, Siam Sq Soi 6, good range of French patisseries; *Sweet Corner*, Siam Intercontinental Hotel, Rama I Rd, one of the best in Bangkok; *Swedish Bake*, Siam Square Soi 2, good Danish pastries.

Chinese: most Thai restaurants sell Chinese food, but there are also many dedicated Chinese establishments. **Siam Square** has a large number, particularly those specializing in shark's fin soup. For shark's fin try the *Scala Shark's Fin* (reputed to be the best of the bunch), *Bangkok Shark's Fin*, and the *Penang Shark's Fin* all opp the Scala Cinema, Siam Square Soi 1. ♦♦♦♦-♦♦♦*Kirin*, 226/1 Siam Square Soi 2, over 20 years old, traditional Chi-

Price guide		
	US$	**Baht**
♦♦♦♦♦	20	500+
♦♦♦♦	15+	375+
♦♦♦	5-15	125-375
♦♦	2-5	50-125
♦	under 2	under 50

nese decor, good atmosphere; ♦♦♦*Art House*, 87 Sukhumvit Soi 55 (Soi Thonglor), country house with traditional Chinese furnishings, surrounded by gardens, particularly good seafood; ♦♦♦*China*, 231/3 Rachdamri Soi Sarasin, Bangkok's oldest Chinese restaurant, serving full range of Chinese cuisine; ♦♦♦*Chinese Seafood Restaurant*, 33/1-5 16 Wall St Tower, Surawong Rd, Cantonese and Szechuan; ♦♦♦*Joo Long Lao*, 2/1 Sukhumvit Soi 2, spacious, with wide choice of dishes, rec; ♦♦♦*Lung Wah*, 848/13 Rama lll Rd, large restaurant, with good reputation, serves shark's fin and other seafood, also serves Thai; ♦♦♦*Pata*, 26 Siam Square Soi 3; ♦♦♦*Shangarila*, 154/4-7 Silom Rd, T 2340861, bustling Shanghai restaurant with dim sum lunch; ♦♦♦*Sunshine Noodle Square*, 39/27-30 Siam Square Soi 5, opened in 1996, clean and cool design and nouvelle Chinese cuisine – open 24 hrs; ♦♦*Tongkee*, 308-314 Sukhumvit Rd (opp Soi 19), Kwangtung food, popular with Thais.

Fast Food: Bangkok now has a large number of Western fast food outlets, such as *Pizza Hut*, *McDonalds*, *Kentucky Fried Chicken*, *Mister Donut*, *Dunkin' Donuts*, *Shakey's*, *Baskin Robbins* and *Burger King*. These are located in the main shopping and tourist areas – Siam Square, Silom/Patpong rds, and Ploenchit Rd, for example.

Foodstalls: scattered across the city for a rice or noodle dish, where a meal will cost ฿15-30 instead of a minimum of ฿75 in the restaurants. For example, on the roads between Silom and Surawong Rd, or down Soi Somkid, next to Ploenchit Rd, or opp on Soi Tonson.

Italian: ♦♦♦♦*L'Opera*, 55 Sukhumvit Soi 39, T 2585606, Italian restaurant with Italian manager, conservatory, good food (excellent salted baked fish), professional service, lively atmosphere, popular, booking essential, rec; ♦♦♦♦*Paesano*, 96/7 Soi Tonson (off Soi Langsuan), Ploenchit Rd, T 2522834, average Italian food, sometimes good, in friendly atmosphere, very popular with locals; ♦♦♦*Gino's*, 13 Sukhumvit Soi 15, Italian food in bright and airy surroundings, set lunch is good value; ◆◆◆*Ristorante Sorrento*, 66 North Sathorn Rd, excellent Italian food; ◆◆◆*Roberto's 18*, 36 Sukhumvit, Soi 18, Italian; ◆◆◆*Terrazzo*, *Sukhothai Hotel*, 13/3 South Sathorn Rd, T 2870222, stylish al fresco Italian restaurant overlooking the pool, wonderful Italian breads and good pasta dishes, rec; ◆◆◆*Trattoria Da Roberto*, 37/9 Plaza Arcade, Patpong 2 Rd, T 2336851, authentic Italian setting; ◆◆◆*Vito's Spaghetteria*, Basement, Gaysorn Plaza, Ploenchit Rd (next to *Le Meridien Hotel*), bright and breezy pasta bar, make up your own dish by combining 10 types of pasta with 12 sauces and 29 fresh condiments, smallish servings but good for a hurried lunch.

French: ◆◆◆◆*Beccassine*, Sukhumvit, Soi Sawatdee, English and French home cooking, rec; ◆◆◆◆*Diva*, 49 Sukhumvit Soi 49, T 2587879, excellent French restaurant, with very good Italian dishes and crepe suzette which should not be missed, friendly service, attractive surroundings, good value, rec; ◆◆◆◆*La Grenouille*, 220/4 Sukhumvit Soi 1, T 2539080, traditional French cuisine, French chef and manager, small restaurant makes booking essential, French wines and French atmosphere, rec; ◆◆◆◆*Le Banyan*, 59 Sukhumvit Soi 8, T 2535556, excellent French food; ◆◆◆◆*L'Hexagone*, 4 Sukhumvit Soi 55 (Soi Thonglor), T 3812187, French cuisine, in 'posh' surroundings; ◆◆◆*Brussels Restaurant*, 23/4 Sukhumvit Soi 4, small and friendly, also serves Thai food; ◆◆◆*Chez Daniel Le Normand*, 1/9 Sukhumvit Soi 24, top class French restaurant; ◆◆◆*Classique Cuisine*, 122 Sukhumvit Soi 49, classic French cuisine; ◆◆◆*Le Bordeaux*, 1/38 Sukhumvit Soi 39, T 2589766, range of French dishes; ◆◆◆*Le Café Français*, 22 Sukhumvit Soi 24, French seafood; ◆◆◆*Le Café de Paris*, Patpong 2, traditional French food, rec; ◆◆◆*Restaurant Des Arts Nouveaux*, 127 Soi Charoensuk, Sukhumvit Soi 55, art nouveau interior, top class French cuisine; ◆◆◆*Stanley's French Restaurant*, 20/20-21 Ruamrudee Village, good French food, special Sun brunch, closed Mon.

Other International: ◆◆◆◆*Neil's Tavern*, 58/4 Wittayu, Soi Ruamrudee, T 2566644, best steak in town, popular with expats; ◆◆◆◆*Wit's Oyster Bar*, 20/10 Ruamrudee Village, T 2519455, Bangkok's first and only Oyster Bar, run by eccentric Thai, one of the few places where you can eat late, good salmon fishcakes, international cuisine; ◆◆◆*Bei Otto*, 1 Sukhumvit Soi 20,

Thailand's best known German restaurant, sausages made on the premises, good provincial food, large helpings; ◆◆◆*Bobby's Arms*, 2nd Flr, Car Park Bldg, 114/1-4 Patpong 2 Rd, T 2336828, British pub food; ◆◆◆*Bourbon Street*, 29/4-6 Sukhumvit Soi 22 (behind Washington Theatre), Cajun specialities include gumbo, jambalaya and red fish, along with steaks and Mexican dishes, served in a/c restaurant with VDOs and central bar – good for breakfast, excellent pancakes; ◆◆◆*Den Hvide Svane*, Sukhumvit Soi 8, Scandinavian and Thai dishes, former are good, efficient and friendly service; ◆◆◆*Gourmet Gallery*, 6/1 Soi Promsri 1 (between Sukhumvit Soi 39 and 40), interesting interior, with art work for sale, unusual menu of European and American food; ◆◆◆*Hard Rock Café*, 424/3-6 Siam Sq Soi 11, home-from-home for all burger-starved farangs, overpriced, videos, live music sometimes, and all the expected paraphernalia, a couple of Thai dishes have been included, large portions and good atmosphere. ◆◆◆*Haus Munchen*, 4 Sukhumvit Soi 15, T 2525776, German food in quasi-Bavarian lodge, connoisseurs maintain cuisine is authentic enough; ◆◆◆*Longhorn*, 120/9 Sukhumvit Soi 23, Cajun and Creole food; ◆◆◆*Senor Pico*, *Rembrandt Hotel*, 18 Sukhumvit Rd, Mexican, pseudo-Mexican decor, staff dressed Mexican style, large, rather uncosy restaurant, average cuisine, live music; ◆◆◆*Tia Maria*, 14/18 Patpong Soi 1, best Mexican restaurant in Bangkok; ◆◆*Caravan Coffee House*, Siam Sq Soi 5, large range of coffee or tea, food includes pizza, curry and some Thai food; ◆◆*Crazy Horse*, 5 Patpong 2 Rd, simple decor, but good French food, open until 0400; ◆◆*Harmonique*, 22 Charoen Krung, small elegant coffee shop with good music, fruit drinks and coffee.

South Asian (Indian): ◆◆◆◆*Rang Mahal*, *Rembrandt Hotel*, Sukhumvit Soi 18, T 2617100, best Indian food in town, very popular with the Indian community and spectacular views from the roof top position, sophisticated, elegant and ... expensive; ◆◆◆*Himali Cha Cha*, 1229/11 Charoen Krung, T 2351569, good choice of Indian cuisine, mountainous meals for the very hungry, originally set up by Cha Cha and now run by his son – 'from generation to generation' as it is quaintly put; ◆◆◆*Moghul Room*, 1/16 Sukhumvit Soi 11, wide choice of Indian and Muslim food; ◆◆◆*Mrs. Balbir's*, 155/18 Sukhumvit Soi 11, T 2532281, North Indian food orchestrated by Mrs Balbir, an Indian originally from Malaysia, regular customers just keep going back, chicken dishes are succulent, Mrs Balbir also runs cookery classes; ♦♦*Bangkok Brindawan*, 15 Sukhumvit Soi 35, S Indian, Sat lunch set-price buffet; ♦♦*Nawab*, 64/39 Soi Wat Suan Plu, Charoen Krung, N and S Indian dishes; ♦*Samrat*, 273-275 Chakraphet Rd, Pratuleck Lek, Indian and Pakistani food in restaurant down quiet lane off Chakraphet Rd, cheap and tasty, rec; ♦*Tamil Nadu*, 5/1 Silom Soi (Tambisa) 11, T 2356336, good, but limited South Indian menu, cheap and filling, *dosas* are rec, there are 4 or 5 **Indian** restaurants in a row on Sukhumvit Soi 11.

Vietnamese: ♦♦♦♦*Pho*, 2F Alma Link Building, 25 Soi Chidlom, T 2518900 (another branch at 3rd floor, Sukhumvit Plaza, Sukhumvit Soi 12, T 2525601), supporters claim this place serves the best Vietnamese in town, modern trendy setting, non-smoking area; ♦♦♦*Le Cam-Ly*, 2nd Flr, 1 Patpong Bldg, Surawong Rd; ♦♦♦*Le Dalat*, 47/1 Sukhumvit Soi 23, T 25841912, same management as Le Cam-Ly, reputed to serve the best Vietnamese food in Bangkok, arrive early or management may hassle; ♦♦♦*Sweet Basil*, 1 Silom Soi Srivieng (opp Bangkok Christian College), T 2383088, another branch at 5/1 Sukhumvit Soi 63 (Ekamai), T 3812834; ♦♦*Saigon-Rimsai*, 413/9 Sukhumvit Soi 55, Vietnamese and some Thai dishes, friendly atmosphere.

Japanese and Korean: ♦♦♦*Akamon*, 233 Sukhumvit Soi 21, Japanese; ♦♦♦*Kobune*, 3rd Fl, Mahboonkhrong (MBK) Centre, Rama 1 Rd, Japanese, Sushi Bar or sunken tables, rec; ♦♦♦*Otafuku*, 484 Siam Sq Soi 6, Henry Dunant Rd, Sushi Bar or low tables, Japanese; ♦♦*New Korea*, 41/1 Soi Chuam Rewang, Sukhumvit Sois 15-19, excellent Korean food in small restaurant, rec.

Indonesian and Burmese: ♦♦♦*Bali*, 20/11 Ruamrudee Village, Soi Ruamrudee, Ploenchit Rd, only authentic Indonesian in Bangkok, friendly proprietress; ♦♦♦*Batavia*, 1/2 Convent Rd, T 2667164, 'imported' Indonesian chefs, good classic dishes like *saté*, *gado-gado* (vegetable with peanut sauce and rice) and *ayam goreng* (deep fried chicken); ♦♦♦*Mandalay*, 23/17 Ploenchit Soi Ruamrudee, authentic Burmese food, most gastronomes of the country reckon the food is the best in the capital, rec.

Middle Eastern: ♦♦♦*Akbar*, 1/4 Sukhumvit Soi 3, T 2533479, Indian, Pakistani and Arabic; ♦♦♦*Nasir al-Masri*, 4-6 Sukhumvit Soi Nana Nua, T 2535582, reputedly the best Eastern (Egyptian) food in Bangkok, *felafal*, *tabouli*, *humus*, fre-

quented by large numbers of Arabs who come to Sayed Saad Qutub Nasir for a taste of home.

Asian: ♦♦*Ambassador Food Centre*, Ambassador Hotel, Sukhumvit Rd. A vast self-service, up-market hawkers' centre with a large selection of Asian foods at reasonable prices: Thai, Chinese, Japanese, Vietnamese etc, rec.

Lao/Isan food: ♦♦♦♦*La Normandie*, Oriental Hotel, 48 Oriental Ave, T 2360400, despite many competitors, *La Normandie* maintains extremely high standards of cuisine and service, guest chefs from around the world, jacket and tie required in the evening, very refined (and expensive); ♦♦♦*Bane Lao*, Naphasup Ya-ak I, off Sukhumvit Soi 36, Laotian open-air restaurant (doubles as a travel agent for Laos), Laotian band, haphazard but friendly service; ♦♦♦*Sarah Jane's*, 36/2 Soi Lang Suan, Ploenchit Rd, T 2526572, run by American lady, married to a Thai, best Thai salad in town and good duck, Isan food especially noteworthy, excellent value, rec; ♦♦*Isn't Classic*, 154 Silom Rd, excellent BBQ, king prawns and Isan specialities like spicy papaya salad (*somtam*).

Vegetarian: ♦♦♦*Whole Earth*, 93/3 Ploenchit Soi Lang Suan, T 2525574 (another branch at 71 Sukhumvit Soi 26, T 2584900), Thailand's best known vegetarian restaurant, eclectic menu from Thai to Indian dishes, live music, ask to sit at the back downstairs, or sit Thai-style upstairs.

Thai: ♦♦♦♦♦*Dusit Thani Thai Restaurant*, 946 Rama IV Rd, beautiful surroundings – like an old Thai palace, exquisite Thai food, very expensive wines; ♦♦♦♦♦*Spice Market*, Regent Hotel, 155 Rachdamri Rd, T 2516127, Westernized Thai, typical hotel decoration, arguably the city's best Thai food – simply delectable; ♦♦♦♦*Bussaracum*, 35 Soi Phiphat off Convent Rd, T 2358915, changing menu, popular, rec; ♦♦♦♦*D'jit Pochana Oriental*, 1082 Phahonyothin Rd, T 2795000, extensive range of dishes, large and rather industrial but the food is good; ♦♦♦♦–♦♦♦there are several excellent restaurants in *Silom Village*, a shopping mall, on Silom Rd (N side, opp Pan Rd), excellent range of food from hundreds of stalls, all cooked in front of you, enjoyable village atmosphere, rec; ♦♦♦♦–♦♦♦*Once Upon a Time*, 67 Soi Anumanrachaton, T 2338493, set in attractive traditional Thai house (between Silom and Surawong rds); ♦♦♦♦–♦♦♦*Bua Restaurant*, Convent Rd (off Silom Rd), classy postmodern Thai restaurant with starched white table linen and cool, minimalist lines, the food also reflects the decor (or the other way around?):

refined and immaculately prepared; ◆◆◆*Ban Chiang*, 14 Srivdieng Rd, T 2367045, quite hard to find – ask for directions, old style Thai house, large menu of traditionally-prepared food; ◆◆◆*Ban Khun Phor*, 458/7-9 Siam Square Soi 8, T 2501732, good Thai food in stylish surroundings; ◆◆◆*Ban Krua*, 29/1 Saladaeng Soi 1, Silom Rd, simple decor, friendly atmosphere, a/c room or open-air garden, traditional Thai food; ◆◆◆*Ban Thai*, Soi 32 or Ruen Thep, Silom Village, Silom Rd, T 2585403, with classical dancing and music; ◆◆◆*Banana Leaf*, Silom complex (basement floor), Silom Rd, T 3213124, excellent and very popular Thai restaurant with some unusual dishes, including *kai manaaw* (chicken in lime sauce), *nam tok muu* (spicy pork salad, Isan style) and fresh spring rolls 'Banana Leaf', booking recommended for lunch; ◆◆◆*Garden Restaurant*, 324/1 Phahonyothin Rd, open-air restaurant or the air-conditioned comfort of a wood panelled room, also serves Chinese, Japanese and International; ◆◆◆*Kaloang*, 2 Sri Ayutthaya Rd, T 2819228. Two dining areas, one on a pier, the other on a boat on the Chao Phraya River, attractive atmosphere, delicious food, rec.; ◆◆◆*Lemon Grass*, 5/1 Sukhumvit Soi 24, T 2588637, Thai style house, rather dark interior but very stylish, one step up from Cabbages and Condoms, rec; ◆◆◆*Moon Shadow*, 145 Gaysorn Rd, good seafood, choice of dining-rooms – a/c or open-air; ◆◆◆*Seafood Market*, Sukhumvit Soi 24, this famous restaurant has recently moved to new premises, and is said to be both larger and better, "if it swims we have it", choose your seafood from the 'supermarket' and then have it cooked to your own specifications before consuming the creatures at the table, popular; ◆◆◆*Seven Seas*, Sukhumvit Soi 33, T 2597662, quirky 'nouvelle' Thai food, popular with young sophisticated and avant garde Thais; ◆◆◆*Side Walk*, 855/2 Silom Rd (opp Central Dept Store), grilled specialities, also serves French, rec; ◆◆◆*Tum Nak Thai*, 131 Rajdapisek Rd, T 2746420, 'largest' restaurant in the world, 3,000 seats, rather out of the way (₿100 by taxi from city centre), classical dancing from 2000-2130; ◆◆◆-◆◆*Ban Somrudee* 228/6-7 Siam Square Soi 2, T 2512085; ◆◆*Ban Bung*, 32/10 Mu 2 Intramara 45, Rachadapisek, well known garden restaurant of northern-style pavilions, row around the lake to build up an appetite; ◆◆*Ban Mai*, 121 Sukhumvit Soi 22, Sub-Soi 2, old Thai-style decorations in an attractive house with friendly atmosphere,

good value; ◆◆*Cabbages and Condoms*, Sukhumvit Soi 12 (around 400m down the soi), Population and Community Development Association (PDA) restaurant so all proceeds go to this charity, eat rice in the Condom Room, drink in the Vasectomy Room, good *tom yam kung* and honey-roast chicken, curries all rather similar, good value, rec; ◆◆*Princess Terrace*, Rama I Soi Kasemsan Nung (1), Thai and French food with BBQ specialities served in small restaurant with friendly service and open terrace down quiet lane, rec; ◆◆*Puang Kaew*, 108 Sukhumvit Soi 23, T 5238172, large, unusual menu, also serves Chinese; ◆◆*Rung Pueng*, 37 Saladaeng, Soi 2, Silom Rd, traditional Thai food at reasonable prices; ◆◆*Sanuk Nuek*, 397/1 Sukhumvit Soi 55 (Soi Thonglor), T 4935590, small restaurant with unusual decorations, live folk music, well priced; ◆◆*September*, 120/1-2 Sukhumvit Soi 23, art nouveau setting, also serves Chinese and European, good value for money; ◆◆*Suda*, 6-6/1 Sukhumvit Rd, Soi 14, rec; ◆◆*Wannakarm*, 98 Sukhumvit Soi 23, T 2596499, well established, very Thai restaurant, grim decor, no English spoken, but rated food.

Travellers' food available in the guesthouse/travellers' hotel areas (see above). *Hello* in Khaosan Rd has been recommended, the portions of food are a good size and they have a useful notice board for leaving messages. Nearly all the restaurants in Khaosan Rd show videos all afternoon and evening. If on a tight budget it is much more sensible to eat in Thai restaurants and stalls where it should be possible to have a good meal for ₿10-20.

● **Bars**

The greatest concentration of bars are in the two 'red light' districts of Bangkok – Patpong (between Silom and Surawong rds) and Soi Cowboy (Sukhumvit). Patpong was transformed from a street of 'tea houses' (brothels serving local dients) into a high-tech lane of go-go bars in 1969 when an American made a major investment. In fact there are two streets, side-by-side, Patpong 1 and Patpong 2. Patpong 1 is the larger and more active, with a host of stalls down the middle at night (see page 192); Patpong 2 supports cocktail bars and, appropriately, pharmacies and clinics for STDs, as well as a few go-go bars. The *Derby King* is one of the most popular with expats and serves what are reputed to be the best club sandwiches in Asia, if not the world. Opposite Patpong, along Convent Rd is *Delaney's* (see Silom map), an Irish pub with draft

Guinness from Malaysia (where it is brewed) and a limited menu, good atmosphere and well-patronized by Bangkok's expats – sofas for lounging and reading (upstairs). Soi Cowboy is named after the first bar here, the *Cowboy Bar*, established by a retired US Airforce officer. Although some of the bars obviously also offer other forms of entertainment (something that quickly becomes blindingly obvious), there are, believe it or not, some excellent and very reasonably priced bars in these two areas. A small beer will cost ¢45-65, with good (if loud) music and perhaps videos thrown in for free. However, if opting for a bar with a 'show', be prepared to pay considerably more.

Warning Front men will assure customers that there is no entrance charge and a beer is only ¢60, but you can be certain that they will try to fleece you on the way out and can become aggressive if you refuse to pay. Even experienced Bangkok travellers find themselves in this predicament. Massages and more can also be obtained at many places in the Patpong and Soi Cowboy areas. **NB** AIDS is a significant and growing problem in Thailand so it is strongly recommended that customers practice safe sex.

A particularly civilized place to have a beer and watch the sun go down is on the verandah of the *Oriental Hotel*, by the banks of the Chao Phraya River, expensive, but romantic; ♦♦♦*Basement Pub* (and restaurant), 946 Rama IV Rd, live music, also serves international food, open 1800-2400; ♦♦♦*Black Scene*, 120/29-30 Sukhumvit Soi 23, live jazz, also serves Thai and French food, open 1700-1300; ♦♦♦*Bobby's Arms*, 2nd Flr, Car Park Bldg, Patpong 2 Rd, English pub and grill, with jazz on Sun from 2000, open 1100-0100; *Gitanes*, 52 Soi Pasana 1, Sukhumvit Soi 63. Live music, open 1800-0100; *King's Castle*, Patpong 1 Rd, another long-standing bar with core of regulars; *Royal Salute*, Patpong 2 Rd, cocktail bar where local farangs end their working days.

Hemingway Bar and Grill, 159/5-8 Sukhumvit Soi 55, live jazz and country music at the w/e, plus Thai and American food, open 1800-0100; ♦♦*Old West Saloon*, 231/17 Rachdamri Soi Sarasin, live country music, also serves international and Thai food, open 1700-0100. ♦♦*Picasso Pub*, 1950-52 Ramkamhaeng Rd, Bangkapi. Live music, also serves Thai food, open 1800-0300; ♦♦*Round Midnight*, 106/12 Soi Langsuan, live blues and jazz, some excellent bands play here, packed at week-

ends, good atmosphere and worth the trip, also serves Thai and Italian food, open 1700-0400; *Trader Vic's*, *Royal Marriott Garden Hotel*; ♦♦*Trumpet Pub* (and restaurant), 7 Sukhumvit Soi 24, live blues and jazz, also serves Thai food, open 1900-0200. **Note** For bars with live music also see *Music*, below, under *Entertainment*, page 191.

● **Airline offices**
For airport enquiries call, T 2860190. Aeroflot, Regent House, 183 Rachdamri Rd, T 2510617; **Air China**, 2nd Flr, CP Bldg, 313 Silom Rd, T 6310731; **Air France**, Grd Flr, Charn Issara Tower, 942 Rama IV Rd, T 2339477; **Air India**, 16th Flr, Amarin Tower, 500 Ploenchit Rd, T 2350557; **Air Lanka**, Grd Flr, Charn Issara Tower, 942 Rama IV Rd, T 2369292; **Alitalia**, 8th Flr, Boonmitr Bldg, 138 Silom Rd, T 2334000; **American Airlines**, 518/5 Ploenchit Rd, T 2511393; **Asiana Airlines**, 14th Flr, BB Bldg, 54 Asoke Rd, T 2607700; **Bangkok Airways**, Queen Sirikit National Convention Centre, New Rajdapisek Rd, Klongtoey, T 2293434; **Bangladesh Biman**, Grd Flr, Chongkolnee Bldg, 56 Surawong Rd, T 2357643; **British Airways**, 2nd Flr, Charn Issara Tower, 942 Rama IV Rd, T 2360038; **Canadian Airlines**, 6th Flr, Maneeya Bldg, 518/5 Ploenchit Rd, T 2514521; **Cathay Pacific**, 11th Flr, Ploenchit Tower, 898 Ploenchit Rd, T 2630606; **China Airlines**, 4th Flr, Peninsula Plaza, 153 Rachdamri Rd, T 2534242; **Continental Airlines**, CP Tower, 313 Silom Rd, T 2310113; **Delta Airlines**, 7th Flr, Patpong Bldg, Surawong Rd, T 2376838; **Egyptair**, CP Tower, 313 Silom Rd, T 2310504; **Finnair**, 12 Flr, Sathorn City Tower, 175 Sathorn Tai Rd, T 6396671; **Garuda**, 27th Flr, Lumpini Tower, 1168 Rama IV Rd, T 2856470; **Gulf Air**, Grd Flr, Maneeya Bldg, 518 Ploenchit Rd, T 2547931; **Japan Airlines**, 254/1 Ratchadapisek Rd, T 2741411; **KLM**, 12th Flr, Maneeya Centre Bldg, 518/5 Ploenchit Rd, T 2548325; **Korean Air**, Grd Flr, Kong Bunma Bldg (opp *Narai Hotel*), 699 Silom Rd, T 2359220; **Kuwait Airways**, 12th Flr, RS Tower, 121/50-51 Ratchadapisek Rd, T 6412864; **Lao Aviation**, 491 17 Ground Flr, Silom Plaza, Silom Rd, T 2369822; **Lufthansa**, 18th Flr, Q-House (Asoke), Sukhumvit Rd Soi 21, T 2642400; **MAS** (*Malaysian Airlines*), 20th Flr, Ploenchit Tower, 898 Ploenchit Rd, T 2630565; **Myanmar Airways**, Charn Issara Tower, 942 Rama IV Rd, T 2342985; **Pakistan International**, 52 Surawong Rd, T 2342961; **Philippine Airlines**, Chongkolnee Bldg, 56 Surawong Rd,

T 2332350; **Qantas**, 11th Flr, Charn Issara Tower, 942 Rama IV Rd, T 2675188; **Royal Brunei**, 4th Flr, Charn Issara Tower, 942 Rama IV Rd, T 2330056; **Royal Nepal Airlines**, Sivadon Bldg, 1/4 Convent Rd, T 2333921; **Sabena**, 3rd Flr, CP Tower, 313 Silom Rd, T 2382201; **SAS**, 8th Flr, Glas Haus I, Sukhumvit Rd Soi 25, T 2600444; **Saudi**, 3rd Flr, Main Bldg, Don Muang Airport, T 5352341; **Singapore Airlines**, 12th Flr, Silom Centre, 2 Silom Rd, T 2360440; **Swissair**, 2nd Flr, 1-7 FE Zuellig Bldg, Silom Rd, T 2332930; **Thai**, 485 Silom Rd, T 2333810; **TWA**, 12th Flr, Charn Issara Tower, 942 Rama IV Rd, T 2337290; **Vietnam Airlines**, 584 Ploenchit Rd, T 2514242.

● **Banks & money changers**
There are countless exchange booths in all the tourist areas open 7 days a week, mostly 0800-1530, some from 0800-2100. Rates vary only marginally between banks, although if changing a large sum, it is worth shopping around.

● **Embassies**
Australia, 37 Sathorn Tai Rd, T 2872680; **Brunei**, 154 Ekamai Soi 14, Sukhumvit 63, T 3815914, F 3815921; **Cambodia**, 185 Rachdamri Rd, T 2546630; **Canada**, 12th Flr, Boonmitr Bldg, 138 Silom Rd, T 2341561/8; **Denmark**, 10 Sathorn Tai Soi Attakarnprasit, T 2132021; **Finland**, 16th Flr, Amarin Plaza, 500 Ploenchit Rd, T 2569306; **France**, 35 Customs House Lane, Charoen Krung, T 2668250. (There is also a French consulate at 29 Sathorn Tai Rd, T 2856104.) **Germany**, 9 Sathorn Tai Rd, T 2132331; **India**, Sukhumvit Rd Soi 23, T 2580300; **Indonesia**, 600-602 Phetburi Rd, T 2523135; **Israel**, 25th Flr, Ocean Tower II, 75 Soi Wattana, Sukhumvit 19, T 2604850; **Greece**, 79 Sukhumvit Soi 4, T 2542936, F 2542937; **Italy**, 399 Nang Linchi Rd, T 2854090; **Japan**, 1674 New Phetburi Rd, T 2526151; **Laos**, 502/1-3 Soi Ramkhamhaeng 39, T 5396667; **Malaysia**, 15th Flr, Regent House, 183 Rachdamri Rd, T 2541700; **Myanmar** (Burma), 132 Sathorn Nua Rd, T 2332237; **Nepal**, 189 Sukhumvit Soi 71, T 3917240; **Netherlands**, 106 Witthayu Rd, T 2547701; **New Zealand**, 93 Witthayu Rd, T 2518165; **Norway**, 1st Flr, Bank of America Bldg, Witthayu Rd, T 2530390; **People's Republic of China**, 57 Ratchadapisek Rd, Dindaeng, T 2457032; **Philippines**, 760 Sukhumvit Rd, T 2590139; **Singapore**, 129 Sathorn Tai Rd, T 2862111; **South Africa**, 6th Flr, Park Place, 231 Soi Sarasin, Rachdamri Rd, T 2538473; **Spain**, 93 Witthayu Rd, T 2526112; **Sweden**, 20th Flr, Pacific Place, 140 Sukhumvit Rd, T 2544954; **UK**, 1031 Witthayu Rd, T 2530191/9; **USA**, 95 Witthayu Rd, T 2525040; **Vietnam**, 83/1 Witthayu Rd, T 2515835.

● **Church services**
Evangelical Church, Sukhumvit Soi 10 (0930 Sun service); the *International Church* (interdenominational), 67 Sukhumvit Soi 19 (0800 Sun service); *Baptist Church*, 2172/146 Phahonyothin Soi 36 (1800 Sun service); *Holy Redeemer*, 123/19 Wittayu Soi Ruam Rudee (Catholic, 5 services on Sun); *Christ Church*, 11 Convent Rd (Anglican – Episcopalian – Ecumenical) (3 Sun services at 0730, 1000 and 1800).

● **Entertainment**
Art galleries: *The Artist's Gallery*, 60 Pan Rd, off Silom, selection of international works of art. *The Neilson Hays Library*, 195 Surawong Rd, has a changing programme of exhibitions.

Buddhism: the headquarters of the World Fellowship of Buddhists is at 33 Sukhumvit Rd (between Soi 1 and Soi 3). Meditation classes are held in English on Wed at 1700-2000; lectures on Buddhism are held on the first Wed of each month at 1800-2000.

Cinemas: most cinemas have daily showings at 1200, 1400, 1700, 1915 and 2115, with a 1300 matinee on weekends and holidays. Cinemas with English soundtracks include *Central Theatre 2*, T 5411065, *Lido*, T 2526729, *Pantip*, T 2512390, *Pata*, T 4230568, *Mackenna*, T 2517163, *Washington 1*, T 2582045, *Washington 2*, T 2582008, *Scala*, T 2512861, *Villa*, T 2589291. *The Alliance Française*, 29 Sathorn Tai Rd, T 2132122 shows French films. Remember to stand for the National Anthem, which is played before every performance. Details of showings from English language newspapers.

Cultural centres: British Council, 254 Chulalongkorn Soi 64 (Siam Square), T 6116830, F 2535311, for films, books and other Anglo-centric entertainment; Check in 'What's On' section of *Sunday Bangkok Post's* magazine for programme of events; **Alliance Française**, 29 Sathorn Tai Rd; **Goethe Institute**, 18/1 Sathorn Tai Soi Atthakan Prasit; **Siam Society**, 131 Soi 21 (Asoke) Sukhumvit, T 2583494, open Tues-Sat. Promotes Thai culture and organizes trips within (and beyond) Thailand.

Meditation: *Wat Mahathat*, facing Sanaam

Luang, is Bangkok's most renowned meditation centre. Anyone interested is welcome to attend the daily classes – the centre is located in Khana 5 of the monastery. Apart from Wat Mahathat, classes are also held at *Wat Bowonniwet* in Banglamphu on Phra Sumen Rd (see the Bangkok – Old City map), and at the *Thai Meditation Centre* in the World Fellowship of Buddhists building on 33 Sukhumvit Rd, T 2511188.

Music: (see also **Bars**, page 188, for more places with live music): *Blues-Jazz*, 25 Sukhumvit Soi 53, open Mon-Sun 1900-0200, three house bands play really good blues and jazz, food available, drinks a little on the steep side. *Blue Moon*, 73 Sukhumvit 55 (Thonglor), open Mon-Sun 1800-0300, for country, rhythm, jazz and blues – particularly Fri and Sun for jazz – some food available. *Brown Sugar*, 231/20 Sarasin Rd (opp Lumpini Park), open Mon-Fri 1100-0100, Sat and Sun 1700-0200, five regular bands play excellent jazz, a place for Bangkok's trendies to hang out and be cool. *Cool Tango*, 23/51 Block F, Royal City Av (between Phetburi and Rama IX rds), open Tue-Sat 1100-0200, Sun 1800-0200, excellent resident rock band, great atmosphere, happy hour(s) 1800-2100. *Front Page*, 14/10 Soi Saladaeng 1, open Mon-Fri 1000-0100, Sat and Sun 1800-0100, populated, as the name might suggest, by journos who like to hunt in packs more than most, music is country, folk and blues, food available. *Hard Rock Café*, 424/3-6 Siam Sq Soi 11, open Mon-Sun 1100-0200, speaks for itself, burgers, beer and rock covers played by reasonable house band, food is expensive for Bangkok though. *Magic Castle*, 212/33 Sukhumvit Plaza Soi 12, open Mon-Thu 1800-0100, Fri and Sat 1800-0200, mostly blues, some rock, good place for a relaxed beer with skilfully performed covers. *Picasso Pub*, 1950-5 Ramkhomhaeng Rd (close to Soi 8), open Mon-Sun 1900-0300, house rock band, adept at playing covers. *Round Midnight*, 106/12 Soi Langsuan, open Mon-Thu 1900-0230, Fri and Sat 1900-0400, jazz, blues and rock bands.

Thai Performing Arts: classical dancing and music is often performed at restaurants after a 'traditional' Thai meal has been served. Many tour companies or travel agents organize these 'cultural evenings'. *National Theatre*, Na Phrathat Rd, (T 2214885 for programme). Thai classical dramas, dancing and music on the last Fri of each month at 1730 and periodically on other days. *Thailand Cultural Centre*, Rach-

daphisek Rd, Huai Khwang, T 2470028 for programme of events. *College of Dramatic Arts*, nr National Theatre, T 2241391. *Baan Thai Restaurant*, 7 Sukhumvit Soi 32, T 2585403, 2100-2145. *Chao Phraya Restaurant*, Pinklao Bridge, Arun Amarin Rd, T 4742389; *Maneeya's Lotus Room*, Ploenchit Rd, T 2526312, 2015-2100; *Piman Restaurant*, 46 Sukhumvit Soi 49, T 2587866, 2045-2130; *Ruen Thep*, Silom Village Trade Centre, T 2339447, 2020-2120; *Suwannahong Restaurant*, Sri Ayutthaya Rd, T 2454448, 2015-2115; *Tum-Nak-Thai Restaurant*, 131 Rachdaphisek Rd, T 2773828 2030-2130.

● **Hospitals & medical services**
Bangkok Adventist Hospital, 430 Phitsanulok Rd, Dusit, T 2811422/2821100; *Bangkok General Hospital*, New Phetburi Soi 47, T 3180066; *Bangkok Nursing Home*, 9 Convent Rd, T 2332610; *St. Louis Hospital*, 215 Sathorn Tai Rd, T 2120033. **Health clinics**: *Dental Polyclinic*, New Phetburi Rd, T 3145070; *Dental Hospital*, 88/88 Sukhumvit 49, T 2605000, F 2605026, good, but expensive; *Clinic Banglamphu*, 187 Chakrapong Rd, T 2827479.

● **Immigration**
Sathorn Tai Soi Suanphlu, T 2873101.

● **Libraries**
British Council Library, 254 Chulalongkorn Soi 64 (Siam Square). Open Tue-Sat 1000-1930, membership library with good selection of English language books. **NB** In Oct 1996 Queen Elizabeth II opened the new British Council offices and it was rumoured that the library had been cut in the interests of economy; *National Library*, Samsen Rd, close to Sri Ayutthaya Rd, open Mon-Sun 0930-1930; *Neilson Hays Library*, 195 Surawong Rd, T 2331731, next door to British Club. Open: 0930-1600 Mon-Sat, 0930-1230 Sun. A small library of English-language books housed in an elegant building dating from 1922. It is a private membership library, but welcomes visitors who might want to see the building and browse; occasional exhibitions are held here. Open 0930-1600 Mon-Sat, 0930-1230 Sun; *Siam Society Library*, 131 Sukhumvit Soi 21 (Asoke), open Tue-Sat 0900-1700, membership library with excellent collection of Thai and foreign language books and periodicals (especially English) on Thailand and mainland south east Asia.

● **Meditation and Yoga**

The *Dharma Study Foundation*, 128 Soi Thonglor 4, Sukhumvit Soi 55, T 3916006, open 0900-1800 Mon-Fri and the *World Fellowship of Buddhists*, 33 Sukhumvit Rd (between sois 1 and 3), T 2511188, open 0900-1630 Mon-Fri, both offer classes in meditation and some religious discussions. Yoga classes available at *Sunee Yoga Centre*, 2nd Flr, Pratunam Centre, 78/4 Rachprarop Rd, T 2549768, open 1000-1200 and 1700-1900 Mon-Sat.

● **Post & telecommunications**

Area code: 02.

Central GPO (*Praysani Klang* for taxi drivers): 1160 Charoen Krung, opp the *Ramada Hotel*. Open 0800-2000 Mon-Fri and 0800-1300 weekend and holidays. The money and postal order service is open 0800-1700, Mon-Fri, 0800-1200 Sat. Closed on Sun and holidays. 24 hrs telegram and telephone service (phone rates are reduced 2100-0700) and a packing service.

● **Shopping**

Most shops do not open until 1000-1100. Nancy Chandler's *Map of Bangkok* is the best shopping guide. Bangkok still stocks a wonderful range of goods, but do not expect to pick up a bargain – prices are high. Stallholders, entirely understandably, are out for all they can get – so bargain hard here. The traditional street market, although not dying out, is now supplemented by other types of shopping. Given the heat, the evolution of the air conditioned shopping arcade and air conditioned department store in Bangkok was just a matter of time. Some arcades target the wealthier shopper, and are dominated by brand name goods and designer ware. Others are not much more than street side stalls transplanted to an arcade environment. Most department stores are now fixed price.

Bangkok's main shopping areas are:

1. Sukhumvit: Sukhumvit Rd, and the sois to the N are lined with shops and stalls, especially around the *Ambassador* and *Landmark* hotels. Many tailors and made-to-measure shoe shops are to be found in this area.

2. Central: 2 areas close to each other centred on Rama I and Ploenchit rds. At the intersection of Phayathai and Rama I rds there is Siam Square (for teenage trendy Western clothing, bags, belts, jewellery, bookshops, some antique shops and American fast food chains) and the massive – and highly popular – Mah Boonkhrong Centre (MBK), with countless small shops and stalls and the Tokyu Department Store. Siam Square used to be great for cheap clothes, leather goods etc, but each year it inches further up market: there are now branches of *Timberland*, the *Body Shop*, *Kookäi* and various designer outlets here. Peninsular Plaza, between the *Hyatt Erawan* and *Regent* hotels is considered the smartest shopping plaza in Bangkok. For those looking for fashion clothes and accessories, this is probably the best area. A short distance to the E, centred on Ploenchit/Rachprarop rds, are more shopping arcades and large department stores, including the World Trade Centre, Thai Daimaru, Robinsons, Gaysorn Plaza (exclusive shopping arcade), Naraiphan shopping centre (more of a market stall affair, geared to tourists, in the basement) and Central Chidlom (which burnt down in a catastrophic fire in 1995 but which should be rebuilt/renovated – although in 1996 it was still waiting for work to begin). North along Rachprasong Rd, crossing over Khlong Saensap, at the intersection with Phetburi Rd is the Pratunam market, good for fabrics and clothing.

3. Patpong/Silom: Patpong is more of a night market (opening at 2100), the streets are packed with stalls selling the usual array of stall goods which seem to stay the same from year to year (fake designer clothing, watches, bags etc). **NB** Bargain hard. The E end of Silom has a scattering of similar stalls open during the day time, and Robinsons Department Store. Surawong Rd (at the other end of Patpong) has Thai silk, antiques and a few handicraft shops.

4. West Silom/Charoen Krung (New Rd): antiques, jewellery, silk, stamps, coins and bronzeware. Stalls set up here at 2100. A 15 min walk N along Charoen Krung (close to the *Orchid Sheraton Hotel*) is the River City Shopping Plaza, specializing in art and antiques.

5. Banglamphu/Khaosan Road: vast variety of low-priced goods, such as ready-made clothes, shoes, bags, jewellery and cassette tapes.

6. Lardphrao-Phahonyothin: some distance N of town, not far from the Weekend Market (see page 172) is the huge Central Plaza shopping complex. It houses a branch of the Central Department Store and has many boutiques and gift shops.

Department Stores: *Central* is the largest chain of department stores in Bangkok, with a range of Thai and imported goods at fixed prices; credit cards are accepted. Main shops on Silom Rd, Ploenchit Rd (Chidlom Branch – which burnt down in 1995 but should be renovated), and in the Central Plaza, just N of the Northern bus terminal. Other department stores include *Thai*

Buying gems and jewellery

More people lose their money through gem and jewellery scams in Thailand than in any other way (60% of complaints to the TAT involve gem scams). **DO NOT** fall for any story about gem sales, special holidays, tax breaks – no matter how convincing. **NEVER** buy gems from people on the street (or beach) and try not to be taken to a shop by an intermediary. **ANY** unsolicited approach is likely to be a scam. The problem is perceived to be so serious that in some countries Thai embassies are handing out warning leaflets with visas.

Rules of thumb to avoid being cheated

● Choose a specialist store in a relatively prestigious part of town (the TAT will informally recommend stores).
● Note that no stores are authorized by the TAT or by the Thai government; if they claim as much they are lying.
● It is advisable to buy from shops who are members of the Thai Gem and Jewellery Traders Association.
● Avoid touts.
● Never be rushed into a purchase.
● Do not believe stories about vast profits from re-selling gems at home. They are lies.
● Do not agree to have items mailed ("for safety").
● If buying a valuable gem, a certificate of identification is a good insurance policy. The Department of Mineral Resources (Rama VI Rd, T 2461694) and the Asian Institute of Gemological Sciences (484 Rachadapisek Rd, T 5132112) will both examine stones and give such certificates.
● Compare prices; competition is stiff among the reputable shops; be suspicious of 'bargain' prices.
● Ask for a receipt detailing the stone and recording the price.

For more information (and background reading on Thailand) the 'Buyer's Guide to Thai Gems and Jewellery', by John Hoskin can be bought at Asia Books.

Daimaru on Rachdamri and Sukhumvit (opp Soi 71), *Robinson's* on corner of Silom and Rama IV rds, Sukhumvit (nr Soi 19) and Rachdamri rds, *Tokyu* in MBK Tower on Rama I Rd, *Sogo* in the Amarin Plaza on Ploenchit Rd, and *Zen*, World Trade Centre, corner of Rama I and Rajdamri rds.

Supermarkets: *Central Department Store* (see above), *Robinsons* – open until midnight (see above), *Villa Supermarket*, between Sois 33 and 35, Sukhumvit Rd (and branches elsewhere in town) – for everything you are unable to find anywhere else, *Isetan*, (World Trade Centre), Rachdamri Rd.

Markets: the markets in Bangkok are an excellent place to browse, take photographs and pick up bargains. They are part of the life blood of the city, and the encroachment of more organized shops and the effects of the re-developer's demolition ball are eating away at one of Bangkok's finest traditions. Nancy Chandler's map of Bangkok, available from most bookshops, is the most useful guide to the markets of the capital. The largest is the *Weekend Market* at Chatuchak Park (see page 172). The *Tewes Market*, nr the National Library, is a photographers dream; a daily market, selling flowers and plants. *Pratunam Market* is spread over a large area around Rachprarop and Phetburi rds, and is famous for clothing and fabric. Half of it was recently bulldozed for redevelopment, but there is still a multitude of stalls here. The *Bai Yoke Market* is next door and sells mostly fashion garments for teenagers – lots of lycra. A short distance S of here on Rachprarop Rd is the *Naraiphan Shopping Centre and Narayana Bazaar* an indoor stall/shopping centre affair (concentrated in the basement) geared to tourists and *farang* residents. *Nakhon Kasem* known as the *Thieves Market*, in the heart of Chinatown, houses a number of 'antique' shops selling brassware, old electric fans and woodcarvings (tough bargaining recommended, and don't expect everything to be genuine – see page 164). Close by are the stalls of *Sampeng Lane* (see page 166), specializing in toys, stationery, clothes and household goods, and the *Pahurat Cloth Market* (see page 164) – a small slice of India in Thailand, with mounds of sarongs, batiks, buttons and bows. *Bangrak Market*, S of the General Post Office, nr the river and the *Shangri-La Hotel*, sells exotic fruit, clothing, seafood and flowers. *Pak Khlong Market* is a wholesale market selling fresh produce, orchids and cut flowers and is situated nr the Memorial Bridge (see page 164). *Phahonyothin Market* is Bangkok's newest, opp the Northern bus terminal, and sells potted plants and orchids. *Banglamphu Market* is close to Khaosan Rd, the backpackers' haven, on Chakrapong and Phra Sumen rds. Stalls here sell clothing, shoes, food and household goods. The nearby *Khaosan Road Market* (if it can be called such) is much more geared to the needs and desires of the foreign tourist: CDs and cassettes, batik shirts, leather goods and so on. *Patpong Market*, arranged down the middle of Patpong Rd, linking Silom and Surawong rds, opens up about 1700 and is geared to tourists, selling handicrafts, T-shirts, leather goods, fake watches, cassettes and VDOs. *Penang Market*, Khlong Toey, situated under the expressway close to the railway line specializes in electronic equipment from hi-fis to computers, with a spattering of other goods as well. A specialist market is the *Stamp Market* next to the GPO on Charoen Krung which operates on Sun only. Collectors come here to buy or exchange stamps.

● **Tour companies & travel agents**
Travel agents abound in the tourist and hotel areas of the city – Khaosan Rd/Banglamphu, Sukhumvit, Soi Ngam Duphli, and Silom (several down Pan Rd, a soi opp Silom Village). All major hotels will have their own in-house agent. Most will book airline, bus and train tickets, arrange tours, and book hotel rooms. Because there are so many to choose from, it is worth shopping around for the best deal. For companies specialising in tours and other travel arrangements to Cambodia, see page223).

● **Tourist offices**
Tourist Authority of Thailand (TAT), Rachdamnern Nok Ave (at intersection with Chakrapatdipong Rd), T 2815051. There is also a smaller office at 372 Bamrung Muang Rd, T 2260060. Open Mon-Sun, 0830-1630. **NB** The main office on Rachdamnern Nok Ave opened after some delay in mid-1996. For the time being the TAT are also keeping their office on Bamrung Muang Rd open, although it may close and/or be relocated in 1997 or 1998. In addition there is a counter at Don Muang airport (in the Arrivals Hall, T 5238972) and

offices at 1 Napralarn Rd, T 2260056, and the Chatuchak Weekend Market (Kampaeng Phet Rd). The main office is very helpful and provides a great deal of information for independent travellers – certainly worth a visit.

A number of good, informative, English language magazines providing listings of what to do and where to go in Bangkok have started up recently. The best is undoubtedly *Bangkok Metro*, published monthly (฿80). It is well designed and produced and covers topics from music and nightlife, to sports and fitness, to business and children. Less independent, and with less quality information, is the oddly named *Guide of Bangkok* or GoB. Its advantage is that it is free.

● **Tourist Police**
Unico House, Ploenchit Soi Lang Suan, T 1699 or 6521721. There are also dedicated tourist police offices in the main tourist areas.

● **Traditional Thai Massage**
Many hotels offer this service; guesthouses also, although most masseuses are not trained. The most famous centre is at Wat Pho (see page 159), a Mecca for the training of masseuses. Wat Pho specializes in the more muscular Southern style. The Northern-style is less exhausting, more soothing. Other centres offering quality massages by properly trained practioners include: Marble House, 37/18-19 Soi Surawong Plaza (opp Montien Hotel), T 2353519, open 0100-2400 Mon-Sun, ฿300 for 2 hrs, ฿450 for 3 hrs and Vejakorn, 37/25 Surawong Plaza, Surawong Rd, T 2375576, open Mon-Sun 1000-2400, ฿260 for 2 hrs, ฿390 for 3 hrs.

● **Transport**
Local Bus: this is the cheapest way to get around town. A bus map marking the routes is indispensable. The *Bangkok Thailand* map and *Latest tours guide to Bangkok and Thailand* are available from most bookshops as well as many hotel and travel agents/ tour companies. Major bus stops also have maps of routes and instructions in English displayed. Standard non-a/c buses (coloured blue) cost ฿2.50. Beware of pickpockets on these often crowded buses. Red-coloured express buses are slightly more expensive (฿3.50), slightly less crowded, and do not stop at all bus stops. A/c buses cost ฿6-16 depending on distance. Travelling all the way from Silom Rd to the airport by a/c bus, for example, costs ฿14; most inner city journeys cost ฿6. There are also smaller a/c

'micro buses' (a bit of a misnomer as they are not micro at all, not even 'mini'), which follow the same routes but are generally faster and less crowded because officially they are only meant to let passengers aboard if a seat is vacant. They charge a flat fare of ฿25. **NB** More people have their belongings stolen on Bangkok's city buses than almost anywhere else.

Elevated railway: an elevated railway being built by Ital-Thai is under construction and should be opened in 1997/1998.

Express boats: travel between Nonthaburi in the N and Wat Rajsingkorn (nr Krungthep bridge) in the S. Fares are calculated by zone and range from ฿4-15. At peak hours boats leave every 10 mins, off-peak about 15-25 mins (see map, page 169 for piers). The journey from one end of the route to the other takes 75 mins. Note that boats flying red or green pennants do not stop at all piers (they also exact a ฿1 express surcharge). Also, boats will only stop if passengers wish to board or alight, so make your destination known.

Ferries: small ferries take passengers across the Chao Phraya River, ฿1 (see map on page 169 for piers).

Khlong or long-tailed boats: can be rented for ฿200/hour, or more (see page 168).

Motorcycle taxi: a relatively new innovation in Bangkok (and now present in other towns in Thailand) they are the fastest, and most terrifying, way to get from A to B. Riders wear numbered vests and tend to congregate in particular areas; agree a fare, hop on the back, and hope for the best. Their 'devil may care' attitude has made them bitter enemies of many other road users. Expect to pay ฿10-20.

Taxi: most taxis are metered (they must have a/c to register) – look for the 'Taxi Meter' illuminated sign on the roof. There are a number of unmarked, unofficial taxis which are to be found around the tourist sites. Flag fall is ฿35 for a journey of 2km or less and it should cost ฿40-100 for most trips in the city. If the travel speed is less than 6 km/hr – always a distinct possibility in the traffic choked capital – a surcharge of ฿1 per minute is automatically added. Sometimes taxis refuse to use the meter – insist they do so. Taxi drivers should not be tipped. For most tourists the arrival of the metered taxi has lowered prices as it has eliminated the need to bargain – check, though, that the meter is 'zeroed' before setting off.

Tuk-tuk: the formerly ubiquitous motorized saamlor is rapidly becoming a piece of history in Bangkok, although they can still always be found

nr tourist sites. Best for short journeys: they are uncomfortable and, being open to the elements, you are likely to be asphyxiated by car fumes. Bargaining is essential and the fare must be negotiated before boarding, most journeys cost at least ฿40. Both tuk-tuk and taxi drivers may try to take you to restaurants or shops – do not be persuaded; they are often mediocre places charging high prices.

Long distance Bangkok lies at the heart of Thailand's transport network. Virtually all trains and buses end up here and it is possible to reach anywhere in the country from the capital. Bangkok is also a regional transport hub, and there are flights to most international destinations. For international transportation, see page 199.

Air Don Muang Airport is 25 km N of the city. Regular connections on **Thai** to many of the provincial capitals. For airport details see page 200. There are a number of Thai offices in Bangkok, Head Office for domestic flights is 89 Vibhavadi Rangsit Rd, T 5130121, but this is inconveniently located N of town. Two more central offices are at 6 Lan Luang Rd (T 2800070) and 485 Silom Rd. Tickets can also be bought at most travel agents. **Bangkok Airways** flies to Koh Samui, Hua Hin, Phuket, Sukhothai, Chiang Mai, Ranong, Hat Yai, U-Tapao (Pattaya) and Mae Hong Son. They have an office in the domestic terminal at Don Muang, and two offices in town: Queen Sirikit National Convention Centre, New Rachadapisek Rd, T 2293456; and llll Ploenchit Rd, T 2542903.

Train Bangkok has two main railway stations. The primary station, catering for most destinations, is Hualamphong, Rama IV Rd, T 2237010/2237020; condensed railway timetables in English can be picked up from the information counter in the main concourse. Trains to Nakhon Pathom and Kanchanaburi leave from the Bangkok Noi or Thonburi station on the other side of the Chao Phraya River.

Road Bus: there are three main bus stations in Bangkok serving the N and NE, the E, and the S and W. Destinations in the Central Plains are also served from these terminals – places N of Bangkok from the northern bus terminal, SW of Bangkok from the southern terminal, and SE from the eastern terminal. The **Northern bus terminal** or *Mor Chit*, Phahonyothin Rd, T 2712961, serves all destinations in the N and NE as well as towns in the Central Plains that lie N of Bangkok like Ayutthaya and

Lopburi. Getting to *Mor Chit* by public transport is comparatively easy as many a/c (Nos 2, 3, 9, 10, 29 and 39) and non-a/c buses travel along Phahonyothin Rd. The new non-a/c **Southern bus terminal** is on Phra Pinklao Rd (T 4110061) nr the intersection with Route 338. Buses for the W (places like Nakhon Pathom and Kanchanaburi) and the S leave from here. A/c town bus No 7 travels to the terminal. A/c buses to the S and W leave from the terminal on Charan Santiwong Rd, nr Bangkok Noi Train Station in Thonburi, T 4351199. The **Eastern bus terminal**, Sukhumvit Rd (Soi Ekamai), between Soi 40 and Soi 42, T 3912504 serves Pattaya and other destinations in the Eastern region.

Buses leave for most major destinations throughout the day, and often well into the night. There are overnight buses on the longer routes – Chiang Mai, Hat Yai, Chiang Rai, Phuket, Ubon Ratchathani. Even the smallest provincial towns such as Mahasarakham have deluxe a/c buses connecting them with Bangkok. Note that in addition to the government-operated buses there are many private companies which run 'tour' buses to most of the major tourist destinations. Tickets bought through travel agents will normally be for these private tour buses, which leave from offices all over the city as well as from the public bus terminals listed above. Shop around as prices may vary. Note that although passengers may be picked up from their hotel/guesthouse therefore saving on the ride (and inconvenience) of getting out to the bus terminal the private buses are generally less reliable and less safe. Many pick-up passengers at Khaosan Rd, for example.

THAILAND – INFORMATION FOR TRAVELLERS

BEFORE TRAVELLING

ENTRY REQUIREMENTS

● **Visas**

All tourists must possess passports valid for at least 6 months longer than their intended stay in Thailand.

30 day visa exemptions No visa is required for tourists arriving by air, holding a confirmed onward air ticket and who intend to stay for up to 30 days (not extendable). (Until 1995 tourists were only permitted to stay for 14 days.) Visitors are fined ฿100/day each day they exceed the 30 day limit. The same applies to tourists who arrive via the Thai-Malaysian border by sea, rail or road. This applies to nationals of the following countries: Algeria, Argentina, Australia, Austria, Bahrain, Belgium, Brazil, Brunei, Canada, Denmark, Djibouti, Egypt, Fiji, Finland, France, Germany, Greece, Iceland, Indonesia, Ireland, Israel, Italy, Japan, Kenya, Kuwait, Luxembourg, Malaysia, Mauritania, Mexico, Morocco, Myanmar (Burma), Netherlands, New Zealand, Oman, Papua New Guinea, Philippines, Portugal, Qatar, Republic of Korea, Saudi Arabia, Senegal, Singapore, Slovenia, South Africa, Spain, Sweden, Switzerland, Tunisia, Turkey, UAE, UK, USA, Vanuatu, Western Samoa, Yemen. Malaysian nationals arriving by road from Malaysia do not need evidence of onward journey.

Visas on arrival There is now a new visa booth at Don Muang (Bangkok) Airport itself, at customs control. Visitors without visas can have one issued here and there is even a photo booth to provide passport snaps (one photograph required). However, the desk only provides tourist visas valid for 15 days (฿300), which nationals of many countries do not require in any case (see above). The facility is only useful for nationals of those countries which are not exempted from having an entry visa. These number 76 in total. Applicants must also have an outbound (return) ticket. There are similar desks at Chiang Mai, Phuket and Hat Yai airports.

3 month visa exemptions Nationals from South Korea, New Zealand, Sweden, Denmark, Norway and Finland visiting as a tourist do not require a visa for visits of up to 3 months, and those from Hong Kong for a visit of up to 15 days.

Tourist visas These are valid for 90 days from date of entry (single entry); **transit visas** for 30 days (single entry). **Visa extensions** are obtainable from the Immigration Department in Bangkok (see below) for ฿500. The process used to be interminable, but the system is now much improved and relatively painless. Extensions can also be issued in other towns, such as Koh Samui and Chiang Mai. Applicants must bring two photocopies of their passport ID page and the page on which their tourist visa is stamped, together with three passport photographs. It is also advisable to dress neatly. It may be easier to leave the country and then re-enter having obtained a new tourist visa. Visas are issued by all Thai embassies and consulates.

Passport control at Don Muang Airport during peak arrival periods (usually 1200-1400) can be choked with visitors – be prepared for a wait of an hour or more before reaching the arrivals hall.

90-day non-immigrant visas These are also issued and can be obtained in the applicant's home country (about US$30). A letter from the applicant's company or organization guaranteeing their repatriation should be submitted at the same time.

In the UK there is now a visa information line, operating 24 hrs a day, T 0891 600 150.

● **Procedure for lost or stolen passport**

1. File a report with the local police.

2. Take the report to your local embassy or consulate and apply for a new travel document or passport. (If there is no representation, visit the Passport Division of the Ministry of Foreign Affairs.)

3. Take the new passport plus the police report to Section 4, Subdivision 4, Immigration Bureau, room 311 (3rd floor), Old Building, Soi Suan Plu, Sathorn Tai Rd, Bangkok, T 2873911, for a new visa stamp.

● **Immigration Department**

Soi Suan Plu, Thanon Sathorn Tai, Bangkok 10120, T 2873101. Open: 0930-1630 Mon-Fri, 0830-1200 Sat (tourists only).

● **Vaccinations**

No vaccinations required, unless coming from an infected area (if visitors have been in a yellow fever infected area in the 10 days before arrival, and do not have a vaccination certificate, they will be vaccinated and kept in quarantine for 6 days, or deported. See health section below for details.

● **Representation overseas**

Australia, 111 Empire Circuit, Yarralumla, Canberra, ACT 2600, T (06) 2731149, 2732937; **Austria**, Weimarer Strasse 68, 1180 Vienna, T (0222) 3103423; **Belgium**, Square du Val de la Cambre 2, 1050 Brussels, T 2 6406810; **Canada**, 180 Island Park Drive, Ottawa, Ontario, K1Y 0A2, T (613) 722 4444; **Denmark**, Norgesmindevej 18, 2900 Hellerup, Copenhagen, T (31) 6250101; **France**, 8 Rue Greuze, 75116 Paris, T 47043222; **Germany**, Uberstrasse 65, 5300 Bonn 2, T (0228) 355065; **Italy**, Via Nomentana, 132, 00162 Rome, T (396) 8320729; **Japan**, 3-14-6, Kami-Osaki, Shinagawa-ku, Tokyo 141, T (03) 3441-1386; **Laos**, Route Phonekheng, PO Box 128, Vientiane, T 2508; **Malaysia**, 206 Jl Ampang, 50450 Kuala Lumpur, T (03) 2488222; **Myanmar**, 91, Pyay Rd, Rangoon, T 21713; **Nepal**, Jyoti Kendra Building, Thapathali, PO Box 3333, Kathmandu, T 213910; **Netherlands**, 1 Buitenrustweg, 2517 KD, The Hague, T (070) 3452088; **New Zealand**, 2 Cook St, PO Box 17-226, Karori, T 768618; **Norway**, Munkedamsveien 59B, 0270 Oslo 2, T (02) 832517-8; **Spain**, Calle del Segre, 29, 20 A, 28002 Madrid, T (341) 5632903; **Sweden**, Sandhamnsgatan 36 (5th Floor), PO Box 27065, 10251 Stockholm, T (08) 6672160; **Switzerland**, Eigerstrasse 60 (3rd Floor), 3007 Bern, T (031) 462281; **UK**, 29-30 Queens Gate, London, SW7 5JB, T 0171 589 0173; **USA**, 2300 Kalorama Rd NW, Washington, DC 20008, T (202) 4837200.

Exchange rates: Jan 1997	
Currency	**Baht**
US$	25
£	41
DM	16
¥	0.23
Malaysian $	10
Singapore $	18
Hong Kong $	3.3
Swiss Franc	19
Dutch Guilder	15
French Franc	4.8
Lire	0.016
Australian $	20
New Zealand $	18

HEALTH

Vaccinations: no vaccinations are required, but cholera immunization and a tetanus booster are advisable. A gamma globulin injection (against hepatitis) is also recommended. There is a vaccination clinic in the Science Division of the Thai Red Cross Society, at the corner of Rama IV and Henri Dunant rds, Bangkok, T 2520161.

● **Medical facilities**

For full listing of hospitals, check the Yellow Pages, or listings under Useful addresses in each town. Hospitals in Bangkok are of a reasonable (Western) standard.

● **Food and water**

Tap water is not recommended for drinking. Cut fruit or uncooked vegetables from roadside stalls may not always be clean.

● **Travelling with children**

(For more information and a check-list, see the Rounding Up section.) Disposable nappies are now widely available in Thailand, although they are expensive. Powdered milks and a good range of powdered foods are on sale in most supermarkets. Bottled water is available everywhere. Fruit is a good source of nutrition and is also widely available. Anti-malarials are recommended (quarter to half dosage by some doctors) if travelling outside the main cities and tourist destinations although opinions – as on most issues connected with malaria – seem to differ. Check with your doctor or telephone your country's centre for tropical diseases.

MONEY

● **ATMs (cash dispensers)**

American Express can be used at Bangkok Bank, JCB at Siam Commercial Bank, Master Card at Siam Commercial, Visa at Bangkok Bank.

● **Credit cards**

Major credit cards such as American Express, Visa, Diners Club, Carte Blanche, Master Charge/Access are accepted in leading hotels, restaurants, department stores and several large stores for tourists. Visitors may have some problems upcountry where the use of credit cards is less common. Generally, Visa and Mastercard are more widely accepted than American Express; the Bangkok Bank takes Amex, but several banks accept Visa and Mastercard. Amex's higher commission also puts off many shopkeepers. **Notification of credit card**

loss: American Express, IBM Bldg, Phahon-yothin Rd, T 2730022; Diners Club, Dusit Thani Bldg, Rama IV Rd, T 2332645, 2335775; JCB T 2561361, 2561351; Visa and Master Card, Thai Farmers Bank Bldg, Phahonyothin Rd, T 2701801-10.

● **Cost of living**

Visitors staying in first class hotels and eating in hotel restaurants will probably spend a minimum of ฿1500/day. Tourists staying in cheaper air-conditioned accommodation, and eating in local restaurants will probably spend about ฿500-750/day. A backpacker, staying in fan-cooled guesthouses and eating cheaply, might expect to be able to live on ฿200/day. In Bangkok, expect to pay 20-30% more.

● **Currency**

The unit of Thai currency is the **baht** (฿), which is divided into 100 **satang**. Notes in circulation include ฿20 (green), ฿50 (blue), ฿100 (red), ฿500 (purple) and new ฿1,000 (orange and grey). Coins include 25 satang and 50 satang, and ฿1, ฿5, and ฿10. The two smaller coins are gradually disappearing from circulation and the 25 satang coin, equivalent to the princely sum of US$0.001 (1 cent), is rare.

● **Exchange rates**

It is best to change money at banks or money changers which give better rates than hotels. First class hotels have 24 hrs money changers. There is a charge of ฿13/cheque when changing TCs (passport required). Indonesian Rupiah and Nepalese Rupees cannot be exchanged for Thai currency.

GETTING THERE

AIR

The majority of visitors arrive in Thailand through Bangkok's Don Muang airport. There are also international chartered flights to Chiang Mai in the N and to Phuket in the S (see below). More than 35 airlines and charter companies fly to Bangkok, and Thailand is easily accessible from Europe, North America, Australasia and the Middle East as well as from other Asian countries. **Thai International** is the national airline.

● **Links with Indochina and Myanmar (Burma)**

Bangkok is a transport hub for air connections with Phnom Penh, Yangon – (Rangoon, My-anmar/Burma), Vientiane (Laos), and Hanoi and Ho Chi Minh City/Saigon (Vietnam). Partly as a result it also has a concentration of tour companies specializing in Indochina/Myanmar and is a good place to arrange a visa.

TRAIN

Regular rail services link Singapore and Bangkok, via Kuala Lumpur, Butterworth and the major southern Thai towns. Express a/c trains take two days from Kuala Lumpur, 34 hrs from Kuala Lumpur, 24 hrs from Butterworth (opp Penang). The *Magic Arrow Express* leaves Singapore on Sun, Tues and Thur, Bangkok-Singapore (฿899-1,965), Bangkok-Kuala Lumpur (฿659-1,432) and to Ipoh (฿530-1,145). An additional train from Butterworth departs at 1340, arriving Bangkok 0835 the next day. The train from Bangkok to Butterworth departs 1515, arriving Butterworth 1225 (฿457-1,147). All tickets should be booked in advance. The most luxurious way to journey by train to Thailand is aboard the *Eastern & Oriental (E&O) Express*. The a/c train of 22 carriages including a salon car, dining car, bar and observation deck and carrying just 132 passengers runs once a week from Singapore to Bangkok and back. Luxurious carriages, fine wines and food designed for European rather than Asian sensibilities make this not just a

Arranging visas for Indochina and Myanmar			
	LENGTH OF VISA	**WORKING DAYS TO ARRANGE**	**COST**
Vietnam	4 weeks	4 days	฿1,100-1,300
Laos	2 weeks	7 days	฿1,300-1,600
Cambodia	4 weeks	7 days	฿500-800
Myanmar (Burma)	4 weeks	2 days	฿300-500

NB Above details were collected in Oct 1996

mode of transport but an experience. The journey takes 43 hrs with stops in Kuala Lumpur, Butterworth and Padang Besar. But such luxury is expensive: US$1,130-2,950. For information call Bangkok 2514862; London (0171) 9286000; US (800) 5242420; Singapore (065) 2272068.

ROAD

The main road access is to and from Malaysia. The principal land border crossings into Malaysia are nr Betong in Yala Province and from Sungei Golok in Narathiwat Province. In Apr 1994 the Friendship Bridge linking Nong Khai with Laos opened – and became the first bridge across the Mekong River. To cross into Laos here foreigners need to obtain a visa in Bangkok – although a consulate is due to open in Nong Khai.

BOAT

No regular, scheduled cruise liners sail to Thailand any longer but it is sometimes possible to enter Thailand on a freighter, arriving at Khlong Toey Port. The Bangkok Post publishes a weekly shipping post with details on ships leaving the kingdom.

CUSTOMS

● **Duty free allowance**

250 gr of cigars or cigarettes (or 200 cigarettes) and 1 litre of wine or spirits. One still camera with five rolls of film or one movie camera with three rolls of 8mm or 16mm film.

● **Currency regulations**

Non-residents can bring in up to ฿2,000 pp and unlimited foreign currency although amounts exceeding US$10,000 must be declared. Maximum amount permitted to take out of the country is ฿50,000 pp.

● **Prohibited items**

All narcotics; obscene literature, pornography; fire arms (except with a permit from the Police Department or local registration office).

Some species of plants and animals are prohibited, for more information contact the Royal Forestry Department, Phahonyothin Rd, Bangkok, T 5792776. Permission of entry for animals by air is obtainable at the airport. An application must be made to the Department of Livestock Development, Bangkok, T 2515136 for entry by sea. Vaccination certificates are required; dogs and cats need rabies certificates.

ON ARRIVAL

● **Airport information**

Don Muang airport lies 25 km N of Bangkok. There are two international terminals (adjoining one another) and one domestic terminal. Terminal 1 serves Asia, and Terminal 2 the rest of the world. A 0.5 km-long covered walkway links the domestic and international terminals. Facilities include: banks and currency exchange, post office, left luggage (฿20/item/day – max 4 months), hotel booking agency, airport information, airport clinic, lost and found baggage service, duty-free shops, restaurants and bars including a whole slate of newly-opened fast food outlets – Burger King, Svensson's, Pizza Hut and Upper Crust. **NB** Food is expensive here – cheap food is available across the footbridge at the railway station. The Airport Hotel is linked to the international terminal by a walkway. It provides a 'ministay' service for passengers who wish to 'freshen-up' and take a room for up to 3 hrs between 0800 and 1800 (฿400 T 5661020/1). **International flight information**: T 5351386 for departures, T 5351301 for arrivals. **Domestic flight information**: T 5351253. The new domestic terminal has a hotel booking counter, post office, currency exchange counters, restaurant and bookshop. An elevated a/c walkway connects the international and domestic terminals; a shuttle bus is sometimes available, beware – taxis grossly overcharge for a drive of under 1 km.

Airport accommodation: A Amari Airport, 333 Chert Wudthakas Rd, T 5661020, F 5661941, a/c, restaurants, pool, connected to airport by foot-bridge; rooms look onto attractive gardens, useful hotel for transit passengersm short-term stays for wash and rest available; A Rama Gardens, 9/9 Vibhavadi Rangsit Rd, Bangkaen (7 km from the airport), T 561002, F 5611025, a/c, restaurants, two attractive, large pools, out of town on road to airport, inconvenient for most except those merely stopping-over for a few hours, but spacious grounds with fitness centre, tennis, squash, golf, putting.

Transport to town By taxi: official taxi booking service in the arrivals hall. There are two desks. One for the more expensive official airport taxis (newer, more luxurious vehicles); one for public taxis. The former cost ฿400 downtown; ฿300 to the northern bus terminal; ฿450 to the southern bus terminal; ฿1,500 to Pattaya. Note that airport flunkies sometimes try to direct passengers to this more expensive 'limousine' service: walk through the barriers to the public taxi desk. A public taxi to downtown should cost about half these prices – roughly ฿150-200 with ฿50 extra if using the new elevated expressway. Note that there are both metered and unmetered public taxis; the fare for the latter will be quoted when you state your destination at the desk. If taking a metered taxi, the coupon from the booking desk will quote no fare – ensure that the meter is used or you may find that the trip costs ฿300 instead of ฿200, keep hold of your coupon – some taxi drivers try to pocket it – as it details the obligations of taxi drivers. **Warning** There have been cases of visitors being robbed in unofficial taxis. To tell whether your vehicle is a registered taxi, check the colour of the number plate. Official airport limousines have green plates, public taxis have yellow plates – and a white plate means the vehicle is not registered as a taxi. The sedan service into town costs ฿500-650. Cars are newer, more comfortable and better maintained than the average city taxi. It takes 30 mins to 1 hr to central Bangkok, depending on the time of day and the state of the traffic. The new elevated expressway reduces journey time to 20 mins – ask the taxi driver to take this route if you wish to save time but note that there is a toll fee – ฿20 and ฿30 for the two sections of this elevated road. Also note that there have been some complaints about taxi drivers at the domestic terminal forming a cartel, refusing to use their meters and charging a fixed rate considerably above the meter rate.

By bus: until 1996 buses were the cheapest but also the slowest way into town. But in Apr a new a/c airport bus service was introduced – ฿70 to Silom Rd (service A1), Sanaam Luang (service A2) (most convenient for Khaosan road guesthouses) and Phra Khanong (service A3). The service operates every 15 mins, 0500-2300. **Stops are as follows:** Silom service **(A1):** Don Muang Tollway, Din Daeng, Pratunam, Lumpini Park, Silom. **Sanaam Luang service (A2):** Don Muang Tollway, Din Daeng, Victory Monument, Phayathai, Phetburi, Lan Luang, Democracy Monument, Sanaam Luang. **Phra Khanong service (A3):** Don Muang Tollway, Din Daeng, Sukhumit, Ekamai, Phra Khanong. While hotel stops are: **Silom service (A1):** *Century, Indra, Anoma, Grand Hyatt, Erawan, Regent, Dusit Thani,* and *Narai* hotels. **Sanaam Luang service (A2):** Victory Monument, *Siam City Hotel*, Soi King Phet, Saphan Khao, *Majestic* and *Rattanakosin* hotels. **Phra Khanong service (A3):** Amari Building, *Ambassador* and *Delta Grand Pacific* hotels, Bang Chan Glass House, *Novotel*, Soi Ekkamai (Sukhumuit). **NB** Return buses have slightly different stops.

Although many visitors will see ฿70 as money well spent there will still be the hardened few who will opt for the regular bus service, which is just as cheap and slow as it ever was, 1½-3 hrs (depending on time of day) (฿7-15). The bus stop is 50m N of the arrivals hall. Buses are crowded during rush-hours and there is little room for luggage. Bus 59 goes to Khaosan Rd, bus 29 goes to Bangkok's Hualamphong railway station, via the Northern bus terminal and Siam Square. A/c bus 10 goes to Samsen Rd and Silom Rd via the Northern bus terminal, a/c bus 4 goes to Silom Rd, a/c bus 13 goes to Sukhumvit Rd and the Eastern bus terminal, a/c bus 29 goes to the Northern bus terminal, Siam Square and Hualamphong railway station. **By minibus:** ฿100 to major hotels, ฿60 shuttle bus to the *Asia Hotel* on Phayathai Rd. ฿50-80 to Khaosan Rd, depending on the time of day. Direct buses to Pattaya at 0900, 1200 and 1700, ฿180. **By train:** the station is on the other side of the N-S highway from the airport. Regular trains into Bangkok's Hualamphong station, ฿5 for ordinary train, 3rd clas (the cheapest option). But only 6 ordinary trains per day. For 'rapid' and 'express' a supplementary charge of ฿20-50 is levied. The State Railways of Thailand runs an 'Airport Express' 5 times a day (but not on Sat and Sun), with a/c shuttle bus from Don Muang station to airport terminal, 35 mins (฿100). **Hotel pick-up services:** many of the more expensive hotels operate airport pick-up services if informed of your arrival ahead of time.

● **Airport tax**
Payable on departure – ฿250 for international flights, ฿30 for domestic flights.

● **Clothing**
In towns and at religious sights, it is courteous to avoid wearing shorts and singlets (or sleeveless shirts). Visitors who are inappropriately dressed may not be allowed into temples. Thais always look neat and clean. *Mai rieb-roi* means 'not neat' and is considered a great insult. Beach resorts are a law unto themselves – casual clothes are the norm, although nudity is still very much frowned upon by Thais. In the

most expensive restaurants in Bangkok diners may well be expected to wear a jacket and tie.

● **Conduct**

Thais are generally very understanding of the foibles and habits of foreigners (*farangs*) and will forgive and forget most indiscretions. However, there are a number of 'dos and don'ts' which are worth observing:

Common greeting *Wai*: hands are held together as if in prayer, and the higher the wai, the more respectful the greeting. By watching Thai's wai it is possible to ascertain their relative seniority. Again, foreigners are not expected to conform to this custom – a simple wai at chest to chin height is all that is required. When *farangs* and Thais do business it is common to shake hands.

Heads, heart and feet Try not to openly point your feet at anyone – feet are viewed as spiritually the lowest part of the body. At the same time, never touch anyone's head which is the holiest, as well as the highest, part. Among Thais, the personal characteristic of *jai yen* is very highly regarded; literally, this means to have a 'cool heart'. It embodies calmness, having an even temper and not displaying emotion. Although foreigners generally receive special dispensation, and are not expected to conform to Thai customs (all *farang* are thought to have 'hot hearts'), it is important to try and keep calm in any disagreement – losing one's temper leads to loss of face and subsequent loss of respect.

The monarchy Never criticize any member of the royal family or the institution itself. The monarchy is held in very high esteem.

Monastery (*wat*) etiquette Remove shoes on entering, do not climb over Buddha images or have pictures taken in front of one. Wear modest clothing – women should not expose their shoulders or wear dresses that are too short (see below, clothing). Females should never hand anything directly to monks, or venture into the monks' quarters.

Smoking Prohibited on domestic flights, public buses and in cinemas.

Further reading A useful book delving deeper into the do's and don'ts of living in Thailand is Robert and Nanthapa Cooper's *Culture shock: Thailand*, Time Books International: Singapore (1990). It is available from most bookshops.

● **Emergencies**

Police 191, 123; **Tourist Police** 195; **Fire** 199; **Ambulance** 2522171-5. **Tourist Police head office**: Unico House, Ploenchit Soi Lang Suan, Bangkok, T 6521721-6. **Tourist Assistance Centre**, Rachdamnern Nok Ave, Bangkok, T 2828129.

● **Hours of business**

Banks: 0830-1530 Mon-Fri. **Currency exchange services**: 0830-2200 Mon-Sun in Bangkok and Pattaya, 0830-1930 in Phuket and 0830-1630 Mon-Fri in other towns. **Government offices**: 0830-1200, 1300-1630 Mon-Fri. **Tourist offices**: 0830-1630 Mon-Sun. **Shops**: 0830-1700, larger shops: 1000-1900 or 2100.

● **Official time**

7 hrs ahead of GMT.

● **Tipping**

Generally unnecessary. A 10% service charge is now expected on room, food and drinks bills in the smarter hotels as well as a tip for any personal service. Increasingly, the more expensive restaurants add a 10% service charge; others expect a small tip.

● **Voltage**

220 volts (50 cycles) throughout Thailand. Most first and tourist class hotels have outlets for shavers and hair dryers. Adaptors are recommended, as almost all sockets are two pronged.

WHERE TO STAY

As a premier tourist destination and one of the world's fastest-growing economies, Thailand has a large selection of hotels – including some of the very best in the world. However, outside the tourist centres, there is still an absence of adequate 'Western style' accommodation. Most 'Thai' hotels are distinctly lacking in character and are poorly maintained. Due to the popularity of the country with backpackers, there are also a large number of small guesthouses, geared to Westerners serving Western food and catering to the foibles of foreigners.

● **Hotels**

Hotels are listed under eight categories, according to the *average* price of a double/twin room for one night. It should be noted that many hotels will have a range of rooms, some with air-conditioning (a/c) and attached bathroom facilities, others with just a fan and shared facilities. A service charge of 10% and government tax of 11% will usually be added to the bill in the more expensive hotels (categories B-L). Ask whether the quoted price includes tax when checking-in. **NB** During the off-season, hotels in tourist destinations may halve their room rates so it is always worthwhile bargaining.

FOOD AND DRINK

FOOD

Thai cuisine is an intermingling of Tai, Chinese, and to a lesser extent, Indian cuisines. This helps to explain why restaurants produce dishes which must be some of the (spicy) hottest in the world, as well as some which are rather bland. Despite these various influences, Thai cooking is distinctive. Thais have managed to combine the best of each tradition, adapting elements to fit their own preferences. Remarkably, considering how ubiquitous it is in Thai cooking, the chilli pepper is a New World fruit and was not introduced into Thailand until the late 16th century (along with the pineapple and papaya).

When a Thai asks another Thai whether he has eaten he will ask, literally, whether he has 'eaten rice' (kin khaaw). Similarly, the accompanying dishes are referred to as food 'with the rice'. A Thai meal is based around rice, and many wealthy Bangkokians own farms upcountry where they cultivate their favourite variety. A meal usually consists (along with the rice) of a soup like tom yam kung (prawn soup), kaeng (a curry) and krueng kieng (a number of side dishes). Generally, Thai food is chilli-hot, and aromatic herbs and grasses (like lemon grass) are used to give a distinctive flavour. Nam pla (fish sauce) and nam prik (nam pla, chillies, garlic, sugar, shrimps and lime juice) are two condiments that are taken with almost all meals. Food is eaten with a spoon and fork, and dishes are usually served all at once; it is unimportant to a Thai that food be hot. Try the open-air foodstalls to be found in every town which are frequented by middle-class Thais as well as the poor and where a meal costs only ฿15-20. Many small restaurants have no menus. Away from the main tourist spots, 'Western' breakfasts are commonly unavailable, so be prepared to eat Thai-style (noodle or rice soup or fried rice). Finally, due to Thailand's large Chinese population (or at least Thais with Chinese roots), there are also many Chinese-style restaurants whose cuisine is variously 'Thai-ified'.

Tourist centres also provide good European, American and Japanese food at reasonable prices. Bangkok boasts some superb restaurants. Less expensive Western fastfood restaurants can also be found – McDonalds, Pizza Hut, Kentucky Fried Chicken and others.

DRINK

● Drinking water

Water in smaller restaurants can be risky, so many people recommend that visitors drink bottled water (widely available) or **hot tea**.

● Soft drinks

Coffee is also now consumed throughout Thailand (usually served with coffeemate or creamer). In stalls and restaurants, coffee come with a glass of Chinese tea. Soft drinks are widely available. Many roadside stalls prepare **fresh fruit juices** in liquidizers (bun) while hotels produce all the usual cocktails.

● Alcohol

Spirits Major brands of spirits are served in most hotels and bars, although not always off the tourist path. The most popular spirit among Thais is **Mekhong** – **local cane whisky** – which can be drunk straight or with mixers. It can seem rather sweet to the Western palate but it is the cheapest form of alcohol.

Beer The most popular local beer is Singha beer brewed by Boon Rowd. It's alcohol content is high of 6% must be partly to blame. Among expatriates, the most popular Thai beer is the more expensive Kloster brand (similar to a light German beer) with an alcohol content of 5.7%. Singha introduced a light beer called Singha Gold a few years ago which is quite similar to Kloster. Amarit is a third, rather less widely available, brand but popular with foreigners. Two new 'local' beers (in the sense that they are locally brewed) to enter the fray are Heineken and Carlsberg. The beer is sweeter and lighter than Singha and Kloster but still strong with an alcohol content of 6%. Yet another new local beer, although it appears to have only a very small segment of the market (as yet), and is hard to find is: Bier Chang or Elephant Beer. Beer is relatively expensive in Thai terms as it is heavily taxed by the government. In a café, expect to pay ฿30-50 for a small beer, in a coffee shop or bar ฿40-65, and in a hotel bar or restaurant, more than ฿60.

Wine Thais are fast developing a penchant for wines. Imported wines are expensive by international standards and Thai wines are pretty ghastly – overall. An exception is Chateau de Loei which is produced in the northeastern province of Loei by Chaijudh Karnasuta with the expert assistance of French wine maker.

COMMUNICATIONS

● **Postal services**

Local postal charges: ฿1 (postcard) and ฿2 (letter, 20 g). **International postal charges**: Europe and Australasia – ฿9 (postcard), ฿12.50 (letter, 10 g); US – ฿9 (postcard), ฿14.50 (letter, 10 g). Airletters cost ฿8.50. Poste Restante: correspondents should write the family name in capital letters and underline it, to avoid confusion.

Outside Bangkok, most post offices are open from 0800-1630 Mon-Fri and only the larger ones will be open on Sat.

Fax services: now widely available in most towns. Postal and telex/fax services are available in most large hotels.

● **Telephone services**

From Bangkok there is direct dialling to most countries. Outside Bangkok, it is best to go to a local telephone exchange for 'phoning outside the country.

Codes: local area codes vary according to province, they are listed under "Post & telecommunications" in each town; the code can also be found at the front of the telephone directory.

Directory inquiries: domestic long distance including Malaysia and Vientiane (Laos) – 101, Greater Bangkok BMA – 183, international calls T 2350030-5, although hotel operators will invariably help make the call if asked.

Callboxes cost ฿1. All telephone numbers marked in the text with a prefix 'B' mean that they are Bangkok numbers.

ENTERTAINMENT

● **Newspapers**

Until recently there were two major English language daily papers – the Bangkok Post and the Nation Review (known as The Nation). They provide good international news coverage and are Thailand's best known broadsheets.

● **Television and radio**

Five TV channels, with English language sound track available on FM. Channel 3 – 105.5 MHz, Channel 7 – 103.5 MHz, Channel 9 – 107 MHz and Channel 11 – 88 MHz. The Bangkok Post stars programmes where English soundtrack is available on FM. Shortwave radio can receive the BBC World Service, Voice of America, Radio Moscow, see page 222.

HOLIDAYS AND FESTIVALS

Festivals with month only are movable; a booklet of holidays and festivals is available from most TAT offices.

Jan: New Year's Day (1st: public holiday).

Feb: Magha Puja (full-moon: public holiday) Buddhist holy day, celebrates the occasion when the Buddha's disciples miraculously gathered together to hear him preach. Culminates in a candle-lit procession around the temple bot (or ordination hall). The faithful make offerings and gain merit. Chinese New Year (movable, end of Jan/beginning of Feb) celebrated by Thailand's large Chinese population. The festival extends over 15 days; spirits are appeased, and offerings are made to the ancestors and to the spirits. Good wishes and lucky money are exchanged, and Chinese-run shops and businesses shut down.

Apr: Chakri Day (6th: public holiday) commemorates the founding of the present Chakri Dynasty. Songkran (movable: public holiday) marks the beginning of the Buddhist New Year and is particularly big in the N (Chiang Mai, Lampang, Lamphun and Chiang Rai). It is a 3 to 5 day celebration, with parades, dancing and folk entertainment. The first day represents the last chance for a 'spring clean'. Rubbish is burnt, in the belief that old and dirty things will cause misfortune in the coming year. The wat is the focal point. Revered Buddha images are carried through the streets, accompanied by singers and dancers. The second day is the main water-throwing day (originally an act of homage to ancestors and family elders). Young people pay respect by pouring scented water over the elders heads. The older generation sprinkle water over Buddha images. Gifts are given. This uninhibited water-throwing continues for all 3 days (although it is now banned in Bangkok). On the third day birds, fish and turtles are all released, to gain merit and in remembrance of departed souls.

May: Coronation Day (5th: public holiday) commemorates the present King Bhumibol's crowning in 1950. Ploughing Ceremony (movable: public holiday) performed by the King at Sanaam Luang near the Grand Palace in Bangkok. Brahmanic in origin, it traditionally marks the auspicious date when farmers could begin preparing their riceland. Impressive bulls decorated with flowers pull a sacred gold plough.

Jun: *Visakha Puja* (full-moon: public holiday) holiest of all Buddhist days, it marks the Buddha's birth, enlightenment and death. Candle-lit processions are held at most temples.

Aug: *The Queen's Birthday* (12th: public holiday). *Asalha Puja and Khao Phansa* (full-moon: public holiday) – commemorates the Buddha's first sermon to his disciples and marks the beginning of the Buddhist Lent. Monks reside in their monasteries for the 3 month Buddhist Rains Retreat to study and meditate, and young men temporarily become monks. Ordination ceremonies all over the country and villagers give white cotton robes to the monks to wear during the Lent ritual bathing.

Oct: *Ok Phansa* (3 lunar months after Asalha Puja) marks the end of the Buddhist Lent and the beginning of Krathin, when gifts – usually a new set of cotton robes – are offered to the monks. Particularly venerated monks are sometimes given silk robes as a sign of respect and esteem. Krathin itself is celebrated over two days. It marks the end of the monks' retreat and the re-entry of novices into secular society. Processions and fairs are held all over the country; villagers wear their best clothes

and food, money, pillows and bed linen are offered to the monks of the local wat. *Chulalongkorn Day* (23rd: public holiday) honours King Chulalongkorn (1868-1910), perhaps Thailand's most beloved and revered king.

Nov: *Loi Krathong* (full-moon) a *krathong* is a small model boat made to contain a candle, incense and flowers. The festival comes at the end of the rainy season and honours the goddess of water. The little boats are pushed out onto canals, lakes and rivers. Sadly, few krathongs are now made of leaves: polystyrene has taken over and the morning after Loi Krathong lakes and river banks are littered with the wrecks of the night's festivities. **NB** The 'quaint' candles in flower pots sold in many shops at this time, are in fact large firecrackers.

Dec: *The King's Birthday* (5th: public holiday). Flags and portraits of the King are erected all over Bangkok, especially down Rachdamnern Ave and around the Grand Palace. *Constitution Day* (10th: public holiday). *New Year's Eve* (31st: public holiday).

NB Regional and local festivals are noted in appropriate sections.

Information for travellers

BEFORE TRAVELLING

Regulations for tourists and businessmen are in a constant state of flux. The advice given below was checked in 1996, but visitors must be ready for the possibility that new or altered regulations have come into force since then.

ENTRY REQUIREMENTS

● **Visas**

Visas for stays up to 28 days can be obtained on arrival at Pochentong airport, Phnom Penh. Fill in the application form in the arrival hall and hand over 1 photo, with your passport. Although *officially* free of charge visitors normally have to pay US$20.

Cambodia has a growing number of embassies, so obtaining a visa abroad is getting easier. At the embassy in Germany, it is now possible to acquire 3 month visas in less than 10 mins. Bangkok and Saigon (Vietnam) are the best places to obtain visas for independent travel (but leave a week to arrange). Nationals of most countries can join tours but citizens of the US, Israel, South Africa, China and South Korea must all have individual, rather than group visas, which take longer to process.

Vietnam visas If arriving overland from Vietnam, be sure that your Vietnam visa has Moc Bai as the exit point, otherwise you will be turned away at the border. The Immigration Police office, at 254 Nguyen Trai St in Saigon can change the exit point on your passport. It takes 24 hrs and costs US$5.

NB: at the beginning of 1997, as this book went to press, the border crossing between Cambodia and Vietnam at Moc Bai was closed. Check on the status of the crossing before embarking from Phnom Penh or Saigon/Ho Chi Minh City.

Visa extensions can be secured through the Immigration Office, 5 Oknha Men St, takes 1 day. **Foreign Ministry** at the intersection of 240 St and Sisowath Quay, T 24641; **Ministry of Tourism**, 3 Monivong Blvd, T 26107; **Phnom Penh Tourism**, 313 Sisowath Quay, T 23949/25349 or a travel agency in Phnom Penh. Extensions cost US$20 for 1 week, US$40 for a month, US$100 for 6 months. Fines are US$3/day for not renewing your visa.

● **Vaccinations**

No vaccinations required except cholera if coming from an infected area. It is advisable to be vaccinated for typhoid, cholera, tetanus and hepatitis. Take all possible precautions against malaria (see page 208).

● **Travelling outside Phnom Penh**

Travellers do not need permits to visit areas outside Phnom Penh. However, it is wise to check with the Ministry of Tourism, the Foreign Ministry or with guesthouses re the security situation before travelling outside Phnom Penh. Visitors should also consider registering with their national embassy who can advise on the current travel situation. Two Britons and an Australian were kidnapped at gunpoint in Apr 1994 on the road from Phnom Penh to Sihanoukville. Stretches of roads are often controlled by Khmers Rouges or bandits and travellers have been forced to pay large bribes. Visitors travelling by road, or river, are advised to join a convoy wherever possible. Do not travel at night under any circumstances, and for long distance road trips it is advisable to set off early in the day. The temples at Angkor lie near scenes of recent fighting between the Khmers Rouges and government troops. Up-market tour groups continue to visit Angkor, arriving by plane and touring by private bus but individuals are advised to check the situation. Facilities and transport are limited outside the capital. Travellers recommend taking shared taxis. Rt 1, Rt 2, Rt 3 and Rt 4 are generally regarded as safe but Rt 5 to Kompong Chhang is less so.

● **Tourist information**
There are two agencies in Phnom Penh: the **Ministry of Tourism** (or General Directorate of Tourism) and **Phnom Penh Tourism** (see Phnom Penh section, page 101 for addresses). They both organize tours to Angkor Wat and rent out cars. Ministry of Tourism produce a small, but good brochure.

WHEN TO GO
● **Best time to visit**
In the winter months, from Nov to Apr, temperatures average 25-32°C. The cool, dry NE monsoon blows during this period, which makes it a pleasant time to visit. The summer months, from May to Oct, are hot, wet and humid; the temperature hovers around 33°C and humidity is usually 90%. However, even in the wet season, it rarely rains heavily before lunch.

● **Clothing**
Women traditionally wear embroidered or patterned cotton sarongs, called *samphots*. Men also wear samphots but, these days, many prefer Western-style clothes. In the years when Pol Pot enforced 'social equality', everyone was forced to wear black. The *krama*, a checked cloth, worn as a turban or shawl is worn by most Khmers. Most kramas are black and white but the Khmers Rouges wear red and white checks. Take cool casual clothes. Cambodians are very modest and women should take care to cover their arms and legs, particularly when visiting wats.

HEALTH
● **Vaccinations**
No innoculations are required except a cholera vaccination if coming from an infected area. It is, however, advisable to take full precautions before travelling to Cambodia. Tetanus, polio, hepatitis, rabies, typhoid and cholera injections are recommended.

● **Malaria**
Malarial drugs are a vital prerequisite for tourists in Cambodia. Much of the population is afflicted with malaria and there is little medicine available. **NB** A virulent malaria – resistant to all drugs, is present in Cambodia.

● **Food and water**
Avoid all but thoroughly boiled or sterilized water. It is advisable not to use ice. Beware of uncooked vegetables and fruit which cannot be peeled.

● **AIDS**
Prevalent among prostitutes, a survey in the western provinces found 60% of prostitutes and 10% of military and police HIV-positive, another in Sihanoukville revealed 39% HIV-positive, and an estimated 50% of Phnom Penh's prostitutes are affected. Of a sample of Phnom Penh's blood donors in Jan 1995, nearly 7% were HIV-positive. Locally sold condoms (*No 1's*, produced by Population Service International) are considered reliable but, shall we

say, 'geared to local conditions'. Western men are advised to bring their own. See page 226 for further background information on prostitution and AIDS.

● **Medical facilities**
Like most social institutions, health services were completely dismantled during the Pol Pot regime: 2 decades on, hospitals are still few and far between, medical facilities are poor and medicines are in short supply. Patients are often expected to buy their own medicines on the black market. Many of the pharmacies sell drugs which are well past their sell-by date or 'hot' pharmaceuticals – stolen from aid agencies. If you need emergency treatment, take the first plane to Bangkok. It is wise to carry a first aid pack.

● **Travelling with children**
Bring all essentials with you; it is not advisable to travel with children outside Phnom Penh.

● **Further health information**
See main section on health, page 225.

MONEY
● **Currency**
The riel (CR) is the official currency. At the beginning of 1997 there were 2,700 riel to US$1.

In mid-1995 the government introduced new paper currency, printed in France, these notes are of larger denomination than the old, which are still in circulation. The new notes are 1,000, 2,000, 5,000, 10,000, 50,000 and 100,000. In Nov 1996 US$1 = 2,300 riel. It is advisable to take small denomination US$ notes, which are easier to change; virtually all services/goods can be paid for in dollars, although the government is trying to phase out their use. Menus are usually priced in dollars and payment in riel is often at a disadvantageous rate. Airline tickets, visas, airport tax and other such payments are usually in US$ – payment in riel may be impossible. There is little point in changing money. You should be able to change any major cash currency including Thai baht.

Cambodia operates strict currency controls. Riel cannot be taken out of the country.

● **Travellers cheques**
Travellers cheques are difficult to change – although it is possible at banks and the *Diamond Hotel* – commission is high. It is possible to change US$, Sterling, French francs, TCs (American Express, Thomas Cook, Visa, Citicorp). Foreign Trade Bank charges 1%, Thai Farmers Bank 3%.

● **Credit cards**
Facilities for drawing cash on visa/mastercard are now widespread both in Phnom Penh and Siem Reap. Some large tour operators may allow use of credit cards but airline tickets must be paid for in cash.

● **Black market**
Hard currency is traded openly, rates are only a little better than the bank.

GETTING THERE

AIR
The vast majority of tourists arrive in Cambodia by air. All international flights land at Pochentong Airport, Phnom Penh. In Dec 1994 the two incumbent Cambodian airlines (CIA and Kampuchea Airlines) were disbanded in favour of a brand new national carrier, **Royal Air Cambodge**. Routes available have increased substantially: there are connections via Bangkok, Saigon, Hong Kong, Kuala Lumpur, Singapore, Guangzhou (China) and Vientiane. Thai International, Malaysian Airlines, Vietnam Airlines, Silk Air and Dragonair also work the routes. Subject to revision there are twice daily connections with Saigon (US$75), connections with Hanoi via Saigon (US$240), twice weekly connections with Vientiane (US$130), 6 flights a week with Kuala Lumpur (US$195), 4 times a week to Hong Kong (US$240), twice daily connections with Singapore (US$200) and up to 3 connections per day to Bangkok (US$130). All prices are one way.

ROAD
It is possible to travel the 245 km from **Saigon** to Phnom Penh on Route 1, via the border crossing at Moc Bai. (Note, though, that this crossing was closed as this book went to press at the beginning of 1997.) Buses leave from Saigon (next to the *Rex Hotel*) to Phnom Penh, 7-9 hrs, incl 2-3 hrs at the border. Buses leave from Phnom Penh from Psar Depot Market; non a/c buses leave on Mon, Tues, Wed (US$5) and a/c buses on Thur, Fri, Sat, 12 hrs (US$12). Shared taxis also go to the border, 6 hrs (US$4 pp). There is no problem obtaining a visa for Vietnam in Phnom Penh (although it is more expensive (US$55) and takes 5 days. The border is only open from 0630 to 1800.

The road between **Bangkok** and Phom Penh (via Poipet) is officially open with foreign ministry approval but in practice it is usually not possible. It takes 10 days to get a visa from the Phnom Penh office (US$20). Taxis cost ø1,500 from Poipet to Phnom Penh.

At present it is still not possible for tourists to enter Cambodia from **Southern Laos**.

TRAIN AND BOAT

Rail travel is forbidden at present. The port is not usually open to visitors. It is possible for yachts to harbour at Sihanoukville (Kompong Som) but contact a Cambodian Consulate first. There are vague plans to open the Bangkok-Phnom Penh railway line.

CUSTOMS

● **Duty free allowance**

200 cigarettes, 1 bottle of spirits and perfume for personal use.

ON ARRIVAL

● **Airport information**

Phnom Penh's tiny Pochentong International Airport is 12 km from the city. The buildings have recently been redeveloped. The runway is being extended to cater for the ever-increasing number of visitors. Facilities include a good restaurant run by a Canadian-Cambodian couple. The menu includes traditional Khmer dishes, international food, delicious pastries and tropical fruit salads. There is also a helpful tourist information desk (who will make hotel reservations) and a foreign exchange counter.

Transport to town By taxi: red fleet taxis operate into town, US$7-10. **By moto**: US$2-3. For pre-arranged tours or those who have hired guides there is a pick-up service.

● **Airport tax**

US$15 for international flights, US$5 for domestic.

● **Conduct**

Wats As in all Buddhist countries in the region, it is important to make sure your arms and legs are covered when visiting wats or religious sites. It is considerate to ask permission before

Mine safety

Very few foreign visitors have been injured, maimed or killed by land mines in Cambodia. Most that have, were members of the UNTAC mission. However, mines do pose an ever-present danger (see the box on page 68) and as tourists venture further off the beaten track so the risks increase proportionately. The following is a short checklist of ways to avoid injury taken from a special supplement in the *Phnom Penh Post* published to coincide with Cambodia's first Mine Awareness Day in Feb 1995:

● Ask local people whether mines are a problem in an area before venturing out by inquiring '*mian min teh?*'. It is worth asking the question of more than one local just to make sure.

● Stick to known safe paths.

● Use a guide wherever possible.

● Do not remove the mine warning signs (some tourists, incredibly, have taken to removing signs as souvenirs).

● Do not touch mines.

● If you find yourself in a mine field retrace your steps <u>exactly</u>, stepping into each of your foot marks.

Illustration from *Support Ban Mine Campaign* poster

entering the main sanctuaries – and take off your shoes. When sitting down, your feet should point away from the altar and the main image. If talking to a monk, one's head should be lower than his. A small donation is often appropriate.

Form of address Old men are addressed as *ta* (or, less commonly, *bang*) and old women *yeay* (or *bang srey*), but those of your own age can be called by name.

Greeting Cambodians use their traditional greeting – the 'wai', bowing with their hands held together. As a foreigner, shaking hands is perfectly acceptable.

In private homes It is polite to take your shoes off on entering a house and a small present goes down well if you are invited for a meal.

General Displays of anger or exasperation are considered unacceptable and therefore reflect very badly on the individual. Accordingly, even in adversity, Khmers (like the Thais) will keep smiling. Displays of affection are also considered embarrassing. Try not to pat children on the head. To beckon someone, use your hand with the palm facing downwards. Pointing is rude.

● **Hours of business**
Government offices: 0730-1200, 1400-1800 Mon-Fri. **Banks**: 0730-1030, 1400-1600 Mon-Fri, 0730-1030 Sat.

● **Official time**
7 hrs ahead of GMT.

● **Photography**
It is polite to ask permission before taking photographs; some people take offence.

It can be difficult to buy colour slide film so it is advisable to bring what you need, colour print film is widely available in Phnom Penh and Angkor. Some photo stores will also print film, but at your own risk.

● **Safety**
As this book went to press at the end of 1996, the only areas that were really open to visitors were Phnom Penh, Siem Reap (Angkor) and Sihanoukville. It is not advisable to venture outside these areas. Tourists should be very cautious when walking in the countryside: land mines and other unexploded ordnance is a ubiquitous hazard. **DO NOT TOUCH!** Take a guide in areas that have been heavily bombed or mined and stick to well-used paths, especially around Siem Reap. There are said to be more than 7 million anti-personnel mines bur-

ied around the country (see page 68). Tourists are advised not to travel after dark.

It is advisable not to walk through Phnom Penh after dark, as many areas have no street lighting and frequent power cuts plunge the city into total darkness. Petty theft is a serious problem in Phnom Penh and other towns. Gangs of disabled people are forced to find a living on the streets, as they get no help from the government, and are well practised in the art of coercion. Shopkeepers are the usual victims, but tourists should be wary. See the advice contained in the tinted box '**Mean Streets**' and how to avoid them, see page 85.

On 11 April 1994 three westerners, two Britons and an Australian, were abducted on Route 4 SW of Phnom Penh and murdered by the Khmers Rouges. At the end of Jul, three more foreign tourists, this time a Briton, an Australian and a Frenchman were kidnapped by the Khmers Rouges while travelling by train in the southern province of Kompot and also murdered. Note that travelling off the main routes holds distinct dangers. Telephone your embassy before venturing off the beaten track, for the latest news and advice. Backpackers accustomed to the relative freedom of movement in Vietnam will find their movements seriously curtailed in Cambodia. The difficulties and dangers of travel, and the degree to which the situation changes week-by-week is illustrated in the following security bulletin issued to NGOs and other workers and organizations in the country in 1997:

"first hand reports indicate there are much larger numbers of soldiers adjacent to the main roads these last few weeks. Invariably that means an increase in checkpoints and the possibility of problems/delays in travelling. Therefore, advice is to avoid travel outside Phnom Penh unless necessary for your work. Around the country, Route 1 to Svay Rieng and Vietnam in the South East is passable. Route 4 is reportedly very busy traffic wise. Route 5 between Pursat-Battambang still required a full-day for travelling to allow time for mishaps and delays otherwise Route 5 Phnom Penh-Poipet is passable without much difficulty. This is not the case on Route 6 Sisophon-Siem Reap: it took one vehicle 8 hrs to make this trip last week and 6 hrs is the norm. Avoid the road if you can is the message. The road to Chikreng is open and you can get to Stung in Kompong Thom, but (lack of) security still makes this route a no-go. Route 7 to Kompong Cham is open again although bribes of 10,000 riel are required of all traffic to cross one bridge in Bateay district en route. Loads of over a tonne are not permitted. Route 67 to Banteai Srei is closed, unless you have permission to work there from the Governor. Sar Sar Sdam to Angkor Chum is open, Angkor Chum onto Varin is closed. Sotnikum to Popeal is open but Popeal to Svay Leu is closed. Route 68 is for essential travel only N of Kralanh.

Another average slice of time in Phnom Penh: 12 June-22 June 1996

June 12: Four armed men carjacked a Toyota Land Cruiser after they held up the driver of the Singapore Embassy in front of Regent Park Hotel.

June 13: Kim Sophal, 28, was shot and killed when his gang tried to break into a doctor's house at midnight. Dr Pov Sovann Than, 46, fired a gun many times from his bed and injured a few of the robbers outside his home in Tra Paing village.

June 15: Oun Arng, 18, from Koh Kong province, was taken to a Phnom Penh hospital after she drank poison. Her family believed Arng drank the poison after having been scolded by her older sister for losing a gold ring.

June 15: A *Cambodia Daily* security guard was hit by a truck and severely injured while driving his motorbike from the newspaper's offices. Doctors at Kosamak hospital were forced to amputate his right leg.

June 17: RCAF soldier Ek Sopharn, 34, was arrested after he used explosives to fish in the Basak River near Kbarl Thnal Bridge. Sopharn confessed he stole TNT powder from his regiment and built the grenade himself.

June 17: Ou Sophart, 50, was arrested for selling two virgin girls, one aged 15 and the other 14, at a Tuol Kork brothel. The two young girls from Pursat province were sold for $150 each.

June 18: Tine Horn, 10, was killed and two other boys were taken to hospital after a rocket-propelled grenade (RPG) they were playing with exploded. The 10-year-old found the RGP near his home in Angkor Seth village, Kandal province. Witnesses said they saw Tine Horn pound the grenade, causing it to explode.

June 18: Sin Vang, 29, was arrested by local police after a 10 mm bomb exploded inside his burning home. Police also found a homemade gun inside the house in Chroy Changvar district.

June 19: A 5-year-old boy was shot and killed by two robbers in Teuk Thlar village. His father was injured three times in his waist, and once in the left hand and leg when he tried to take his moto back from the robbers. The suspects left the motorbike and ran away before local villagers arrived.

June 20: A married couple were shot five times each and killed inside their home in Tuol Svay Prei district early in the morning by unidentified gunmen. Police said they don't know whether the killing was a robbery or revenge.

June 21: Sim Sokha, 33, was found unconscious by police and taken to Kosamak hospital. After waking, Sokha said he was poisoned and robbed of his moto while drinking beer with his moto-taxi customer.

June 22: An unidentified man was found dead in the Tonlé Sap River in front of a petrol station in Khlaing Sang village. His wrists had been tied to a bamboo stake and he had stayed submerged for 3 days. Police said they could not find the murderers and paid 60,000 riel to bury the body.

Source: *Phnom Penh Post*, 28 June-11 July 1996.

CAM_BX06

Route 69 to Thmour Pouk is open but is in bad condition and few users. There is a boat operating between Battambang and Siem Reap every other day, but please note it travels through an area closed to UN personnel and has to be at your own risk."

● Shopping

Cambodia is known for certain crafts: silverware, textiles, worked ivory, wooden sculptures, pottery and basketwork. Many of the hotels in Phnom Penh run small boutiques selling postcards and local handicrafts.

Textiles: The royal Cambodian court supported a vast retinue of weavers and wore sumptuous silk textiles, embellished with gold-patterned yarns in colours corresponding to the days of the week. They also wove beautiful scarves for the royal ballet troupe. *Samphots* (twice the size of a sarong, wrapped around the hips and pulled between the legs to form loose trousers) were traditionally woven in Cambodia. The same simple pictorial designs used on samphots were also woven into large banners for festivals. Banners for funerals have temple designs with a row of elephants underneath. *Matmii* – ikat – is also commonly found in Cambodia. It may have been an ancient import from Java) and is made by tie-dyeing the threads before weaving (see page 51). Matmii is also found in central and southern Laos and in Northeastern Thailand. The Cambodian civil war has levied a heavy toll on traditional crafts, such as weaving. *Kramas* – checked cotton scarves – can be found in local markets but little else is available.

Silverwork: Cambodian craftsmen are well known for their high-quality silver work, exemplified by betelnut boxes and jewellery. Dancers' anklets, decorated with tiny silver bells are popular buys.

Handicrafts: Other crafts include bamboo work, wooden panels with carvings of the Ramayana and temple rubbings. Stone and cement copies of Khmer sculptures are also popular buys. Many precious and semi-precious stones are for sale – although guarantees of authenticity are not so readily available.

● Tipping

Tipping is very rare and is only necessary if someone has given particularly good service. However, it is greatly appreciated as salaries are so low. A small present is often a good idea, rather than a tip.

● Voltage

220 volts, 60 cycles in Phnom Penh, 110 volts, 50 cycles in some other towns. Power cuts and power surges are commonplace – torches come in useful.

● Weights and measures

Metric system along with local systems of measurement.

WHERE TO STAY

● Accommodation

The hotel building boom triggered by the UN presence and over-optimistic predictions of tourist arrivals has resulted in a number of excellent hotels in Phnom Penh. Pessimistic reports on the security situation combined with UNTAC's withdrawal mean that supply is cur-

Hotel classifications

A+ US$100-200 International: business services (fax, translation, seminar rooms etc), sports facilities (gym, swimming pool etc), Asian and Western restaurants, bars, and discotheques.

A US$50-100 First class: business, sports and recreational facilities, with a range of restaurants and bars.

B US$25-50 (67,500-135,000 riel) Tourist class: most rooms will have a/c and an attached bathroom, swimming pool, restaurants and 24-hr coffee shop/room service. Cable films.

C US$15-25 (40,500-67,500 riel) Economy: no a/c, attached bathrooms. Restaurant and room service. No sports facilities.

D US$8-15 (21,600-40,500 riel) Budget: no a/c, attached bathroom. Bed linen and towels, and there may be a restaurant.

E US$4-8 (10,800-21,600 riel) Guesthouse: fan-cooled rooms, shared bathroom facilities. 'Squat' toilets. Bed linen but no towels. Rooms are small, facilities few.

F Less than US$4 (10,800 riel) Guesthouse: fan-cooled rooms, usually with shared bathroom facilities. Squat toilets. Variable standards of cleanliness.

NB The riel equivalents are calculated from the Jan 1997 exchange rate.

C3_BX01

rently well ahead of demand for rooms and consequently bargains abound. There is a small group of hotels, including **Cambodiana** and the **Royal Phnom Penh** that can be considered truly 4-star international and a huge number of good 3-star hotels. Outside Phnom Penh hotels tend to be pretty basic. Air-conditioned rooms are usually around US$20 upwards and fan-cooled rooms are about US$10 and below. Hotels charge a 10% tax on all bills.

FOOD AND DRINK

● Food

The Cambodian verb 'to eat', *sii bay*, translates literally as 'eat rice' – and rice is the central ingredient of any meal. Dried, salted fish is the most common accompaniment. Other than fish, Cambodians eat poultry, beef, pork and game. *An sam chruk* is a Cambodian favourite: a fat roll of sticky-rice filled with soya-bean cake and chopped pork. Local legend has it that *an sam chruk* was invented by the Buddha himself. *Khao phonne*, a noodle dish, is also a popular Cambodian meal.

A typical Cambodian meal consists of a bowl of fried or steamed rice, mixed with bits of fish and seasoned with chillies, mint or garlic. Most of the fish is fresh-water from the Tonlé Sap. Bits of fish are often eaten with *tuk trey*, a spicy sauce with ground peanuts. More elaborate meals include barbecued shrimp, roasted sunflower seeds and such delicacies as *pong tea kon* (duck eggs, which are eaten just before they hatch) and *chong roet* (crunchy cicadas). Soup accompanies most meals and is eaten at the same time as the main dishes. *Amok* is another popular dish. It is served in paste or soup form and consists of boneless fish mixed with coconut and flavoured with spices – delicious – but being highly time consuming to prepare is not widely available, try it whenever you see it on a menu.

The UN's presence in Phnom Penh resulted in many new restaurants opening and the selection has improved dramatically in the past few years. The choice of restaurants outside Phnom Penh is limited.

The French gastronomic influence is still in evidence – fresh French bread can be bought daily in Phnom Penh. Western food, as well as Khmer, Chinese and Vietnamese, is available at all the hotels and quite a few restaurants. European style breakfasts are only available in the more expensive hotels otherwise you can eat a local breakfast of sliced roast pork, rice and a bowl of clear soup. Seafood is readily obtainable. Outside Phnom Penh, roadside stalls are the most you can expect. There are very few restaurants serving Cambodian food but plenty of stalls do (expect to pay about US$1 or 25 riel).

Food in Cambodia is relatively cheap. Expect to pay between US$2-6/head in most places.

● Drink

Tea is the national drink and is drunk without sugar or milk. Coffee is also available black or 'crème' with tinned milk. Ubiquitous coke is available as well as other soft, fizzy drinks. Imported soft drinks are available in the larger towns. Soda water with lemon, *soda kroch chhmar*, is a popular drink. Bottled water is widely available. Local and imported beers (the latter at no great mark up) are available. Of the locally brewed beers the two most common are *Angkor Beer* and *VB – Victoria Bitter* – both available on draught, in bottles and cans. There is a limited selection of spirits in some of the main hotels.

GETTING AROUND

● Practicalities

It's best to travel up country by air. Roads are badly maintained and often blocked by bandits. The train network is constantly disrupted and is subject to attack. Check safety areas before leaving Phnom Penh.

AIR

Bookings should be made as soon as possible during the tourist season. All services are op-

Restaurant classifications

✦✦✦✦ Over US$15 (40,500 riel) for a meal. A 3-course meal in a restaurant with pleasant decor. Beers, wines and spirits available.

✦✦✦ US$5-15 (13,500-40,500 riel) for a meal. Two courses, not including alcohol, reasonable surroundings.

✦✦ US$2-5 (5,400-13,500 riel) for a meal, probably only a single course, surroundings spartan but adequate.

✦ Under US$2 (under 5,400 riel). Single course, often makeshift surroundings such as a steet kiosk with simple benches and tables.

C3_BX02

erated by **Royal Air Cambodge** which flies new French-built ATR 72s. Tickets are available from travel agents and can be a cheaper and much faster way of purchasing a ticket than visiting the Airline. The baggage allowance for domestic flights is 10 kg pp.

From Phnom Penh:

	US$ Return	US$ One Way
Siem Reap	110	55
Battambang	90	45
Koh Kong	100	50
Stung Treng	90	45
Rattanakiri	100	55
Sihanoukville	75	40

TRAIN

Cambodia's railway system is poorly developed. There are 2 main lines from Phnom Penh: one goes to the Thai border at Poipet and the other links with the coast at Sihanoukville/Kompong Som. Much of the rail network was destroyed during the civil war. The irregular services are unreliable and plagued with the problem of unexploded mines and as this book went to press, rail travel was forbidden for foreigners.

ROAD

There is a basic road network, about 2,000 km in total. An extensive programme of road upgrading and maintenance is taking place. For example the Khmer-American Friendship Highway which runs from Phnom Penh to Kompong Som (first built in the 1960s) is now tarmac from start to finish. The Japanese in particular have put considerable resources into road building. However, bridges are often in a more perilous state being susceptible to Khmers Rouges attacks. The main roads are numbered 1-10 (see country map). Times from Phnom Penh to Pursat 3½ hrs; Pursat to Battambang 1½ hrs and Battambang to Sisophon 2½ hrs. From Sisophon to Aranyaprathet on the Thai border is 45 mins on a surfaced road. The road from Sisophon to Siem Reap is in an appalling condition and takes 3 hrs. As yet the road from Phnom Penh to Siem Reap is only surfaced as far as 20 km outside Phnom Penh. Again the Japanese are working on it. The main roads are generally tarmac or laterite.

The rainy season often makes many roads unpassable. There are buses and shared taxis to most parts of the country, although all services are unreliable. Shared taxis cost about 6,000 riel/100 km, and tend to leave early in the morning. Most travellers reckon shared taxi is the best way to get around.

There are often "road blocks" on routes out of Phnom Penh, where armed men oblige travellers to pay small fees of around 200 riel, or cigarettes, before proceeding. In a shared taxi the driver will take care of these additional costs.

Shared taxi **fares from Phnom Penh:**

Battambang	US$5
Kompong Cham	US$3
Kompong Som	US$3
Siem Reap	US$6
Kratie	US$5

CAR HIRE

There are no taxis in Cambodia but cars can usually be hired from one of the government ministries (US$25-30/day) or from the *Cambodiana Hotel* (US$50/day).

OTHER LOCAL TRANSPORT

● **Hitchhiking**

There are very few vehicles, so hitching is only on trucks ... but inadvisable at present because of bandits.

● **Cyclo**

It is customary to pay more for a cyclo in the mid-day heat. Cyclo and **moto** (motorcycle taxi) are the main form of transport in Phnom Penh. Cyclos can be hired for around (US$1/hour). Motos for US$5/day.

BOAT

Western embassies and Cambodian government do **not** recommend boat travel; most aid agencies forbid it. Boats are an important means of transport in Cambodia. The Mekong is navigable by small sea-going vessels as far as the capital and then by smaller boats up-river. Boats can be taken to Siem Reap (Angkor), Kratie (and a slow boat on to Stung Treng), Kompong Cham and Kompong Chhnang. There are check points on stretches, eg between Stung Treng and Kratie and foreigners are often expected to cough up dollars.

Express Boat fares **from Phnom Penh:**

Kompong Cham	US$8
Kratie	US$14
Siem Reap	US$25

COMMUNICATIONS

● Language

The national language is Khmer. Unlike other Southeast Asian languages it has no tones. The script is derived from the S Indian alphabet. English is used increasingly and French is widely spoken by the older generation. Outside Phnom Penh language can be a problem for those with no knowledge of Cambodian.

● Postal services

International service is slow, but it is reasonably priced and fairly reliable. Letters arrive and leave for Bangkok on Mon and Thur. Post from the UK takes between 5 and 15 days. It is recommended that mail be posted from the main Post Office in Phnom Penh, although there are post boxes everywhere.

International postal charge: 1,800 riels for 20 g airmail letter to Europe and the US.

Telegram and telex service and **Internal telephone service**: main Post Office in Phnom Penh.

● Telephone services

Local: poor service, but improving with Australian help, there are now more than 60 pay phones in the capital; phonecards now on sale for around US$2, US$5, US$20, U$50 or US$100. Owing to the delays in having a telephone line connected many businesses use mobile phones – numbers prefixed 015 or 018 are mobile phones.

International: there are links to the rest of the world via Australia – it is sometimes possible to get straight through on this line but it is often a long wait. Most calls must be placed through the operator. It is not possible to place collect calls. A number of hotels, restaurants and bars (*FCCC*), now have IDD service for telephone and fax. Overseas calls can also be made from the Post Office on 13 St, Phnom Penh. Both fax and telephone are charged at US$4.20/minute, Mon-Fri and US3.20/minute at the weekend.

ENTERTAINMENT

● Newspapers

During the UN operation in 1992/93, a number of new titles appeared on Phnom Penh's streets. The circulation of the old Party newspaper, the *Pacheachun* (which was Cambodia's only daily), shrank drastically in 1991 due to the shortage of newsprint, formerly supplied by the Soviet Union. With the UN there as human rights guardians, a number of newsletters were produced by opposition parties, giving Cambodians their first taste of news from non-government sources in years. For a while, the Cambodian press was relatively free, although sadly this freedom proved shortlived: in Jul 1995 the National Assembly voted 90-4 in favour of legislation which allows the government to lock up its more outspoken critics.

The principal 3 English-language newspapers are the *Phnom Penh Post* (fortnightly), which is regarded as the best of the 3, the *Cambodia Daily*, published 5 times a week, it covers international and national news and the *Cambodiana Times*, the government newspaper, published weekly. Local journalist Khien Kannanarith brought out the *Kampuchea Weekly*. The centre pages of the *Phnom Penh Post* have a good city map and the quality of journalism is high with some fine investigative reporting. The *Cambodian Times* is published in English every week. *Bangkok Post* available from stalls in Phnom Penh.

Political rivalries are fought out in the pages of the Khmer press notably between *Koh Santepheap* (Cambodian People's Party) and *Damneung Pelpreuk* (Funcinpec) which often degenerate into personal slanging matches with the odd hand-grenade chucked into opposition newspaper offices. Other incidents between rival organs, including the deaths of a number of journalists have dismayed observers who see the press playing into the hands of the government.

● TELEVISION

Many of the large hotels have satellite TV.

HOLIDAYS AND FESTIVALS

There are some 30 public holidays celebrated each year in Cambodia. Most are celebrated with public parades and special events to commemorate the particular holiday. The largest holidays also see many Khmers loosing off their guns, to the extent that red tracer fills the sky. The habit of firing weapons also extends to nights with a full moon and the onset of the rainy season. It is best to stay indoors at such times, as the concept of what goes up must come down does not seem to be recognized in Cambodia.

Jan: *Chinese and Vietnamese New Year* (movable), celebrated by the Chinese and Vietnamese communities; *National Day* (7th: public holiday), celebration of the fall of the Khmers

Rouges in 1979 (it is also the anniversary of the beginning of the Vietnamese occupation of the country leading some people to lobby against it being declared a national holiday); *Anniversary of the last sermon of Buddha* (movable).

Mar: *Women's Day* (8th: public holiday), processions, floats and banners in main towns.

Apr: *Cambodian New Year* (13th), predictions are made for the forthcoming year, the celebration is to show gratitude to the departing demi-god and to welcome the new one, every household erects a small altar in front to welcome a new demi-god; *Independence Day* (17th: public holiday), celebrates the fall of the Lon Nol government (17 April 1975) floats and parades through Phnom Penh; *Chaul Chhnam* (movable), 3-day celebration, which involves an inevitable drenching, to welcome in the new year, a similar festival to *Pimai* in Laos and *Songkran* in Thailand'; *Visak Bauchea* (movable – full moon), most important Buddhist festival; a triple anniversary commemorating Buddha's birth, enlightenment and his Parenivana (state of final bliss).

May: *Labour Day* (1st: public holiday), no great event; *Genocide Day* (9th: public holiday), to remember the atrocities of the Khmers Rouges in which up to a million Cambodians lost their lives, the main ceremony is held at Choeng Ek.

Jun: *Anniversary of the Founding of the Revolutionary Armed Forces of Kampuchea* (19th), founded in 1951, main parades and celebrations are in Phnom Penh; *Anniversary of the founding of the People's Revolutionary Party of Cambodia* (28th), founded in 1951, again, the main parades and celebrations are in Phnom Penh.

Jul: *Chol Vassa* – the start of the rainy season retreat – a Buddhist 'lent' – time for meditation.

Sep: *End of Buddhist 'Lent'* (movable), in certain areas it is celebrated with boat races; *Prachum Ben* (movable), in remembrance of the dead, offerings are made to ancestors.

Oct/Nov: *Water Festival, Bon Om Tuk* (movable) or *Festival of the Reversing Current* to celebrate the movement of the waters of the Tonlé Sap (see page 135), boat races in Phnom Penh, the festival dates back to the 12th century when King Jayavarman VII and his navy defeated water-borne invaders, most wats have ceremonial canoes which are rowed by the monks to summon the Naga King. Under the Cambodian monarchy, the king would command the waters to retreat, the festival was only revived in 1990; the festival coincides with *Ok Ambok* (The Pounding of Rice) – which stems from a myth of a female giant who can control the weather and Sampeah Preah Khai, dedicated to a rabbit who took his own life in a fire to feed a dying man, some celebrants look for the rabbit's figure drawn in the moon.

Nov: *King Sihanouk's Birthday* (1st), public offices and museums close for about a week.

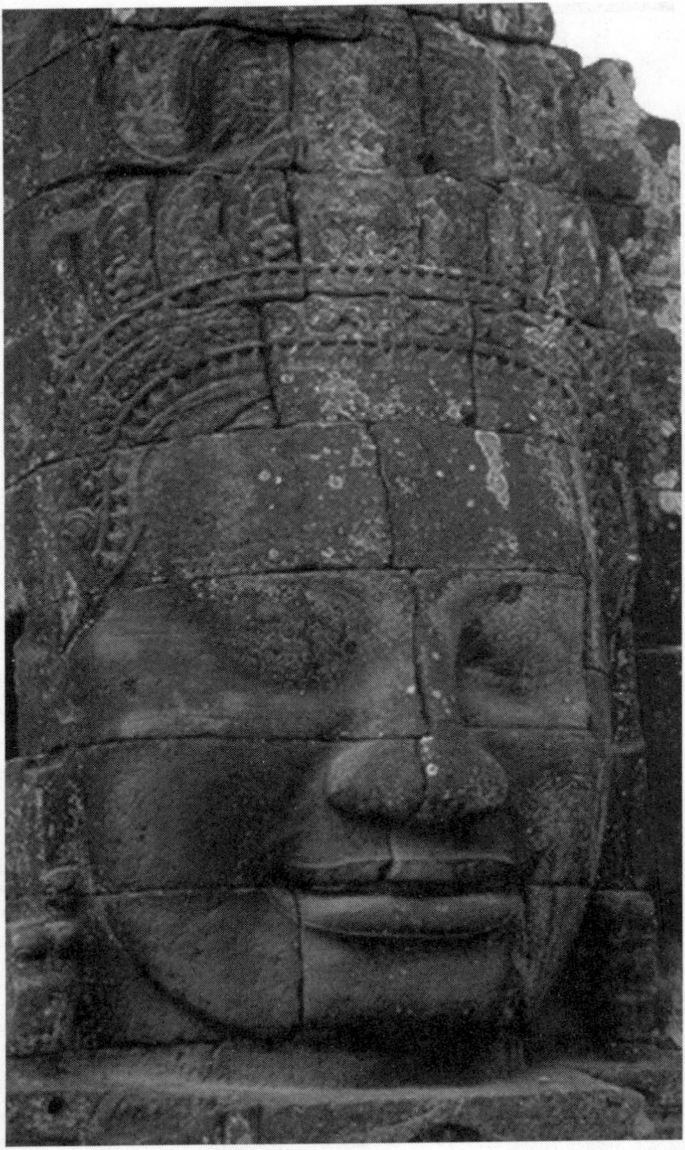

Rounding up

ACKNOWLEDGEMENTS

Duncan Shearer, Phnom Penh; Bollarino Roberto, Italy; Pierre Francis, Belgium; Dirk Zeiler, Germany; Denise Heywood, UK; Robert Robbins, New York, USA; Patrick and Nicole Millischer, Paris, France; Andrea Fiedler, Germany; Jochen Bink, Germany; Jack Turner, UK; M Sweeney, USA.

READING AND LISTENING

PUBLICATIONS ON THE REGION

Magazines

Asiaweek (weekly). A light weight *Far Eastern Economic Review*; rather like a regional *Time* magazine in style.

The Far Eastern Economic Review (weekly). Authoritative Hong Kong-based regional magazine; their correspondents based in each country provide knowledgeable, in-depth analysis particularly on economics and politics. The reporting is highly detailed and sometimes rather heavy going.

Books

Cambridge History of Southeast Asia (1992). Two volume edited study, long and expensive with contributions from most of the leading historians of the region. A thematic and regional approach is taken, not a country one, although the history is fairly conventional. Published by Cambridge University Press: Cambridge.

Dingwall, Alastair (1994) *Traveller's literary companion to South-east Asia*, In Print: Brighton. Experts on Southeast Asian language and literature select extracts from novels and other books by western and regional writers. The extracts are annoyingly brief, but it gives a good overview of what is available.

Dumarçay, Jacques (1991) *The palaces of South-East Asia: architecture and customs*, OUP: Singapore. A broad summary of palace art and architecture in both mainland and island Southeast Asia.

Fenton, James (1988) *All the wrong places: adrift in the politics of Asia*, Penguin: London. British journalist James Fenton skilfully and entertainingly recounts his experiences in Vietnam, Cambodia, the Philippines and Korea.

Fraser-Lu, Sylvia (1988) *Handwoven textiles of South-East Asia*, OUP: Singapore. Well-illustrated, large-format book with informative text.

Higham, Charles (1989) *The archaeology of mainland Southeast Asia from 10,000 BC to the fall of Angkor*, Cambridge University Press: Cambridge. Best summary of changing views of the archaeology of the mainland.

Keyes, Charles F (1977) *The golden peninsula: culture and adaptation in mainland Southeast Asia*, Macmillan: New York. Academic, yet readable summary of the threads of continuity and change in Southeast Asia's culture.

King, Ben F and Dickinson, EC (1975) *A field guide to the birds of South-East Asia*, Collins: London. Best regional guide to the birds of the region.

Miettinen, Jukko O (1992) *Classical dance and theatre in South-East Asia*, OUP, Singapore. Expensive, but accessible survey of dance and theatre, mostly focusing on Indonesia, Thailand and Burma.

Osborne, Milton (1979) *Southeast Asia: an introductory history*, Allen & Unwin: Sydney. Good introductory history, clearly written, pub-

220

lished in a portable paperback edition.

Rawson, Philip (1967) *The art of Southeast Asia*, Thames & Hudson: London. Portable general art history of Cambodia, Vietnam, Thailand, Laos, Burma, Java and Bali; by necessity, rather superficial.

Reid, Anthony (1988) *Southeast Asia in the age of commerce 1450-1680: the lands below the winds*, Yale University Press: New Haven. Perhaps the best history of everyday life in Southeast Asia, looking at such themes as physical well-being, material culture and social organization.

Reid, Anthony (1993) *Southeast Asia in the age of commerce 1450-1680: expansion and crisis*, Yale University Press: New Haven. Volume 2 in this excellent history of the region.

Rigg, Jonathan (1997) *Southeast Asia: the human landscape of modernization and development*, London: Routledge. A book which covers both the market and former command economies (ie Myanmar, Vietnam, Laos and Cambodia) of the region. It focuses on how people in the region have responded to the challenges and tensions of modernization.

SarDesai, DR (1989) *Southeast Asia: past and present*, Macmillan: London. Skilful but at times frustratingly thin history of the region from the 1st century to the withdrawal of US forces from Vietnam.

Savage, Victor R (1984) *Western impressions of nature and landscape in Southeast Asia*, Singapore University Press: Singapore. Based on a geography PhD thesis, the book is a mine of quotations and observations from Western travellers.

Sesser, Stan (1993) *The lands of charm and cruelty: travels in Southeast Asia*, Picador: Basingstoke. A series of collected narratives first published in the *New Yorker* including essays on Singapore, Laos, Cambodia, Burma and Borneo. Finely observed and thoughtful, the book is an excellent travel companion. The chapter on Laos is as good an introduction as you are likely to find.

Steinberg, DJ *et al* (1987) *In search of Southeast Asia: a modern history*, University of Hawaii Press: Honolulu. The best standard history of the region; it skilfully examines and assesses general processes of change and their impacts from the arrival of the Europeans in the region.

Waterson, Roxana (1990) *The living house: an anthropology of architecture in South-East Asia*, OUP: Singapore. Illustrated, academic book on Southeast Asian architecture, fascinating material for those interested in such things.

BOOKS ON CAMBODIA

Novels

Drabble, Margaret (1992) *The gates of ivory*, London: Penguin. The third part of a trilogy which deals with Cambodia during the period of the civil war while the Vietnamese 'occupied' Phnom Penh and the Khmers Rouges controlled much of the countryside. The other two volumes in the trilogy are *The radiant way*, and *A natural curiosity*).

History

Chou Ta-kuan (1993) *The customs of Cambodia*, Siam Society: Bangkok. This is not a Culture Shock! type of book but a volume written in 1296-1297 by Chou Ta-kuan, a Chinese emissary to the kingdom of Angkor. It is a potted, first hand account of life and livelihoods in the 13th century. Widely available in Bangkok.

Cambodia during the Indochina war and under the Khmers Rouges

Chandler, David P (1991) *The tragedy of Cambodian history: politics, war and revolution since 1945*, Yale University Press: New Haven.

Chandler, David P (1992) *Brother Number One: A political biography of Pol Pot*, Westview Press: Colorado.

Chanda, Nayan (1986) *Brother enemy: the war after the war*, Macmillan: New York. Exhaustive and engrossing account of 'the third Indochina war'; puts Cambodian conflict into regional perspective; vivid journalistic style.

Criddle, Joan & Butt Mam, T (1987) *To destroy you is no loss: the odyssey of a Cambodian family*, Doubleday.

Jackson, K (edit) (1989) *Cambodia 1975-1978: rendez-vous with death*, Princetown University Press.

May, Someth (1986) *Cambodian witness*, Faber and Faber: London. A chilling personal account of the Pol Pot period. Of Someth May's family of 14 only 4 survived the terrible years of the Khmers Rouges.

Ponchaud, Francois (1978) *Cambodia year zero* (translation from French), Penguin: London.

Shawcross, William (1979; revised 1986) *Sideshow: Kissinger, Nixon and the destruction of Cambodia*, Chatto & Windus: London. Excellent, balanced and very readable investigative work on American involvement in the Cambodian 'sideshow'; it runs through to cover the Pol Pot period. The best place to start mugging up on modern history.

Shawcross, William (1984) *The quality of mercy: Cambodia, holocaust and the modern conscience*, Fontana: London.

Shawcross, William (1994) *Cambodia's new deal*. A new book by Shawcross examining the UN-brokered peace deal and the country's progress since the elections. A good companion to his much better known *Sideshow*.

Swain, Jon (1995) *River of time*, London: Minerva. Jon Swain was a journalist in Indochina during the Vietnam War and then stayed on to be one of the few foreigners to witness the fall of Phnom Penh to the Khmers Rouges. This book covers Laos and Vietnam as well as Cambodia. The chapters on Cambodia are excellent and Swain's account of Indochina during this traumatic period is enthralling.

Szymusiak, Moldya (1986) *The stones cry out: a Cambodian childhood*, London: Jonathan Cape. A book recounting the recent tragedy of Cambodia from the perspective of one person. It has been translated from the French original.

Var Hong Ashe (1975) *From Phnom Penh to paradise*, Hodder & Stoughton: London.

Vickery, M (1984) *Cambodia 1975-1982*, George Allen & Unwin. Scholarly work by one of the West's foremost scholars on Cambodia.

Travel, geography and guides

De Carne, Louis (1872) *Travels in Indochina and the Chinese Empire*, London: Chapman Hall. Recounts De Carne's experiences in Laos in 1872, some years before the country was colonised by the French.

Hoskins, John (1991) *The Mekong*, Bangkok: Post Publishing. A large format coffee table book with good photographs and a modest text. Widely available in Bangkok.

Lewis, Norman (1951) *A dragon apparent: travels in Indochina*, Jonathan Cape: London. Republished by Eland Books. Possibly Norman Lewis' best known travel book. Witty and perceptive, about a fifth is based on his travels in Cambodia. Cheap second hand volumes widely available and also republished in paperback. Gives a good feel of Cambodia 'before the fall'.

Mouhot, Henri (1986) *Travels in Indochina*, Bangkok: White Lotus. An account of Laos by France's most famous explorer of Southeast Asia. He tried to discover a 'back door' into China by travelling up the Mekong River, but died of malaria in Luang Prabang in 1860. The book has been republished by White Lotus and is easily available in Bangkok; there is also a more expensive reprint available from OUP (Kuala Lumpur).

WIG (1995) *Guide to Phnom Penh*, Phnom Penh: Women's International Group. First edition of a new guide to Phnom Penh, good for expats and long term visitors with lots of practical information on how to live in Cambodia, widely available in the city.

Zepp, Ray, *Less travelled Cambodia*, excellent read for intrepid travellers, with lots of accurate information on provincial towns no one ever goes to and sound advice on security.

Economics, politics, society and development

Elizabeth Becker (1986) *When the war was over*, Simon & Schuster.

Fitzsimmons, T (ed) (1959), *Cambodia, its people, its society, its culture*, HRAF Press: New Haven.

Art and architecture

Coedès, George (1975) *Angkor*. The classic account of Angkor, now rather dated in terms of the picture it paints of this former empire.

Newsletters

Indochina Newsletter (monthly) from Asia Resource Centre, c/o 2161 Massachusetts Ave, Cambridge, MA02140, USA.

MAPS OF CAMBODIA

Regional maps: Bartholomew Southeast Asia (1:5,800,000); Nelles Southeast Asia (1:4,000,000); Hildebrand Thailand, Burma, Malaysia and Singapore (1:2,800,000).

Country maps: Periplus Cambodia (1:1,100,000); Nelles Vietnam, Laos and Cambodia (1:1,500,000); Bartholomew Vietnam, Laos and Cambodia (1:2,000,000).

City maps: the Periplus Cambodia map also has a good map of Phnom Penh (1:17,000) and a detailed map of Angkor (1:95,000).

Other maps: Tactical Pilotage Charts (TPC, US Airforce) (1:500,000); Operational Navigational Charts (ONC, US Airforce) (1:500,000). Both of these are particularly good at showing relief features (useful for planning treks); less good on roads, towns and facilities.

THE INTERNET

Cambodia and Southeast Asia on the Internet

Listed below are Internet addresses which access information on Asia generally, the Southeast Asian region, or Cambodia. **Newsgroups** tend to be informal talking shops offering information from hotels and sights through to wide-ranging discussions on just about any topic. **Mailing lists** have a more academic clientele, and probably are not worth plugging into unless you have a specific interest in the subject concerned. **Web sites** offer a whole range of information on a vast variety of topics. Below is only a selection.

Newsgroups on USENET with a Southeast Asian focus

Newsgroups are discussion fora on the USENET. Not every computer linked to the Internet has access to USENET – your computer needs Net News and a News reader. Newsgroups are informal fora for discussion; they are occasionally irreverent, usually interesting.

● **Asia general**

alt.asian.movies
alt.buddha.short.fat.guy
rec.travel.asia
soc.religion.eastern
talk.religion.buddhism

● **Southeast Asia**

soc.culture.asean

Mailing lists

These are discussion groups with a more academic content; some may be moderate – ie the content of messages is checked by an editor. Mailing lists communicate using E-mail. The focus of the groups are in italics.

● **Asia general**

actmus-1@ubvm.bitnet
[Asian Contemporary Music Discussion Group]
apex-1@uheevm.bitnet
[Asia-Pacific Exchange]
buddha-1@ulkyvm.bitnet
[Buddhist Academic Discussion Forum]

● **Southeast Asia**

seanet-1@nusvm.bitnet
[Southeast Asian Studies List]
seasia-1@msu.bitnet
[Southeast Asia Discussion List]

Southeast Asia on the World Wide Web – Web sites

Web sites are on the World Wide Web. They can now be browsed using a graphical mouse-based hypertext system. The two in use are Mosaic and the newer, Netscape. They allow the user to browse through the WWW easily. Note, however, that images (especially) take time to download and if on the Web during the time of the day when the US is alive and kicking expect to spend a very long time twiddling your thumbs. The subject of the web site is in brackets after the address.

● **Asia general**

http://none.coolware.com/infoasia/
[run by Infoasia which is a commercial firm that helps US and European firms get into Asia]
http://www.city.net/regions/asia
[pointer to information on Asian countries]
http://www.branch.com:80/silkroute/
[information on hotels, travel, news and business in Asia]
http://www.singapore.com/pata

[Pacific Asia Travel Association – stacks of info on travel in the Pacific Asian region including stats, markets, products etc]

● **Southeast Asia**

http://emailhost.ait.ac.th/asia/asia. html
[clickable map of mainland Southeast Asia with pointer to sources of other information on the region]
http://www.pactoc.net.au/index/resindex.htm
[Pacific talk homepage with lots of topics and links]
http://libweb.library.wise.edu/guides/SEAsia/library.htm
[the 'Gateway to Southeast Asia', lots of links]
http://www.leidenuniv.nl/pun/ubhtm/ mjkintro.htm
[library of 100 slides of Thailand (Phimai, Chiang Mai, Lamphun) and other mainland Southeast Asian countries]

Terms

E-mail = Electronic mail
WWW = World Wide Web or, simply, the Web
HTML = Hypertext Markup Language
URL = Uniform Resource Locators

Sources: the above was collated from *Internet news* published in the *IIAS Newsletter* [International Institute for Asian Studies Newsletter], Summer 1995; *IIAS Newsletter*, Spring 1996 and *Asian Studies Newsletter*, June/July 1996.

SHORT WAVE RADIO GUIDE

British Broadcasting Corporation (BBC, London) *Southeast Asian service* 3915, 6195, 9570, 9740, 11750, 11955, 15360; *Singapore service* 88.9MHz; *East Asian service* 5995, 6195, 7180, 9740, 11715, 11750, 11945, 11955, 15140, 15280, 15360, 17830, 21715.
Voice of America (VoA, Washington) *Southeast Asian service* 1143, 1575, 7120, 9760, 9770, 15185, 15425; *Indonesian service* 6110, 11760, 15425.
Radio Beijing *Southeast Asian service (English)* 11600, 11660.
Radio Japan (Tokyo) *Southeast Asian service (English)* 11815, 17810, 21610.

Radio

The BBC World Service's *Dateline East Asia* provides probably the best news and views on Asia (available on 100 FM). Also with a strong Asia focus are the broadcasts of the ABC (Australian Broadcasting Corporation).

Useful addresses

EMBASSIES

Australia
5 Canterbury Cr, Deakin-ACT 2600, T 273 1259

Bulgaria
Mladost 1, Block Salvador Allende Residenzz, Sofia, T 757135

China
Dong Zhi Men Wai Dajio, 100600 Peking, T 5322101

Cuba
7001 Sta Ave Esq, 70 Miramar, Havana, T 336400

Czech Republic
Na Habalec 1, 16900 Prague 6, T 352603

France
11 Ave Charles Floquet, 75007, Paris, T 456 64023

Germany
Arnold Zweing Str 10, 13189 Berlin, T 711853

Hungary
Rath Gyorgyu 48, 1122 Budapest XII, T 155 5165

India
B47 Saomi Nagar, New Delhi 110017, T 642 3782

Indonesia
Panin Bank Plaza, Jln 52 Palmerrah Utara, Jakarta 11480, T 548 3716

Japan
8.6.9. Akasaka, Minato Ku, Tokyo 107, T 3478 0861

Laos
Bane Saphanthong Noua, BP34, Vientiane, T 314951. Note that we have received reports that the Cambodian embassy in Vientiane take so long to process visa applications that it sometimes exceeds the length of time visitors are allowed to stay in Laos!

North Korea
Rue de L'Universitie, Mounsou, Daedongang, Pyongyang, T 817 283.

Russia
Starokpuchenny Per 16, Moscow, T/F 956 6573

Thailand
185 Rajadamri Rd, Bangkok 10500, T 254 6630

USA
4500, 16th St, NW Washington, DC20011, T (202) 726 7742, F (202) 726 8381

Vietnam
71 Tran Hung Dao St, Hanoi, T 8253789 or 41 Phung Khac Khoan St, Saigon, T 8292751, it is possible to apply for a visa in Saigon and collect it in Hanoi and vice versa.

TOUR OPERATORS

BANGKOK

Diethelm
Kian Gwan Bldg II, 140/1 Witthayu (Wireless) Rd, T 2559150, F 2560248

Exotissimo
21/17 Sukhumvit Rd, T 2535240

M K Ways
18/4 Saint Louis Soi 3, Sathorn Tai Rd, T 2122532, F 2545583

Transindo Ltd
9th flr, Thasos Bldg, 1675 Chan Rd, T 2873241, F 2873245. operates the daily direct Bangkok-Phnom Penh air link (chartering Bangkok Airways planes), rec.

Siam Wings
173/1-3 Surawong Rd, T 2354757, F 2366808.

Tour East
Rajapark Bldg, 10th Flr, 163 Soi Asoke, T 2593160, F 2583236

Vista Travel
244/4 Khaosan Rd, T 2800348, F 2800348

VIETNAM

Saigon Tourist
49 Le Thanh Ton St, T 298914. Expensive short tours to the main sights.

UK

Asia World
3rd Floor, Waterloo House, 11-17 Chertsey Rd, Woking, Surrey GU21 5AB, T 01483 730808, F 01483 721919

Abercrombie and Kent
Sloane Sq House, Holbein Place, London SW1W 8NS, T 0171 730 9600, F 0171 730 9376

Explore Worldwide
1 Frederick St, Aldershot, GU11 1LQ, T 01252 344161, F 01252 343170

Indochina Travel
Chiswick Gate, 598-608 Chiswick High Rd, London W4 5RT, T 0181 995 8280, F 0181 995 5346, rec

Regent Holidays
15 John St, Bristol, BS1 2HR, T 0117 921 1711, F 0117 925 4866, rec.

Useful words and phrases

THERE ARE a number of sounds in Khmer, or Cambodian, which have no equivalent in English. The transcription given here is only an approximation of the sound in Khmer and is taken from David Smyth and Tran Kien's (1991) *Courtesy and survival in Cambodia*, School of Oriental & African Studies: London.

CONSONANTS

bp a sharp 'p', somewhere between 'p' and 'b' in English; **dt** a sharp 't', somewhere between 't' and 'd' in English; **j** as in 'jump'; **g** as in 'get'; **ng** as in 'ring'

VOWELS

a as in 'ago'; **ah** as in 'car'; **ai** as in 'Thai'; **ao** as in 'Lao'; **ay** as in 'pay'; **ee** as in 'see'; **eu** as in 'uugh'; **i** as in 'fin'; **o** as in 'long'; **oh** as in 'loan'; **oo** as in 'boot'; **OO** as in 'cook'; **u** as in 'run'

USEFUL WORDS AND PHRASES

Yes　baht [male speakers]
　　　jah [female speakers]
No　(ot) dtay
Thank you (very much)
　or-gOOn (j'run)
Hello　jOOm ree-up soo-a
Goodbye　lee-a hai
Excuse me/Sorry!
　som dto(h)
Where's the..? ...ai nah?
How much is...
　...t'lai bpon-mahn?
It doesn't matter, never mind, that's all right
　mun ay dtay
I don't understand
　mun yoo-ul dtay

TRAVEL

That's expensive
　t'lai na(h)
Will you go for...riel?
　...ree-ul bahn dtay?
Is it far?
　ch'ngai dtay?
Turn left/right
　bot dtoh kahng
　ch'wayng/s'dum
Go straight on
　dtoh dtrong

TIME

morning　bpreuk
midday　t'ngai dtrong
night　yOOp
today　t'ngai ni(h)
tomorrow　sa-aik
yesterday　m'serl mern

NUMBERS

1	moo-ay	**2**	bpee
3	bay	**4**	boo-un
5	bprum		

6　bprum moo-ay
7　bprum bpee or bprum bpeul
8　bprum bay
9　bprum boo-un
10　dop
11　dop moo-ay
12　dop bpee...etc
16　dop bprum moo-ay
20　m'pay
30　sahm seup
40　sai seup
50　hah seup
60　hok seup
70　jert seup
80　bpait seup
90　gao seup
100　moo-ay roy
1,000　moo-ay bpohn
10,000　moo-ay meun
100,000　moo-ay sain
1,000,000　moo-ay lee-un

BASIC VOCABULARY

bank　ta-nee-a-gee-a
day　t'ngai
delicious　ch'ngun
doctor　bpairt
food　m'hohp
hospital　mOOn-dti-bpairt
Khmer Rouge
　k-mai gra-horm
market　p'sah
post office
　brai-sa-nee-ya-tahn
toilet　borng-goo-un
water　dteuk

Health

THE TRAVELLER to Cambodia is inevitably exposed to health risks not encountered in North America, Western Europe or Australasia. Cambodia has a tropical climate; nevertheless the acquisition of true tropical disease by the visitor is probably conditioned as much by the rural nature and standard of hygiene of the country than by the climate. There is an obvious difference in health risks between the business traveller staying in international class hotels and the backpacker staying in basic guesthouses in more out of the way places. There are no hard and fast rules to follow; you will often have to make your own judgements on the healthiness or otherwise of your surroundings.

Medical care

The quality of medical care in Cambodia is highly variable. Away from Phnom Penh it is, generally speaking, very poor indeed. In Bangkok, medical care is adequate (and rapidly improving) for most exigencies, although Singapore and Hong Kong offer the best facilities for serious illness. In rural areas there are systems and traditions of medicine wholly different from the Western model and you may be confronted with less orthodox forms of treatment such as herbal medicine and acupuncture. At least you can be sure that local practitioners have a lot of experience with the particular diseases of their region. If you are in Phnom Penh it may be worthwhile calling on your embassy to provide a list of recommended doctors.

Medicines

If you are a long way away from medical help, a certain amount of self administered medication may be necessary and you will find many of the drugs available have familiar names. However, always check the date stamping (sell-by date) and buy from reputable pharmacists because the shelf life of some items, especially vaccines and antibiotics, is markedly reduced in hot conditions. Unfortunately, many locally produced drugs are not subjected to quality control procedures and so can be unreliable. There have, in addition, been cases of substitution of inert materials for active drugs. With the following precautions and advice you should keep as healthy as usual. Make local enquiries about health risks if you are apprehensive and take the general advice of European, Australian or North American families who have lived or are living in the area.

BEFORE YOU GO

Take out medical insurance. You should also have a dental check-up, obtain a spare glasses prescription and, if you suffer from a long-standing condition, such as diabetes, high blood pressure, heart/lung disease or a nervous disorder, arrange for a check-up with your doctor who can at the same time provide you with a letter explaining details of your medical disorder. Check the current practice for malaria prophylaxis (prevention) for the countries you intend to visit.

INOCULATIONS

Smallpox vaccination is no longer required. Neither is cholera vaccination, despite the fact that the disease occurs – but not at present in epidemic form – in some of these countries. Yellow fever vaccination is not required either, although you may be asked for a certificate if you have been in a country affected by yellow fever immediately before travelling to Southeast Asia. The following vaccinations are recommended:

Typhoid (monovalent) One dose followed by a booster 1 month later. Immunity from this course lasts 2-3 years. An oral preparation is also available.

Poliomyelitis This is a live vaccine generally given orally but a full course consists of three doses with a booster in tropical regions every 3-5 years.

Tetanus One dose should be given, with a booster at 6 weeks and another at 6 months. 10 yearly boosters thereafter are recommended.

Meningitis and Japanese B encephalitis (JVE) There is an extremely small risk of these rather serious diseases; both are seasonal and vary according to region. Meningitis can occur in epidemic form; JVE is a viral disease transmitted from pigs to man by mosquitos. For details of the vaccinations, consult a travel clinic.

Children should, in addition to the above, be properly protected against diphtheria, whooping cough, mumps and measles. Teenage girls, if they have not had the disease, should be given a rubella (German measles) vaccination. Consult your doctor for advice on BCG inoculation against tuberculosis: the disease is still common in the region.

INFECTIOUS HEPATITIS (JAUNDICE)

This is common and seems to be frequently caught by travellers. The main symptoms are stomach pains, lack of appetite, nausea, lassitude and yellowness of the eyes and skin. Medically speaking there are two types: the less serious but more common is *hepatitis A* for which the best protection is careful preparation of food, the avoidance of contaminated drinking water and scrupulous attention to toilet hygiene. Human normal immunoglobulin (gammaglobulin) confers considerable protection against the disease and is particularly useful in epidemics. It should be obtained from a reputable source and is certainly recommended for travellers who intend to travel and live rough. The injection should be given as close as possible to your departure and as the dose depends on the likely time you are to spend in potentially infected areas, the manufacturers' instructions should be followed. A vaccination against hepatitis A has recently become generally available and is safe and effective. Three shots are given over 6 months and confer excellent protection against the disease for up to 10 years. Eventually this vaccine is likely to supersede the use of gammaglobulin.

The other, more serious, version is *hepatitis B* which is acquired as a sexually transmitted disease, from a blood transfusion or an injection with an unclean needle, or possibly by insect bites. The symptoms are the same as hepatitis A but the incubation period is much longer.

You may have had jaundice before or you may have had hepatitis of either type before without becoming jaundiced, in which case it is possible that you could be immune to either hepatitis A or B (or C or a number of other letters). This immunity can be tested for before you travel. If you are not immune to hepatitis B already, a vaccine is available (3 shots over 6 months) and if you are not immune to hepatitis A already, then you should consider having gammaglobulin or a vaccination.

AIDS

This is increasingly prevalent in Cambodia (and Thailand). It is not wholly confined to the well known high risk sections of the population ie homosexual men, intravenous drug abusers, prostitutes and the children of infected mothers. Heterosexual transmission is probably now the dominant mode of infection and so the main risk to travellers is from casual sex. The same precautions should be taken as when encountering any sexually transmitted disease. In Thailand and increasingly in Cambodia, almost the entire population of female prostitutes is HIV positive and in other parts intravenous drug abuse is common. The AIDS virus (HIV) can be passed via unsterile needles which have been previously used to inject an HIV positive patient, but the risk of this is very small indeed. It would, however, be sensible to check that needles have been properly sterilized or disposable needles used. The chance of picking up hepatitis B in this way is much more of a danger. Be wary of carrying disposable needles. Customs officials may find them suspicious. The risk of receiving a blood transfusion with blood infected with the HIV virus is greater than from dirty needles because of the amount of fluid exchanged. Supplies of blood for transfusion are supposed to be screened for HIV in all reputable hospitals so the risk should be small. Catching the virus which causes AIDS does not necessarily produce an illness in itself; the only way to be sure if you feel you have been put at risk is to have a blood test for HIV antibodies on your return to a place where there are reliable laboratory facilities. However, the test does not become positive for many weeks.

COMMON PROBLEMS

HEAT AND COLD

Full acclimatization to tropical temperatures takes about 2 weeks and during this period it is normal to feel relatively apathetic, esp-ecially if the humidity is high. Drink plenty of water (up to 15 litres a day are required when working physically hard in the tropics). Use salt on your food and avoid extreme exertion. Tepid showers are more cooling than hot or cold ones. Large hats do not cool you down but do prevent sunburn. Remember that, especially in highland areas, there can be a large and sudden drop in temperature between sun and shade and between night and day so dress accordingly. Loose-fitting cotton clothes are best for hot weather. Warm jackets and woollens are often necessary after dark at high altitude.

INTESTINAL UPSETS

Practically nobody escapes intestinal infections, so be prepared for them. Most of the time they are due to the insanitary preparation of food. Do not eat uncooked fish, vegetables or meat (especially pork), fruit without the skin (always peel fruit yourself), or food that is exposed to flies (particularly salads). Tap water may be unsafe, especially in the monsoon seasons and the same goes for stream water or well water. Filtered or bottled water is usually available and safe but you cannot always rely on it. If your hotel has a **central** hot water supply, this is safe to drink after cooling. Ice should be made from boiled water but rarely is, so stand your glass on the ice cubes instead of putting them in the drink. Dirty water should first be strained through a filter bag (available from camping shops) and then boiled or treated. Bringing the water to a rolling boil at sea level is sufficient. In the highlands, you have to boil the water a bit longer to ensure that all the microbes are killed (because water boils at a lower temperature at altitude). Various sterilizing methods can be used and there are proprietary preparations

containing chlorine or iodine compounds. Pasteurised or heat-treated milk is now fairly widely available as is ice cream and yoghurt produced by the same methods. Unpasteurised milk products, including cheese, are sources of tuberculosis, brucellosis, listeria and food poisoning germs. You can render fresh milk safe by heating it to 62°C for 30 mins followed by rapid cooling or by boiling. Matured or processed cheeses are safer than fresh varieties.

Fish and shellfish are popular foods but can be the source of health problems. Shellfish which are eaten raw will transmit food poisoning or hepatitis if they have been living in contaminated water. Certain fish accumulate toxins in their bodies at certain times of the year, which give rise to illness when they are eaten. The phenomenon known as 'red tide' can also affect fish and shellfish which eat large quantities of tiny sea creatures and thereby become poisonous. The only way to guard against this is to keep as well informed as possible about fish and shellfish quality in the area you are visiting. Most countries impose a ban on fishing in periods when red tide is prevalent, although this is often flouted.

Diarrhoea is usually the result of food poisoning, but can occasionally result from contaminated water. There are various causes – viruses, bacteria, protozoa (like amoeba), salmonella and cholera organisms. It may take one of several forms coming on suddenly or rather slowly. It may be accompanied by vomiting or severe abdominal pain, and the passage of blood or mucus (when it is called dysentery).

All kinds of diarrhoea, whether or not accompanied by vomiting, respond favourably to the replacement of water and salts taken as frequent small sips of some kind of rehydration solution. There are proprietary preparations consisting of sachets of oral rehydration electrolyte powder which are dissolved in water, or you can make up your own by adding half a teaspoonful of salt (3.5 grams) and 4 tablespoons of sugar (40 grams) to a litre of boiled water. If it is possible to time the onset of diarrhoea to the minute, then it is probably viral or bacterial and/or the onset of dysentery. The treatment in addition to rehydration is Ciprofloxacin (500 mgs every 12 hrs). The drug is now widely available as are various similar ones.

If the diarrhoea has come on slowly or intermittently, then it is more likely to be protozoal, i.e. caused by amoeba (amoebic dysentery) or giardia, and antibiotics will have no effect. These cases are best treated by a doctor as should any diarrhoea continuing for more than 3 days. If there are severe stomach cramps, the following drugs may help: Loperamide (*Imodium*, *Arret*) and Diphenoxylate with Atropine (*Lomotil*). The drug usually used for giardia or amoeba is Metronidazole (*Flagyl*) or Tinidazole (*Fasigyu*).

The lynchpins of treatment for diarrhoea are rest, fluid and salt replacement, antibiotics such as Ciprofloxacin for the bacterial types, and special diagnostic tests and medical treatment for amoeba and giardia infections. Salmonella infections and cholera can be devastating diseases and it would be wise to get to a hospital as soon as possible if these were suspected. Fasting, peculiar diets and the consumption of large quantities of yoghurt have not been found useful in calming travellers' diarrhoea or in rehabilitating inflamed bowels. Oral rehydration has, especially in children, been a lifesaving technique and as there is some evidence that alcohol and milk might prolong diarrhoea they should probably be avoided during, and immediately after, an attack. There are ways of preventing travellers' diarrhoea for short periods of time when visiting these countries by taking antibiotics but these are ineffective against viruses and, to some extent, against protozoa. This technique should not be used other than in exceptional circumstances. Some preventatives such as Enterovioform can have serious side effects if taken for long periods.

INSECTS

These can be a great nuisance. Some, of course, are carriers of serious diseases such as malaria, dengue fever or filariasis and various worm infections. The best way of keeping mosquitos away at night is to sleep off the ground with a mosquito net and to burn mosquito coils containing Pyrethrum. Aerosol sprays or a 'flit gun' may be effective as are insecticidal tablets which are heated on a mat which is plugged into the wall socket (if taking your own, check the voltage of the area you are visiting so that you can take an appliance that will work; similarly, check that your electrical adaptor is suitable for the repellent plug; note that they are widely available in the region).

You can, in addition, use personal insect repellent of which the best contain a high concentration of diethyltoluamide (DET). Liquid is best for arms and face (take care around eyes and make sure you do not dissolve the plastic of your spectacles). Aerosol spray on clothes and ankles deter mites and ticks. Liquid DET suspended in water can be used to impregnate cotton clothes and mosquito nets. The latter are now available in wide mesh form which are lighter to carry and less claustrophobic to sleep under.

If you are bitten, itching may be relieved by cool baths and anti-histamine tables (take care with alcohol or when driving), corticosteroid creams (great care – never use if any hint of septic poisoning) or by judicious scratching. Calamine lotion and cream have limited effectiveness and anti-histamine creams have a tendency to cause skin allergies and are therefore not generally recommended. Bites which become infected (a common problem in the tropics) should be treated with a local antiseptic or antibiotic cream such as Cetrimide, as should infected scratches. Skin infestations with body lice, crabs and scabies are unfortunately easy to pick up. Use gamma benzene hexachloride for lice and benzyl benzoate for scabies. Crotamiton cream alleviates itching and also kills a number of skin parasites. Malathion lotion is good for lice but avoid the highly toxic full strength Malathion which is used as an agricultural insecticide.

MALARIA

Malaria is prevalent in Cambodia and remains a serious disease and you are advised to protect yourself against mosquito bites as above and to take prophylactic (preventative) drugs. Start taking the tablets a few days before exposure and continue to take them 6 weeks after leaving the malarial zone. Remember to give the drugs to babies and children, pregnant women also.

The subject of malaria prevention is becoming more complex as the malaria parasite becomes immune to some of the older drugs. Nowhere is this more apparent than in Southeast Asia – and especially in parts of Cambodia. In particular, there has been an increase in the proportion of cases of falciparum malaria which are resistant to the normally used drugs. It would not be an exaggeration to say that we are near to the situation where some cases of malaria will be untreatable with presently available drugs.

Before you travel you must check with a reputable agency the likelihood and type of malaria in the countries which you intend to visit. Take their advice on prophylaxis but be prepared to receive conflicting advice. Because of the rapidly changing situation in the Southeast Asian region, the names and dosage of the drugs have not been included. But Chloroquine and Proguanil may still be recommended for the areas where malaria is still fully sensitive; while Doxycycline, Mefloquine and Quinghaosu are presently being used in resistant areas. Quinine, Halofantrine and tetracycline drugs remain the mainstay of treatment.

It is still possible to catch malaria even when taking prophylactic drugs, although this is unlikely. If you do develop symptoms (high fever, shivering, severe headache, and sometimes diarrhoea) seek medical advice immediately. The risk of the disease is obviously greater the further you move from the cities into rural areas, with primitive facilities and standing water.

SUNBURN AND HEAT STROKE

The burning power of the tropical sun is phenomenal, especially in highland areas. Always wear a wide-brimmed hat, and use some form of sun cream or lotion on untanned skin. Normal temperate zone suntan lotions (protection factors up to 7) are not much good. You need to use the types designed specifically for the tropics or for mountaineers or skiers, with a protection factor between 7 and 15 or higher. Glare from the sun can cause conjunctivitis so wear sunglasses, particularly on beaches.

There are several varieties of heat stroke. The most common cause is severe dehydration. Avoid this by drinking lots of non-alcoholic fluid, and adding salt to your food.

SNAKE AND OTHER BITES AND STINGS

If you are unlucky enough to be bitten by a venomous snake, spider, scorpion, centipede or sea creature, try (within limits) to catch or kill the animal for identification. Reactions to be expected are shock, swelling, pain and bruising around the bite, soreness of the regional lymph glands, nausea, vomiting and fever. If in addition any of the following symptoms should follow closely, get the victim to a doctor without delay: numbness, tingling of the face, muscular spasms, convulsions, shortness of breath or haemorrhage. Commercial snake-bite or scorpion-sting kits may be available but these are only useful against the specific type of snake or scorpion for which they are designed. The serum has to be given intravenously so is not much good unless you have had some practice in making injections into veins. If the bite is on a limb, immobilize it and apply a tight bandage between the bite and the body, releasing it for 90 seconds every 15 minutes. Reassurance of the victim is very important because death from snake bite is very rare. Do not slash the bite area and try to suck out the poison because this sort of heroism does more harm than good. Hospitals usually hold stocks of snake-bite serum. The best precaution is not walk in long grass with bare feet, sandals, or in shorts.

When swimming in an area where there are poisonous fish such as stone or scorpion fish (also called by a variety of local names) or sea urchins on rocky coasts, tread carefully or wear plimsolls/trainers. The sting of such fish is intensely painful. This can be relieved by immersing the injured part of the body in water as hot as you can bear for as long as it remains painful. This is not always very practical and you must take care not to scald yourself, but it does work. Avoid spiders and scorpions by keeping your bed away from the wall, look under lavatory seats and inside your shoes in the morning. In the rare event of being bitten, consult a doctor.

OTHER AFFLICTIONS

Remember that **rabies** is endemic in Cambodia. If you are bitten by a domestic or wild animal, do not leave things to chance. Scrub the wound with soap and water and/or disinfectant, try to have the animal captured (within limits) or at least determine its ownership where possible and seek medical assistance at once. The course of treatment depends on whether you have already been satisfactorily vaccinated against rabies. If you have (and this is worthwhile if you are spending lengths of time in developing countries) then some further doses of vaccine are all that is required. Human diploid cell vaccine is the best, but expensive: other, older kinds of vaccine such as that derived from duck embryos may be the only types available. These are effective, much cheaper and interchangeable generally with the human derived types. If not already vaccinated then anti-rabies serum (immúnoglobulin) may be required in addition. It is wise to finish the course of treatment whether the animal survives or not.

Dengue fever is present in Cambodia. It is a viral disease transmitted by mosquito and causes severe headaches and body pains. Complicated types of dengue known as haemorrhagic fevers occur throughout Asia but usually in persons who have caught the disease a second time. Thus, although it is a very serious type it is rarely caught by visitors. There is no treatment, you must just avoid mosquito bites.

Intestinal worms are common and the more serious ones, such as hook worm can be contracted by walking barefoot on infested earth or beaches.

Influenza and **respiratory diseases** are common, perhaps made worse by polluted cities and rapid temperature and climatic changes – accentuated by air-conditioning.

Prickly heat is a very common itchy rash, best avoided by frequent washing and by wearing loose clothing and is helped by the use of talcum powder, allowing the skin to dry thoroughly after washing.

Athlete's foot and other **fungal infections** are best treated by sunshine and a proprietary preparation such as Tolnaftate.

WHEN YOU RETURN HOME

On returning home, remember to take anti-malarial tablets for 6 weeks. If you have had attacks of diarrhoea, it is worth having a stool specimen tested in case you have picked up amoebic dysentery. If you have been living rough, a blood test may also be worthwhile to detect worms and other parasites.

FURTHER HEALTH INFORMATION

Information regarding country-by-country malaria risk can be obtained from the World Health Organization (WHO) or in Britain from the Ross Institute, London School of Hygiene and Tropical Medicine, Keppel Street, London WC1E 7HT which also publishes a highly recommended book: *The preservation of personal health in warm climates*. The Centres for Disease Control (CDC) in Atlanta, Georgia, USA will provide equivalent information. The organization MASTA (Medical Advisory Service for Travellers Abroad) also based at the London School of Hygiene and Tropical Medicine (T 0171 631-4408) will provide up-to-date country-by-country information on health risks. Further information on medical problems overseas can be obtained from the new edition of *Travellers health, how to stay healthy abroad*, edited by Richard Dawood (Oxford University Press, 1992). This revised and updated edition is highly recommended, especially to the intrepid traveller. A more general publication, with hints on health and much more besides, is John Hatt's new edition of *The tropical traveller* (Penguin, 1993).

The above information has been compiled by Dr David Snashall, Senior Lecturer in Occupational Health, United Medical Schools of Guy's and St Thomas' Hospitals and Chief Medical Adviser, Foreign and Commonwealth Office, London.

Fares and timetables

Domestic flight schedules

Time	Days	Flight/Airline
Phnom Penh to Siem Reap:		
0645-0730	1,2,3,4,5,6,7	VJ320
0650-0735	1,2,3,4,5,6,7	VJ360
0655-0740	1,2,3,4,5,6,7	VJ350
0915-1100	1,4,7	VJ436
0915-1000	2,6	VJ438
1440-1525	1,2,3,4,5,6,7	VJ370
1540-1625	1,2,3,4,5,6,7	VJ340
1550-1635	1,2,3,4,5,6,7	VJ330
Siem Reap to Phnom Penh:		
0755-0840	1,2,3,4,5,6,7	VJ321
0800-0845	1,2,3,4,5,6,7	VJ361
0805-0850	1,2,3,4,5,6,7	VJ351
1030-1215	2,6	VJ438/9
1130-1215	1,4,7	VJ437
1550-1635	1,2,3,4,5,6,7	VJ371
Phnom Penh to Battambang:		
0915-1000	1,4,7	VJ436
0915-1100	2,6	VJ438
0915-1000	3,5	VJ432
Battambang to Phnom Penh:		
1030-1115	1,4,7	VJ436/7
1130-1215	2,6	VJ439
1030-1115	3,5	VJ433
Phnom Penh to Rattanakiri:		
0905-1055	1,4	VJ208
1135-1235	3,6	VJ206
1140-1240	5	VJ200
Rattanakiri to Phnom Penh:		
1120-1220	1,4	VJ209
1300-1450	3,6	VJ206/7
1310-1410	5	VJ201
Phnom Penh to Sihanoukville:		
1135-1210	5	VJ606
1135-1305	2,7	VJ604
Sihanoukville to Phnom Penh		
1235-1405	5	VJ604/5
1330-1405	2,7	VJ607

Time	Days	Flight/Airline
Phnom Penh to Koh Kong:		
1135-1210	2,7	Vj604
1135-1305	5	VJ606
Koh Kong to Phnom Penh:		
1235-1405	2,7	VJ604/5
1330-1405	5	VJ607
Phnom Penh to Stung Treng:		
0905-0950	1,4	VJ208
0905-0950	2	VJ202
1135-1340	3,6	VJ206
Stung Treng to Phnom Penh:		
1015-1220	1,4	VJ208/9
1015-1220	2	VJ203
1405-1450	3,6	VJ207
Phnom Penh to Mondulkiri:		
1135-1225	1,4	VJ204
Mondulkiri to Phnom Penh		
1250-1340	1,4	VJ205

Schedule valid until 31 March 1997.

NB 1 = Mon; 2 = Tues; 3 = Wed; 4 = Thur; 5 = Fri; 6 = Sat; 7 = Sun.

CAM_TB02

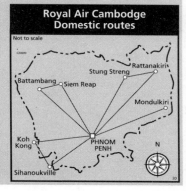

Royal Air Cambodge Domestic routes

Not to scale

Glossary

A

Achar
Cambodian spiritual adviser

Amitabha
the Buddha of the Past (see Avalokitsvara)

Amulet
protective medallion

Apsara
celestial dancers who entertain the gods and are sensual rewards of kings and heroes who die bravely; important in temple decoration, especially at Angkor (see page 112)

Arhat
a person who has perfected himself; images of former monks are sometimes carved into arhat

Avadana
Buddhist narrative, telling of the deeds of saintly souls

Avalokitsvara
also known as Amitabha and Lokeshvara, the name literally means 'World Lord'; he is the compassionate male Bodhisattva, the saviour of Mahayana Buddhism and represents the central force of creation in the universe; usually portrayed with a lotus and water flask

B

Bai sema
boundary stones marking consecrated ground around a Buddhist bot

Baray
artificial lake or reservoir

Batik
a form of resist dyeing

Bhikku
Buddhist monk

Bodhi
the tree under which the Buddha achieved enlightenment (*Ficus religiosa*)

Bodhisattva
a future Buddha. In Mahayana Buddhism, someone who has attained enlightenment, but who postpones nirvana to help others reach it.

Brahma
the Creator, one of the gods of the Hindu trinity, usually represented with four faces, and often mounted on a hamsa

Brahmin
a Hindu priest

Bun
to make merit

C

Caryatid
elephants, often used as buttressing decorations

Champa
rival empire of the Khmer, of Hindu culture, based in present day Vietnam

Chat
honorific umbrella or royal multi-tiered parasol

Chedi
from the Sanskrit *cetiya* (Pali, *caitya*) meaning memorial. Usually a religious monument (often bell-shaped) containing relics of the Buddha or other holy remains. Used interchangeably with stupa

Chenla
Chinese name for Cambodia before the Khmer era

D

Deva
a Hindu-derived male god

Devata
a Hindu-derived goddess

Dharma
the Buddhist law

Dipterocarp
family of trees (*Dipterocarpaceae*) characteristic of Southeast Asia's forests

F

Funan
the oldest Indianised state of Indochina and precursor to Chenla

G

Ganesh
elephant-headed son of Siva

Garuda
mythical divine bird, with predatory beak and claws, and human body; the king of birds, enemy of naga and mount of Vishnu (see page 112).

Gautama
the historic Buddha

Geomancy
the art of divination by lines and figures

Gopura
crowned or covered gate, entrance to a religious area

H

Hamsa
sacred goose, Brahma's mount; in Buddhism it represents the flight of the doctrine

Hinayana
'Lesser Vehicle', major Buddhist sect in Southeast Asia, usually termed Theravada Buddhism (see page 59)

I

Ikat
tie-dyeing method of patterning cloth (see page 51)

Indra
the Vedic god of the heavens, weather and war; usually mounted on a three headed elephant

J

Jataka(s)
the birth stories of the Buddha; they normally number 547, although an additional 3 were added in Burma for reasons of symmetry in mural painting and sculpture; the last 10 are the most important

K

Kala (makara)
literally, 'death' or 'black'; a demon ordered to consume itself; often sculpted with grinning face and bulging eyes over entranceways to act as a door guardian; also known as kirtamukha

Kambuja
Cambodia

Kathin/krathin
a one month period during the eighth lunar month when lay people present new robes and other gifts to monks

Ketumula
flame-like motif above the Buddha head

Kinaree
half-human, half-bird, usually depicted as a heavenly musician

Kirtamukha
see kala

Koutdi
see kuti

Krishna
incarnation of Vishnu

L

Laterite
bright red tropical soil/stone commonly used in construction of Khmer monuments

Linga
phallic symbol and one of the forms of Siva. Embedded in a pedestal shaped to allow drainage of lustral water poured over it, the linga typically has a succession of cross sections: from square at the base through octagonal to round. These symbolise, in order, the trinity of Brahma, Vishnu and Siva

Lintel
a load-bearing stone spanning a doorway; often heavily carved

Lokeshvara
see Avalokitsvara

M

Mahabharata
a Hindu epic text written about 2,000 years ago

Mahayana
'Greater Vehicle', major Buddhist sect (see page 59)

Maitreya
the future Buddha

Makara
a mythological aquatic reptile, somewhat like a crocodile and sometimes with an elephant's trunk; often found along with the kala framing doorways

Mandala
a focus for meditation; a representation of the cosmos

Mara
personification of evil and tempter of the Buddha

Meru
sacred or cosmic mountain at the centre of the world in Hindu-Buddhist cosmology; home of the gods (see page 109)

Mondop
from the sanskrit, *mandapa*. A cube-shaped building, often topped with a cone-like structure, used to contain an object of worship like a footprint of the Buddha

Mudra
symbolic gesture of the hands of the Buddha (see page 46)

N

Naga
benevolent mythical water serpent, enemy of Garuda (see page 112)

Naga makara
fusion of naga and makara

Nalagiri
the elephant let loose to attack the Buddha, who calmed him

Nandi/nandin
bull, mount of Siva

Nirvana
release from the cycle of suffering in Buddhist belief; 'enlightenment'

P

paddy/padi
unhulled rice

Pali
the sacred language of Theravada Buddhism

Parvati
consort of Siva

Phnom/phanom
Khmer for hill/mountain

Pradaksina
pilgrims' clockwise circumambulation of holy structure

Prah
sacred

Prang
form of stupa built in Khmer style, shaped like a corncob

Prasada
stepped pyramid (see prasat)

Prasat

residence of a king or of the gods (sanctuary tower), from the Indian prasada (see page 107)

R

Rama
incarnation of Vishnu, hero of the Indian epic, the *Ramayana*

Ramakien
Thai version of the *Ramayana* (see page 62)

S

Sakyamuni
the historic Buddha

Sal
the Indian sal tree (*Shorea robusta*), under which the historic Buddha was born

Sangha
the Buddhist order of monks

Singha
mythical guardian lion (see page 112)

Siva
the Destroyer, one of the three gods of the Hindu trinity; the sacred linga was worshipped as a symbol of Siva

Sravasti
the miracle at Sravasti when the Buddha subdues the heretics in front of a mango tree

Stele
inscribed stone panel

Stucco
plaster, often heavily moulded

Stupa
chedi (see page 107)

T

Tavatimsa
heaven of the 33 gods at the summit of Mount Meru

Theravada
'Way of the Elders'; major Buddhist sect also known as Hinayana Buddhism ('Lesser Vehicle') (see page 60)

Traiphum
the three worlds of Buddhist cosmology – heaven, hell and earth

Trimurti
the Hindu trinity of gods: Brahma, the Creator, Vishnu the Preserver and Siva the Destroyer

Tripitaka
Theravada Buddhism's Pali canon

U

Ubosoth
see bot

Urna
the dot or curl on the Buddha's forehead, one of the distinctive physical marks of the Enlightened One

Usnisa
the Buddha's top knot or 'wisdom bump', one of the physical marks of the Enlightened One

V

Vahana
'vehicle', a mythical beast, upon which a deva or god rides

Viharn
from Sanskrit *vihara*, an assembly hall in a Buddhist monastery; may contain Buddha images and is similar in style to the bot

Vishnu
the Protector, one of the gods of the Hindu trinity, generally with four arms holding a disc, conch shell, ball and club

Tinted boxes

Index

SAINT BENEDICT SCHOOL
DUFFIELD ROAD
DERBY DE22 1JD

Maps and illustrations

Map Symbols

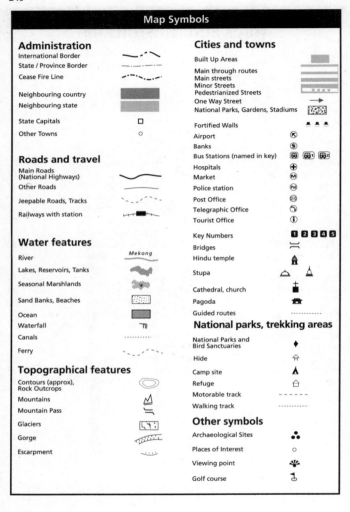

Administration

International Border
State / Province Border
Cease Fire Line

Neighbouring country
Neighbouring state

State Capitals
Other Towns

Roads and travel

Main Roads
(National Highways)
Other Roads

Jeepable Roads, Tracks

Railways with station

Water features

River   *Mekong*

Lakes, Reservoirs, Tanks

Seasonal Marshlands

Sand Banks, Beaches

Ocean
Waterfall

Canals

Ferry

Topographical features

Contours (approx),
Rock Outcrops

Mountains

Mountain Pass

Glaciers

Gorge

Escarpment

Cities and towns

Built Up Areas

Main through routes
Main streets
Minor Streets
Pedestrianized Streets
One Way Street
National Parks, Gardens, Stadiums

Fortified Walls

Airport
Banks
Bus Stations (named in key)
Hospitals
Market
Police station
Post Office
Telegraphic Office
Tourist Office

Key Numbers
Bridges
Hindu temple

Stupa

Cathedral, church

Pagoda

Guided routes

National parks, trekking areas

National Parks and
Bird Sanctuaries

Hide

Camp site

Refuge

Motorable track

Walking track

Other symbols

Archaeological Sites

Places of Interest

Viewing point

Golf course

Footprint Handbooks

All of us at Footprint Handbooks hope you have enjoyed reading and travelling with this Handbook, one of the first published in the new Footprint series. Many of you will be familiar with us as Trade & Travel, a name that has served us well for years. For you and for those who have only just discovered the Handbooks, we thought it would be interesting to chronicle the story of our development from the early 1920's.

It all started 75 years ago in 1921, with the publication of the Anglo-South American Handbook. In 1924 the South American Handbook was created. This has been published each year for the last 73 years and is the longest running guidebook in the English language, immortalised by Graham Greene as "the best travel guide in existence".

One of the key strengths of the South American Handbook over the years, has been the extraordinary contact we have had with our readers through their hundreds of letters to us in Bath. From these letters we learnt that you wanted more Handbooks of the same quality to other parts of the world.

In 1989 my brother Patrick and I set about developing a series modelled on the South American Handbook. Our aim was to create the ultimate practical guidebook series for all travellers, providing expert knowledge of far flung places, explaining culture, places and people in a balanced, lively and clear way. The whole idea hinged, of course, on finding writers who were in tune with our thinking. Serendipity stepped in at exactly the right moment: we were able to bring together a talented group of people who know the countries we cover inside out and whose enthusiasm for travelling in them needed to be communicated.

The series started to grow. We felt that the time was right to look again at the identity that had brought us all this way. After much searching we commissioned London designers Newell & Sorrell to look at all the issues. Their solution was a new identity for the Handbooks representing the books in all their aspects, looking after all the good things already achieved and taking us into the new millennium.

The result is Footprint Handbooks: a new name and mark, simple yet assertive, bold, stylish and instantly recognisable. The images we use conjure up the essence of real travel and communicate the qualities of the Handbooks in a straightforward and evocative way.

For us here in Bath, it has been an exciting exercise working through this dramatic change. Already the 'new us' fits like our favourite travelling clothes and we cannot wait to get more and more Footprint Handbooks onto the book shelves and out onto the road.

James Dawson

The Footprint list

Andalucía Handbook
Cambodia Handbook
Caribbean Islands Handbook
Chile Handbook
East Africa Handbook
Ecuador Handbook
  with the Galápagos
Egypt Handbook
India Handbook
Indonesia Handbook
Laos Handbook
Malaysia & Singapore Handbook
Mexico & Central America
  Handbook
Morocco Handbook
  with Mauritania
Myanmar (Burma) Handbook
Namibia Handbook
Pakistan Handbook
Peru Handbook
South Africa Handbook
South American Handbook
Sri Lanka Handbook
Thailand Handbook
Tibet Handbook
Tunisia Handbook with Libya
Vietnam Handbook
Zimbabwe & Malawi Handbook
  with Botswana, Moçambique &
  Zambia

New in Autumn 1997
Israel Handbook
Nepal Handbook

In the pipeline
Argentina Handbook
Brazil Handbook
Colombia Handbook
Cuba Handbook
Jordan, Syria & Lebanon Handbook
Venezuela Handbook

Footprint T-shirt

The Footprint T-shirt is available in 100% cotton in various colours.

Mail Order

Footprint Handbooks are available worldwide in good bookstores. They can also be ordered directly from us in Bath (see below for address). Please contact us if you have difficulty finding a title.

The Footprint Handbook website will be coming to keep you up to date with all the latest news from us (http://www.footprint-handbooks.co.uk). For the most up-to-date information and to join our mailing list please contact us at:

Footprint Handbooks
6 Riverside Court
Lower Bristol Road
Bath BA2 3DZ, England
T +44(0)1225 469141
F +44(0)1225 469461
E Mail handbooks@footprint.cix.co.uk